Forschungen zum Alten Testament

Edited by

Konrad Schmid (Zürich) · Mark S. Smith (Princeton)
Andrew Teeter (Harvard)

162

Alma Brodersen

The Beginning of the Biblical Canon and Ben Sira

Mohr Siebeck

Alma Brodersen, born 1986; 2006–12 Studies of Protestant Theology in Mainz, Munich, and Oxford; 2016 Doctorate at the University of Oxford; 2016–19 Postdoctoral Researcher at LMU Munich; since 2019 Postdoctoral Researcher and Lecturer at the University of Bern; 2022 Habilitation at LMU Munich.
orcid.org/0000-0002-3350-8869

The prepress production of this book and the eBook were published with the support of the Swiss National Science Foundation.

ISBN 978-3-16-161599-3 / eISBN 978-3-16-161992-2
DOI 10.1628/978-3-16-161992-2

ISSN 0940-4155 / eISSN 2568-8359 (Forschungen zum Alten Testament)

The Deutsche Nationalbibliothek lists this publication in the Deutsche Nationalbibliographie; detailed bibliographic data are available at *http://dnb.dnb.de.*

© 2022 Mohr Siebeck Tübingen, Germany. www.mohrsiebeck.com

This work is licensed under the license "Attribution-NonCommercial-NoDerivatives 4.0 International" (CC BY-NC-ND 4.0). A complete version of the license text can be found at https://creativecommons.org/licenses/by-nc-nd/4.0/. Any use not covered by the above license is prohibited and illegal without the permission of the publisher.

The book was typeset by Martin Fischer in Tübingen using Minion typeface, printed on non-aging paper by Gulde Druck in Tübingen, and bound by Buchbinderei Spinner in Ottersweier. Published by Mohr Siebeck Tübingen, Germany. www.mohrsiebeck.com.

Printed in Germany.

Preface

Questions about the beginning of the biblical canon and Ben Sira already came to my attention during my studies on Psalms which led to a doctorate at the University of Oxford in 2016 (published as *The End of the Psalter* by De Gruyter in 2017 and reprinted by Baylor University Press in 2018). The first steps towards the present study of the beginning of the biblical canon and Ben Sira were funded by the Agnes-Ament-Foundation Munich. Postdoctoral positions at LMU Munich from 2016 to 2019 and at the University of Bern since 2019 allowed me to complete it.

This book now presents a revised version of my *Habilitationsschrift* which was accepted by the Faculty of Protestant Theology of LMU Munich in January 2022. I am very grateful to Friedhelm Hartenstein (LMU Munich), who encouraged and supported the study in every possible way. He as well as Loren T. Stuckenbruck (LMU Munich), Markus Witte (Humboldt-Universität, Berlin), and Benjamin G. Wright (Lehigh University, Bethlehem, PA) kindly served as its assessors for *Habilitation* at LMU Munich, and I am thankful for their detailed constructive feedback.

At LMU Munich, I took immense benefit from being a postdoctoral fellow at the Graduate School for Ancient Studies *Distant Worlds*, funded by the German Research Foundation (Deutsche Forschungsgemeinschaft), where I led an interdisciplinary group of doctoral students focussing on ancient norms. I am grateful to the scholars and staff at the Graduate School as well as the Faculty of Protestant Theology, the Faculty of Catholic Theology, and the Munich Center of Ancient Worlds (Münchner Zentrum für Antike Welten), especially Anne Friederike Becker, Katharina Herrmann, Martin Hose, Kathrin Liess, Jonathan Spanos, Verena Schulz, and Veronika Weidner. At the University of Bern, Andreas Wagner comprehensively supported my work even during a global pandemic. I am thankful for all the valuable assistance and feedback I received in and beyond the University of Bern's Faculty of Theology, especially by Judith Göppinger, Steffen Götze, and Nancy Rahn. Conferences and meetings in person and online allowed me to continue discussions with scholars worldwide, especially John Barton, Helge Bezold, Kylie Crabbe, Ekaterina Kozlova, Sonja Noll, Birge-Dorothea Pelz, and Laura Quick. My parents and my partner proofread the entire book, and all of my family and my friends gave me their constant and loving support.

VI *Preface*

The publication of this book was made possible by the editors of *Forschungen zum Alten Testament*, especially Konrad Schmid, and the staff at Mohr Siebeck, especially Elena Müller. The Swiss National Science Foundation made this book freely available online by funding its open access publication through Mohr Siebeck. I hope that the published book will help to further advance the scholarly discussions which shaped it.

University of Bern, April 2022   Alma Brodersen

Table of Contents

Preface V
Abbreviations XIII

1. The Beginning of the Biblical Canon and Ben Sira 1

  1.1 Introduction 1
  1.2 Languages 6
    1.2.1 Versions of the Book of Ben Sira 6
    1.2.2 Comparative Study of Hebrew and Greek 9
  1.3 Canonical Categories 10
    1.3.1 History of the Canon of the Hebrew Bible 10
    1.3.2 Canon 11
    1.3.3 Bible 14
    1.3.4 Scriptures 15
    1.3.5 Authoritative Texts 17
    1.3.6 Criteria for Textual Authority 18
    1.3.7 Ben Sira and Canonical Categories 20
    1.3.8 Study of Authoritative Texts 21
  1.4 Intertextual References 22
    1.4.1 References to the Hebrew Bible in Ben Sira? 22
    1.4.2 Lists for Ben Sira 24
    1.4.3 Intertextuality 25
    1.4.4 Criteria for Intertextuality 27
    1.4.5 Ben Sira and Texts outside the Hebrew Bible 32
    1.4.6 Study of Historical Contexts including Dead Sea Scrolls ... 33
  1.5 Aim and Structure of the Study 34

2. Historical Contexts of Ben Sira 35

  2.1 Date and Historical Setting of Ben Sira 35
  2.2 Writing at the Time of Ben Sira 38
    2.2.1 Orality and Literacy 38
    2.2.2 Materiality 40
    2.2.3 Literature 43
    2.2.4 1 Enoch and Jubilees 49

VIII   *Table of Contents*

2.3 Writing in the Book of Ben Sira 52
    2.3.1 Teaching Setting 52
    2.3.2 Hebrew Book of Ben Sira 52
    2.3.3 Greek Book of Ben Sira 54
    2.3.4 Orality and Literacy and Ben Sira 55
    2.3.5 Materiality and Ben Sira 57
2.4 Conclusion 58

3. Greek Prologue to Ben Sira 59

3.1 Introduction 59
3.2 Greek Text and Translation 59
3.3 Analysis 61
    3.3.1 Manuscripts and Date 61
    3.3.2 Context 66
    3.3.3 Genre 67
    3.3.4 Structure 67
3.4 Key Terms: Law, Prophets, and Writings 69
    3.4.1 Greek Prologue to Ben Sira 69
    3.4.2 Hebrew and Greek Terms 70
    3.4.3 Hebrew Book of Ben Sira 72
    3.4.4 Greek Book of Ben Sira 74
    3.4.5 Summary of Uses 77
3.5 The Prologue and the Question of Canon 78
    3.5.1 Canonical References? 78
    3.5.2 Tripartite Canon? 78
    3.5.3 Bipartite Canon? 82
    3.5.4 One-Part Canon? 84
    3.5.5 No Canon? 85
    3.5.6 Open Canon including Ben Sira? 86
    3.5.7 Greek Canon? 92
3.6 Conclusion 95

4. Ben Sira 38:24–39:11 99

4.1 Introduction 99
4.2 Hebrew Text and Translation 99
4.3 Greek Text and Translation 100
4.4 Comparative Analysis 103
    4.4.1 Manuscripts and Date 103
    4.4.2 Context 104
    4.4.3 Genre 104
    4.4.4 Structure 105

Table of Contents IX

4.5 Sir 38:24–39:11 and the Question of Canon 107
    4.5.1 Canonical References? 107
    4.5.2 Tripartite Canon? 108
    4.5.3 Bipartite Canon? 109
    4.5.4 One-Part Canon? 110
    4.5.5 No Canon? 111
    4.5.6 Open Canon including Ben Sira? 112
    4.5.7 Greek Canon? 112
4.6 Conclusion 113

5. Ben Sira 44–50: Survey 115

5.1 Introduction 115
5.2 Textual Basis 115
5.3 Comparative Analysis 116
    5.3.1 Manuscripts and Date 116
    5.3.2 Context 117
    5.3.3 Genre 118
    5.3.4 Structure 119
5.4 Sir 44–50 and the Question of Canon 122
    5.4.1 Canonical References? 122
    5.4.2 Tripartite Canon? 122
    5.4.3 Bipartite Canon? 123
    5.4.4 One-Part Canon? 125
    5.4.5 No Canon? 126
    5.4.6 Open Canon including Ben Sira? 126
    5.4.7 Greek Canon? 126
    5.4.8 Summary of Arguments 126
5.5 Figures and the Question of Quotation 127
    5.5.1 Order of Figures in Sir 44–50 127
    5.5.2 Question of Quotation in Sir 48:10 134
    5.5.3 Beyond the Hebrew Bible 141
5.6 Conclusion 141

6. Ben Sira 44–50: Case Studies 143

6.1 Selection of Case Studies 143
6.2 Enoch (Sir 44:16; 49:14) 144
    6.2.1 Hebrew and Greek Text 144
    6.2.2 References to Genesis 5:21–24? 146
    6.2.3 Comparison with the Hebrew Bible and the Greek Septuagint.. 147
    6.2.4 Comparison with the Dead Sea Scrolls 149
    6.2.5 Comparison within the Book of Ben Sira 156
    6.2.6 Conclusion 157

X Table of Contents

6.3 Judges (Sir 46:11–12) 159
   6.3.1 Hebrew and Greek Text 159
   6.3.2 References to the Book of Judges? 159
   6.3.3 Comparison with the Hebrew Bible 160
   6.3.4 Comparison with the Greek Septuagint 162
   6.3.5 Comparison with the Dead Sea Scrolls 163
   6.3.6 Comparison within the Book of Ben Sira 164
   6.3.7 Conclusion 164
6.4 Isaiah (Sir 48:17–25) 165
   6.4.1 Hebrew and Greek Text 165
   6.4.2 References to the Book of Isaiah? 167
   6.4.3 Comparison with the Hebrew Bible 168
   6.4.4 Comparison with the Greek Septuagint 172
   6.4.5 Comparison with the Dead Sea Scrolls 174
   6.4.6 Comparison within the Book of Ben Sira 175
   6.4.7 Conclusion 176
6.5 Job (Sir 49:9) 177
   6.5.1 Hebrew and Greek Text 177
   6.5.2 References to the Books of Ezekiel and Job? 178
   6.5.3 Comparison with the Hebrew Bible 178
   6.5.4 Comparison with the Greek Septuagint 179
   6.5.5 Comparison with the Dead Sea Scrolls 179
   6.5.6 Comparison within the Book of Ben Sira 180
   6.5.7 Conclusion 180
6.6 Twelve Prophets (Sir 49:10) 180
   6.6.1 Hebrew and Greek Text 180
   6.6.2 References to the Book of the Twelve Prophets? 181
   6.6.3 Comparison with the Hebrew Bible 182
   6.6.4 Comparison with the Greek Septuagint 182
   6.6.5 Comparison with the Dead Sea Scrolls 183
   6.6.6 Comparison within the Book of Ben Sira 184
   6.6.7 Conclusion 184
6.7 Conclusion 185

7. Results 187

7.1 The Beginning of the Biblical Canon and Ben Sira 187
   7.1.1 Hebrew and Greek Sources 187
   7.1.2 Anachronism of Biblical Canon 188
   7.1.3 Key Passages: Greek Prologue, Sir 38:24–39:11, Sir 44–50 188

7.2 Implications 189
    7.2.1 Historical Implications 189
    7.2.2 Methodological Implications 190
7.3 Concluding Summary 191

Bibliography 193

Index of Sources 239
Index of Subjects 253

Abbreviations

BHQ   Biblia Hebraica Quinta (GELSTON 2010 / TAL 2015)
BHS   Biblia Hebraica Stuttgartensia (ELLIGER/RUDOLPH 1997)
l.   Line(s)
LXX   Septuagint (RAHLFS/HANHART 2006, for Sir^{LXX} ZIEGLER 1980;
     book titles as for MT in order to ease comparison)
MT   Masoretic Text of the Hebrew Bible (ELLIGER/RUDOLPH 1997 [BHS])
NETS   New English Translation of the Septuagint (PIETERSMA/WRIGHT 2007,
     for Sir^{LXX} WRIGHT 2007b)
NRSV   New Revised Standard Version (*NRSV* 1989)
Sir   Book of Ben Sira in Hebrew (RENDSBURG/BINSTEIN 2013)
Sir^{LXX} Book of Ben Sira in Greek (ZIEGLER 1980)

General abbreviations follow *The SBL Handbook of Style: Second Edition, For Biblical Studies and Related Disciplines.* 2014. Atlanta, GA: SBL Press.

All translations are the author's unless specified otherwise.

1. The Beginning of the Biblical Canon and Ben Sira

1.1 Introduction

The Book of Ben Sira is usually regarded to show the beginning of the biblical canon. Dated to the early the 2nd century BCE, the Book of Ben Sira is taken as the earliest reference to the canon of the Hebrew Bible / Old Testament.[1]

Today, the canon of the Hebrew Bible consists of three parts, each of which contains a number of different books: the "Law" (Hebrew תּוֹרָה "law", also called Torah or Pentateuch), the "Prophets" (Hebrew נְבִיאִים "prophets"), and the "Writings" (Hebrew כְּתוּבִים "writings"), in this order, with the "Prophets" subdivided into "Former Prophets" (Hebrew נְבִיאִים רָאשׁוֹנִים "former prophets") and "Latter Prophets" (Hebrew נְבִיאִים אַחֲרוֹנִים "latter prophets").[2] In the Old Testament, the division of books into three parts and the order of these parts differs: "Historical Books" starting with the Pentateuch are followed by "Didactic Books" and then "Prophetic Books", with the "Prophetic Books" corresponding to the "Latter Prophets", and the "Former Prophets" included in the "Historical Books".[3]

The Book of Ben Sira (also known as "Jesus Sirach" or "Ecclesiasticus" based on the Greek and Latin traditions)[4] is an ancient text which contains advice for a wise life and references to the God of Israel.[5] Today, the Book of Ben Sira is a part of the "Apocrypha" or "Deuterocanonical Books" of the Old Testament and

---

[1] Today, the Old Testament in some Christian traditions includes books which are not included in the Jewish Hebrew Bible, but the two terms mostly refer to the same texts. Cf. for this and the non-pejorative use of the term "Old Testament" BERLEJUNG 2012a, 18–22.

[2] On this tripartite division of the Hebrew Bible today cf. FISCHER 1998, 1408; LISS 2019, 1–3; SCHMITT 2011; HUPPING et al. 2008, 2–4, 91–93. The three parts (without the subdivision of the "Prophets") are named in the Babylonian Talmud in Sanhedrin 90b, cf. STRACK/BILLERBECK 1928, 417–418, 422. The Babylonian Talmud can be dated to a long period beginning in the 3rd and culminating in the 7th–8th century CE, cf. BECKER 2001, 626–627. For the history of the canon of the Hebrew Bible see Chapter 1.3.1.

[3] For an overview of this division and order cf. BERLEJUNG 2012a, 18–22. The "Didactic Books" are also called "Poetic Books", cf. SCHMITT 2011, 158–160, or "Wisdom Books", cf. HUPPING et al. 2008, 6–7.

[4] Cf. WITTE 2012b, 726; WRIGHT 2019, 187.

[5] For the overall structure of the Book of Ben Sira cf. the suggestions summarized by UEBERSCHAER 2007, 25–27; BECKER/FABRY/REITEMEYER 2011, 2165–2168. The book's advice for a wise life is also seen to be without any strict structure, cf. e.g. SNAITH 1974, 3; SKEHAN/DI LELLA 1987, 4.

2   *1. The Beginning of the Biblical Canon and Ben Sira*

thus forms a part of the Old Testament in some Christian Bibles (e. g. in Greek Orthodox or Roman Catholic traditions) but is not included in the Jewish Hebrew Bible and other Christian Bibles (e. g. in Lutheran or Reformed traditions).[6] The ancient Book of Ben Sira can be dated with relative certainty compared to other books in the Hebrew Bible / Old Testament.[7] It was written in Hebrew in the early 2nd century BCE and translated into Greek probably later in the same century.[8] In the ancient Greek translation of the whole Hebrew Bible / Old Testament called Septuagint (and abbreviated LXX),[9] the Book of Ben Sira is transmitted in Greek on several manuscripts, and other translations are also extant.[10] In spectacular rediscoveries in a Genizah near Cairo (from 1896) and in Qumran and Masada near the Dead Sea (from 1956/1964), fragmentary Hebrew manuscripts of the Book of Ben Sira came to light, and today many but not all parts of the book are also available in Hebrew. The Greek translation preserved in the Septuagint (LXX) remains the oldest complete source available today.[11] Therefore, the counting of 51 chapters and their verses in the Book of Ben Sira is based on the Septuagint.[12]

The Book of Ben Sira is the oldest book included in (some) later Bibles which mentions its author by name.[13] In Hebrew, in Sir 50:27 the author is called שמעון בן ישוע בן אלעזר בן סירא "Simeon son of Yeshua son of Eleazar son of Sira". In Sir 51:30 the author has the same name but also, before that and additionally, שמעון בן ישוע שנקרא בן סירא "Simeon son of Yeshua who is called son of Sira".[14] In the Greek translation of the Book of Ben Sira, Sir 50:27[LXX] mentions Ἰησοῦς υἱὸς Σιραχ Ελεαζαρ ὁ Ιεροσολυμίτης "Jesus son of Sirach, [son of] of Eleazar,

---

[6] Cf. on Ben Sira WITTE 2012b, 726, 738–739; WRIGHT 2019, 189–191; on the "Apocrypha" or "Deuterocanonical Books" of the Old Testament generally BERLEJUNG 2012a, 15–22.

[7] For the difficulties of dating texts in the Hebrew Bible / Old Testament in general cf. BERLEJUNG 2012a, 8–9.

[8] For details on the date of the Book of Ben Sira see Chapter 2.1, on the date of its Greek translation see Chapter 1.2.1, on the date of its Greek Prologue see Chapter 3.3.1.

[9] On the Septuagint in general cf. BERLEJUNG 2012a, 15–16; BOYD-TAYLOR 2021, 13–14; ROSS 2021, 4–5. On the order of books in the Septuagint see Chapter 3 Note 256.

[10] For details see Chapter 1.2.

[11] Cf. WITTE 2012b, 732–734; WRIGHT 2019, 192.

[12] For differences in counting regarding Sir 30–36 cf. WITTE 2012b, 726. MROCZEK 2016, 103–106, 112, notes that the concept of one unified and original "Book of Ben Sira" does not fit the idea of overflowing wisdom or the different extant manuscripts, and "project" would be a better term than "book". However, since the manuscripts do mostly contain the same content, and preserve written texts, the term "Book of Ben Sira" is still a helpful summarizing term, while the textual sources are then differentiated in the present study, see Chapter 1.2.

[13] Even if this name is not the actual name of the author, the book's date and content still allow for a study of its relation to the biblical canon. WRIGHT/MROCZEK 2021, 213–218, take the name to be the actual name of the author, but argue that the use of the author's name is unusual in contemporary writings and reflects the author's claim to his own importance, and also that the author cannot simply be identified with the first person "I" in the Book of Ben Sira.

[14] Cf. RENDSBURG/BINSTEIN 2013, Manuscript B XX recto, XXI verso. On the Hebrew manuscripts see Chapter 1.2.

1.1 Introduction

the Jerusalemite". Subscriptions after Sir 51:30[LXX] on Greek manuscripts mostly include variations of Ἰησοῦς υἱὸς Σιραχ "Jesus son of Sirach".[15] "Ben Sira", a transcription of the Hebrew בן סירא "son of Sira" which is translated into Greek as υἱὸς Σιραχ "son of Sirach", is a name that refers to an ancestor named "Sira / Sirach".[16] The names "Simeon", "Yeshua / Jesus", "Ben Sira", "Sirach", and "Jesus Sirach" all refer to the same person, the latter three are also used to refer to this person's book.[17] The Hebrew Book of Ben Sira was probably written in Jerusalem.[18] The Greek translation of the Book of Ben Sira begins with a Prologue whose first person narrator claims to be the grandson of Ben Sira and the translator of Ben Sira's book. This person (whose name is not mentioned) calls the author of the Book of Ben Sira ὁ πάππος μου Ἰησοῦς "my grandfather Jesus" (Prologue l. 7),[19] and writes that he translated Ben Sira's book in Egypt (Prologue l. 28).[20]

The Book of Ben Sira is usually seen today as the starting point for the history of the tripartite canon of the Hebrew Bible / Old Testament.[21] For example, in the German encyclopedia *Theologische Realenzyklopädie*, Wanke writes in the entry on "Bible":

"In the work of *Ben Sira* (around 190) we have the oldest evidence of collections of writings which were included in the later Jewish canon. His Praise of the Fathers (Sir 44–49) is based on the collection of the normative, historical and prophetic tradition in the form of the Pentateuch, the books Josh – Kgs, Isa, Jer, Eze, and the Twelve Prophets. For Ben Sira we cannot yet talk about a canon in its strict sense, but the fact that these writings were seen as fundamental guidance moves them close to what was later called canon. In addition to the writings just mentioned, Ben Sira knew other Old Testament writings. This can initially be deduced from the numerous allusions to them within the book, and is then explicitly confirmed by the *grandson of Ben Sira*. In the Prologue which the grandson placed before his Greek translation of the book (after 117 BCE), he does not only state that many and great things are given διὰ τοῦ νόμου καὶ τῶν προφητῶν καὶ τῶν ἄλλων τῶν κατ᾽ αὐτοὺς ἠκολουθηκότων [through the Law, the Prophets, and the others which followed after them], but also highlights that his grandfather devoted himself to the thorough study τοῦ νόμου καὶ τῶν προφητῶν καὶ τῶν ἄλλων πατρίων βιβλίων [of the

---

[15] Cf. ZIEGLER 1980, 124, 362, 368. On the Greek text see Chapter 1.2.

[16] The Aramaic word סירא can mean "coat of mail" (i.e. armour), "thorn", or "court", cf. JASTROW 1903, s.v. סִירָא, סִירָה. The Greek χ at the end may be a marker that the word cannot be declined, thus SCHÜRER 1986, 201 (referring to DALMAN 1905, 202 n. 3), or a transcription of the letter א, thus PETERS 1913, XXVIII (referring to NESTLE 1901, 332).

[17] Cf. REITEMEYER 2011, 2159–2160; WITTE 2012b, 726.

[18] See Chapter 2 Note 3.

[19] DIEBNER 1982, 8–11, argues that the name Ἰησοῦς "Jesus" in l. 7 shows that the grandson is not who he says he is, i.e., not the grandson of Ben Sira, as not "Jesus" but "Simeon" was the grandfather's real first name. However, as Diebner himself notes, the grandfather was not necessarily called by his own first name ("who is called son of Sira").

[20] See Chapter 3 Note 15.

[21] Cf. STEINMANN 1999, 84; SCHMITT 2011, 159–160; LISS 2019, 5. This is also noted by WITTE 2012a, 231–232.

4   *1. The Beginning of the Biblical Canon and Ben Sira*

Law, the Prophets, and the other traditional books]. He finally points out that Law, Prophets, and τὰ λοιπὰ τῶν βιβλίων [the remaining books] are often different when translated as compared to the original language. These remarks by the grandson mention for the first time another group of writings in addition to the Law and the Prophets, writings which were equated with them. We can, however, only speculate about the scope of this third collection. Nevertheless, the popularity and reputation which the Book of Ben Sira subsequently acquired led to the establishment of the tripartite division of the canon regardless of the question which books were in each case counted among the Prophets or the *kᵉtûbîm* [Writings]."[22]

Similarly, in the entry on "Bible" in the encyclopedia *Religion Past and Present* (translated from the German *Religion in Geschichte und Gegenwart*), Becker writes:

"The beginning of the prologue to Sirach (c. 130 BCE) is already familiar with the threefold division into 'the laws, the prophets, and the other (books) which followed them,' or 'the other books of the fathers,' 'the other books.' Not only 'the law,' but 'the prophets' too form a clearly defined group of texts with a fixed name. Sirach's grandson probably had in mind here the books of Joshua, Judges, Samuel, Kings, Isaiah, Jeremiah, Ezekiel, and the twelve prophets, which are presupposed in his 'praise of the fathers' (Sir 46–49). The third section, which complements the 'law and the prophets,' has no fixed name in the prologue to Sirach."[23]

---

[22] Wanke 1980, 3–4 (square brackets and emphases in German original), German original: "Im Werk des *Jesus Sirach* (um 190) haben wir das älteste Zeugnis für das Vorhandensein von Schriftensammlungen, wie sie im späteren jüdischen Kanon Aufnahme fanden. Seinem Lobpreis der Väter (Sir 44–49) liegt die Sammlung der normativen, geschichtlichen und prophetischen Tradition in Gestalt des Pentateuchs, der Bücher Jos – Reg, Jes, Jer, Ez und des Dodekapropheton zugrunde. Von einem Kanon im strengen Sinn kann bei Sirach zwar noch nicht die Rede sein, daß jedoch die genannten Schriften als grundlegende Orientierung angesehen wurden, rückt sie in die Nähe dessen, was später unter Kanon verstanden wurde. Neben den genannten Büchern waren dem Jesus Sirach auch noch andere alttestamentliche Schriften bekannt. Das ergibt sich zunächst aus den zahlreichen Anspielungen des Buches auf sie und wird schließlich durch den *Enkel des Jesus Sirach* ausdrücklich bestätigt. Im Prolog, den der Enkel seiner griechischen Übersetzung des Buches (nach 117 v. Chr.) vorausschickte, stellt er nicht nur fest, daß Vieles und Großes διὰ τοῦ νόμου καὶ τῶν προφητῶν καὶ τῶν ἄλλων τῶν κατ᾽ αὐτοὺς ἠκολουθηκότων [durch das Gesetz, die Propheten und die andern, die ihnen nachgefolgt sind] gegeben wurde, sondern hebt auch hervor, daß sein Großvater sich dem intensiven Studium τοῦ νόμου καὶ τῶν προφητῶν καὶ τῶν ἄλλων πατρίων βιβλίων [des Gesetzes, der Propheten und der anderen überkommenen Bücher] gewidmet hat. Er weist schließlich darauf hin, daß Gesetz, Propheten und τὰ λοιπὰ τῶν βιβλίων [die übrigen Bücher] übersetzt oft anders lauten als in der Ursprache. Mit diesen Äußerungen des Enkels ist erstmals neben dem Gesetz und den Propheten eine weitere Gruppe von Schriften genannt, die jenen gleichgestellt wurden. Über den Umfang dieser dritten Sammlung können allerdings nur Vermutungen angestellt werden. Die Bekanntheit und das Ansehen, die das Buch Sir in der Folgezeit erlangte, haben aber dazu geführt, daß sich die Dreiteilung des Kanons unabhängig davon durchsetzte, welche Bücher jeweils den Propheten bzw. den *kᵉtûbîm* [Schriften] zugeteilt wurden."

[23] Becker 2012, 2 (German original Becker 1998, 1409).

1.1 Introduction 5

That the tripartite canon starts with Ben Sira is also often stated in current textbooks on the Hebrew Bible / Old Testament. For example, ARNOLD writes in his *Introduction to the Old Testament*:

"it is likely that already as early as the second century BCE the three-part structure familiar now in the Jewish Bible was set. The book of Ecclesiasticus (also known as the Wisdom of Ben Sira, or simply, Sirach) is a second-century book preserved in the Roman Catholic canon, and relying on the Torah, the Prophets, the Psalms, Proverbs, Job, Ezra, and Nehemiah. The author's grandson added a preface referring to 'the Law and the Prophets and the others that followed them.' Of the three parts – Law, Prophets, Writings – the first two seem to have arrived at canonical status by the second century BCE. The third portion probably had not yet been given a name and likely was not yet a closed list of approved books."[24]

In the *T&T Clark Handbook of the Old Testament* (translated from the German *Grundwissen Altes Testament*), WITTE in his introduction to Ben Sira emphasizes the importance of the Prologue for the history of the canon:

"the prologue refers to an existing collection of the sacred texts of Judaism (→ *canon*) consisting of the Torah, the Nevi'im and 'other writings'".[25]

ZENGER explains in his German introduction to the Old Testament:

"The division into three parts as a theological concept is older than the completed canon whose scope was generally accepted around 100 CE, although after 200 BCE discussions and deviations were limited to the part of the 'Writings' [...] The *fundamental* division into three parts is first indicated in Sir 38:34b–39:1 (around 190 BCE); around 117 BCE this is presupposed in the prologue which the grandson of Ben Sira writes as an introduction to the Greek translation of the book which his grandfather wrote in Hebrew."[26]

As these examples from encyclopedias and textbooks illustrate, there are two main reasons for seeing Ben Sira as the first evidence for a tripartite canon of the Hebrew Bible / Old Testament. First, two key passages, the Greek Prologue to Ben Sira and Sir 38:34–39:1^{LXX}, are seen to contain mentions of this canon. Second, Ben Sira, especially in the the third key passage "Praise of the Ancestors"

---

[24] ARNOLD 2014, 22–23.

[25] WITTE 2012b, 728 (cf. the most recent edition of the German original WITTE 2019a, 558: "Der vom Enkel Ben Siras verfasste Prolog [...] verweist [...] auf eine zu seiner Zeit existierende, aus Tora, Nebiim und 'übrigen Schriften' bestehende Sammlung der heiligen Texte des Judentums (→ *Kanon*)"). In the same handbook, BERLEJUNG 2012a, 17, places Sir 44–50 at the beginning of the history of the canon.

[26] ZENGER 2008, 23 (emphasis in German original), German original: "Die Dreiteilung als theologisches Konzept ist älter als der abgeschlossene Kanon, dessen Umfang um 100 n. Chr. allgemein akzeptiert wurde, wobei sich die Diskussionen bzw. die Abweichungen nach 200 v. Chr. nur noch im Bereich der 'Schriften' abspielten [...] Die *grundsätzliche* Dreiteilung deutet sich erstmals in Sir 38,34b–39,1 (um 190 v. Chr.) an; sie wird um 117 v. Chr. im Prolog, den der Enkel des Jesus Sirach als Einleitung zur griechischen Übersetzung des von seinem Großvater auf Hebräisch verfassten Buches schreibt, vorausgesetzt." The same quote is also found in the current edition ZENGER/FREVEL 2016, 24.

6   *1. The Beginning of the Biblical Canon and Ben Sira*

(Sir 44–50), is thought to refer to almost all books which today are included in the Hebrew Bible.[27]

However, these examples also show that there are a number of problems in seeing Ben Sira as the oldest evidence for the canon of the Hebrew Bible. First, it is not always noted that Sir 38:34–39:1[LXX] is only extant in Greek and not in Hebrew.[28] Second, the term "canon" is used to refer to the Hebrew Bible divided into Law, Prophets, and Writings, but it is unclear if this is a division existing at the time of Ben Sira[29] or, in hindsight, the beginning of a division known as a canon in later times,[30] while earlier only a bipartite canon may have existed.[31] Third, it is unclear in which way Ben Sira actually refers to earlier texts. The following sections of the present study explain these main problems in taking Ben Sira as the earliest evidence for a tripartite canon: languages, canonical categories, and intertextual references.

1.2 Languages

1.2.1 Versions of the Book of Ben Sira

Today – following rediscoveries in a Genizah near Cairo (from 1896) and in Qumran and Masada near the Dead Sea (from 1956/1964) – large parts of the Book of Ben Sira are available in Hebrew, its original language.[32] Most of the 51 chapters of the Book of Ben Sira are now extant, in part or fully, on Hebrew manuscripts, but seven chapters, namely Sir 1–2, Sir 17, Sir 24, and Sir 27–29, are not preserved in Hebrew at all.[33] The oldest extant manuscript of a part of the Book of Ben Sira is the fragmentary Masada Manuscript (Mas1h, Mas Sir) which probably dates from the first half of the 1st century BCE and must have been written before 73 CE when Masada was destroyed. Mas1h contains parts of Sir 39–44.[34] In Qumran, parts of the Book of Ben Sira are attested on 2Q18 (2QSir; second half

---

[27] The key passages of the Prologue and Sir 44–50 (specifically Sir 49:8–10 with "Ezekiel, Job, and the Twelve Prophets") are also listed as the oldest primary sources for the Hebrew Bible / Old Testament canon outside the Hebrew Bible itself in MCDONALD 2002, 580; MCDONALD 2007, 431.

[28] Thus ZENGER 2008, 23 (see Note 26).

[29] Thus implied by BECKER 2012, 2 (see Note 23); WITTE 2012b, 728 (see Note 25); ARNOLD 2014, 22–23 (see Note 24).

[30] Thus implied by WANKE 1980, 3–4 (see Note 22); ZENGER 2008, 23 (see Note 26).

[31] Thus implied by ARNOLD 2014, 22–23 (see Note 24).

[32] For more details on Ben Sira in the Genizah cf. WÜRTHWEIN 1988, 13–14, 42–43; REIF 1997; in Qumran cf. SANDERS 1965, 3, 79–85, Plate XIII–XIV; in Masada cf. YADIN 1999.

[33] For a detailed list of passages extant in Hebrew in the order of chapters in Sir cf. BLACHORSKY [2014]. For a list of passages in each manuscript cf. BEENTJES 1997, 13–19.

[34] Cf. YADIN 1999, 157 (middle or late Hasmonean script, first half of the 1st century BCE, possibly 100–75 BCE), 212–225.

1.2 Languages

of the 1st century BCE), a fragment containing only a few letters of Sir 6,[35] and on 11Q5 (11QPsª; first half of the 1st century CE), a longer scroll containing – amongst many psalms, most but not all of which are found today in the Hebrew Bible in a different sequence – parts of Sir 51.[36] Most of the Hebrew text of the Book of Ben Sira is extant on partly damaged manuscripts found in a Genizah near Cairo. These Genizah manuscripts are called Manuscripts A to F in modern research. They date from the 10th to 13th century CE: Manuscript B is dated to the turn of the 10th and 11th century CE, Manuscripts A, D, E, and F are dated to the turn of the 11th and 12th century CE, and Manuscript C to the 12th to 13th century CE.[37]

The Greek translation preserved in the Septuagint (LXX) remains the oldest complete source of Ben Sira available today.[38] It is usually dated to the late 2nd century BCE based on its Prologue (see Chapter 3.3.1). The content of the Greek translation itself does not indicate a later date than the late 2nd century BCE,[39] but it may have been made in more than one stage.[40] The oldest extant Greek fragments for Ben Sira date to the 3rd century CE, and full Greek manuscripts are extant from the 4th century CE, especially Codex Vaticanus (B) and Codex Sinaiticus (S).[41]

None of the extant manuscripts in Hebrew or Greek date as far back as the times of the Hebrew Book of Ben Sira in the early 2nd century BCE (see Chapter 2.1) or its Greek translation in the late 2nd century BCE (see Chapter 3.3.1). They may contain later influences, both in Hebrew and Greek, including harmonizations with the later Hebrew and Greek biblical canons.[42] At the same time, the Hebrew text on the Masada Manuscript from the 1st century BCE is largely identical with that on Manuscript B from the turn of the 10th and 11th century CE,[43] which can be taken of a sign of a relatively stable textual transmission.[44] In any case, extant manuscripts are the only textual basis available today.

---

[35] Cf. BAILLET 1962, 75–77.

[36] Cf. SANDERS 1965, 5, 79–85.

[37] Cf. OLSZOWY-SCHLANGER 2018, 77, 85–86, 92 (against BEENTJES 1997, 5–6).

[38] For a critical edition of the Greek Septuagint text of Ben Sira in the Göttingen Septuagint cf. ZIEGLER 1980. For different placings and numberings for the chapters Sir 30–36LXX cf. ZIEGLER 1980, 27, 29.

[39] Cf. for aspects of the Greek translation related to cultural differences UEBERSCHAER 2016, 450–451.

[40] Cf. MARBÖCK 2003, 112; UEBERSCHAER 2016, 442–444, 447.

[41] Cf. ZIEGLER 1980, 7, 10, in combination with SEPTUAGINTA-UNTERNEHMEN 2012, 1, 15; CORLEY 2019, 214–215.

[42] Cf. WRIGHT 2019, 195; REYMOND 2019, 207–208. On examples of possible "biblical harmonizations" in Hebrew which are reconstructed from different extant manuscripts as well as the difficulties of such reconstructions cf. AITKEN 2018, 148–151, 159. For examples of possible secondary assimilations in the Greek Septuagint see Chapter 3 Note 108 and Chapter 6 Note 196.

[43] Cf. YADIN 1999, 168–169; REYMOND 2019, 199. For examples of minor differences see Chapter 5.3.1.

[44] Cf. MORLA 2012, 19–23.

8   *1. The Beginning of the Biblical Canon and Ben Sira*

In research on Ben Sira, the Hebrew sources are sometimes divided into H-I and H-II, the Greek sources into G-I and G-II.[45] G-II is not actually found in any manuscript but its existence is deduced from different additions in some Septuagint manuscripts.[46] The Septuagint thus represents mostly G-I but also G-II. Similarly, the extant Hebrew manuscripts are thought to mostly represent H-I, with some additions belonging to H-II which may partly represent a basis of G-II.[47] For the key passages of the Prologue to Ben Sira, Sir 38:24–39:11, and Sir 44–50, the reconstruction of G-II overall is not relevant.[48] Additions in Hebrew manuscripts are discussed individually.[49]

In commentaries on Ben Sira, the two languages of Hebrew and Greek are often mixed: where a Hebrew text is extant, this is used, and the gaps are then filled with Greek passages.[50] However, a separate interpretation of the two languages is desirable as it avoids mixing different linguistic, literary, historical, and theological backgrounds.[51]

In addition to Hebrew and Greek, the Book of Ben Sira is transmitted in other languages, especially in Syriac and Latin.[52] The Syriac Peshitta translation dates from the 2nd or 3rd century CE, with manuscripts preserved from the 6th or 7th century CE onwards.[53] The Syriac Peshitta translation is probably based on a Hebrew text which cannot be reconstructed.[54] The Latin version, partly preserved in the Vetus Latina and fully in the Vulgate, is probably based on a Greek translation which is different from the extant Greek texts, and dates from the 2nd or

---

[45] Cf. WITTE 2012b, 732–734; REYMOND 2019, 205–206.

[46] Cf. ZIEGLER 1980, 69 (additions in Gr II printed in small print in the edition), 73–75 (Gr II not found on a single manuscript but deduced from different additions found in several manuscripts), 113 (Gr I = translation made by the grandson, Gr II = later translation); BÖHMISCH 1997, 87–89; KEARNS 2011, 47–52; CORLEY 2019, 221–223.

[47] Cf. KEARNS 2011, 49, 52–54, esp. 54 (H-II contains fewer additions than G-II); ZIEGLER 1980, 83 (there are examples where the Hebrew Manuscript B equals the Hebrew original of G-I and Manuscript A equals the Hebrew original of G-II). Cf. also BÖHMISCH 1997, 87–89. In addition to H-I/II or G-I/II, other text forms have also been reconstructed, cf. BÖHMISCH 1997, 87–92, esp. 92.

[48] Only the last two lines of Sir 50:29^{LXX} are printed in small print in ZIEGLER 1980, 362, to mark them as a reconstructed part of G-II, cf. ZIEGLER 1980, 69.

[49] See Chapters 4.4.1 and 5.3.1.

[50] Cf. WITTE 2015a, 26–28.

[51] Thus also BÖHMISCH 1997, 87–92, esp. 92; WITTE 2015a, 28, 37.

[52] For current work on a synopsis of the Book of Ben Sira in the four languages of Hebrew, Greek, Syriac, and Latin, with German translations for each version, cf. GESCHE/RABO/LUSTIG [2018].

[53] Cf. VAN PEURSEN 2007, 3–4, 12, 131–133; VAN PEURSEN 2019, 233, 235. Further studies on the date of the Syriac Peshitta translation would be desirable, cf. WITTE 2015b, 6–7; WITTE 2017b, 11–12. For a Syriac diplomatic edition of a facsimile of the Peshitta Codex Ambrosianus (6/7th century CE) with English and Spanish translations cf. CALDUCH-BENAGES/FERRER/LIESEN 2003, esp. 56, 60–61.

[54] Cf. VAN PEURSEN 2007, 16–18; OWENS 1989, 40–41; OWENS 2011, 177–179; VAN PEURSEN 2019, 239–240.

3rd century CE, with manuscripts of parts of the Latin version preserved from the 6th century CE onwards.[55] Later translations into Coptic, Ethiopic, Armenian, Georgian, Slavonic, Arabic, and Palestinian-Christian Aramaic, are mostly based on Greek translations.[56] All translations except for the Greek translation postdate the Second Temple Period,[57] and come from different historical contexts which include Christianity in the Common Era.

1.2.2 Comparative Study of Hebrew and Greek

A separate interpretation of the Hebrew and Greek versions of the Book of Ben Sira is especially important when studying questions of canon since the later Hebrew and Greek canons of the Hebrew Bible / Old Testament also differ.[58] The present study analyses Hebrew and Greek passages separately before comparing them to each other.[59]

Other complete extant versions of the Book of Ben Sira, especially in Syriac and Latin, are not analysed separately in the present study for two main reasons. First, arguments relating to the beginning of the biblical canon of the Hebrew Bible / Old Testament and Ben Sira are based only on the Hebrew and Greek text of the Book of Ben Sira.[60] Second, Syriac and Latin as well as other translations are much younger than the Greek translation. They postdate the Second Temple Period and come from different historical contexts which include Christianity in the Common Era. While it is possible that later translations preserve ancient details no longer found in the Hebrew and Greek sources available today, the reconstruction of such details is faced with problems including the later historical contexts of the translations.[61] Studies of Syriac, Latin, and other translations of the Book of Ben Sira have to take these different historical contexts into account,[62] and further studies would be desirable. Specifically regarding the beginning of the biblical canon, the different historical contexts for the time of Syriac, Latin,

---

[55] Cf. GREGORY 2019, 243–247. For Latin critical editions cf. THIELE 1987 and FORTE 2014/2021 (Vetus Latina, not yet complete) and *Biblia Sacra* 1964 (Vulgate).

[56] Cf. for an overview WRIGHT 2019, 187–188, 191–194.

[57] On the Second Temple Period see Chapter 2.1.

[58] Cf. WITTE 2015b, 10; WITTE 2017b, 18. On the Hebrew and Greek canon see Notes 2 and 3.

[59] This approach is also taken by MULDER 2003, 23–24.

[60] See Chapter 1.1.

[61] For example, for the Syriac Peshitta translation, OWENS 1989, 40–41, states that it "in some passages preserves the best text", but also immediately notes several problems in reconstructing such a text. There are significant differences between the extant Syriac and Hebrew texts, see Note 54. VAN PEURSEN 2019, 240, argues that the "text-critical value" of the Syriac Peshitta translation is "considerably limited", and it rather serves as a witness to the "textual history and reception of the book", demonstrating "how the book was adapted to ever new views and circumstances." For the complicated "text-critical value" of the Latin version with its Greek basis cf. GREGORY 2019, 254–255. For problems regarding rabbinic quotations of Ben Sira cf. LABENDZ 2006, 381. Also cf. MORLA 2012, 22–23.

[62] Cf. VAN PEURSEN 2007, 97 (Syriac); WITTE 2019b, 5, 36 (Hebrew, Greek, Latin, Syriac).

10   *1. The Beginning of the Biblical Canon and Ben Sira*

and other translations also include different canons, especially a Christian biblical canon. For example, the Syriac Peshitta translation of the Book of Ben Sira was probably influenced by the Syriac New Testament.[63] In contrast, the present study assesses the question of the beginning of the canon of the Hebrew Bible / Old Testament and Ben Sira in the Second Temple Period. It therefore uses the Hebrew and Greek texts of the Book of Ben Sira as its basis.

For the Hebrew texts, the transcriptions of the manuscripts found in the Cairo Genizah and in Qumran and Masada as presented in RENDSBURG/BINSTEIN 2013 (www.bensira.org) are used.[64] Where there are differences beyond spelling to photographs of the manuscripts supplied there, between extant manuscripts, or to the earlier edition BEENTJES 1997,[65] these are noted individually. For the Greek text, the critical edition of the Göttingen Septuagint ZIEGLER 1980 is used.[66] Where there are major differences noted in the critical apparatus there (including major differences in later translations), or differences beyond spelling to the text of the shorter updated edition RAHLFS/HANHART 2006,[67] these are noted individually. All translations into English are the author's unless specified otherwise. Comparisons with the modern English translations "New Revised Standard Version" (NRSV)[68] and "A New English Translation of the Septuagint" (NETS)[69] are specified in each case.

1.3 Canonical Categories

1.3.1 History of the Canon of the Hebrew Bible

For the canon of the Hebrew Bible, there is a prominent reconstruction of its history with a successive canonization of Law (5th/4th century BCE), Prophets (3rd/2nd century BCE), and Writings (end of the 1st century CE), in this order.[70] This reconstruction, however, is criticized in recent research for two main reasons.[71]

---

[63] Cf. OWENS 2011, 195–196. For example, in Sir 38:24 and Sir 48:10 (on the Hebrew and Greek see Chapter 4 and Chapter 5.5.2), the Syriac Peshitta translation seems to be influenced by New Testament passages, cf. OWENS 2011, 187–190, 192–193; VAN PEURSEN 2019, 237. On a similar New Testament influence on the Latin translation cf. WITTE 2019b, 8–9.

[64] RENDSBURG/BINSTEIN 2013.

[65] BEENTJES 1997 with the corrections in BEENTJES 2002.

[66] ZIEGLER 1980. Also see Note 38.

[67] RAHLFS/HANHART 2006.

[68] *NRSV* 1989.

[69] PIETERSMA/WRIGHT 2007, for Ben Sira WRIGHT 2007b. NETS is also available online (http://ccat.sas.upenn.edu/nets/edition).

[70] Thus STECK 1992, 16–17, 25; GRABBE 2006, 327, 336; SCHMID/SCHRÖTER 2019, 169, 199, 358. This view is found since the 19th century CE, e.g. in GRAETZ 1871, 147–173 (mentioned by LANGE 2006, 286–287) and RYLE 1892, xiii–11 (mentioned by OSSÁNDON WIDOW 2019, 12).

[71] On additional criticisms regarding the lack of evidence for a council in Yavneh in the 1st

First, it is anachronistically based on today's tripartite division rather than on ancient textual developments.[72] Second, it is, again anachronistically, based on a unitary view of ancient Judaism rather than on ancient evidence for its plurality.[73] In current research, a closed canon is most often dated either before or after the destruction of the Second Temple in Jerusalem in 70 CE.[74] For a date before 70 CE, it is often argued that the Maccabean revolts in the mid-2nd century BCE led to a major shift in the authority of texts later included in the Hebrew Bible.[75] Some scholars argue that a tripartite[76] or bipartite[77] canon was closed at this time. For a date after 70 CE,[78] the Maccabean revolts are seen as only one step towards canon which was completed in the 1st century CE.[79]

The Book of Ben Sira and its Prologue play an important role in dating the canon of the Hebrew Bible. Some scholars take Sir 44–49 as a *terminus ad quem* for the closing of the Prophets section of the canon,[80] while this is criticized by others.[81] The Greek Prologue is sometimes taken as indicating a shift in textual authority following the Maccabean revolts.[82] The present study does not aim to rewrite the whole history of the biblical canon, but to focus on the earliest piece of evidence in it: the Book of Ben Sira. Regarding this question of the beginning of the biblical canon and Ben Sira, the following sections will discuss terms and concepts related to "the biblical canon".

1.3.2 Canon

Regarding the term "canon", in Ancient Greek κανών "rule" could refer to a physical ruler, abstract rules such as criteria or norms, or tangible rules such as models or tables.[83] In Christianity, κανών "rule" came to denote a rule of faith in the 2nd/3rd century CE, and ecclesiastical law and then sacred texts in the 4th

---

century CE cf. LANGE 2006, 286–287; OSSÁNDON WIDOW 2019, 11–12; regarding the intention to explain the exclusion of the Book of Daniel from the "Prophets" cf. OSSÁNDON WIDOW 2019, 12; BARTON 2019, 222.

[72] Cf. BARTON 2019, 221–222.

[73] Cf. CARR 1996, 25–27. Some scholars argue that before 70 CE there were group-specific canons, thus STECK 1992, 21 (only for the Writings); FABRY 1999, 267.

[74] Cf. for an overview of current research OSSÁNDON WIDOW 2019, 5–15, 205–207.

[75] Thus LANGE 2004, 67, 83, 107; BAUKS 2019, 38. On historical contexts see Chapter 2.

[76] Thus BECKWITH 1985, 152; VAN DER KOOIJ 1998, 32, 38.

[77] Thus CARR 2005, 253–254 (against CARR 1996), 272; CARR 2011, 166–179; GRABBE 2006, 336.

[78] Thus CARR 1996, 49, 56; OSSÁNDON WIDOW 2019, 205–206.

[79] Thus LANGE 2006, 290. For the 1st century CE date of the canon of the Hebrew Bible cf. LANGE 2009, 27, 32.

[80] Thus LEIMAN 1976, 27; STECK 1992, 18 (only bipartite canon); VAN DER KOOIJ 1998, 38–39.

[81] Thus CARR 1996, 28, 39.

[82] Thus VAN DER KOOIJ 1998, 37.

[83] Cf. ASSMANN 1992, 103–114; LIDDELL/SCOTT/JONES [1940], s. v. κανών.

century CE.[84] Today, "canon" usually denotes a normative collection of texts considered authoritative and sacred in religious traditions.[85] It can also be used today for collections of texts playing a central role in an academic discipline such as Classics.[86] The use of the term "canon" for a normative collection of sacred texts in centuries before the Common Era is anachronistic since the term is not used in this sense in antiquity.[87] In which form the concept of a canon existed before the Common Era is debated.

Current research on the Hebrew Bible / Old Testament uses the term "canon" with two main definitions.[88] The first is a narrow definition: (1) "canon" refers to a closed collection of authoritative and sacred writings to which nothing can be added and from which nothing can be taken away.[89] The second is a broader definition: (2) "canon" refers to writings which are considered authoritative in religious traditions.[90] "Canon" in the second definition is also often seen as the starting point of a "canonical process" ending with a "canon" in the first definition.[91] This sometimes leads to the conflation of both definitions: in order to become part of an exclusive list, writings need to be recognized as canonical before they become a part of this list.[92] The possibility of an open collection, in which some writings were definitely included but none excluded, is also sometimes considered to have existed before a closed collection.[93]

The first, narrow definition of canon is given by ULRICH as follows:

"canon is the definitive list of inspired, authoritative books which constitute the recognized and accepted body of sacred scripture of a major religious group, that definitive list being the result of inclusive and exclusive decisions after serious deliberation."[94]

---

[84] Cf. SCHINDLER 2001, 767–770.

[85] Cf. PEZZOLI-OLGIATI 2001, 767. In general English usage today, "canon" may refer to a rule, to a body of works considered important, to church law and a closed list of holy books (in addition to other meanings such as musical canons), cf. OXFORD ENGLISH DICTIONARY [OED] ONLINE 1888/2021.

[86] Such academic canons are often debated, cf. on this issue in Classics GÜTHENKE/HOLMES 2018; FRANKLINOS/FULKERSON 2020, 5.

[87] Thus also LANGE 2008, 57; OSSÁNDON WIDOW 2019, 22–23.

[88] From modern dictionaries, ULRICH 2002b, 25–33, esp. 28, deduces two similar definitions: (1) an authoritative list of books and (2) a rule of faith in authoritative books. Also cf. KRAFT 1996, 202.

[89] Cf. BARTON 1986, 56. LEIMAN 1976, 14, offers a modern definition of canon: "A canonical book is a book accepted by Jews as authoritative for religious practice and/or doctrine, and whose authority is binding upon the Jewish people for all generations." He further distinguishes between "inspired canonical literature" (the "Hebrew Scriptures") and "uninspired canonical literature" (which includes the Mishnah), cf. LEIMAN 1976, 14–15.

[90] Cf. BARTON 1996, 83.

[91] Cf. COLPE 1987, 83–84; ULRICH 1992, 270, 274; CARR 1996, 23–24; BARTON 1997, 12; ULRICH 2002b, 30; LANGE 2008, 57–58 (referring to ULRICH 1992); LIM 2013, 4.

[92] Cf. ALEXANDER 2007, 12–13, 23.

[93] See Note 90. Cf. also STEINMANN 1999, 18–19 (open canon and closed canon).

[94] ULRICH 2002b, 29, similarly ULRICH 2003a, 58. Cf. also ULRICH 1992, 270–275 (criticizing

1.3 Canonical Categories

There are at least two problems with this narrow definition. First, it implies an authority such as an institution or other body for "deliberation" in "a major religious group". Such authoritative institutions may not have existed at all times in antiquity.[95] Rather than being the result of specific decisions, the authority of texts may have grown organically within communities.[96] Second, the narrow definition may be too limited in its modern geographic focus. For example, ULRICH states:

"Clearly the contents of the canon are different for different faith communities, but the concept of canon is the same for each. Jews, Catholics, Protestants, and others will list different books in their canons, but the definition remains the same for all."[97]

However, not just the lists, but the concepts of canon differ today. For example, the Ethiopian Orthodox Tewahedo Church does not use a fixed list of books, as ASALE describes:

"The concept of canon, according to the EOTC [Ethiopian Orthodox Tewahedo Church], is not a list of books with nothing to be added or removed, but is rather an inclusive collection of ancient sacred books [...] any ancient writing that is coherent with the dogma of the church can be part of the canon. [...] It [the church] is satisfied with the tradition of eighty-one canonical books [...] without worrying that this number is neither unambiguous nor definitive. Thus, one may conclude that the central concept of the 'canon' of Scripture for the EOTC does not mainly reflect a list of specific books that would constitute authoritative Scripture; rather, it denotes 'the apostolic criteria' [...] as claimed by the church, that determine whether a given book can be part of that authoritative Scripture. In other words, the concept of the EOTC 'canon' of Scripture arises more from the ancient concept of canon as a rule of faith than the later understanding of canon as a fixed list of books."[98]

Thus, even today, "canon" does not everywhere refer to a closed collection of books in which some are definitely included and others definitely excluded.

For the centuries before the Common Era, a narrow definition of canon is often rejected in modern research.[99] An even narrower definition, according to

---

"open canon" as a confusing term); ULRICH 2002b, 32–34. A list of definitions from theological dictionaries ("Jewish, Catholic, and Protestant dictionaries as well as dictionaries in English, French, German, and Spanish", ULRICH 2003a, 58) can be found ULRICH 2003a, 78–79 and also ULRICH 2002b, 26–28. Similarly, FLINT defines canon as a closed list, cf. FLINT 1997, 21; FLINT 2003, 270.

[95] Cf. LIM 2010, 304 (against ULRICH 2002b, 29). For example, OSSÁNDON WIDOW notes that the oldest extant mentions of an explicit number (though not a list) of books important in Judaism – Josephus and 4 Ezra at the end of the 1st century CE – do not mention any institutional authority, cf. OSSÁNDON WIDOW 2019, 3, 204–205.

[96] This is also recognized by ULRICH 1994, 84 (intrinsic rather than imposed authority of texts).

[97] ULRICH 2002b, 23. Cf. similarly COLPE 1987, 90.

[98] ASALE 2016, 219–220. Also cf. BAYNES 2012, 799, 801–802; BARTON 2013, 147. Specifically for 1 Enoch and its relation to an Ethiopian Orthodox canon cf. STUCKENBRUCK 2013a.

[99] Cf. BARTON 1986, 55 (see Note 124), 57; ULRICH 1992, 274–275; FLINT 2003, 271; VAN DER

14   *1. The Beginning of the Biblical Canon and Ben Sira*

which the text of each word and not just the list of writings is fixed, is almost always rejected for centuries before the Common Era.[100] A more stable text is dated to the second half of the 1st century CE.[101] Even then, texts as handwritten objects still show a large degree of fluidity.[102]

The rejection of a narrow definition of canon for the centuries before the Common Era is mainly due to the spectacular rediscovery of the Dead Sea Scrolls since 1947.[103] The Dead Sea Scrolls comprise around a thousand mostly fragmentary manuscripts in Hebrew, Aramaic, Greek, and Nabataean, from the 3rd century BCE to the 1st century CE, only some of which contain texts included today in biblical canons of the Hebrew Bible / Old Testament, while most contain other texts.[104] Regarding texts later included in the Hebrew Bible, manuscripts among the Dead Sea Scrolls contain a variety of different forms of the same texts.[105] Given their plurality of texts and text forms, the Dead Sea Scrolls have called historical reconstructions of one unitary canon into question.[106]

1.3.3 Bible

As the expressions "biblical canon" or "canon of Hebrew Bible" show, "canon" is often connected with "Bible". The term "Bible" (based on the Greek word βιβλίον "book" with the plural form βιβλία "books" and its Latin derivative *biblia* "Bible") today designates the Hebrew Bible in Judaism, and the combined Old Testament and New Testament in Christianity.[107] In the present study, the focus lies on the Hebrew Bible / Old Testament.[108]

For the centuries before the Common Era, "Bible" – just as "canon" – is usually seen as an anachronistic term,[109] based on the development from multiple scrolls before the Common Era to a single codex from the 4th century CE onwards.[110] The production of the Bible as one book between two covers was only possible when

---

KOOIJ 2003, 28; BORCHARDT 2014, 64–65; STEMBERGER 2019, 36; STUCKENBRUCK 2020, 2–3. Few scholars disagree generally, for example SCHIFFMAN 1995, 169.

[100] Cf. SCHRADER 1994, 83; KRAFT 1996, 202; ULRICH 1992, 274; ULRICH 1999, 93; ULRICH 2002b, 30; LANGE 2006, 284; STEMBERGER 2019, 36. Few scholars disagree, for example SCHIFFMAN 1995, 173 (proto-Masoretic texts dominant).

[101] Cf. LANGE 2009, 27, 32.

[102] Cf. on textual fluidity LUNDHAUG/LIED 2017, 9–10.

[103] Cf. SANDERS 1972, 118; VANDERKAM 2002, 91–92.

[104] Cf. LANGE 2003, 1884–1885.

[105] Cf. MROCZEK 2016, 3.

[106] Cf. CARR 1996, 25–26, 63.

[107] Cf. SCHNELLE 2012, 1 (German original SCHNELLE 1998, 1407); LISS 2019, 1.

[108] See Note 1.

[109] Thus also ZAHN 2011a, 95–96; MROCZEK 2016, 4; OSSÁNDON WIDOW 2019, 19–23; STUCKENBRUCK 2020, 10.

[110] Cf. ULRICH 2002b, 29; ULRICH 1994, 77, 79; ULRICH 2003a, 62. Cf. also BROOKE 2007, 81; OSSÁNDON WIDOW 2019, 18.

1.3 Canonical Categories

codices came into use (for details see Chapter 2.2.2). While a codex could contain a whole Bible, scrolls did not have such a capacity. Nevertheless, some scrolls may have been more important than others, as ULRICH notes:

"instead of envisioning a 'Bible,' a single-volume anthology bound with the books in a permanent order, we might more accurately envision a jar of scrolls."[111]

Probably, even several jars of scrolls would have been needed to keep all the books now in the Hebrew Bible: at least the "scroll jar" found near Qumran in Cave 1 probably only contained three scrolls.[112]

Based on studies of the Dead Sea Scrolls, many scholars argue that the anachronistic use of the term "Bible" should be altogether avoided for centuries before the Common Era.[113] Nevertheless, the term and category "biblical" is still dominant in research on the Second Temple Period, and only some studies avoid the the anachronism of using it.[114] As MROCZEK notes, removing modern "biblical spectacles" remains an important task in order to understand Second Temple texts in their ancient contexts.[115]

1.3.4 Scriptures

Given the diversity of writings found in the Dead Sea Scrolls, "scripture(s)" (in singular and plural forms, occasionally with a capital S) is sometimes suggested as an alternative to the term "canon". Based on the expression (כ)אשר כתוב "(as) written" which is found in the Dead Sea Scrolls, the term "Scripture" is suggested by FLINT for "a writing that was considered divinely revealed, uniquely authoritative, and believed to be [of] ancient origin".[116] Other scholars use the combined terms "authoritative scriptures"[117] or "authoritative Scripture"[118] although this combination is not used in ancient sources.[119] The term "scriptures"

---

[111] ULRICH 1999, 90.

[112] Cf. DE VAUX 1955, 12–13; MAGNESS 2004, 146, 156; VANDERKAM 2010, 4. Also cf. BOCCACCINI 2012, 45–51 (against "biblical literature" as a canonical term). The "shelf of scrolls" mentioned in ULRICH 1994, 80 ("It may help to envision a large jar of scrolls or a shelf of scrolls.") may be a more helpful image for modern minds.

[113] Cf. FLINT 1997, 21–22, 24–25 (still using "biblical" and "non-biblical" as the best practical classification of Dead Sea Scrolls, but noting that the Ethiopian church would regard different texts as "biblical"); VANDERKAM 2002, 109; FLINT 2003, 271; VANDERKAM 2010, 194–195. On terms such as "rewritten Bible" also cf. NAJMAN/TIGCHELAAR 2014.

[114] Cf. MROCZEK 2015, 3–5, 33–34; MROCZEK 2016, 7–14, 22–23, 135–139 (pointing out the biblical focus of FELDMAN/KUGEL/SCHIFFMAN 2013).

[115] Thus MROCZEK 2015, 3 ("biblicizing lenses"), 5 ("biblical 'spectacles'"); MROCZEK 2016, 13 ("biblical – and bookish – spectacles"), 15 ("biblical lenses"), 22 ("biblical spectacles").

[116] Cf. FLINT 2003, 272 . Cf. similarly FLINT 1997, 25.

[117] Cf. LANGE 2002, 27; BROOKE 2007, 82 ; LIM 2013, 4. Also see Note 120.

[118] Cf. ULRICH 2003a, 65–66, 76–77 ("authoritative Scriptures", "authoritative Scripture").

[119] Cf. LIM 2013, 3–4 (referring to ULRICH 2002b, 33.

is noted as an alternative to "canon" which does not include the notion of a closed exclusive collection.[120] For example, BARTON argues that "scriptures" refers to a group of books with authoritative status to which others may be added, while "canon" is an exclusive group of such books.[121] BARTON then suggests to use the term "canon" for closed collections of authoritative writings, and "scriptures" for authoritative writings,[122] although he recognizes that "canon" can still be used for centuries before the Common Era in its broader sense.[123] ZAHN stresses that using a lower-case "s" in "scriptures" is important to mark that scriptures in antiquity may differ from those later included in biblical canons.[124] To distinguish "scriptures" from other texts in antiquity, their supposed ancient origin[125] or their authority for an ancient religious community[126] are seen by some scholars as distinguishing aspects. But sometimes, where the term "scripture" is used, its content is unchanged to "canon" or "Bible".[127] For example, SCHMID argues that "the literature of the Old Testament" was largely written "by scholars of scripture for scholars of scripture" who were able to recognize many allusions.[128] However, in this argument, the Old Testament is at the same time written and alluded to, thus not yet existing and already existing. The difference between the canon of the Old Testament and "scripture" is not clear, while in ancient texts allusions are also made to literature not included in the Old Testament (see Chapter 2.2.3). Thus, the use of the term "scriptures" does not necessarily avoid the anachronism of "canon" and "Bible".

---

[120] Cf. VANDERKAM 2002, 109 ("authoritative writings", "scripture"); FLINT 2003, 271–272 ("Scripture"); ULRICH 2003a, 65–66 ("authoritative Scripture"); LANGE 2004, 57–58 ("authoritative literature"). In German, STÖKL BEN EZRA 2016, 175, 188 uses "Heilige Schriften" ("Holy Scriptures") and "autoritative Schriften" ("authoritative scriptures").

[121] Cf. BARTON 1986, 56 (see Note 90). Cf. similarly CAMPBELL 2000, 181.

[122] Cf. BARTON 1986, 57, 281 n. 53 (referring to SUNDBERG 1968, 147); SUNDBERG 1968, 147; BARTON 2013, 152.

[123] Cf. BARTON 1986, 62.

[124] Cf. ZAHN 2011a, 96–97. For example, BARTON sometimes uses "Scripture" with a capital S, cf. BARTON 1986, 55; BARTON 1996, 72.

[125] Cf. FLINT 2003, 273. This idea of an ancient origin of texts also applies to texts considered authoritative in the modern Ethiopian Orthodox Tewahedo Church, cf. ASALE 2016, 219–220 (see Note 98).

[126] Thus ULRICH 1994, 79. Cf. also KRAFT 1996, 201–202.

[127] This is also noted by ZAHN 2011a, 99; MROCZEK 2016, 121–122.

[128] Cf. SCHMID 2011, 53 (German original: "die alttestamentliche Literatur", "von Schriftgelehrten für Schriftgelehrte"). This concept is criticized by STIPP 2021, 147, 154–155.

1.3.5 Authoritative Texts

"Authoritative writings",[129] "authoritative texts",[130] or "authoritative literature"[131] are sometimes used instead of "scriptures".[132] These terms could refer to any authoritative texts (e.g. laws), whether or not they appear in predominantely religious contexts. Therefore, many scholars distinguish between "scriptures" and "authoritative writings", where "scriptures" are authoritative in a religious context, and "authoritative writings" are authoritative more generally.[133] However, a strict distinction between "religious" and "non-religious" contexts is criticized as anachronistic for antiquity.[134] Other anachronisms also have to be avoided. For example, using another alternative term, CRAWFORD explicitly equates "the classical literature of ancient Israel" with "the biblical books".[135] Based on the old age and the "high status" of this "classical literature of ancient Israel", CRAWFORD excludes some books such as Daniel.[136] At the same time, she does not include books outside the Hebrew Bible such as 1 Enoch (on 1 Enoch see Chapter 2.2.4) even though they could fit her criteria for "classical literature of ancient Israel".

Even if anachronistic concepts are avoided, it is often unclear what exactly is meant by the "authority" of ancient texts.[137] For whom and in what respect are texts authoritative in antiquity? Where does textual authority come from? And how can it be recognized? For an assessment of the beginning of the biblical canon and Ben Sira, the last question is of particular importance. Only if textual

---

[129] Thus VanderKam 2002, 92, 109.

[130] Thus García Martínez 2010, 22.

[131] Thus Lange 2004, 107 (precursor rather than synonym to scripture, but for the same texts: in Maccabean times, "authoritative literature gained a dignity of its own and became scripture").

[132] Terms such as "authoritative", "normative", and "official recognition" are also used for ancient texts now included in the Hebrew Bible, for example by Barton 2019, 221–223.

[133] Thus Flint 1997, 26; Ulrich 2000, 117; Ulrich 2002b, 29. Ulrich – unlike Flint – does not use "scripture" for the canonical process before the 1st century ce, and instead speaks of "a category of sacred, authoritative books to which further entries could be added", cf. Ulrich 1992, 275 (see Note 99).

[134] For example, Colpe 1987, 80–84, sharply distinguishes between holy and profane ancient texts (similarly Colpe 1988, 202). Carr 2005, 289–290, argues that a such a sharp distinction is anachronistic for ancient texts. On this issue also cf. Zahn 2011a, 98–100. Even so, Zahn uses "any text or group of texts considered sacred and authoritative by a particular religious tradition" as a definition of "scriptural", cf. Zahn 2011a, 97. And even in the later Hebrew Bible, the Song of Songs is sometimes seen as a non-religious text, and yet included in the biblical canon, cf. Colpe 1987, 83–84.

[135] Crawford 2019, 9–10.

[136] Cf. Crawford 2019, 11.

[137] This is criticized by Borchardt 2015, 182–183. Cf. similarly Popović 2010, 1–2; Zahn 2011a, 95–102; Zahn 2020a, 197–198.

18   *1. The Beginning of the Biblical Canon and Ben Sira*

authority can be recognized at all in the Book of Ben Sira, specific views on texts and their authority can be further analysed.[138]

1.3.6 Criteria for Textual Authority

Authoritative texts, unlike texts which form a part of a canon in its narrow sense, cannot simply be found on a list. It is also not enough for texts to be known or alluded to for them to also be authoritative texts,[139] as allusions do not have to be positive but can be made to texts which are criticized. Rather, the following four criteria are often applied in current research, especially on the Dead Sea Scrolls, to determine the authoritative status of writings in antiquity.[140]

(1) A large number of extant ancient manuscripts is often used as a criterion for authoritative texts.[141] – Indeed, the number of ancient manuscripts of the same text may reflect its importance in antiquity: the more manuscripts exist of any one text, the higher its importance is likely to be. However, many manuscripts are not preserved at all, and those which are may be extant by coincidence rather than due to their importance. The number of extant manuscripts does not necessarily correspond with textual authority.[142] Almost all extant ancient manuscripts of texts later included in the Hebrew Bible were found in the desert near the Dead Sea, and they may not be representative for other regions and communities. Regarding books contained in the later Hebrew Bible, the extant Dead Sea Scrolls include parts of all books except Esther, and based on the number of manuscripts, Psalms, Deuteronomy, Genesis, and Isaiah are especially important.[143] However, the number of manuscripts also shows the importance of 1 Enoch and Jubilees (see Chapter 2.2.4) which are not included in the Hebrew Bible.[144] In addition, writings existed for which no manuscripts are pre-

---

[138] On the relation of "authoritative texts" and "oral authority" cf. MILLER 2019, 21, 23–24, 77–115, 277.

[139] This is also noted by OSSÁNDON WIDOW 2019, 178, although this distinction is not applied there 178–179. Cf. similarly WITTE 2012a, 246.

[140] For later times, other criteria are also used. For example, COLPE uses the use of texts in non-textual, non-daily practice of a community as the most important indication for texts to be considered holy, as well as the texts' content (claims of dignity, antiquity, or inspiration) and the careful written transmission of the texts. HARTENSTEIN 2019, 4, 13, 22, 34, also stresses the importance of practice and community in both ancient and modern times. Both COLPE 1987, 81, and HARTENSTEIN 2019, 15, also point to universal, ahistorical contents. COLPE 1988, 184–186, discusses descriptional, functional, and ontological levels of definitions of holy writings. WITTE 2017a, 329, defines holy writings as texts which contain existential meaning, point towards a transcendent reality, are used in special settings by a community, and are affiliated by that community with a person holding a special connection to their deity.

[141] Thus ULRICH 2000, 119; ULRICH 2003a, 66; BARTON 2013, 153.

[142] Cf. VAN DER WOUDE 1992, 157: "Writings which one keeps in one's library need not be representative of one's own views.". This is also quoted by LIM 2010, 306.

[143] Cf. TOV 2012, 95–98.

[144] Cf. ULRICH 2003a, 71–72, 80.

1.3 Canonical Categories

served today,[145] and oral tradition played an important role in the transmission of written texts (see Chapter 2.2.1).

(2) The fact of the use of texts in other texts is another criterion, especially the use of texts in quotations introducing them as authoritative (e. g. as words of God or as a written source),[146] but also the use of texts in quotation,[147] commentary,[148] rewriting,[149] and translation,[150] as well as an influence of language.[151] – Indeed, quotations introduced as words of God point towards divine authority, while quotations introduced as taken from a written source presuppose an authority of these sources which is not necessarily divine, as do quotations without introductions. The most prominent commentaries in the Dead Sea Scrolls are the Pesharim (which, however, are younger than Ben Sira)[152] which contain explicit quotations followed by interpretations for extended amounts of consecutive verses.[153] While in the Pesharim the commentary is also divinely revealed and thus authoritative,[154] the distinction between the quoted text and the commentary is clearly marked. "Rewriting" of texts presupposes the importance of these texts, but "rewritten" texts can also be authoritative themselves.[155] Translations show the importance of a text, but not necessarily its authority. The influence of language is hard to detect (it could, for example, derive from oral tradition rather than written texts) and also does not necessarily point towards the authority of texts.[156]

(3) The way of the use of texts in other texts is seen as a criterion for their authority, namely exemplification (figures found in texts later included in the Hebrew Bible are used to illustrate how a good life is to be lived),[157] explanation of inconsistencies,[158] allegorical interpretation,[159] interpretation of small details,[160]

---

[145] For examples mentioned in Jub 21:10 and 2 Kgs 20:20 see Chapters 6.2.4 and 6.4.7. Also see Chapter 2 Note 125.

[146] Thus VanderKam 1998, 389–395; Ulrich 2000, 119. Cf. also the modern criterion by Leiman 1976, 15–16 (for his definition of canon see Note 89).

[147] Thus Ulrich 2003a, 66; García Martínez 2010, 22; Barton 2013, 153–154.

[148] Thus Ulrich 2000, 119; Ulrich 2003a, 66; García Martínez 2010, 22; Lim 2010, 305–307; Barton 2013, 153–154.

[149] Thus García Martínez 2010, 22.

[150] Thus Ulrich 2003a, 66; Barton 2013, 154.

[151] Thus Ulrich 2000, 119.

[152] See Chapter 2 Note 131.

[153] Cf. Lim 2010, 305–307. On Pesharim in general cf. Berrin 2000.

[154] Cf. VanderKam 1998, 386–387; Lim 2010, 306.

[155] Cf. Zahn 2010, esp. 329–330.

[156] Cf. VanderKam 1998, 389.

[157] Thus Barton 2013, 154.

[158] Thus Barton 2013, 155.

[159] Thus Barton 2013, 155–156.

[160] Thus Barton 2013, 155–157.

interpretation showing timeless relevance,[161] interpretation as divine revelation,[162] interpretation revealing hidden meanings,[163] and calls to study.[164] – Indeed, there can be explicit mentions of texts, though such mentions are not restricted to texts now in the Hebrew Bible.[165] However, texts which contain topics or figures also found in other texts do not necessarily point to a direct relation between two texts, as there are oral means of transmitting such content.

(4) The presumed antiquity of texts is seen to show their authority. – Since authority is connected with ancient ancestral traditions,[166] explicit mentions of the great antiquity of texts can be seen as a sign of authority. However, the context of such mentions has to be taken into account.

Overall, the four most common criteria for identifying authoritative texts in antiquity are (1) the number of extant ancient manuscripts, (2) the fact of the use in other ancient texts, (3) the way of the use in other ancient texts, and (4) presumed antiquity.[167] The criteria do not necessarily suffice to identify authoritative texts, and have to be examined in each individual case. For Ben Sira, it has to be asked if and how any authoritative texts are mentioned in the Hebrew and Greek versions of the book.

1.3.7 Ben Sira and Canonical Categories

As shown in Chapter 1.1, in current research Ben Sira is usually connected with a biblical canon in its narrow sense. The distinction between authoritative texts and a closed canon is only sometimes applied in research on Ben Sira.[168] In addition, it is sometimes noted that authoritative texts at Ben Sira's time may not be the same as those later included in the Hebrew Bible.[169] For example, TREBOLLE in the article "Canon of the Old Testament" in the *New Interpreter's Dictionary of the Bible* calls for caution:

"Just as there was a plurality of Jewish groups during this time [the Second Temple Period], there seems to have been a plurality in conceptions of Scripture. The evidence from Sirach (Sir 38:34–39:1 and 44–49) and from Qumran warns us to be cautious in our views about what may have been included in the category of authoritative 'Scripture' near the turn of the era and what was already excluded."[170]

---

[161] Thus BARTON 2013, 157–158.

[162] Thus LIM 2010, 306; POPOVIĆ 2010, 2.

[163] Thus LIM 2010, 306.

[164] Thus VANDERKAM 1998, 387.

[165] See Note 145.

[166] Thus POPOVIĆ 2010, 2.

[167] At least the first criterion is also used for authoritative texts unrelated to religious authority, cf. for a canon of ancient Greek literature NETZ 2018, 14.

[168] Thus WITTE 2012a, 248.

[169] Thus WITTE 2012a, 247; ASKIN 2018b, 6–7.

[170] TREBOLLE BARRERA 2006, 554.

1.3 Canonical Categories

Nevertheless, even scholars noting that no canon or Bible existed in Ben Sira's time often assume that the biblical texts were used by Ben Sira.[171] For example, WRIGHT argues:

"The term 'biblical' is also a term of convenience and denotes only a text that ended up in the Hebrew Bible. I do not think that Ben Sira had a Bible in any modern sense of the term. [...] He almost certainly was acquainted with a much wider corpus than what we now call the Bible, and they also would have been part of his network of intertextual connections. [...] Unfortunately, there are many cases where we simply do not know if Ben Sira used sources for the Praise of the Ancestors that were not accepted into the Jewish Bible, whereas we can potentially identify texts that later became part of the Hebrew biblical canon (whether or not Ben Sira considered them canonical), and we can ask questions about how those specific texts exerted pressure on what he eventually produced."[172]

To "exert pressure", as WRIGHT states, the later biblical writings must have been in existence as authoritative texts, and their influence must be detectable in the Book of Ben Sira. Overall, while the anachronism of the terms "canon" and "Bible" is sometimes recognized in current research on Ben Sira, authoritative texts for Ben Sira are mostly still identified with those in the Hebrew Bible.

1.3.8 Study of Authoritative Texts

Asking about the beginning of the biblical canon takes a later phenomenon and asks about its development towards a result known today. However, at the time at which the beginning is usually placed, multiple developments leading to different results are more likely. The rediscovered Dead Sea Scrolls show that "canon" and "Bible" are anachronistic terms for the 2nd century BCE. It is necessary to use broader terms such as "authoritative texts", and make their relation to later canons and Bibles explicit.[173] Rather than asking only which texts later included in the biblical canon were already known to Ben Sira, the present study broadly asks whether Ben Sira refers to any texts, and if so, which texts are referred to and in which way. To find out if there are any references to "authoritative texts" (using the broadest term currently employed in scholarship on these issues, see Chapter 1.3.5), the present study applies the criteria for recognizing ancient authoritative texts (see Chapter 1.3.6) in each analysis.

In scholarly literature on Ben Sira, "canon" is applied in both its narrow sense as a closed group of authoritative texts and in its broad sense as an open group of authoritative texts, and the distinction between these two concepts is not always clear. In order to portray the different uses in secondary literature on Ben

---

[171] Thus CORLEY 2011, 57, 69–70; UEBERSCHAER 2007, 137, 220–221, n. 142; LIM 2013, 183–185 (see Notes 177, 188); SCHMIDT 2019, 57–60, 193–194, 384–397.

[172] WRIGHT 2008, 188–189.

[173] E.g. by using expressions such as "also contained in the later Hebrew Bible" rather than just the term "biblical", against LIM 2010, 304. Cf. also ULRICH 1994, 78.

1. The Beginning of the Biblical Canon and Ben Sira

Sira, the present study uses the term "canon" to denote a group of authoritative texts, without deciding whether such a group needs to have fixed boundaries or a fixed text.

1.4 Intertextual References

1.4.1 References to the Hebrew Bible in Ben Sira?

The Book of Ben Sira is usually seen to contain references to other texts which are now included in the canon of the Hebrew Bible.[174] This view is expressed in research published shortly after the first rediscovery of Hebrew Ben Sira manuscripts,[175] in several later studies,[176] and in recent research.[177] According to this view, Ben Sira knew and used almost all of the books included in the Hebrew Bible, with the exception of Daniel[178] / Ruth[179] / Esther and Daniel[180] / Ruth, Daniel, and Ezra[181] / Ruth, Esther, Daniel, and Ezra[182] / Ruth, Song of Songs, Esther, and Daniel[183] / Ruth, Song of Songs, Esther, Daniel, and Ezra.[184] Other books like Leviticus are also sometimes excluded.[185] The great variety of exceptions already shows that the underlying view is far from obvious. Most lists of exceptions include Daniel, as the Book of Daniel is usually dated to the mid-2nd century BCE and is thus younger than the Book of Ben Sira.[186]

Ben Sira's assumed use of texts later included in the Hebrew Bible is then often used to argue for the existence of a canon at the time of Ben Sira,[187] or at least the contemporary authority of texts which were subsequently included in the

---

[174] For an overview cf. WITTE 2015b, 9–10; WITTE 2017b, 16–18.

[175] Cf. SCHECHTER 1899, 34–35; SMEND 1906, XIX–XX; BOX/OESTERLEY 1913, 268, 279; EBERHARTER 1925, 8.

[176] Cf. LEIMAN 1976, 29; SKEHAN/DI LELLA 1987, 40–41; KISTER 1999, 160; PERDUE 2004, 135.

[177] Cf. WITTE 2012a, 242; LIM 2013, 185, 187; MERMELSTEIN 2014, 28; ADAMS 2016, 100; ZAPFF 2019, 118.

[178] Thus SCHECHTER 1899, 34–35.

[179] Thus STEINMANN 1999, 49.

[180] Thus KOOLE 1965, 396.

[181] Thus SKEHAN/DI LELLA 1987, 40–41.

[182] Thus MOPSIK 2003, 48.

[183] Thus LEIMAN 1976, 29; RÜGER 1984, 65; LIM 2013, 105, 230 (referring to RÜGER 1984 and BEENTJES 2006a). LIM 2013, 105, argues against BEENTJES 2006a, 172 (see Note 184) that Ezra is included as Ezra-Nehemiah.

[184] Thus BEENTJES 2006a, 172; WITTE 2012a, 242.

[185] Thus ADAMS 2008, 201.

[186] Cf. for the date of Daniel WITTE 2012c, 654 (final redaction of Daniel during the time of Antiochus IV, around 167–165 BCE).

[187] Cf. STEINMANN 1999, 49–50.

later canon of the Hebrew Bible.[188] It is also used to argue for the contemporary importance of the same books included in the Hebrew Bible that also seem to have been important at Qumran.[189] It is also frequently argued that Ben Sira depends much more on the books now included in the Hebrew Bible than on any other source.[190] Similarly, it is often assumed that the translator of Ben Sira knew large parts of the Greek Septuagint translation,[191] especially of the Pentateuch and Prophets.[192]

Differences between the Hebrew Bible and the Book of Ben Sira in words and content are often recognized as prominent.[193] However, such differences are usually explained as Ben Sira's own invention.[194] For example, Ben Sira is described by BEENTJES as "a creative author who in a very selective and conscious way adopted and elaborated the Holy Scriptures of his day into his own book".[195] Only recently has this view of Ben Sira's intentional deviation from the Hebrew Bible been criticized with ORPANA's call to "situating his work in the larger discourse of his time by noting similarities to compositions from the same general time period".[196] That Ben Sira knew and used most of the books now in the Hebrew Bible is mostly still seen as a "commonplace in biblical studies" (DI LELLA),[197] to the point that only how, not if, Ben Sira used texts now in the Hebrew Bible is asked as a research question.[198]

However, there are several fundamental problems with the view that Ben Sira refers to almost all books in the later Hebrew Bible. The most obvious problem is that there is not a single explicit quotation or mention of any books now in the Hebrew Bible in the whole Book of Ben Sira.[199] This is noted, for example, by KRAFT who states that there are "no explicit references to scriptural passages"[200]

---

[188] Cf. LIM 2013, 106, 183–184 (all books of bipartite and some of tripartite canon but canon still open).

[189] Cf. AITKEN 2000, 191 (referring to BROOKE 1997b). Cf. BROOKE 1997b, 266.

[190] Cf. SKEHAN/DI LELLA 1987, 49–50; STEINMANN 1999, 42 (referring to SKEHAN/DI LELLA 1987, 49–50); CRENSHAW 1997a, 625.

[191] Cf. CORLEY 2013, 11.

[192] Cf. SMEND 1906, LXIII; BOX/OESTERLEY 1913, 287 (referring to SMEND 1906).

[193] Cf. STEMBERGER 2019, 36.

[194] Cf. KISTER 1999, 160, 186–187; SAUER 2000, 32; REITERER 2007, 346; BERG 2013, 143, 181; WITTE 2015b, 9–10, 19; WITTE 2017b, 16–18, 30; WITTE 2020, 400–402. For further examples see Chapter 5 Notes 93–99.

[195] BEENTJES 2017b, 123.

[196] ORPANA 2016, 5, against BERG 2013 (see Note 194).

[197] Cf. DI LELLA 2006, 151. Also see Note 177.

[198] Thus CIRAFESI 2017, 104: "In regard to the poem's reuse of scripture, the question is not *if* the poem is alluding to [..., texts in Hebrew Bible] – this appears to be acknowledged by scholars frequently enough. The question, rather, is *how* do the allusions function together as a compounded whole?" (emphases in original).

[199] On Sir 48:10 see Chapter 5.5.2.

[200] Cf. KRAFT 1996, 211. This is also noted by UEBERSCHAER 2007, 226–227, esp. n. 170, who, however, still assumes allusions (see Note 207). MOPSIK 2003, 46, interprets the lack of quo-

24   *1. The Beginning of the Biblical Canon and Ben Sira*

in the Book of Ben Sira. However, even where the lack of any explicit quotations is mentioned, Ben Sira's knowledge of the Hebrew Bible is still assumed.[201] As the following section of the present study shows, the assumed references are largely based on later lists of assumed references to texts in the Hebrew Bible rather than on any explicit mentions and quotations of texts in the Book of Ben Sira itself.

1.4.2 Lists for Ben Sira

The view that Ben Sira knew almost all the books included in the later Hebrew Bible is largely based on modern lists of assumed references to texts in the Hebrew Bible.[202] Comprehensive lists of assumed references from Ben Sira to the later Hebrew Bible by SCHECHTER 1899,[203] GASSER 1903,[204] and EBERHARTER 1911,[205] all predate the rediscovery of the Dead Sea Scrolls. Nevertheless, these outdated lists still form the basis of much later[206] and current[207] research stating that Ben Sira knew almost the entire Hebrew Bible. These lists also simply list intertextual references without further analysis. This was already criticized by SNAITH in 1967.[208] More recently, BEENTJES has noted that the lists by SCHECHTER 1899, GASSER 1903, and EBERHARTER 1911 lack methodological explanations.[209] WRIGHT has criticized that the modern knowledge of the Hebrew Bible influences interpretations of Ben Sira.[210] Nevertheless, studies and

---

tations as showing Ben Sira's reverence towards older texts which for him are too holy to be quoted. However, this presumes an unchangeable canon, which is problematic (see Chapter 1.3).

[201] Thus STEMBERGER 2019, 36.

[202] This is also noted by WRIGHT 2012, 363 (referring to SCHECHTER/TAYLOR 1899).

[203] SCHECHTER 1899, 12–38. SCHECHTER 1899, 38–39, notes: "In fact the impression produced by the perusal of B[en] S[ira]'s original on the student who is at all familiar with the Hebrew Scriptures is that of reading the work of a post-canonical author, who already knew his Bible and was constantly quoting it." Cf. also SCHECHTER 1908b, 47.

[204] GASSER 1903, 199–254.

[205] EBERHARTER 1911, 4–54.

[206] Cf. PETERS 1913, XLVII (referring to GASSER 1903 and EBERHARTER 1911); MIDDENDORP 1973, 49–91, esp. 50 n. 1 (referring to GASSER 1903 and EBERHARTER 1911); LEIMAN 1976, 29, 149 n. 134 (referring to SCHECHTER 1908a and EBERHARTER 1911); STEINMANN 1999, 39 (referring to SCHECHTER/TAYLOR 1899); SAUER 1981, 492 (referring to EBERHARTER 1911); MULDER 2003, 368–369 (referring to the 1979 reprint of SCHECHTER/TAYLOR 1899). LEIMAN and SAUER also refer to KOOLE 1965, an article (without lists of references) written before the publication of the Masada findings (KOOLE 1965, 374 n. 4 refers to newspaper articles on YADIN's findings).

[207] Cf. UEBERSCHAER 2007, 218 n. 129, 226–227 n. 170 (referring to EBERHARTER 1911); WITTE 2012a, 242 (referring, although critically, to EBERHARTER 1911).

[208] Cf. SNAITH 1967, 11. WRIGHT 2012, 364, notes that SNAITH still uses canonical categories. Also cf. the criticism by STADELMANN 1980, 252–255, who, however, also argues that Ben Sira interpreted the Old Testament.

[209] BEENTJES 2006c, 187 (referring to SCHECHTER 1899, GASSER 1903, EBERHARTER 1911). Thus also BEENTJES 2006g, 12; BEENTJES 2006a, 175; BEENTJES 2017b, 103; BEENTJES 2017a, 143.

[210] Cf. WRIGHT 2012, 385: "We also need to guard against connecting any allusion or mention of something that we now know as biblical with Ben Sira's use of a biblical book. So, although

1.4 Intertextual References

commentaries continue to merely list passages similar in their words or content between Ben Sira and texts in the Hebrew Bible, without any analysis, and without including any texts beyond the Hebrew Bible.[211] However, listing texts in the Hebrew Bible which are similar to the Book of Ben Sira in their words or content does not suffice to show Ben Sira's knowledge and use of texts now in the Hebrew Bible. Rather, intertextual references from Ben Sira's text to texts now in the Hebrew Bible have to be shown.

1.4.3 Intertextuality

The question of intertextual references in the Book of Ben Sira can be placed in a wider debate on intertextuality in the Hebrew Bible and other ancient texts.[212] In this debate, approaches to intertextuality and the Hebrew Bible fall into two main groups: author-oriented and reader-oriented approaches.[213] Author-oriented approaches focus on diachronic questions, asking which older or contemporary ancient texts are referenced by the authors of ancient texts (meaning written texts extant today, although oral transmission is sometimes noted to be important in antiquity).[214] Reader-oriented approaches focus on synchronic questions, asking which other texts (including younger texts) or concepts (not necessarily in the form of written texts) a text's readers connect with it at the time of reading. For the argument that Ben Sira as an author used texts now in the Hebrew Bible, a diachronic author-oriented approach is necessary.

Sir 16:7 alludes to some form of the myth that we find in Gen 6:1–4, the short scope of Ben Sira's reference and the distinct differences between it and the biblical text should instill caution about claiming that Ben Sira was using Genesis. In his account of Noah, Ben Sira probably knew the Genesis account. [...] Perhaps the Mosaic Torah formed a canon for him (in whole or in part), but it is not clear that Ben Sira had an exclusivistic view of those works. [...] If we think that Ben Sira would have used only the Mosaic Torah in 16:7–10, then these verses demonstrate something of how he interpreted the biblical texts. If he drew from other 'nonbiblical' sources for these stories, then we know much less about his interpretive strategies." Similarly, Marböck 2000, 314–315, criticizes the list in Middendorp 1973, 66–69, but still takes the Hebrew Bible as the only source of comparison, for example when referring to the significance of expressions which appear in it only once.

[211] Cf. Middendorp 1973, 49–91, esp. 50 n. 1 (referring to Gasser 1903 and Eberharter 1911); Sauer 1981, 492 (referring to Eberharter 1911), 507 (similar passages introduced by "vgl." ["cf."]); Steinmann 1999, 37–38 (list of "Ancestors Praised by Ben Sira and His Biblical Sources" without analysis); Grabbe 2004, 338–340 (list of "Ben Sira's References to Hebrew Bible Passages" without analysis); Grabbe 2006, 324–326 (list of "Ben Sira's References to Hebrew Bible Passages" without analysis); Lim 2013, 208–212 = appendix 5 (list of "Scriptural References in Sirach 44–50" without analysis).

[212] Cf. for overviews on intertextuality regarding the Hebrew Bible Miller 2011, 284–285; Krause 2014, 37–66; regarding the New Testament Emadi 2015, 8, 21; regarding antiquity in general Bendlin 1998, 1044–1047.

[213] Cf. Miller 2011, 285–288; Carr 2012, 521–523.

[214] Cf. Carr 2011, 425–426; Stipp 2021, 145–146, 154–155. For orality and literacy see Chapter 2.2.1.

26   *1. The Beginning of the Biblical Canon and Ben Sira*

In author-oriented approaches to intertextuality, there are several general difficulties for the identification of intertextual references in ancient texts, particularly the issue of orality,[215] the plurality of extant written sources,[216] the loss of written sources (for example, texts may refer to texts no longer extant, or two extant texts could not depend on each other but a third, lost text),[217] and the possibility that texts may have changed in their transmission process.[218] Another specific problem of author-oriented approaches is that they usually search for the authors' intent.[219] But generally, no one can look into another's mind,[220] and there is an especially large gap between the authors of ancient texts and modern readers.[221] Rather, a process of detecting possible intent always involves a triangle of authors, texts, and readers.[222] References not intended by the authors may be seen by later readers in ancient texts. Nevertheless, sometimes ancient authors explicitly mark where they refer to other texts, e. g. by using a quotation formula. References which are explicitly marked in texts can be regarded as intentional whether or not the authors' names are transmitted.[223] Debates about inter-textuality regarding the Hebrew Bible and other ancient texts sometimes distinguish between intentional references (such as explicitly marked quotations) and unintentional references, but use the same criteria based on the texts to identify both intentional and unintentional references.[224] For Ben Sira and the Hebrew Bible, it is also sometimes attempted to distinguish intentional use and unintentional dependance.[225] But given the lack of explicit mentions and quotations of texts in the Book of Ben Sira, intentionality is difficult to assess. At the same time, for the argument that Ben Sira knew texts now in the Hebrew Bible, unintentional references would also suffice: whether intertextual references are intended or unintended is less important than their reference to specific texts.

In debates regarding the Hebrew Bible references are often only sought in texts included in it today,[226] even though there was a much wider range of texts in antiquity only some of which are preserved, and an even wider context of

---

[215] See Chapter 2.2.1.

[216] See Chapter 1.3.2, esp. Note 100.

[217] Cf. STIPP 2021, 144–145, 154–155.

[218] Cf. ZAHN 2020a, 85–88, 96–97.

[219] Cf. BEYER 2014, 20; KRAUSE 2014, 43.

[220] Cf. KELLY 2017, 26.

[221] Cf. BENDLIN 1998, 1046–1047.

[222] Cf. BEYER 2014, 13–14; KELLY 2017, 26.

[223] For Ben Sira's names see Chapter 1.1.

[224] In a study of New Testament texts by HAYS, intentional references are called "allusion" while unintentional references are called "echoes", and allusions are noted to be detectable with greater certainty than echoes but using the same criteria, cf. HAYS 1989, 29. On criteria see Chapter 1.4.4.

[225] Cf. SCHULTZ 1999, 154.

[226] Cf. BEYER 2014, 20–21; KRAUSE 2014, 37, 45.

non-textual entities.[227] This canonical restriction is sometimes backed up by the supposed lack of extant ancient Hebrew texts outside the Hebrew Bible,[228] or the argument that texts canonical today must have been important in antiquity.[229] Both arguments are criticized in studies based on the Dead Sea Scrolls: other Hebrew texts not today included in the Hebrew Bible are extant, and some are used in ways underlining their importance in antiquity.[230] For Ben Sira, the question of a canonical restriction is particularly important as the book is regarded as the first evidence of a canon not attested before it. At the same time, any comparison of other texts with Ben Sira is usually restricted to the Hebrew Bible.[231] Calls to include literature beyond the Hebrew Bible in comparisons with Ben Sira are few and recent.[232] The view that Ben Sira knew and used the Hebrew Bible is dominant.[233]

1.4.4 Criteria for Intertextuality

Similarities between texts in their words and contents can be due to common knowledge or traditions rather than marking references to specific texts.[234] In author-oriented approaches to intertextuality, criteria are formulated to distinguish intertextual references from other more coincidental similarities between texts. There are no standard criteria, and identifying intertextual references is a qualitative art rather than a quantitative assessment.[235] However, as a guidance in this art, criteria are either explicitly formulated as guidelines or employed implicitly in assessments of intertextual references.[236]

Regarding the Hebrew Bible and related other ancient texts, shared words are usually considered to be the first and most important criterion.[237] The syn-

---

[227] Cf. CARR 2012, 521–523.

[228] Cf. BEYER 2014, 11, 20–21; NILSEN 2018, 60.

[229] Cf. KYNES 2012, 46.

[230] Cf. ZAHN 2016, 108, 119–120; ZAHN 2020a, 119–120.

[231] For example, SNAITH 1967, 3, 11, while recognizing the possibility of lost ancient texts, still uses canonical boundaries (also see Note 208). The same is true for SCHULTZ who criticizes SNAITH, cf. SCHULTZ 1999, 152 (referring to SNAITH 1967), 213–215.

[232] Cf. HARDING 2016, 457: "In Sirach, then, the question of intertextuality cannot be reduced to identifying the influence of particular passages in the Tanakh on particular passages in Sirach. What is required is a case-by-case analysis of the relationship between the manuscripts and versions of both Sirach and the works that now form the Tanakh, and of the different patterns of influence of both Jewish and non-Jewish works on both the Hebrew of Sirach and its earliest translation."

[233] See Notes 177, 194, 197–198.

[234] Cf. BRODERSEN/NEUMANN/WILLGREN 2020, 3.

[235] Cf. MILLER 2011, 298; EMADI 2015, 21.

[236] Cf. KRAUSE 2014, 65–66.

[237] Cf. for an overview MILLER 2011, 284, 295; for examples of criteria SCHULTZ 1999, 222; LEONARD 2008, 246; KYNES 2012, 37; ZAHN 2012, 243–246; BEYER 2014, 21–22; KRAUSE 2014, 58; BRODERSEN 2017, 25; BAUKS 2019, 20–23; ZAHN 2020a, 51–52; STIPP 2021, 155. The criterion

28   *1. The Beginning of the Biblical Canon and Ben Sira*

tactical similarity of shared words (the same forms, or the same or inverted order of shared words, including whole phrases and paragraphs) is often seen as an even stronger criterion.[238] Rare words which are shared are usually seen as a stronger criterion than frequently used words,[239] although this criterion has to be used with caution due to the fragmentary transmission of ancient texts: rare words sometimes become less rare when more ancient manuscripts with these words are rediscovered.[240] Shared contents and structural similarities are mostly seen as a supporting criterion where shared words are present,[241] but sometimes also independently.[242] Where criteria for an intertextual reference are fulfilled, and other explanations such as the use of formulas are excluded, the direction of textual dependence then has to be determined:[243] one text can refer to another or vice versa, or both texts can be contemporary and possibly written by the same authors.[244] The same criteria are used for intentional and unintentional intertextual references: where there are fewer indications of their fulfilment, references are seen as unintentional, but still as references to specific texts.[245] Using shared words as a criterion for references is possible only where two texts are written in the same language. Therefore, the criterion of shared words is regarded of different importance for texts in the same or in different languages.[246] For texts in the same language such as Hebrew, shared words and their order and frequency are seen as more important than similarities in content, but for texts in other languages, the focus lies on similarities in content.[247] Based on the main lines of the debate on intertextuality, the present study as-

---

of shared words is sometimes criticized as excluding references based on content only, cf. MILLER 2011, 295–296; KYNES 2012, 37.

[238] Cf. for an overview MILLER 2011, 295; for examples of criteria SCHULTZ 1999, 223 ("Rather than setting an arbitrary minimum number of words, it is more useful to seek both verbal *and* syntactical correspondence, that is, phrases and not just words. Otherwise one may be dealing with motifs, themes, images and key concepts, rather than quotation.", emphasis in original); LEONARD 2008, 246 ("Shared phrases suggest a stronger connection than do individual shared terms."); KRAUSE 2014, 58–59; KYNES 2012, 37; ZAHN 2012, 243–246; BRODERSEN 2017, 25; BAUKS 2019, 20–23.

[239] Cf. LEONARD 2008, 246; KYNES 2012, 37; ZAHN 2012, 243–246; BRODERSEN 2017, 25; ZAHN 2020a, 51–52; STIPP 2021, 155.

[240] Cf. BRODERSEN 2017, 25 n. 150.

[241] Cf. KYNES 2012, 37; KRAUSE 2014, 59; BRODERSEN 2017, 25; BAUKS 2019, 20–23; ZAHN 2020a, 51–52.

[242] Cf. for an overview MILLER 2011, 295–298; for examples CARR 2011, 26; BEYER 2014, 21–22.

[243] Cf. CARR 2011, 426–428; KYNES 2012, 38–42, 49–54; KRAUSE 2014, 58–65; BRODERSEN 2017, 26–27; BAUKS 2019, 24; ZAHN 2020a, 85–88.

[244] Cf. KRAUSE 2014, 61; BRODERSEN/NEUMANN/WILLGREN 2020, 3.

[245] Cf. HAYS 1989, 29 (see Note 224); KYNES 2012, 30–33. Similar criteria are used by KRAUSE 2014, 56–61, for references with authorial intent only. In research on Ben Sira, knowledge of texts is more important than intentionality, see Chapter 1.4.3.

[246] Cf. CARR 2017, 44.

[247] Cf. HAYS 2008, 35, 37.

sesses shared words and contents in same-language texts and shared contents in texts in different languages.

Regarding the Book of Ben Sira, criteria for intertextual references are not always specified. For example, KAISER states that "the richly listed parallel texts [...] prove the biblical background of Ben Sira's thoughts and language", but does not give criteria for the texts included in the following list.[248] Where criteria are given, they are sometimes rather general. For instance, ADAMS refers to "the repetition of motifs and language",[249] CRENSHAW to "language" and "ideas" similar to the Hebrew Bible.[250] More specifically, shared words are sometimes regarded as a criterion,[251] or shared words combined with shared content,[252] or rare shared words or contents.[253] SNAITH, following the criticism of unanalyzed lists, mentions similarity in words or contents as a criterion.[254]

Specific criteria for intertextual references in the Book of Ben Sira are given by BEENTJES, DIMANT, and LANGE/WEIGOLD. BEENTJES directly challenges KRAFT's statement that there are "no explicit references to scriptural passages",[255] and gives the following criteria for references in Ben Sira: the introductory formulae הלא "is not?", כי "for", and once in Sir 48:10 הכתוב "the one written" combined with words or content shared with the Hebrew Bible,[256] the use of "inverted quotations" where shared words are used in reverse orders compared to the Hebrew Bible,[257] unique word combinations in Ben Sira also found in the Hebrew Bible,[258] and the "structural use of Scripture" where a passage in Ben Sira is structured by "elements" from "biblical texts".[259] Explicit quotations are defined by DIMANT, and following her also BEENTJES, as "biblical phrases of at least three words, more or less accurately reproduced, and introduced by special terms and explicit references to the source".[260] Shared contents, namely "mention of biblical persons and events", are also seen as a criterion for explicit use of the Hebrew Bible by DIMANT and BEENTJES.[261] With regard to Deuteronomy, BEENTJES identifies "explicit use of the Hebrew Bible by means of

---

[248] KAISER 2005, 157 (German original: "Die reichlich aufgelisteten Paralleltexte weisen [...] den biblischen Hintergrund der Gedanken und der Sprache Ben Siras nach").

[249] Cf. ADAMS 2016, 101.

[250] Cf. CRENSHAW 1997a, 622.

[251] Thus CORLEY/SKEMP/DI LELLA 2004, 157–158.

[252] Thus WITTE 2020, 400–401.

[253] Thus REITERER 2007, 345–347.

[254] Cf. SNAITH 1967, 7. This is criticized by SCHULTZ 1999, 152.

[255] Cf. KRAFT 1996, 211, referred to by BEENTJES 2006a, 173.

[256] Cf. BEENTJES 2006a, 173–175.

[257] Cf. BEENTJES 2006a, 175–177. Against BEENTJES, WEINGART 2015, 161–163, notes that inverted word orders are not a sufficient criterion for the identification of intertextual references.

[258] Cf. BEENTJES 2006a, 180–183.

[259] Cf. BEENTJES 2006a, 177–180, esp. 177–178.

[260] DIMANT 1988, 385, quoted by BEENTJES 2017b, 108.

[261] DIMANT 1988, 400, referred to by BEENTJES 2017b, 108.

30   *1. The Beginning of the Biblical Canon and Ben Sira*

explicit mention of persons and circumstances from the Book of Deuteronomy",[262] using as criteria "same person(s)" and "same circumstances".[263] However, all criteria are based on the anachronistic term "biblical" (see Chapter 1.3.3), and are not designed for texts not included today in the Hebrew Bible. The Hebrew Bible is the only text compared to Ben Sira, and presumed to be older than Ben Sira. The same is true for DIMANT's definition of "implicit quotation" as "a phrase of at least three words, which stems from a specific recognizable biblical context",[264] of "allusion" as "motifs, key-terms and small phrases from a specific and recognizable biblical passage".[265] LANGE/WEIGOLD 2011 provide a list of references from Ben Sira to texts now included in the Hebrew Bible[266] which is based on criteria distinguishing between explicit quotations (explicit reference to a text plus at least two shared words),[267] implicit quotations (uninterrupted sequence of at least four shared words),[268] explicit allusions (explicit reference to a text plus paraphrase),[269] and implicit allusions (at least three, or two rare, shared words).[270] The word order is not usually included in these criteria except in implicit quotations,[271] although the examples given do include shared word orders.[272] However, it is unclear how these criteria are then applied since the distinction between explicit and implicit quotation and explicit and implicit allusion is not included in the long list of references between texts given by LANGE/WEIGOLD, and the list is also restricted to the Hebrew Bible.[273] Overall, the criteria given by BEENTJES, DIMANT and LANGE/WEIGOLD are shared words or shared content solely with the Hebrew Bible, but such a canonical restriction is anachronistic (see Chapter 1.3).

---

[262] BEENTJES 2017b, 108.

[263] BEENTJES 2017b, 108 (these criteria are printed in italics in the original). With regard to Proverbs cf. similarly BEENTJES 2019, 141–144, 148–152.

[264] DIMANT 1988, 401.

[265] DIMANT 1988, 410.

[266] Cf. the list in LANGE/WEIGOLD 2011, 306–316. For the limitation on the Hebrew Bible cf. LANGE/WEIGOLD 2011, 35–36: "This restriction should not suggest that we regard the canon of the Hebrew Bible as closed early in the Second Temple period. On the contrary, based on the evidence provided by the quotations and allusions we think that even the idea of a canon as well as the idea of Scripture developed relatively late in the Second Temple period. Our restriction to the quotations of and allusions to the books of the Hebrew Bible in the present lists is motivated instead by the special importance these quotations and allusions have for the interpretative, textual, and canonical histories of the books of the Hebrew Bible. [...] Should we be able to raise more funds we hope to identify non-biblical quotations and allusions as well."

[267] Cf. LANGE/WEIGOLD 2011, 27.

[268] Cf. LANGE/WEIGOLD 2011, 26.

[269] Cf. LANGE/WEIGOLD 2011, 26.

[270] Cf. LANGE/WEIGOLD 2011, 25.

[271] Cf. LANGE/WEIGOLD 2011, 18.

[272] Cf. LANGE/WEIGOLD 2011, 25–26, 33 ("three linguistically parallel words"), 34 ("Because these five words are scattered over two lines [...] an allusion [...] is far from certain.").

[273] Cf. the list for Ben Sira in LANGE/WEIGOLD 2011, 306–316.

To give an example, it is usually argued that Ben Sira refers to the Book of Proverbs in the Hebrew Bible.[274] The similarities between Ben Sira and the Book of Proverbs are some shared words and contents, not quotations or explicit references to a written text, and could could be based on conincidence[275] or oral tradition.[276] Assumed references to the Book of Proverbs are based on comparisons with the Hebrew Bible only,[277] and sometimes explicitly connected with the argument that Ben Sira knew and copied by hand "biblical manuscripts" (CORLEY),[278] or that he regarded the Book of Proverbs as "sacred and virtually canonical" (SKEHAN/DiLELLA).[279]

For questions regarding intertextual references in general, the restriction to texts canonical today as possible reference texts is anachronistic, and any attempt to identify ancient intertextual references has to take into account the availability of texts in ancient times. Even if references could be ascertained, they would only confirm the existence of the reference texts, not necessarily their authoritative status.[280] This problem is outlined by WRIGHT as follows:

"Traditionally, scholars have invoked Ben Sira as evidence for which books of what later became the Hebrew Bible were 'canonical' in the early part of the second century B.C.E. The usual method has been to look for which books Ben Sira quoted or alluded to. If he 'knew' books that ended up in the canon, so the reasoning goes, then they must have been authoritative, and probably canonical, by his time. Books he did not know were probably not authoritative, and hence not canonical. This approach to canon stems, at least in part, from some early assessments of Sirach that followed the discovery of the Hebrew manuscripts, such as that of Solomon Schechter and Charles Taylor [...]"[281]

For questions regarding the authoritative status of texts, more extensive criteria have to be taken into account (see Chapter 1.3.6).

---

[274] Cf. SKEHAN/DI LELLA 1987, 43–45; CORLEY 2004, 155 (referring to GASSER 1903); BEENTJES 2019, 148–152.

[275] Cf. CORLEY 2004, 158.

[276] See Chapter 2.2.1.

[277] Cf. BEENTJES 2019, 148–152.

[278] Thus CORLEY 2004, 158 n. 9. However, the Book of Ben Sira does not indicate this, see Chapter 2.3.

[279] Thus SKEHAN/DI LELLA 1987, 44–45.

[280] Thus KRAFT 1996, 203, partly also quoted by WRIGHT 2012, 365–366. However, KRAFT still identifies the Pentateuch as a sort of canon based on Sir 24:23[LXX] and Sir 44–50, cf. KRAFT 1996, 203, 211. For a discussion of criteria for authoritative texts see Chapter 1.3.6.

[281] WRIGHT 2012, 363 (referring to SCHECHTER/TAYLOR 1899). Cf. also WRIGHT 2012, 385: "Simple use of a text does not communicate much about its authority, only its availability. Even traditions that originated in works that Ben Sira probably regarded as sacred he was willing to manipulate to his own instructional ends."

1.4.5 Ben Sira and Texts outside the Hebrew Bible

It is sometimes argued that the Book of Ben Sira refers to Greek and Egyptian texts.[282] For example, MIDDENDORP argues for a literary dependence of Ben Sira on many Greek texts, especially by Theognis,[283] but also on the Old Testament.[284] SANDERS argues that Ben Sira knew and used works by Theognis[285] and one passage found in the Homeric Iliad,[286] and works of the Egyptian writer Phibis preserved on Papyrus Insinger[287] as well as the Egyptian "Satire on the Trades".[288] SANDERS notes that Sir 39 explicitly mentions international sources of wisdom,[289] but also stresses Ben Sira's main focus on other texts which he identifies, based on the Prologue, with the Hebrew Bible.[290] Other scholars such as GOFF,[291] KIEWELER,[292] and WICKE-REUTER[293] argue that similarities are due to a common Hellenistic background rather than literary dependence. As for texts in the Hebrew Bible, similarities with Greek literature are often assessed based on lists comparing similar passages.[294] But unlike for texts in the Hebrew Bible, the question of textual authority usually plays no role in comparisons between the Book of Ben Sira and Greek and Egyptian texts.

Hebrew and Aramaic texts not included in the Hebrew Bible – texts which are extant especially in the Dead Sea Scrolls – are less frequently compared to the Book of Ben Sira when searching for intertextual references. But where they are, similarities are sometimes found against the Hebrew Bible. For example, ASKIN argues that Ben Sira may refer to psalms in their sequence found in 11Q5

---

[282] Cf. for a bibliography on Ben Sira's "Relationship to Greek and Egyptian Learning" CORLEY/GREGORY 2016.

[283] Thus MIDDENDORP 1973, 25, 33–34.

[284] Thus MIDDENDORP 1973, 50 (referring to GASSER 1903 and EBERHARTER 1911). MIDDENDORP 1973, 48–49 warns that texts in Ben Sira may have secondarily assimilated to biblical texts.

[285] Thus SANDERS 1983, 27, 38 (referring to MIDDENDORP 1973, 25).

[286] Thus SANDERS 1983, 39. However, SANDERS also notes that this could be a common saying rather than a direct quotation, cf. SANDERS 1983, 27, 41.

[287] Thus SANDERS 1983, 100. Cf. differently GOFF 2005, 150–152, 172 (uncertain date of Papyrus Insinger, no direct dependence).

[288] Thus SANDERS 1983, 69.

[289] Thus SANDERS 1983, 56–57, 59, 105–106.

[290] Thus SANDERS 1983, 26–27, 61.

[291] Thus on Papyrus Insinger GOFF 2005, 172 (see Note 287).

[292] Thus on Greek literature KIEWELER 1992, 269–270 (against MIDDENDORP 1973). KIEWELER 1992, 10, also states that Ben Sira knew the Torah, the Prophets, and Wisdom writings.

[293] Thus on Stoic texts WICKE-REUTER 2000, 275–276. WICKE-REUTER 2000, 217, 220, states that in the Book of Ben Sira the law refers to the Pentateuch.

[294] This is criticized by WICKE-REUTER 2000, 5–7, as not taking into account the context of passages.

(11QPs[a]).[295] It is also discussed if there are references to 1 Enoch.[296] A study conducted by ARGALL comparing Ben Sira and 1 Enoch comes to the conclusion that it cannot be proven that the authors of one text were aware of the other text, and that similarities probably arise from a similar contemporary background with rivalling traditions.[297] WRIGHT similarly argues for a common background with competing groups,[298] and also notes similarities between Jubilees and the Book of Ben Sira in the way they emphasize their own authority.[299] But usually, textual authority is only assumed for texts now in the Hebrew Bible, while other Hebrew or Aramaic literature, even if it also refers to Israel and its God, is not usually seen as an authoritative source for the Book of Ben Sira.[300]

1.4.6 Study of Historical Contexts including Dead Sea Scrolls

Since Ben Sira can be dated to the early 2nd century BCE with relative certainty,[301] questions of possible references to texts can be answered on a specific historical background. This background includes the availability and use of texts as well as material aspects of writing. The present study surveys the general historical background regarding written texts as well as references to writing in the Book of Ben Sira itself, and assesses possible references to texts both in and beyond the Hebrew Bible. While further studies on the relation between the Book of Ben Sira and Greek, Egyptian, and possibly further texts would be desirable, due to the question about the beginning of the biblical canon the present study focusses on literature preserved in the Dead Sea Scrolls in comparisons with the Book of Ben Sira: this literature, like the Book of Ben Sira, refers to ancient Judaism, it is written in similar languages, particularly Hebrew and Aramaic,[302] and has its origins in times and regions chronologically and geographically close to Ben Sira

---

[295] Cf. ASKIN 2016, 45–46, who also highlights the need for further studies on Ben Sira and the Dead Sea Scrolls. On general problems regarding the "textual reuse" studied by ASKIN see Chapters 2.2 and 2.3. For the order of psalms and other texts in 11Q5 (11QPs[a]) cf. SANDERS 1965, 5.

[296] Cf. WITTE 2012a, 239. For details on 1 Enoch see Chapter 2.2.4.

[297] Cf. ARGALL 1995, 8–9, 247, 249–250, 255. Also cf. STUCKENBRUCK 2007, 373–374, 406 (referring to ARGALL 1995), 593. For a discussion cf. WRIGHT 2007a, 163–165.

[298] Thus WRIGHT 2006b, 93, 108, 111–112; WRIGHT 2008, 188–189 (referring to WRIGHT 2006b).

[299] Cf. WRIGHT 2009, 123–126.

[300] For example, MOPSIK 2003, 46–48, notes that references to 1 Enoch are possible and a comparison of Ben Sira with Qumran literature would probably lead to the discovery of new similarities (48), but also that Ben Sira regarded as holy those writings now in the Hebrew Bible (46).

[301] See Note 7 for the difficulties of dating texts in the Hebrew Bible, and Chapter 2.1 for the date of Ben Sira.

[302] For a dictionary of Qumran Aramaic cf. COOK 2015 (cf. also the not yet completed dictionary KRATZ/STEUDEL/KOTTSIEPER 2017/2018), for a grammar of Qumran Aramaic cf. MURAOKA 2011.

(for details see Chapter 2.2.3). In addition, the texts found in the Dead Sea Scrolls are themselves of high importance regarding questions about a biblical canon (see Chapter 1.3), and some regarded as canonical even today (see Chapter 2.2.4). The present study combines scholarship on the Hebrew Bible and on Ben Sira with scholarship on the Dead Sea Scrolls. Rather than comparing Ben Sira with the Hebrew Bible only, it uses the same criteria for intertextual references to assess similarities with texts not now included in the Hebrew Bible.

1.5 Aim and Structure of the Study

The aim of the present study is to answer one main question: Does the Book of Ben Sira really refer to a biblical canon? In order to answer this question, the following steps are taken. First, the Book of Ben Sira is placed in its historical contexts, especially regarding writing (Chapter 2). The passages used most frequently to argue for Ben Sira as the earliest extant evidence of the Hebrew Bible / Old Testament canon are then systematically analyzed: the Greek Prologue (Chapter 3), Sir 38:24–39:11 (Chapter 4), and the "Praise of the Ancestors" Sir 44–50 in both a broad survey (Chapter 5) and detailed case studies (Chapter 6). Chapter 7 presents the results and implications regarding the beginning of the biblical canon and Ben Sira.

2. Historical Contexts of Ben Sira

2.1 Date and Historical Setting of Ben Sira

For the text of the Book of Ben Sira, no originals are preserved, but it is older than its oldest extant material source from the first half of the 1st century BCE (see Chapter 1.2.1). The time and place of the Book of Ben Sira – which is usually regarded as a literary unit[1] – can be reconstructed based on historical references in the book itself and in its Greek translation, and on historical reconstructions based on other ancient sources.[2] The Book of Ben Sira contains explicit references to Israel and its God and temple, for example in Sir 50 (Sir 50:1 היכל "temple", Sir 50:22 ייי אלהי ישראל "YYY the God of Israel"). Sir 50:1 mentions by name שמעון בן יוחנן הכהן "Simeon, the son of Johanan, the priest", in Greek Sir 50:1[LXX] Σιμων Ονίου υἱὸς ἱερεὺς ὁ μέγας "Simon, son of Onias, the High Priest". Sir 50 describes Simon's actions in the temple as well as building works around the temple. As the Book of Ben Sira mentions Israel's temple, and the Greek text of Sir 50:27[LXX] calls the author ὁ Ιεροσολυμίτης "the Jerusalemite", it was most likely written in Jerusalem.[3] That the priest Simeon mentioned in the Hebrew of Sir 50:1 is a High Priest can be deduced from Sir 45:24 and Sir 50:24. In Sir 45:24, כהונה גדולה עד עולם "a high priesthood for duration" is mentioned as a covenant for Phineas and his descendants. In Sir 50:24, ברית פינחס "the covenant of Phineas" is explicitly connected with שמעון "Simon".[4] In Greek, Simon is ex-

---

[1] Cf. UEBERSCHAER 2007, 34. Some parts in Sir 36 and Sir 51 may be later additions, cf. WITTE 2012b, 734–735. Also see Chapter 1.2.1.

[2] The Book of Ben Sira may have grown or been abridged over different periods of time, as partly shown by its versions in different languages, cf. WITTE 2015b, 8–9; WITTE 2017b, 15. However, in research reconstrucing different redactional stages, all these stages are argued to be Ben Sira's own work rather than that of later generations, cf. CORLEY 2008a, 41–45.

[3] Thus BECKER/FABRY/REITEMEYER 2011, 2160–2161. Also cf. WRIGHT 2019, 189.

[4] While the covenant of Phineas is also mentioned in the Greek text in Sir 45:24[LXX], it is missing in Sir 50:24[LXX]. This is sometimes taken as an adaption after Antiochus IV which showed that the covenant was in fact no longer lasting as the Zadokite dynasty of High Priests ended, cf. HAYWARD 1996, 40–41, 81–82; cf. also FREVEL 2018, 383–388. However, for example 1 Macc 2:54[LXX] still refers to Phineas and his covenant for the time after Antiochus IV, cf. KOENEN 2017. Zadok and his sons as priests are only mentioned in Sir 51:12i, while Aaron and Phineas play a prominent role in Sir 50, cf. BABOTA 2014, 276. On the complicated relations of Aaron, Phineas, and Zadok regarding High Priesthood in general cf. SCHAPER 2000; SCHWARTZ 2000; OTTO 2003b.

plicitly described as the ἱερεὺς ὁ μέγας "High Priest" in Sir 50:1[LXX]. From ancient sources outside the Book of Ben Sira, lists of High Priests in Jerusalem can be reconstructed.[5] These lists show that there are two High Priests called Simon who are also a son of Onias: Simon I, son of Onias I, around 300–280 BCE, and Simon II, son of Onias II, around 215–196 BCE.[6] Both of these are thus dated to the 3rd to 2nd centuries BCE.

In the Mediterranean region, the 3rd to 2nd centuries BCE are characterized by a historical period often named "Hellenism" after the expansion of Greek culture surrounding conquests of Alexander the Great in the 4th century BCE until Roman conquests in Egypt in 30 BCE.[7] The Book of Ben Sira mentions elements of Greek culture which fit into Hellenistic times such as good conduct at a συμπόσιον "banquet" (Sir 34:31; 35:5;[8] 49:1[LXX], Hebrew משתה "banquet" in Sir 31:31; 32:5; 49:1).[9] Specifically for Jerusalem and the surrounding regions, the 2nd century BCE also forms a part of a historical period which is often named "Second Temple Judaism" or "Second Temple Period" after the second temple in Jerusalem, built in the 6th century BCE after the destruction of the first temple, and destroyed in 70 CE.[10] The Second Temple Period for regions surrounding Jerusalem can be subdivided into the periods of Persian rule (538–332 BCE), Hellenistic rule (332–63 BCE) – including Ptolemaic (ca. 305–198 BCE), Seleucid (198–140 BCE), and Hasmonean rule (140–63 BCE) – and finally Roman rule (63 BCE–70 CE).[11] In the 3rd to 2nd centuries BCE, Jerusalem and the surrounding region can be described as affected by two main changes of rule. First, in the context of several "Syrian Wars" between Ptolemaic and Seleucid rulers, which also led to damages in Jerusalem and its temple, the rule of Jerusalem changed from Ptolemaic to Seleucid rule around 200 BCE under the Seleucid king Antiochus III Megas (223–187 BCE), who allowed the damages to be repaired.[12] Second, the Seleucid king Antiochus IV Epiphanes (175–164 BCE) took over the temple in

---

[5] Cf. VANDERKAM 2004, 491–493; FREVEL 2018, 384–385.

[6] Cf. FREVEL 2018, 384–385.

[7] On the term "Hellenism" and different dates for this period cf. EDER 1998. For a bibliography on Hellenistic history cf. CHANIOTIS 2009.

[8] Sir 34:31; 35:5[LXX] in ZIEGLER 1980, 273–274, equals Sir 31:31; 32:5[LXX] in RAHLFS/HANHART 2006, Vol. II 431–432.

[9] Thus BOX/OESTERLEY 1913, 293; KIEWELER 1998, 214; WISCHMEYER 1994, 106–109; UEBERSCHAER 2007, 35, 176, 190, 217, 355.

[10] Cf. on the terms "Second Temple Judaism" and "Second Temple Period" REED 2012; STUCKENBRUCK 2020, 1–4. An introduction to Second Temple Judaism can be found in VANDERKAM 2001, comprehensive treatments in FREVEL 2018; GRABBE 2004; GRABBE 2008; GRABBE 2020. On problems surrounding the terms such as "Jews", "Jewish", "Judaism", and "Judaean" in antiquity cf. MASON 2007.

[11] Cf. VANDERKAM 2001, 1–52. A chronological table listing rulers, High Priests, and key events in Egypt, Israel/Palestine, Syria, Rome, and Greece can be found in DAVIES/FINKELSTEIN 1989, 717–721.

[12] Cf. GRABBE 2008, 316–326; FREVEL 2018, 371–372.

2.1 Date and Historical Setting of Ben Sira

Jerusalem and made it into a Hellenistic sanctuary in 167 BCE, and the following Maccabean revolts led to Hasmonean rather than direct Seleucid rule.[13]

Regarding the Book of Ben Sira, the priest Simon mentioned in Sir 50 is usually identified with the High Priest Simon II (around 215–196 BCE).[14] The reasons for identifying Simon in Sir 50:1 with the High Priest Simon II are the following: (1) A calculation of two generations before the date given in the Prologue, in which Ben Sira is mentioned as the translator's grandfather (see Chapter 3.3.1), fits with Simon II.[15] (2) According to the 1st century CE author Josephus (Ant. 12.138–144), king Antiochus (referring to Antiochus III) allowed restoration works to the temple in Jerusalem.[16] This roughly fits the description of the building works in Sir 50.[17]

Simon II is often regarded as a contemporary of Ben Sira due to the detailed descriptions given of his appearance.[18] Simon II is also often thought to have died before Ben Sira wrote his book.[19] Indeed, Sir 50:1[LXX] uses the phrases ἐν ζωῇ αὐτοῦ "in his life" and ἐν ἡμέραις αὐτοῦ "in his days", the Hebrew of Sir 50:1 uses בדורו "in whose generation" and בימיו "in whose days", which points to a time in the past. Ben Sira does not mention the Maccabean revolts under Antiochus IV Epiphanes (175–164 BCE) and is therefore usually thought to have died before these events.[20]

---

[13] Cf. VanderKam 2001, 18–24.

[14] Thus Ryssel 1900, 235–237; Smend 1906, XV; Peters 1913, XXXIII–XXXIV; Box/Oesterley 1913, 293; Eberharter 1925, 3–5; Hamp 1951, 5, 136; Gilbert 1984, 291; Schürer 1986, 202; Skehan/Di Lella 1987, 9; Hengel 1988, 241–242; Crenshaw 1997a, 611; Sauer 2000, 338; Mulder 2003, 354; Zapff 2010, 375; Becker/Fabry/Reitemeyer 2011, 2160–2161; Mulder 2011, 284; Witte 2012b, 737 (with Simon II 218–192 BCE); Corley 2013, 5, 141–144; Wright 2013b, 2208; Wright 2019, 188–189. VanderKam, who argues for an identification of Simon in Sir 50 with Simon I around 300 BCE (cf. VanderKam 2001, 118; VanderKam 2004, 153), notes that Sir 50 may still refer to Simon II (cf. VanderKam 2000, 237; VanderKam 2004, 150, 182). The dates for Simon II differ slightly, e. g. 218–192 BCE in Witte 2012b, 737, cf. VanderKam 2004, 185 n. 203.

[15] Thus Ryssel 1900, 235–237; Smend 1906, XV; Peters 1913, XXXII; Box/Oesterley 1913, 293; Eberharter 1925, 3–5; Hamp 1951, 5; Gilbert 1984, 291; Schürer 1986, 202; Skehan/Di Lella 1987, 9; Williams 1994, 563–564; Crenshaw 1997a, 610–611; Sauer 2000, 22; Ueberschaer 2007, 35–36; Grabbe 2008, 101; Becker/Fabry/Reitemeyer 2011, 2160–2161; Mulder 2011, 282–284; Witte 2012b, 737; Corley 2013, 5; Wright 2013b, 2208–2209. Various possibilities are mentioned but not decided by Forster 1959, esp. 9.

[16] For the Greek text and an English translation of Josephus, Ant. 12.138–144, cf. Marcus 1933, 70–75. On Josephus in general see Note 88.

[17] Thus Ryssel 1900, 235–237; Hamp 1951, 136; Crenshaw 1997a, 858–859; Grabbe 2008, 101, 323–326; Mulder 2011, 282–284.

[18] Thus Hamp 1951, 5; Skehan/Di Lella 1987, 9, 499; Sauer 2000, 338–339; Wright 2013b, 2326.

[19] Thus Schürer 1986, 202; Skehan/Di Lella 1987, 9; Williams 1994, 563–564; Crenshaw 1997a, 611; Hayward 1996, 38; Ueberschaer 2007, 34–25; Zapff 2010, 375; Corley 2013, 5; Wright 2013b, 2208; Wright 2019, 188–189.

[20] Thus Peters 1913, XXXIII–XXXIV; Eberharter 1925, 3–5; Hamp 1951, 5; Schürer 1986, 202; Skehan/Di Lella 1987, 9–10; Hengel 1988, 241–242; Williams 1994, 563–564;

38   *2. Historical Contexts of Ben Sira*

This all leads to a date of the Hebrew Book of Ben Sira in the early 2nd century BCE around 190–175 BCE.[21] Ben Sira is estimated to have written the book late in his life and to have lived from after 250 BCE to before 175 BCE.[22] Thus, he lived under Ptolemaic and Seleucid rule in Jerusalem before the Maccabean revolts and Hasmonean rule. The change from Ptolemaic to Seleucid rules and the related damages and repairs of Jerusalem and its temple can be seen as a key event during Ben Sira's lifetime. In contrast, the Greek translation of the Book of Ben Sira is usually dated to the late 2nd century BCE based on information given in the Greek Prologue (see Chapter 3.3.1).

2.2 Writing at the Time of Ben Sira

2.2.1 Orality and Literacy

Oral tradition played a highly important role in antiquity.[23] In Hellenism, reading and writing were mostly restricted to privileged or professional groups.[24] Even where literacy was present, it was connected with orality.[25] For example, written texts were mostly read out loud,[26] there were oral performances of written texts for wider audiences,[27] and orality also played a key role in teaching and discussing written texts.[28] In Second Temple Judaism, reading and writing were also mostly restricted to privileged or professional groups,[29] and literacy was connected with orality.[30] For example, texts could be memorized by writers,[31]

CRENSHAW 1997a, 611; HAYWARD 1996, 38; SAUER 2000, 338–339; UEBERSCHAER 2007, 35; BECKER/FABRY/REITEMEYER 2011, 2160–2161; WITTE 2012b, 737; CORLEY 2013, 5; WRIGHT 2013b, 2208–2209.

[21] Cf. WITTE 2012b, 737; CORLEY 2013, 5; WITTE 2015b, 9, 19; WITTE 2017b, 16, 29; WRIGHT 2019, 188–189 (196–175 BCE).

[22] Cf. BECKER/FABRY/REITEMEYER 2011, 2160–2161; CORLEY 2013, 5.

[23] This is highlighted in recent media studies, cf. for Biblical studies and media studies PERSON/KEITH 2017; for Classics and media studies MICHELAKIS 2020.

[24] Cf. for Hellenism BINDER 2001, 223; SCHMITT 2005, 951–952.

[25] Cf. RÖSLER 2001. Also see Note 83.

[26] Cf. CAVALLO 1997a, 815.

[27] Cf. GUTZWILLER 2007, 178–179.

[28] Cf. DUBISCHAR 2015, 549–550.

[29] Cf. for Second Temple Judaism KEITH 2020a, 712. It is sometimes argued that professional scribes copied Torah scrolls, thus KEITH 2020a, 712; KEITH 2020b, 831; HESZER 2020, 438. However, scrolls including the whole Pentateuch are materially unlikely, see 2.2.2.

[30] For a bibliography on orality and literacy cf. HEARON 2016. For models of the connection of orality and literacy cf. NIDITCH 1996, 130; PARK 2009, 645–646 (referring to NIDITCH 1996). Orality and literacy are often connected with questions about education and canon formation in antiquity, cf. for a bibliographic overview QUICK 2014.

[31] Cf. SCHMID 2011, 54; CARR 2015, 164–165; KWON 2016, 227; PERSON 2017, 352.

2.2 Writing at the Time of Ben Sira

and references to oral traditions could be made in texts.[32] The Dead Sea Scrolls have their origin in such oral-written contexts.[33]

For the Hebrew Bible, it is debated whether orality or literacy is more important for the formation of its texts. For example, CARR emphasizes the importance of orality and memory.[34] In his book *Writing on the Tablet of the Heart*, CARR notes a connection of textuality and memorization in Prov 3:3 and Prov 7:3 which mention writing on the tablet of the heart (in both verses in the phrase כָּתְבֵם עַל־לוּחַ לִבֶּךָ "write them on the tablet of your heart"), and on the whole stresses the importance of literacy in an interplay of "writing, orality and memory".[35] Such a high importance of written texts in oral-written processes is debated. For example, HORSLEY argues against CARR that writing was not necessary for every part of a process of oral teaching, memorization, and development of material.[36] QUICK notes that different books in the Hebrew Bible may be different regarding their place on the orality-literacy spectrum.[37] And even the verbs כתב "to write" and חרש "to engrave" combined with the expression עַל־לוּחַ לִבָּם "on the tablet of their heart" are also found in Jer 17:1 with reference to the sin of Judah rather than to a written text.

The anachronism of the biblical canon is not necessarily avoided by noting the importance of orality. For example, CARR writes about "oral/written biblical traditions", thus still focussing on the Hebrew Bible rather than on traditions not included in it, and practically identifying oral traditions with some form (which cannot be reconstructed) of the written texts now in the Hebrew Bible.[38] In describing Ben Sira, CARR also explicitly focusses on books in the Hebrew Bible.[39] Similarly, WRIGHT uses the word "text" for "specific content that Ben Sira inherited in some packaged form that we could identify as Genesis or Numbers", thus also practically using the written texts now in the Hebrew Bible as the basis for the "content".[40] In contrast, a continued focus on the canon of the Hebrew Bible in studies of orality has been criticized by NIDITCH, who argues that the focus should be on "oral world mentality" instead of "the Bible as a Book".[41]

Oral tradition is difficult to grasp as voice recordings do not exist for antiquity.[42] While texts now in the Hebrew Bible may well have been transmitted orally in

---

[32] Cf. GARNER 2017, 425–428.

[33] Cf. MILLER 2019, esp. 37–38, 273, 276–279.

[34] Cf. CARR 2005, 8–10, 287–288; CARR 2011, 5.

[35] Cf. CARR 2005, 127–128.

[36] Thus HORSLEY 2007, 106 (against CARR 2005, 126–128).

[37] Cf. QUICK 2014, 29 (referring to CARR 2011).

[38] Cf. CARR 2005, 291–292.

[39] Cf. CARR 2005, 209; CARR 2011, 163, 192–193, 344–345.

[40] Cf. WRIGHT 2013a, 165.

[41] Cf. NIDITCH 2010, 7–8 (against CARR 2005).

[42] This is also noted by MILLER 2019, 37.

40   *2. Historical Contexts of Ben Sira*

some form, this form is unknown today.[43] Any modern reconstruction of oral traditions as well as their complex interplay with written texts in antiquity has to rely on extant written texts.[44] Many ancient written texts are also no longer extant. Nevertheless, there are extant written texts providing evidence for a much wider range of traditions than the Hebrew Bible (see Chapters 2.2.3 and 2.2.4).

2.2.2 Materiality

Texts are preserved written on material artefacts rather than as abstract entities.[45] The Book of Ben Sira today is called a "book" in English, but modern printed books are different material artefacts than ancient books. Ancient material culture shows a shift from scrolls to codices. The oldest extant manuscripts preserving the whole of the Book of Ben Sira are 4th century CE Greek codices (see Chapter 2.1). Such handwritten codices look similar to (very large) modern printed books: they have pages which can be turned with texts on both sides, and can contain a large amount of text. However, codices were not yet used during Ben Sira's time: they only became common around the 2nd to 4th centuries CE.[46] Earlier, from around the 6th to 3rd centuries BCE onwards, texts were written on scrolls usually made out of papyrus or parchment.[47] Most scrolls were between 3 and 10 meters long and did not have the same capacity as later codices.[48]

For example, the whole Hebrew Bible or Septuagint fits into codices such as the Hebrew Codex Leningradensis (L) (11th century CE) or the Greek Codices Vaticanus (B) and Sinaiticus (S) (4th century CE).[49] These codices form the basis of widely used modern editions such as the Hebrew "Biblia Hebraica Stuttgartensia" (BHS)[50] and "Biblia Hebraica Quinta" (BHQ)[51] or the Greek Septuagint edition RAHLFS/HANHART 2006.[52] The longest scrolls preserved among the Dead Sea Scrolls are the Temple Scroll (11Q19, 11QT[a]; first half of the 1st century CE) measuring just over 8 meters, and the Isaiah Scroll 1QIsa[a] (second half of the 1st century BCE), where the text of Isa 1–66 is written on a scroll which is just over 7 meters long.[53] Longer scrolls are not actually extant

---

[43] Cf. on the impossibility of reconstructions also CARR 2005, 292.

[44] Cf. HORSLEY 2007, 110, for a quote see Chapter 5.5.3 Note 169.

[45] This is highlighted in recent material culture studies, cf. HILGERT 2016; KRAUß/ LEIPZIGER/SCHÜCKING-JUNGBLUT 2020; on material culture studies generally KALTHOFF/ CRESS/RÖHL 2016.

[46] Cf. CAVALLO 1997a, 811; CAVALLO 1997b, 52.

[47] Cf. CAVALLO 1997a, 811; CAVALLO 2001, 1047–1049.

[48] Cf. CAVALLO 2001, 1048 (2.5 to 12 meters); CARR 2020, 600–601 (3 to 10 meters).

[49] On these codices cf. TOV 2012, 45, 133.

[50] Cf. ELLIGER/RUDOLPH 1997 [BHS], XII.

[51] Cf. TAL 2015 [BHQ], 5*.

[52] Cf. RAHLFS/HANHART 2006, XI.

[53] Cf. TOV 1998, 71 ("it is possible that several of the scrolls found in Qumran contained more than one book of the Torah, and possibly all of the Torah, in which case they would have

2.2 Writing at the Time of Ben Sira

from a comparable time and place. Should they have existed, they would have been an extreme exception and very difficult to handle.[54] Given the usual scroll lengths, even individual books included in the Hebrew Bible such as the Book of Psalms are too long to fit onto one scroll,[55] let alone whole compositions such as all of the "Prophets" in the Hebrew Bible,[56] or the Hebrew Bible in its entirety. Compositions such as the Pentateuch are sometimes reconstructed as having fitted onto one large scroll of about 25–30 meters.[57] However, there is no extant material evidence for an ancient scroll containing the whole Pentateuch. Fragmentary scrolls among the Dead Sea Scrolls are sometimes reconstructed to contain at least two books of the Pentateuch, but none of these preserve any whole individual books or any actual joins between books of the Pentateuch.[58] The later term "Pentateuch", used from the 2nd century CE, also points to the limitations of ancient scrolls, while also attesting that scrolls could then be seen as belonging together: "Pentateuch" is based on the Greek word πεντάτευχος which combines πέντε "five" and τεῦχος "scroll (jar)", and literally means "five scrolls" – not one scroll.[59] Because scrolls rather than codices were used for writing, the Hebrew Bible could not exist as one material unit before the Common Era. Rather, texts later included in it could only be written on separate scrolls.[60] The importance of ancient material writing culture is recognized in recent research for example by CARR who proposes a "scroll approach"[61] to reconstructing the history of texts included in the Hebrew Bible.

Scrolls could be stored in libraries in antiquity.[62] In Hellenistic times, libraries existed in places of wealth, such as palaces and temples, sometimes also schools or private houses.[63] Around the beginning of the 3rd century BCE, the library

---

measured 25–30 meters. At the same time, the only preserved evidence for long scrolls pertains to 1QIsa[a] and 11QT[a]."), 72 (11QT[a] 8.148 meters; 1QIsa[a] 7.34 meters); TOV 2004, 74–77. For the dates of the scrolls cf. WEBSTER 2002, 385, 422.

[54] Cf. CARR 2020, 609–610.

[55] For example, a book of 150 Psalms was probably too long, cf. PAJUNEN 2014, 143.

[56] Cf. BRANDT 2001, 72.

[57] Thus TOV 1998, 71 (see Note 53); LANGE 2009, 151, 168–169. Against this cf. CARR 2020, 614.

[58] Cf. TOV 1998, 70–71; TOV 2004, 75. Even 4Q11 (4QpaleoGen-Exod[l]) preserves merely one complete letter of what may be Genesis, cf. SKEHAN/ULRICH/SANDERSON 1992, 17, 25, Plate I. SCHMID 2011, 38–40, also notes an average length of 8 to 9 meters for ancient scrolls but still argues that all of Genesis to 2 Kings may have been written onto one ancient scroll. Also see Note 95.

[59] This is also noted by CARR 2020, 608. On the term "Pentateuch" in general cf. OTTO 2003a, 1089–1090.

[60] This is also noted by VAN DER TOORN 2007, 20–23.

[61] CARR 2020, 595.

[62] CRAWFORD 2019, 8, 31–32, notes that a distinction between a "library" with literary and an "archive" with administrative texts does not apply to antiquity.

[63] Cf. NIELSEN 1997, 634; VÖSSING 1997, 640–643; DUBIELZIG 2005, 214–216.

42   2. *Historical Contexts of Ben Sira*

in Alexandria in Egypt collected a very large number of texts[64] – rather than a limited canon. It is unclear if there was a library attached to the Second Temple in Jerusalem, and if so whether it contained the texts now found in the Hebrew Bible. Some scholars assume both.[65] Indeed, there are some indications for the existence of a library in Jerusalem.[66] For example, scribes at the Jerusalem temple are mentioned by the 1st century CE author Josephus (Ant. 12.138–142, esp. 142: οἱ γραμματεῖς τοῦ ἱεροῦ "the scribes of the temple") for the time of Antiochus III around 200 BCE.[67] 2 Macc 2:13–15[LXX] explicitly refers to a library, stating for the time of Judas Maccabaeus (mid-2nd century BCE):[68]

2 Macc 2:13[LXX]	Ἐξηγοῦντο δὲ καὶ ἐν ταῖς ἀναγραφαῖς καὶ ἐν τοῖς ὑπομνηματισμοῖς τοῖς κατὰ τὸν Νεεμιαν τὰ αὐτὰ καὶ ὡς καταβαλλόμενος βιβλιοθήκην ἐπισυνήγαγεν τὰ περὶ τῶν βασιλέων βιβλία καὶ προφητῶν καὶ τὰ τοῦ Δαυιδ καὶ ἐπιστολὰς βασιλέων περὶ ἀναθεμάτων.	These things are also reported in the records and in the memoirs according to Nehemiah, and how founding a library he collected the books about the kings and prophets and those about David, and letters of kings about curses.
2:14[LXX]	ὡσαύτως δὲ καὶ Ιουδας τὰ διαπεπτωκότα διὰ τὸν γεγονότα πόλεμον ἡμῖν ἐπισυνήγαγεν πάντα, καὶ ἔστιν παρ᾽ ἡμῖν.	Similarly Judas also collected all these that had been lost because of the war that had happened to us, and they are with us.
2:15[LXX]	ὧν οὖν ἐὰν χρείαν ἔχητε, τοὺς ἀποκομιοῦντας ὑμῖν ἀποστέλλετε.	So if you have need of them, send those who will bring them for you.

Based on such sources, CRAWFORD argues for the existence of a library in Jerusalem, and states regarding its content:

"This library housed sacred scrolls, definitely Torah scrolls but undoubtedly also the other books that became part of the later Jewish canon, as well as archival material. We cannot be certain what other types of literature may have been stored in the temple library (e.g., books of the later Apocrypha, or other Jewish literary works)."[69]

However, against an equation of a possible library's content with today's Hebrew Bible, the Pentateuch is not mentioned in 2 Macc 2:13[LXX] at all.[70] At the same time,

---

[64] Cf. VÖSSING 1997, 641; BAGNALL 2002, 351–356, 361–362; DUBIELZIG 2005, 214–215; NESSELRATH 2013, 77–78. For a bibliography on the library at Alexandria cf. CLAYMAN 2016.

[65] Thus BECKWITH 1988, 41–42, 70; DAVIES 1998, 87; SCHNIEDEWIND 2004, 182–183; CRAWFORD 2019, 98–100, 315–317.

[66] Cf. for a discussion of these sources as well as rabbinic sources CRAWFORD 2019, 98–100, 315–317.

[67] Thus CRAWFORD 2019, 72–73. For the Greek text and an English translation of Josephus, Ant. 12.138–144, cf. MARCUS 1933, 70–75. On Josephus in general see Note 88, on Antiochus III see Note 12.

[68] Cf. on the date of 2 Macc (late 2nd century BCE) BERLEJUNG 2012b, 759–760.

[69] CRAWFORD 2019, 100. Cf. similarly CRAWFORD 2019, 315–317.

[70] This is also noted by ULRICH 2003b, 213; SCHMID 2011, 45–47; CRAWFORD 2019, 99 n. 162.

books not included in the Hebrew Bible today are explicitly mentioned in 2 Macc 2:13[LXX], namely "records" and "memoirs according to Nehemiah" and "letters of kings about curses". Even taking aside the question whether 2 Macc 2:13[LXX] can be taken as a source for the earlier times of Ben Sira, the verse does not seem to describe a library preserving only the canon of the Hebrew Bible.[71] Nevertheless, a temple library in Jerusalem is often referred to by scholars arguing for a closed canon in Maccabean times.[72]

2.2.3 Literature

In Hellenism, literature[73] was written in poetry and prose, from hymns and epics to texts on mathematics and medicine.[74] Greek was its common language,[75] Alexandria with its library a centre of literature.[76] Written literature played an important role among educated elites.[77] Hellenistic literature is often described by modern scholars as "bookish",[78] as containing allusions to earlier literature, especially Homeric poetry, but also contemporary literature,[79] and as mentioning writing.[80] However, literature such as Homeric poetry is also described as oral in origin and transmission.[81] Hellenistic commentaries on earlier literature are often reconstructed from later sources.[82] Some authors (for example Homer or Hesiod) are mentioned in Hellenistic literature especially frequently – but not always with reference to written texts rather than sayings[83] – and there is no closed canon of written texts.[84]

---

[71] Cf. Mroczek 2015, 26–29.

[72] Thus Beckwith 1985, 82; van der Kooij 1998, 31.

[73] The term "literature" is used for any coherent written text in antiquity, cf. Rüpke 1999.

[74] For a bibliography on Hellenistic literature cf. Clayman 2016.

[75] Cf. Krevans/Sens 2006, 186–189.

[76] Cf. Gutzwiller 2007, 21–23.

[77] Cf. Gutzwiller 2007, 178–179.

[78] Thus Pfeiffer 1968, 102; Krevans/Sens 2006, 194; Gutzwiller 2007, 178.

[79] Cf. Dubielzig 2005, 216; Kühnert/Vogt 2005; Krevans/Sens 2006, 189–196; Gutzwiller 2007, 169–188.

[80] Cf. Gutzwiller 2007, 178–180.

[81] Cf. Bird 2010, 27–34.

[82] For a bibliography on ancient scholarship cf. Butterfield 2017. Most of the Hellenistic commentaries are no longer extant and can only be reconstructed from much later sources, cf. Dickey 2007, 4–6, especially from "scholia", i. e. marginal comments in medieval codices, rather than from scrolls, cf. Dickey 2007, 11–13, 18–23.

[83] For example, Callimachus – a Hellenistic author in Alexandria in the 4th to 3rd centuries BCE, cf. Lehnus 1999 – mentions Ὁμήρειον [...] γράμμα "Homeric writing" (Epigram VII, Mair 1960, 142) as well as αἶνος Ὁμηρικός "Homeric saying" (Aetia Fragment 178, Trypanis 1975, 94). Also cf. Bird 2010, 43: "Those classical authors who quote lines of Homer may well not have depended on written texts at all; their versions of Homer will have derived from one or other of the various and varied performance traditions with which they will have been familiar."

[84] On Greek literature and canon formation cf. Hose 1999, 281–284. On texts used in education cf. Wissmann 2010, 63–64.

44   *2. Historical Contexts of Ben Sira*

For Second Temple Judaism, literature in Hebrew, Greek and other languages is extant, especially since the rediscovery of the Dead Sea Scrolls.[85] However, much of this literature is younger than Ben Sira.[86] Two prominent authors, Philo (ca. 15 BCE to 50 CE)[87] and Josephus (ca. 37/38 CE to 100 CE),[88] wrote in Greek in the 1st century CE, around two whole centuries after Ben Sira whose book was written around 190–175 BCE (see Chapter 2.1). Which literature might have been available before and during the time of Ben Sira?

Most of the texts included in the Hebrew Bible are dated to times before Ben Sira.[89] A prominent exception is the Book of Daniel which was probably completed after the Book of Ben Sira, around 165 BCE.[90] The oldest extant manuscripts of texts included in the Hebrew Bible are found among the Dead Sea Scrolls which were written between the 3rd century BCE and the 2nd century CE.[91] A chronological survey shows that most of the Dead Sea Scrolls manuscripts are dated to the 1st century BCE.[92] Only a few very fragmentary manuscripts are dated before 175 BCE and are thus probably earlier than or at least contemporary with the Book of Ben Sira: 4Q17 (4QExod-Levf), 4Q52 (4QSamb), 4Q46 (4QpaleoDeuts), 4Q15 (4QExodd), 4Q70 (4QJera), 4Q201 (4QEna ar), and 4Q208 (4QEnastra ar).[93] A slightly larger number of manuscripts containing texts included in the Hebrew Bible as well as other texts is dated to the 2nd century BCE and possibly contemporary with the Book of Ben Sira.[94] Among the 3rd to early 2nd century BCE manuscripts, 4Q17 (4QExod-Levf), 4Q201 (4QEna ar), and 4Q208 (4QEnastra ar) are of particular relevance for the question of canon. 4Q17 (4QExod-Levf), a manuscript dated to the mid-3rd century BCE, is reconstructed to have contained Exodus and Leviticus, but Leviticus is reconstructed

---

[85] For a bibliography on Second Temple literature cf. GRABBE 2012.

[86] For an introduction for Second Temple literature in chronological order cf. NICKELSBURG 2005.

[87] For the date of Philo and an overview of his writings cf. RUNIA 2000. Also cf. NIEHOFF 2011, 5: "Lacking independent exegetical sources between the mid second century BCE and the first century CE, vital evidence of the diversity of Alexandrian Judaism comes from Philo."

[88] For the date of Josephus and an overview of his writings cf. WANDREY 1998. Josephus' writings "Antiquitates judaicae" (Ant.) and "Against Apion" (Ag. Ap.) both date from the last decade of the 1st century CE, cf. WANDREY 1998, 1090.

[89] Cf. the chronological overview in GERTZ et al. 2012, 800–802.

[90] See Chapter 1 Note 186.

[91] Cf. TOV 2012, 99. For the exception of silver rolls from the 7th or 6th century BCE with parts of the blessing contained in Num 6:24–26 cf. TOV 2012, 111.

[92] Cf. WEBSTER 2002, 371–375. On the difficulties of dating the Dead Sea Scrolls manuscripts cf. WEBSTER 2002, 351–368. For a chronological survey of texts in the Hebrew Bible only and their similarity to the Masoretic Text cf. LANGE 2009, 30–31.

[93] Cf. WEBSTER 2002, 378 (without 4Q201); DRAWNEL 2019, 70–71 (4Q201).

[94] Cf. WEBSTER 2002, 378–380. A list of Dead Sea Scrolls manuscripts dated before 175 BCE can be found in LANGE 2006, 279–281, although some date ranges there include times after 175 BCE.

2.2 Writing at the Time of Ben Sira

from two small fragments with a few letters which are not joined to the rest of the manuscript.[95] 4Q201 (4QEn[a] ar), dated to the end of the 3rd or beginning of the 2nd century BCE, contains parts of 1 Enoch 1–10 (Book of Watchers; see Chapter 2.2.4. on 1 Enoch).[96] 4Q208 (4QEnastr[a] ar), also dated to the end of the 3rd or beginning of the 2nd century BCE, may be the oldest extant evidence for 1 Enoch 73 (Astronomical Book), and even in case it represents some other text, this text is not included in the Hebrew Bible.[97] Thus, the oldest manuscript evidence shows that some texts now included in the Hebrew Bible existed in the 3rd to early 2nd century BCE, but so did texts not included in the Hebrew Bible. There is no manuscript evidence for a closed canon at this time, not even for a closed Pentateuch.

For the Septuagint, the translation of the Pentateuch is usually dated to the 3rd century BCE.[98] A main basis for this date is the Letter of Aristeas, which probably postdates Ben Sira.[99] Other Septuagint texts are dated later than the Septuagint Pentateuch, from the 2nd century BCE to the 2nd century CE.[100] Overall, there were multiple Greek texts rather than one fixed Septuagint translation in antiquity.[101] There is Greek manuscript evidence for a fragment of Deuteronomy, 4Q122 (4QLXXDeut), from the first half of the 2nd century BCE.[102] Greek fragments of Exodus, Leviticus and Numbers (though not Genesis) are found among the later Dead Sea Scrolls from around 125 BCE until the 1st century CE.[103] A few Greek fragments of Deuteronomy are preserved on a papyrus from the 2nd century BCE; later Greek manuscripts before the Common Era preserve some parts of Genesis, Exodus, Leviticus, Numbers, Deuteronomy, the Epistle of Jeremiah, and the Twelve Prophets.[104]

A number of ancient texts not included in the Hebrew Bible or Septuagint but from similar geographic regions and in related languages are dated earlier than or at least contemporary to Ben Sira.[105] While such texts, their dates of composition,

---

[95] Cf. CROSS 1994, 133–134, 143–144, Plate XXII.

[96] Cf. DRAWNEL 2019, 59–60, 68, 70–71.

[97] Cf. DRAWNEL 2011, 29, 72–73.

[98] Cf. KREUZER 2016, 41; AITKEN 2021, 9–10; BOYD-TAYLOR 2021, 13–17 (noting the issue of textual fluidity).

[99] On the date of the Letter of Aristeas cf. TILLY 2007 (2nd half of the 2nd century BCE); WRIGHT 2015, 28 (150–100 BCE); KREUZER 2016, 41 (around 125 BCE).

[100] Cf. for an overview SIEGERT 2001, 42–43. Also cf. BOYD-TAYLOR 2021, 19.

[101] Cf. BOYD-TAYLOR 2021, 20–22; MEADE 2021, 222–223, 227–228; ROSS 2021, 4–5.

[102] Cf. WEBSTER 2002, 379.

[103] Cf. TOV 2002, 177–178; for the dates of the Greek manuscripts WEBSTER 2002, 387, 394, 397, 410.

[104] Cf. KREUZER/SIGISMUND 2016, 89–90 (and also SIEGERT 2001, 96–98) in combination with SEPTUAGINTA-UNTERNEHMEN 2012, 13, 15, esp. Siglum 957.

[105] For difficulties of dating texts in the Second Temple period in general cf. NICKELSBURG 2005, 3; SIEGERT 2019, 29–30, 47–48, 68–69. Also see Chapter 1 Note 7.

46   *2. Historical Contexts of Ben Sira*

and their contents cannot all be treated in detail here,[106] a brief survey based on all Second Temple literature translated in the three volumes of *Outside the Bible* allows for a broad overview (giving some examples of figures mentioned in these texts in brackets).[107] According to this survey, the composition of several texts can be dated to times in the 3rd century BCE, before the Book of Ben Sira, namely 1 Enoch (mentioning Enoch),[108] Aramaic Levi Document (mentioning Levi),[109] Demetrius the Chronographer (mentioning Jacob and Joseph),[110] Instruction-like Composition B (4Q424, 4QInstruction-like Work; about wisdom),[111] and Tobit (Tobit[LXX]; mentioning priests as sons of Aaron and Levi).[112] Further texts were possibly also composed in the 3rd or early 2nd century BCE, earlier than or contemporary to Ben Sira's book:[113] Artapanus (mentioning Abraham, Moses, and Joseph),[114] Book of Giants (mentioning Enoch),[115] Ezekiel the Tragedian (mentioning Moses),[116] Genesis Apocryphon (1Q20, 1QapGen ar; mentioning Methuselah, Lamech, Enoch, Noah, and Abraham),[117] Jubilees (mentioning Enoch),[118] Musar leMevin, also known as 4QInstruction (about wisdom),[119] New Jerusalem (often compared to Ezekiel but not mentioning this

---

[106] For two more detailed examples, 1 Enoch and Jubilees, see Chapter 2.2.4, for details on 4Q397 (4QMMT[d]) see below.

[107] FELDMAN/KUGEL/SCHIFFMAN 2013. Further studies on the dates of composition of Second Temple literature would be desirable, including issues such as different possible directions of dependence between texts and textual fluidity, cf. for example on 4Q365 (4QRP[c]) ZAHN 2011b, 6 n. 20; ZAHN 2020a, 115–119.

[108] For details on 1 Enoch see Chapter 2.2.4.

[109] Cf. STONE/ESHEL 2013, 1490–1491 ("in the 3rd century BCE or the early 2nd century BCE at the latest", extant among other sources in late Hasmonean or early Herodian Dead Sea Scrolls).

[110] Cf. DITOMMASO 2013, 669–670 ("last decades of the 3rd century BCE", extant in later Christian sources).

[111] Cf. LANGE 2013a, 2414 ("early postexilic times [...] the earliest nonbiblical text from the Qumran library" rather than "after 200 BCE", extant in 4Q424 from the end of the 1st century BCE).

[112] Cf. NICKELSBURG 2013, 2631–2633 ("3rd century BCE", extant in Dead Sea Scrolls fragments and in translations, especially the Septuagint).

[113] A longer list of texts dated before 175 BCE is provided by LANGE 2006, 279–281, but the dates of these texts are not explained further.

[114] Cf. GRUEN 2013, 675–676 ("no later than the early 1st century BCE [...] no earlier than the mid-3rd century BCE", extant in later Christian sources).

[115] Cf. STUCKENBRUCK 2013b, 221 ("during the first third of the 2nd century BCE, though a date during the latter part of the 3rd century BCE is also possible", extant in Dead Sea Scrolls), 222, 226.

[116] Cf. JACOBSON 2013, 730 ("200–100 BCE", extant in later Christian sources), 731.

[117] Cf. MORGENSTERN/SEGAL 2013, 237–238 ("somewhere between the 3rd and 1st centuries BCE", extant on 1Q20 from the 1st century BCE), 241, 243, 251. On Genesis Apocryphon (1Q20, 1QapGen ar) also see Chapter 6.2.4.

[118] For details on Jubilees see Chapter 2.2.4.

[119] Cf. LANGE 2013b, 2418–2419 ("between the later part of the 3rd century BCE and the first half of the 2nd century BCE", extant on Dead Sea Scrolls manuscripts from the late 1st century BCE or early 1st century CE).

name),[120] Philo the Epic Poet (mentioning Abraham and Joseph),[121] Pseudo-Orpheus (possibly mentioning Moses),[122] and Pseudo-Philo, On Samson and On Jonah (mentioning Samson and Jonah).[123] This brief survey points to two aspects of relevance for questions about the beginning of the biblical canon and Ben Sira. First, the texts listed above as earlier than or contemporary to Ben Sira mention many figures also found in the Hebrew Bible.[124] Second, at the same time, they do not seem to contain explicit quotations or mentions of books now in the Hebrew Bible, while there are explicit mentions of books not included in the Hebrew Bible.[125] These phenomena are usually described as intentional deviations from the Hebrew Bible.[126] However, in light of the discussions about canon[127] and oral tradition,[128] it could be questioned if the texts in the Hebrew Bible even formed the basis of these texts. Texts with explicit quotations and comments on texts now in the Hebrew Bible, most prominently the Pesharim, are dated later than Ben Sira, mostly to the 1st century BCE.[129] STUCKENBRUCK argues that for

---

[120] Cf. ANGEL 2013, 3152–3153 ("before the middle fo the 2nd century BCE [...] no earlier than the 3rd century BCE", extant in Dead Sea Scrolls from 50 BCE to 50 CE).

[121] Cf. ATTRIDGE 2013, 726–728 ("3rd or 2nd century BCE", extant in later Christian sources).

[122] Cf. AUNE 2013, 743 ("no earlier than the 3rd century BCE", extant in later Christian sources), 745, 749.

[123] Cf. MURADYAN/TOPCHYAN 2013, 750–752 ("early 2nd century BCE [to] 4th century CE", extant in later Armenian sources).

[124] For example, for the Aramaic Levi Document, which mentions Levi, the different attitude to priesthood compared to Ben Sira is noted by STONE/ESHEL 2013, 1491. Such a debate could be on persons rather than texts.

[125] For writings of Noah mentioned in Jubilees and 1Q20 (1QapGen ar) see Chapter 6.2.4, esp. Note 101. Another example regards Musar LeMevin (MLM, also known as 4QInstruction): LANGE 2013b, 2418, argues that MLM criticizes the book of Ecclesiastes and must therefore be later, but there is no direct mention of Ecclesiastes in MLM. LANGE 2013b, 2419, also argues that it "quotes and alludes to authoritative literature more often than it quotes other Jewish Wisdom texts" which "is a reflection of this increased importance of the Torah". However, the only book actually mentioned in MLM is "the book of remembrance" before God, and "the vision of Hagoh (murmuring) is the book of remembrance" (MLM as translated in LANGE 2013b, 2423). This book is not a part of the Hebrew Bible. Nevertheless, LANGE 2013b, 2424, states: "In allusion to Mal. 3:16, the Torah is described as the 'book of remembrance.' MLM identifies it as the 'vision of Hagoh.'" (emphasis in original). LANGE 2013b, 24232, also states that the "author clearly knows the Pentateuch". LANGE 2006, 288, states that before 175 BCE "quotations and allusions to authoritative literature" in- and outside the Hebrew Bible can be found.

[126] For example, ANGEL 2013, 3153 notes on "New Jerusalem": "Although the author closely followed Ezek. 40–48, he also modified this material extensively." For Ezekiel the Tragedian cf. GRUEN 2010, 416: "Ezekiel retold the story of the Exodus, employing the tragic mode to convey a familiar tale in a new form. He followed closely the narrative and language of the Septuagint (there is nothing to suggest that he consulted the Hebrew version or even knew the language), but did not refrain from injecting elements that went beyond material in the Book of Exodus."

[127] See Chapter 1.3.

[128] See Chapter 2.2.1.

[129] Pesharim manuscripts date from 100 BCE onwards, cf. LIM 2002, 20–22, also cf. e. g. NITZAN 2013, 636 (Pesher Habakkuk manuscript 1QpHab "second half of the 1st century BCE"); TZOREF 2013, 623 (Pesher Nahum manuscript 4Q169, 4QpNah, "latter half of the 1st century

48   *2. Historical Contexts of Ben Sira*

the Second Temple Period, the use of "sacred traditions", "settings" and "figures" are frequently found in extant literature, as well as new revelations, rather than "biblical interpretation" or "rewritten Bible".[130]

For the beginning of the biblical canon, 4Q397 (4QMMT^d), a manuscript of a text called "Miqṣat Maʿaśe Ha-Torah" (MMT, "Some Works of the Torah"), is of particular importance. The MMT text is preserved on six manuscripts (4Q394–399, 4QMMT^a–f) from around 75 BCE to 50 CE.[131] The MMT text may have developed from 159–152 BCE onwards,[132] or have later origins in the Hasmonean period (possibly towards its end in the mid-1st century BCE).[133] The manuscript 4Q397 (4QMMT^d) can be dated to around the end of the 1st century BCE to the beginning of the 1st century CE.[134] 4Q397 (4QMMT^d) is sometimes argued to refer to a tripartite canon of the Hebrew Bible,[135] or at least a bipartite[136] or one-part canon.[137] However, the relevant passage, 4Q397 Fragments 14–21 Line 10, is spread across three fragments whose joins are not preserved. Reconstructed, Line 10 of 4Q397 Fragments 14–21 reads on Fragment 18: כתב]נו אליכה שנבין בספר מושׁה "w[e have written] to you that you will have understanding in the book of Mo[ses]". This is followed on a separate Fragment 17 by ו]בספר[י] "[and] in the book[s of]" and then on Fragment 15 by הנ]ביאים ובדוי[ד] "[the p]rophets and in Dav[id]".[138] Some scholars argue that the small Fragment 17 cannot be placed in this reconstructed sequence with any certainty.[139] In addition to questions about the reconstruction of the passage, it is debated whether the content of the passage refers to a canon of the Hebrew Bible.[140] The first "book" may not refer to the Pentateuch,[141] "prophets" may not refer to all of the Former and Latter Prophets in the

---

BCE"). The text of the Pesharim is dated "roughly between 150 B.C.E. and 68 C.E., and most of the texts probably between 100 and 1 B.C.E.", cf. HORGAN 2002, 1.

[130] Cf. STUCKENBRUCK 2020, 10–12.

[131] Cf. QIMRON/STRUGNELL 1994, 109 (75 BCE to 50 CE); KRATZ 2020a, 23–26 (50 BCE to 30 CE); TIGCHELAAR 2020, 61–64 (75/50 BCE to ca. 25 CE).

[132] Cf. QIMRON/STRUGNELL 1994, 121.

[133] Thus COLLINS 2020, 178. Also cf. the discussion in WEISSENBERG 2009, 15–17. On the date of the Hasmonean period (140–63 BCE) see Note 11.

[134] Cf. QIMRON/STRUGNELL 1994, 21; TIGCHELAAR 2020, 61.

[135] Thus QIMRON/STRUGNELL 1994, 59; SCHIFFMAN 1995, 166; VAN DER KOOIJ 1998, 26–28.

[136] Thus CAMPBELL 2000, 188–190. KRATZ 2020b, 91, argues for a reference to a bipartite canon (Torah and Prophets), and possibly to a one-part canon (Torah = Pentateuch only) in earlier forms of the text.

[137] Thus BROOKE 2007, 84–87, 95–96 (Pentateuch certain).

[138] See QIMRON/STRUGNELL 1994, 27, Plate VI. For similar reconstructions see LIM 2001, 21; QIMRON et al. 2006, 222–223; KRATZ 2020c, 50–51.

[139] Thus ULRICH 2003b, 208–210; WEISSENBERG 2009, 50–51, 206–204 (following ULRICH 2003b).

[140] BERTHELOT 2006, 6, 12, argues that the passage refers to individual authoritative texts now in the Hebrew Bible rather than a canon.

[141] Thus LIM 2001, 27–28 (Exodus missing); WEARNE 2020, 236, 254 (Deuteronomy only).

2.2 Writing at the Time of Ben Sira

Hebrew Bible,[142] and the expression "in David" (without an explicit mention of "books")[143] may not refer to the "Writings" of the Hebrew Bible,[144] and may also not refer to its Psalter.[145] Overall, a reference to a tripartite canon of the Hebrew Bible cannot be substantiated. In any case, MMT postdates the Book of Ben Sira and the rule of Antiochus IV Epiphanes (see Chapter 2.1).

2.2.4 1 Enoch and Jubilees

1 Enoch and Jubilees are especially prominent examples of texts earlier than or contemporary to the Book of Ben Sira. Today, both 1 Enoch and Jubilees are often regarded as canonical in the Ethiopian Orthodox Tewahedo Church.[146] 1 Enoch and Jubilees fulfil all of the criteria often used to identify authoritative texts in antiquity (see Chapter 1.3.6).[147] 1 Enoch is extant in a number of ancient manuscripts (criterion 1: number of extant ancient manuscripts), it is quoted in the New Testament in Jude 14–15 and also used in other ancient texts (criteria 2 and 3: fact and way of use in other texts),[148] and Enoch is described as an ancient ancestor closely following Adam in Jude 14–15 (criterion 4: presumed antiquity). Similarly, Jubilees is extant in a number of ancient manuscripts, used in other ancient texts,[149] and placed in the ancient times of Moses.[150] 1 Enoch and Jubilees thus show that texts beyond the Hebrew Bible can be authoritative both today and at the time of Ben Sira.

1 Enoch is a composite work dating from the 4th century BCE to the 1st century CE.[151] 1 Enoch was written in Aramaic and is preserved in fragmentary Aramaic manuscripts found near the Dead Sea as well as partly in Greek and most fully in Ethiopic (Geʿez, i. e. Ancient Ethiopic) translations. As it is the fullest available version of 1 Enoch, chapters and verses are counted according to the Ethiopic tradition.[152] 1 Enoch consists of several parts often called Book of Watchers (1 En 1–36), Parables of Enoch (1 En 37–71), Astronomical Book (1 En 72–82), Book of Dream Visions (1 En 83–90), Epistle of Enoch (1 En 91–105), Birth of Noah (1 En

---

[142] Thus LIM 2001, 31–34.

[143] Cf. LIM 2001, 26–27.

[144] Thus QIMRON/STRUGNELL 1994, 111–112; LIM 2001, 34–36.

[145] Thus BROOKE 1997a, 85–88; LIM 2001, 312–314; BROOKE 2007, 84–87, 95–96; MROCZEK 2015, 29–31; MROCZEK 2016, 37–38. In contrast, FLINT 2003, 290–291, argues for a reference to the Psalter.

[146] Cf. BAYNES 2012, 801–803, 818. Also see Chapter 1 Note 98.

[147] Thus for 1 Enoch similarly KNIBB 2010, 143–146.

[148] For details on ancient references to 1 Enoch cf. NICKELSBURG 2001, 71–108.

[149] For details on the use of Jubilees in other ancient texts cf. VANDERKAM 2018, 98–121; ZAHN 2020a, 104–110, 133–134.

[150] Cf. VANDERKAM 2018, 125.

[151] Cf. NICKELSBURG 2001, 1.

[152] Cf. SIEGERT 2019, 190–191.

50   *2. Historical Contexts of Ben Sira*

106–107) and Eschatological Admonition (1 En 108).[153] The Book of Watchers (1 En 1–36) and the Astronomical Book (1 En 72–82) are dated to the 3rd century BCE or earlier, and the Epistle of Enoch (1 En 91–105) is dated mostly to the early 2nd century BCE.[154] Thus, these three parts of 1 Enoch are earlier than or at least contemporary with Ben Sira. Material evidence for the Book of Watchers (1 En 1–36) and the Astronomical Book (1 En 72–82) is extant in fragmentary Aramaic manuscripts which date from the 3rd and early 2nd century BCE onwards.[155] The Aramaic fragments of 1 Enoch were found near the Dead Sea, geographically close to Ben Sira's city Jerusalem.[156] The Greek translation of 1 Enoch may date from the late 1st century BCE, and large parts of it are materially attested in manuscripts preserved from the 4th century CE onwards.[157] The Ethiopic translation may have been made from a Greek translation in the 4th to 6th centuries CE, and is preserved on manuscripts from the 15th century CE onwards.[158] The Greek and Ethiopic translations are extant in different forms within these languages.[159] There are also many differences in details between the translations, and it is not possible to reconstruct from extant translations what the ancient Aramaic original of passages not preserved in Aramaic might have contained.[160] A full critical edition including the Aramaic, Greek, and Ethiopic sources of 1 Enoch is not available.[161] Further Ethiopic manuscripts continue to be made accessible for research,[162] and a new edition of the Ethiopic sources is in preparation.[163] A new edition of the Greek translation of 1 Enoch would also be desirable.[164] In the present study, the English translation of 1 Enoch by NICKELSBURG/VANDERKAM 2012, based mostly on Ethiopic texts but also critical reconstructions explained

---

[153] Cf. STUCKENBRUCK 2013a, 7–8.

[154] Cf. NICKELSBURG 2001, 7–8, 25–26. In the Astronomical Book (1 En 72–82), parts of 1 En 80–82 are sometimes considered later additions, cf. NICKELSBURG 2001, 26, 334–335; NICKELSBURG/VANDERKAM 2012a, 339–345, 522, 531–536, 546. Most parts of 1 En 91–105 are probably pre-Maccabean (i. e. before 167 BCE), cf. STUCKENBRUCK 2007, 60–62, 211–216, 616 (Apocalypse of Weeks = 1 En 93:1–10; 91:11–17, and Epistle of Enoch = 1 En 92:1–5; 93:11–14; 94:1–105:2, dated to the pre-Maccabean 2nd century BCE), with a few verses being later, cf. STUCKENBRUCK 2007, 156 (Exhortation = 1 En 91:1–10, 18–19, dated in to the 2nd half of the 2nd century BCE). The Parables of Enoch (1 En 37–71) are dated to the late 1st century BCE, cf. NICKELSBURG 2001, 7–8; NICKELSBURG/VANDERKAM 2012a, 58–63. The Book of Dream Visions (1 En 83–90) is dated to the mid-2nd century BCE, cf. NICKELSBURG 2001, 7–8, 347, 360–361. The Birth of Noah (1 En 106–107) is dated to the middle of the 2nd century BCE, and the Eschatological Admonition (1 En 108) to the 1st century BCE, cf. STUCKENBRUCK 2007, 616, 694.

[155] C. NICKELSBURG 2001, 9–11; STUCKENBRUCK 2007, 5–7. Also see Chapter 2.2.3.

[156] Cf. NICKELSBURG 2001, 65.

[157] Cf. NICKELSBURG 2001, 12–14.

[158] Cf. NICKELSBURG 2001, 15–17; ERHO/STUCKENBRUCK 2013, 132–133.

[159] Cf. BOKHORST 2021, 69–72, 90–94.

[160] Cf. STUCKENBRUCK/ERHO 2019, 4, 12–13; BOKHORST 2021, 33, 42–44.

[161] Cf. NICKELSBURG 2001, 125; STUCKENBRUCK 2007, 17–19; BOKHORST 2021, 3.

[162] Cf. ERHO/STUCKENBRUCK 2013, 129, 132–133.

[163] Cf. STUCKENBRUCK/ERHO 2019, 1.

[164] Cf. BOKHORST 2021, 72–75.

in the extensive commentaries by NICKELSBURG 2001 and NICKELSBURG/ VANDERKAM 2012, is used for general overviews of content.[165] For the Aramaic texts, which are of particular importance for the present study since their texts and manuscripts are close to Ben Sira in time and place, and share a similar language, the edition by DRAWNEL 2019 is used.[166] For the Greek texts, which are of particular importance for the present study since they share their language with the Greek translation of the Book of Ben Sira, the edition by BLACK 1970 is used.[167] The comparative editions and translations of 1 En 14–16 by BOKHORST 2021 and of 1 En 91–108 by STUCKENBRUCK 2007 are additionally consulted for the respective passages of 1 Enoch.[168]

Jubilees can be dated to the mid-2nd century BCE in or near Jerusalem, slightly later than Ben Sira and parts of 1 Enoch.[169] It is attested in Hebrew Dead Sea Scrolls dating to the late 2nd century BCE.[170] Jubilees is often thought to be based on Genesis and Exodus,[171] but also other sources.[172] Jubilees explicitly refers to writings of Enoch,[173] for example in Jub 4:16–17: "Enoch [...] wrote down in a book".[174] However, the writings of Enoch mentioned in Jubilees cannot clearly be identified with parts of 1 Enoch.[175] Jubilees also explicitly mentions other books written by ancestors, while there are no explicit references to texts now in the Hebrew Bible.[176] Written in Hebrew, the 50 chapters of Jubilees are extant most fully in an Ancient Ethiopic (Geʻez) translation,[177] which forms the basis of the edition and commentary by VANDERKAM 2018.[178] The Ethiopic translation, in turn, is most likely a translation of a Greek translation which itself is not preserved.[179] In the present study, the complete English translation including multiple textual traditions by VANDERKAM 2018 is used for general overviews of content.[180] For the Hebrew texts, which are of particular importance for the present study since

---

[165] NICKELSBURG/VANDERKAM 2012b. The translation relates to the comprehensive commentaries NICKELSBURG 2001 and NICKELSBURG/VANDERKAM 2012a, cf. NICKELSBURG/ VANDERKAM 2012b, vii, 13. For the textual basis of the translation cf. NICKELSBURG 2001, 18–20.

[166] DRAWNEL 2019, index 16–19. For a more comprehensive index cf. MILIK 1976, 365–366.

[167] BLACK 1970.

[168] STUCKENBRUCK 2007; BOKHORST 2021.

[169] Cf. VANDERKAM 2018, 25–38.

[170] Cf. VANDERKAM 2018, 4–8.

[171] Thus ZAHN 2020a, 20–22 (Gen 1–Exod 19).

[172] Thus VANDERKAM 1995, 111–112; ZAHN 2020a, 101–104.

[173] Cf. VANDERKAM 1995, 111–112; VANDERKAM 2018, 88–90.

[174] Jub 4:16–17 in the translation VANDERKAM 2018, 235. These parts of the verses are not extant in Hebrew, cf. GARCÍA MARTÍNEZ/TIGCHELAAR/VAN DER WOUDE 1998b, 212–213.

[175] Cf. VANDERKAM 2018, 250–254.

[176] Cf. VANDERKAM 2018, 84–98; against MROCZEK 2016, 140.

[177] Cf. VANDERKAM 2018, 1, 14.

[178] The edition VANDERKAM 1989a and translation VANDERKAM 1989b form the basis of the commentary VANDERKAM 2018 (explained there xxiii–xxiv).

[179] Cf. VANDERKAM 2018, 10.

[180] Cf. VANDERKAM 2018, 1–17.

52   *2. Historical Contexts of Ben Sira*

their texts and manuscripts are close to Ben Sira in time and place, and share the same language, editions of the individual manuscripts are used.[181]

2.3 Writing in the Book of Ben Sira

2.3.1 Teaching Setting

The Book of Ben Sira contains explicit references to teaching.[182] The Book of Ben Sira is usually seen to have its origin in Ben Sira's oral teaching,[183] and to address both Ben Sira's students and following generations of readers.[184] In Sir 51:23, Ben Sira asks those who are not educated to come to him and stay בבית מדרשי "in the house of my study" (Sir 51:23[LXX] ἐν οἴκῳ παιδείας "in the house of education").[185] Ben Sira is usually seen as a teacher who had a positive view of the priestly cult in the temple in Jerusalem and was probably not a priest himself.[186] His students in a private teaching setting were probably young men[187] from rich and influential families in Jerusalem.[188] The Book of Ben Sira explicitly mentions the use of both oral information and written texts for teaching.[189] This will be demonstrated in detail in the following two sections on the Hebrew and Greek Book of Ben Sira.

2.3.2 Hebrew Book of Ben Sira

Explicit references to oral teaching are frequent in the Hebrew Book of Ben Sira.[190] For example (with the lexical forms of key words in Hebrew added in brackets), Sir 3:29 states: "A wise heart (לב) will understand the proverbs of the wise, and an ear (אזן) attending to wisdom will rejoice." Sir 4:24 notes: "wisdom is known through speech (אומר) and understanding through the answer of a

---

[181] VanderKam/Milik 1994a; VanderKam/Milik 1994b; García Martínez/Tigchelaar/van der Woude 1998b.

[182] This is true even if the "I" of the Book is not Ben Sira himself but an exemplary wise teacher, cf. on this issue Wright/Mroczek 2021, 215–216.

[183] Cf. Wischmeyer 1994, 4–5; Ueberschaer 2007, 162.

[184] Cf. Ueberschaer 2007, 160–163, 211–212, 235–236 n. 214.

[185] Cf. Witte 2012b, 737. The authenticity of this verse is debated, but even if the "house of study" is not a specific institution, the Book of Ben Sira fits into a pedagogical context, cf. Mroczek 2016, 100–102. On the term מדרש "study" cf. Mandel 2017, 1–4, 289–294, 303–305, who argues that the term in the Second Temple Period refers to instruction rather than textual interpretation.

[186] Cf. Ueberschaer 2007, 322–337.

[187] Cf. Wischmeyer 1994, 180 (men only); Ueberschaer 2007, 290 (men only), 393.

[188] Cf. Ueberschaer 2007, 172–174, 193, 336. On the debate about the existence of schools cf. Ueberschaer 2007, 91–104. Wischmeyer 1994, 175–177, argues that Ben Sira primarily taught his own son, then also students in a private setting.

[189] Cf. Wischmeyer 1994, 185–186; Crenshaw 1997b, 180, 187; Carr 2005, 208–209.

[190] This is also noted by Wright 2013a, 180–181.

2.3 Writing in the Book of Ben Sira

tongue (לשון)". Sir 6:33 states: "if you are willing to listen (שמע), then incline your ear (אזן), you will be taught". Sir 6:35 states: "Take pleasure in hearing (שמע) every discourse and do not let an understanding proverb escape you." And Sir 16:24 advises: "Listen (שמע) to me and receive my knowledge, and on my words set the heart (לב)".

In contrast, Ben Sira's own book is the only text explicitly mentioned for teaching purposes. For example, Sir 39:32 notes: על כן מראש התיצבתי והתבוננתי ובכתב הנחתי "Therefore from the beginning I placed myself, and I understood, and in writing I set down."[191] Here, Ben Sira only refers to his own writings. Sir 50:27 mentions מוסר שכל ומושל אופנים לשמעון בן ישוע בן אלעזר בן סירא "in-struction of insight and proverb of appropriate occasions by Simeon son of Yeshua son of Eleazar son of Sira", and Sir 50:28 then states אשרי איש באלה יהגה ונותן על לבו יחכם "happy the one who will meditate on these, and the one giving (these) to his heart will be wise",[192] though without an explicit reference to writing or books.[193] No other texts are mentioned at all for Ben Sira's teaching. Writing is important in practical matters: Ben Sira's students are asked to note what they give and receive in transactions concerning number and weight הכל בכתב "all in writing" in Sir 42:7.

The "Praise of the Ancestors" (Sir 44–50) includes ancestors as users of books and as writers: in Sir 44:4 they are described as חכמי שיח בספרתם "wise ones of thinking in their books", and in Sir 44:5 as נושאי משל בכתב "the ones putting a proverb in writing".[194] Sir 44:5 is the only mention of books in the Hebrew Book of Ben Sira. A marginal addition in Manuscript B even corrects בספרתם "in their books" in Sir 44:4 to במספרתם "in their numbers",[195] thus eliminating the mention of books. In any case, no specific texts used or written by the ancestors are mentioned at all. Even if a reference to specific books is implied, they do not have to be books now in the Hebrew Bible. There are extant ancient books outside the Hebrew Bible which are explicitly attributed to ancestors. For example, 1 En 92:1 attributes a book to an ancestor mentioned in Sir 44–50, Enoch. 1 En 92:1 reads: "Written by Enoch the scribe (this complete sign of wisdom) (who is) praised by all people and a leader of the whole earth, to all my sons who will dwell on the earth, and to the last generations who will observe truth and

---

[191] Only in Manuscript B, the Masada Manuscript is damaged there and only contains a final י, cf. RENDSBURG/BINSTEIN 2013, Manuscript B IX verso, Masada Manuscript I.

[192] Cf. RENDSBURG/BINSTEIN 2013, Manuscript B XX recto.

[193] This is also noted by MROCZEK 2016, 89, 92.

[194] Fully in Manuscript B, the Masada Manuscript is damaged and lacks the final ל of משל "proverb" as well as בכתב "in writing" in Sir 44:5, cf. RENDSBURG/BINSTEIN 2013, Manuscript B XIII verso, Masada Manuscript VII.

[195] Cf. RENDSBURG/BINSTEIN 2013, Manuscript B XIII verso.

54   *2. Historical Contexts of Ben Sira*

peace."[196] Other ancient texts also mention writings of the ancestor Noah (see Chapter 6.2.4).

Just as books apart from Ben Sira's own are hardly even mentioned, the verb "to write" is also rare. In the Hebrew Ben Sira the verb כתב "to write" appears in Sir 39:32; 42:7; 44:5; 45:11; 48:10. In Sir 39:32, it refers to Ben Sira's writing, in Sir 42:7 to records of goods given and received, in Sir 44:5 to unnamed written works of the ancestors, in Sir 45:11 to precious stones engraved בכתב "in writing" and attached to vestments in the temple. Sir 48:10 contains – with reference to Elijah who is mentioned in Sir 48:4 – הכתוב "the one written" followed by what is often taken as a quotation of Mal 3:23–24 (see Chapter 5.5.2). The Hebrew Book of Ben Sira additionally contains some words related to writing: the poʿel participle מחוקק "prescribing one" of חקק "to inscribe" in Sir 10:5 refers to a leading person. Sir 38:24 mentions a סופר "scribe" as a profession though writing is not explicitly mentioned as an activity of a scribe (see Chapter 4.4). Overall, books or writing do not play an important role in the Book of Ben Sira.[197]

2.3.3 Greek Book of Ben Sira

Like the Hebrew Book of Ben Sira, the Greek translation contains explicit references to oral teaching, for example in Sir 3:29; 4:24; 6:33; 6:35; 16:24[LXX]. And as in Hebrew, in the Greek translation the noun γραφή "writing" is used in Sir 39:32[LXX] (referring to Ben Sira's writing), Sir 42:7[LXX] (referring to records of goods), Sir 44:5[LXX] (referring to unnamed writings of ancestors, while Sir 44:4[LXX] uses γραμματεία "learning" with reference to ancestors without mentioning books), and Sir 45:11[LXX] (referring to engraved gemstones). Sir 48:10[LXX] (referring to Elijah who is mentioned in Sir 48:4[LXX]) uses καταγράφω "to write down" in a passive participle ὁ καταγραφείς "the one who is written down" (see Chapter 5.5.2). In Sir 10:5[LXX], γραμματεύς "scribe" is used. The same word also appears in Sir 38:24[LXX] where it refers to the profession of a scribe without explicitly mentioning the activity of writing (see Chapter 4.4).

---

[196] 1 En 92:1 in the translation NICKELSBURG/VANDERKAM 2012b, 138; cf. the translation STUCKENBRUCK 2007, 217: "That which was written by Enoch the scribe (which is a complete sign of wisdom) praised by all men, and judge of all the earth: 'To all my sons who will dwell upon the earth and to the last generations who will do uprightness and peace." 1 En 108:1 also describes Enoch as writing a book: "Another book that Enoch wrote for his son Methuselah and for those who would come after him and keep the law in the last days." (1 En 108:1 in the translation NICKELSBURG/VANDERKAM 2012b, 167; cf. the translation STUCKENBRUCK 2007, 695: "Another book, which Enoch wrote for his son Methuselah and for those who come after him and will keep the law in the last days."). STUCKENBRUCK 2007, 696, also notes that the "law" (see Chapter 3.4.2) here may be Enochic rather than Mosaic.

[197] This is also noted by MROCZEK 2016, 89.

2.3 Writing in the Book of Ben Sira

In the Greek Book of Ben Sira, there are two additional explicit mentions of books and writing.[198] Unlike in Hebrew where this verse is not extant, βίβλος "book" appears in Sir 24:23[LXX] referring to God's covenant and Moses' law (for details see Chapter 3.4.4). In Sir 50:27[LXX], βιβλίον "book" refers to Ben Sira's writing, unlike in Hebrew where writing or books are not explicitly mentioned.

The later Greek Prologue to Ben Sira (see Chapter 3) contains a number of additional references to reading and writing. Books are mentioned explicitly several times in the Prologue: l. 10 τὰ βιβλία "the books", l. 25 τὰ βιβλία "the books", l. 30 ἡ βίβλος "the book", l. 33 τὸ βιβλίον "the book".[199] The verb γράφω "to write"[200] is found in l. 6 of the Prologue where it refers to educated people, συγγράφω "to write down"[201] is used in l. 12 referring to Ben Sira's writing.[202] Reading is mentioned using the words ἀναγιγνώσκω "to read"[203] in l. 4, ἀνάγνωσις "reading"[204] in l. 10 and l. 17, and λέγω "to speak" in the context of written texts, thus possibly "to recite" as reading aloud in l. 6 and l. 26.[205] In these mentions of reading, the reading ones in l. 4 are the same as those who love learning according to l. 5 and can recite and write according to l. 6,[206] while οἱ ἔκτος "those outside" in l. 5 are probably those who are outside a circle of reciting and writing lovers of learning.[207] According to l. 10, reading is done by Ben Sira, in l. 17, the readers of the Prologue are addressed. In l. 26, the three categories of books are read, but it is not mentioned by whom they are read. Overall, the later Greek Prologue contains many more explicit mentions of books and writing as well as reading than the Book of Ben Sira itself.

2.3.4 Orality and Literacy and Ben Sira

With explicit references to oral teaching in its written text, the Book of Ben Sira shows a connection of orality and literacy. On the orality-literacy spectrum, Ben

---

[198] The word ζωγραφία "picture" in Sir 38:27[LXX] refers to depictions, see Chapter 4.3. This verse is not fully extant in Hebrew, see Chapter 4.2.

[199] Cf. LIDDELL/SCOTT/JONES [1940], s.v. βιβλίον, s.v. βύβλος. Since there were no codices at the time of Ben Sira and his translator, the translation "book" denotes scrolls rather than bound books, see Chapter 2.2.2.

[200] Cf. LIDDELL/SCOTT/JONES [1940], s.v. γράφω.

[201] Cf. LIDDELL/SCOTT/JONES [1940], s.v. συγγράφω.

[202] The mention of writing in l. 6 is also sometimes taken as a reference to books like that of Ben Sira, Tobit, and "even noncanonical works", cf. SKEHAN/DI LELLA 1987, 133.

[203] Cf. LIDDELL/SCOTT/JONES [1940], s.v. ἀναγιγνώσκω.

[204] Cf. LIDDELL/SCOTT/JONES [1940], s.v. ἀνάγνωσις.

[205] Cf. LIDDELL/SCOTT/JONES [1940], s.v. λέγω (13).

[206] Cf. SKEHAN/DI LELLA 1987, 133: "the learned, the scribes, who can read the Scriptures in the original languages".

[207] Thus MARBÖCK 2010, 41. According to SKEHAN/DI LELLA 1987, 133, the expression "refers to the laity, or those who cannot read the original Scriptures without help". According to CORLEY 2019, 220, due to the context with references to the law it refers "mainly to uneducated Jews rather than to Gentiles".

56   *2. Historical Contexts of Ben Sira*

Sira is usually placed on the literacy end. For example, KOOLE states that Ben Sira cannot possibly have known about Israel's ancestors through oral tradition only since he was "Schriftgelehrter" ("learned in Scripture") and there was a library in Jerusalem.[208] CRENSHAW also argues for Ben Sira's study of "the Scriptures" but does not rule out oral tradition.[209] That Ben Sira's teaching primarily and predominately used and relied on orality rather than literacy is recognized by scholars focussing on Ben Sira's contemporary culture such as UEBERSCHAER and WISCHMEYER.[210] Their studies highlight the important role of practical advice related to contemporary culture in the Book of Ben Sira. Still, UEBERSCHAER states that Ben Sira relies on "the biblical writings" in his teaching,[211] based on the argument that the biblical canon is known by Ben Sira.[212] Similarly, WISCHMEYER explicitly notes that Ben Sira's students do not learn from holy writings but from Ben Sira's oral teaching.[213] Nevertheless, she takes the Prologue to imply that Ben Sira's students read "the Old Testament" and mostly know it by heart,[214] and that Ben Sira himself studies holy writings[215] and knows but does not teach or quote the Torah.[216] While arguing – based on Sir 44–49, Sir 49:10, and the Prologue – that Ben Sira knows most of the Old Testament,[217] WISCHMEYER also notes that he does not know "the concept of a Holy Book"[218] and instead has a focus on the temple cult.[219]

The placement of Ben Sira on the literacy end of the orality-literacy spectrum is mostly influenced by Ben Sira's supposed knowledge of the biblical canon. Ben Sira is only rarely placed on the orality end of the spectrum, but even then written texts, and particularly those now in the Hebrew Bible, are seen as indispendably important for Ben Sira.[220] Such views run into the problems of definitions of biblical canon at the time of Ben Sira (see Chapter 1.3), uncertainty about a Jerusalem library (see Chapter 2.2.2), and frequent mentions of oral transmission and a lack of mentions of specific written texts in the Book of Ben

---

[208] Cf. KOOLE 1965, 379. Cf. similarly SCHREINER 2002, 8.

[209] Cf. CRENSHAW 1997a, 623.

[210] Cf. UEBERSCHAER 2007, 202–203, 209–211 (singing in addition to hearing and speaking); WISCHMEYER 1994, 140–142, 185–186. Cf. also NEWMAN 2018, 43–45 (oral teaching but Ben Sira used Torah and Prophets).

[211] Cf. UEBERSCHAER 2007, 207 (German original: "der biblischen Schriften").

[212] Cf. UEBERSCHAER 2007, 137, 226–227 n. 170 (referring to EBERHARTER 1911). See Chapter 1 Note 207.

[213] Thus WISCHMEYER 1994, 185.

[214] Thus WISCHMEYER 1994, 185 (German original: "das Alte Testament"). WISCHMEYER 1994, 170, also mentions "Old Testament sources" (German original: "atl. Quellen") of Sir 44–49.

[215] Thus WISCHMEYER 1994, 186.

[216] Thus WISCHMEYER 1994, 200.

[217] Thus WISCHMEYER 1994, 257.

[218] WISCHMEYER 1994, 257 (German original: "Die Vorstellung vom Heiligen Buch").

[219] Thus WISCHMEYER 1994, 261–265.

[220] Cf. WRIGHT 2008, 183 (referring to CARR 2005, 8–9), 206.

Sira itself (see Chapter 2.3.2 and 2.3.3). Other scholars such as HORSLEY therefore argue for a higher importance of oral tradition and against canonical limits (see Chapter 5.5.3).

2.3.5 Materiality and Ben Sira

Aspects of the materiality of texts have only recently been brought into research on Ben Sira. For example, ASKIN writes in a 2018 article entitled "What Did Ben Sira's Bible and Desk Look Like?":

"the use of 'Bible' and 'desk' in the title of this study are purposefully anachronistic in order to provoke reflection upon the way in which we often mentally picture ancient scribes and even Hellenistic and Roman writers to have read and written."[221]

ASKIN then shows that against the modern mental image of desks with multiple scrolls, ancient sources close to Ben Sira in time and space indicate that reading and writing usually took place with very little furniture on floors or small stools, on laps or at most small portable tables, outside in courtyards using daylight.[222] No more than one scroll could normally be used at once, which made memorization important.[223] ASKIN also refers to the importance of oral transmission:

"As far as what Ben Sira taught, when appealing to readers (Sir 51:23–30), he says they will learn wisdom from him, and says nothing about the drudgery of copying texts or keeping accounts and inventories."[224]

While the "desk" is thus put into its ancient contexts by ASKIN, regarding "Bible" she builds on studies of "Ben Sira's explicit direct and indirect quotations, explicit and implicit allusions, and echoes of textual sources".[225] ASKIN notes that while Ben Sira may have used sources outside today's Hebrew Bible such as 11Q5 (11QPs^a),[226] "out of known extant textual sources, Ben Sira refers primarily to the texts which became the Hebrew Bible".[227] In most examples, ASKIN uses the Hebrew Bible only as a reference text for Ben Sira.[228] As for libraries, ASKIN argues, based especially on 2 Macc 2:13–15^{LXX} about Nehemiah (see Chapter 2.2.2), for the existence of a temple library in Jerusalem which Ben Sira may have used.[229] However, the Book of Ben Sira does not mention any libraries at all, neither

---

[221] ASKIN 2018a, 3 n. 4.
[222] Cf. ASKIN 2018a, 6, 14–20.
[223] Cf. ASKIN 2018a, 24–26.
[224] ASKIN 2018a, 12.
[225] ASKIN 2018a, 4.
[226] Cf. ASKIN 2018a, 6–7.
[227] ASKIN 2018a, 23.
[228] Cf. ASKIN 2018a, 5.
[229] Cf. ASKIN 2018a, 13, 15.

58   *2. Historical Contexts of Ben Sira*

for Ben Sira's own nor for Nehemia's time.[230] It can thus not be shown that Ben Sira used a library. And even if he did use one without mentioning it, such a library may have contained texts not today included in the Hebrew Bible (see Chapter 2.2.3).

2.4 Conclusion

The Book of Ben Sira has its origin in Jerusalem around 190–175 BCE, a time in the Hellenistic and the Second Temple Period before the Maccabean revolts around 167 BCE. Oral tradition plays an important role during this time. The use of scrolls rather than later codices makes it impossible to write texts as long as the whole Hebrew Bible onto one material object. Extant older or contemporary texts related to ancient Judaism in similar languages and from similar geographic regions are preserved mostly in the Dead Sea Scrolls, and contain some small parts of texts now in the Hebrew Bible as well as a variety of texts not included in it such as parts of 1 Enoch. The present study focusses on this extant written evidence.[231]

The Book of Ben Sira contains several explicit mentions of oral teaching. Writing is mentioned as important for keeping accounts. Ben Sira does not mention any specific texts other than his own book. Only the later Greek Prologue names specific groups of books and contains many more references to writing than the Hebrew and Greek text of the Book of Ben Sira itself.

---

[230] Thus also CRAWFORD 2019, 98 n. 161: "Later references to Nehemiah likewise do not mention a library. For example, Sir 49:13 credits Nehemiah with rebuilding the wall of Jerusalem, setting up its gates, and rebuilding houses, but makes no mention of a library."

[231] Similarly, MROCZEK 2016, 5, argues that, in addition to studies of orality, studies of written texts, but texts outside the Hebrew Bible, are of particular importance for avoiding the anachronism of the biblical canon. Further studies of this question with a focus on orality would be desirable. For example, MILLER 2019, 120–121, in a study of stichographic layouts in Dead Sea Scrolls manuscripts mentions Ben Sira as a part of "authoritative Scripture" on "biblical manuscripts" (although the "lack of a better term" than "biblical" is noted by MILLER 2019, 22).

3. Greek Prologue to Ben Sira

3.1 Introduction

The Greek Prologue to Ben Sira is often seen as referring to a biblical canon.[1] As it is a prologue to the Greek translation of the Book of Ben Sira, it does not exist in Hebrew. This chapter provides an analysis of the Greek text of the Prologue, a discussion of Hebrew and Greek terms related to "Law", "Prophets" and "Writings" in- and outside the Book of Ben Sira and its Prologue, and a systematic assessment of possible canonical references in the Greek Prologue to Ben Sira.

3.2 Greek Text and Translation

The Greek text of the Prologue to Ben Sira presented here follows the Göttingen Septuagint edited by ZIEGLER.[2]

ΠΡΟΛΟΓΟΣ	PROLOGUE
1 Πολλῶν καὶ μεγάλων ἡμῖν διὰ τοῦ νόμου καὶ τῶν προφητῶν	Since many and great things are given to us through the law and the prophets
2 καὶ τῶν ἄλλων τῶν κατ' αὐτοὺς ἠκολουθηκότων δεδομένων,	and the others which followed in accordance with them
3 ὑπὲρ ὧν δέον ἐστὶν ἐπαινεῖν τὸν Ισραηλ παιδείας καὶ σοφίας,	because of which it is necessary to praise Israel for education and wisdom,
4 καὶ ὡς οὐ μόνον αὐτοὺς τοὺς ἀναγινώσκοντας δέον ἐστὶν ἐπιστήμονας γίνεσθαι,	and since it is necessary that not only those reading become understanding themselves,
5 ἀλλὰ καὶ τοῖς ἐκτὸς δύνασθαι τοὺς φιλομαθοῦντας χρησίμους εἶναι	but also that those loving learning are able to be useful to those outside,
6 καὶ λέγοντας καὶ γράφοντας,	those reciting as well as those writing,
7 ὁ πάππος μου Ἰησοῦς ἐπὶ πλεῖον ἑαυτὸν δοὺς	my grandfather Jesus, having given himself still more
8 εἴς τε τὴν τοῦ νόμου	to the reading of the law
9 καὶ τῶν προφητῶν	and the prophets

---

[1] See Chapter 3.5 for details.
[2] Cf. ZIEGLER 1980, 123–126.

60   3. Greek Prologue to Ben Sira

10 καὶ τῶν ἄλλων[3] πατρίων βιβλίων ἀνάγνωσιν	and the other ancestral books,
11 καὶ ἐν τούτοις ἱκανὴν ἕξιν περιποιησάμενος	and having obtained sufficient proficiency in those,
12 προήχθη καὶ αὐτὸς συγγράψαι τι τῶν εἰς παιδείαν καὶ σοφίαν ἀνηκόντων,	was also himself led to write down something of those things pertaining to education and wisdom,
13 ὅπως οἱ φιλομαθεῖς καὶ τούτων ἔνοχοι γενόμενοι	in order that the lovers of learning, becoming connected also with those,
14 πολλῷ μᾶλλον ἐπιπροσθῶσιν διὰ τῆς ἐννόμου[4] βιώσεως.	might gain much more through the lawful manner of life.
15 Παρακέκλησθε οὖν	You are therefore urged
16 μετ᾽ εὐνοίας καὶ προσοχῆς	with goodwill and attention
17 τὴν ἀνάγνωσιν ποιεῖσθαι	to do for yourselves the reading,
18 καὶ συγγνώμην ἔχειν	and to have forbearance
19 ἐφ᾽ οἷς ἂν δοκῶμεν	in those things in which we may potentially seem
20 τῶν κατὰ τὴν ἑρμηνείαν πεφιλοπονημένων τισὶν τῶν λέξεων ἀδυναμεῖν·	to lack power for some of the phrases which have been diligently worked through concerning the translation;
21 οὐ γὰρ ἰσοδυναμεῖ	for they do not have equal power
22 αὐτὰ ἐν ἑαυτοῖς Ἑβραϊστὶ λεγόμενα καὶ ὅταν μεταχθῇ εἰς ἑτέραν γλῶσσαν·	when they are recited in themselves in Hebrew and when they are transferred into another language;
23 οὐ μόνον δὲ ταῦτα,	for not only these,
24 ἀλλὰ καὶ αὐτὸς ὁ νόμος καὶ αἱ προφητεῖαι[5]	but also the law itself and the prophecies
25 καὶ τὰ λοιπὰ τῶν βιβλίων	and the remaining ones of the books
26 οὐ μικρὰν ἔχει τὴν διαφορὰν ἐν ἑαυτοῖς λεγόμενα.	have no small difference when recited in themselves.
27 Ἐν γὰρ τῷ ὀγδόῳ καὶ τριακοστῷ ἔτει ἐπὶ τοῦ Εὐεργέτου βασιλέως	For having in the thirty-eighth year at (the time) of the king Euergetes
28 παραγενηθεὶς εἰς Αἴγυπτον καὶ συγχρονίσας	come to Egypt, and having spent some time,
29 εὑρὼν οὐ μικρᾶς παιδείας ἀφόμοιον	finding a likeness of no little education,
30 ἀναγκαιότατον ἐθέμην καὶ αὐτός τινα προσενέγκασθαι σπουδὴν καὶ φιλοπονίαν τοῦ μεθερμηνεῦσαι τήνδε τὴν βίβλον	as the most necessary thing I also set myself to offer some effort and diligence of translating this book here,
31 πολλὴν ἀγρυπνίαν καὶ ἐπιστήμην προσενεγκάμενος	having brought much sleeplessness and understanding

---

[3] Some Greek manuscripts here add δεόντων "necessary", cf. ZIEGLER 1980, 124.

[4] Some Greek manuscripts instead read ἐκ νόμου "out of law" or ἐν νόμῳ "in law", cf. ZIEGLER 1980, 124.

[5] Some Greek manuscripts and some versions instead of αἱ προφητεῖαι "the prophecies" read οἱ προφῆται "the prophets", cf. ZIEGLER 1980, 125. See Chapter 3.4.1.

32 ἐν τῷ διαστήματι τοῦ χρόνου	in the interval of time
33 πρὸς τὸ ἐπὶ πέρας ἀγαγόντα τὸ βιβλίον ἐκδόσθαι	to, having led it to the end, publishing the book
34 καὶ τοῖς ἐν τῇ παροικίᾳ βουλομένοις φιλομαθεῖν	also for those wanting to love learning in the foreign country
35 προκατασκευαζομένους τὰ ἤθη	so that those preparing the manners
36 ἐννόμως[6] βιοτεύειν.	live lawfully.

3.3 Analysis

3.3.1 Manuscripts and Date

The Greek translation of Ben Sira begins with a Greek Prologue.[7] The Prologue is written in the first person singular. This "I" writes about translating τήνδε τὴν βίβλον "this book here" (l. 30) and calls Ben Sira ὁ πάππος μου Ἰησοῦς "my grandfather Jesus" (l. 7). The earliest extant manuscripts of the Prologue are the Greek Codices Vaticanus (B) and Sinaiticus (S) which date to the 4th century CE,[8] around five to six centuries after the date of the Book of Ben Sira. Instead of the Prologue discussed here, one Greek manuscript, the 13th century CE Minuscule 248, contains a different prologue.[9]

---

[6] Some Greek manuscripts instead read ἐν νόμῳ "in law", cf. ZIEGLER 1980, 126.

[7] The term "Prologue" is used here in line with the most common designation in scholarship, and with the use of the designation πρόλογος "prologue" in most Greek manuscripts, cf. ZIEGLER 1980, 123, 126 (προοίμιον "preface" is used in only a few manuscripts). In categories of ancient rhetorics, προοίμιον "preface" would actually be more fitting because πρόλογος "prologue" is usually used for dramas rather than other literature, cf. ZIMMERMANN 2001, 398, 400, but the terms can be interchanged, cf. MÄNNLEIN-ROBERT 1992, 247–248, 250; LÓPEZ MARQUÉS 1992, 201.

[8] The Prologue discussed here is found in its earliest extant witnesses in the 4th century CE codices B and S (also the 5th century codices A and C), and is missing in some manuscripts from the 12th century CE onwards, cf. ZIEGLER 1980, 123, in combination with SEPTUAGINTA-UNTERNEHMEN 2012, 1, 3–5, 7, 12.

[9] Cf. ZIEGLER 1980, 66, 127. According to ZIEGLER 1980, 53, 65–66, Manuscript 248 is the most important Greek minuscule manuscript of Ben Sira. It is dated to the 13th century CE, cf. SEPTUAGINTA-UNTERNEHMEN 2012, 4. For a German translation of the prologue in Manuscript 248 cf. PETERS 1913, 5; FABRY 2009, 1092; for a commentary FRITZSCHE 1859, 6–9. The prologue in Manuscript 248 is probably taken from a synopsis of all biblical books attributed to Athanasius, cf. ZIEGLER 1980, 66. The almost identical text in this synopsis can be found in MIGNE 1887, 376–377. Athanasius lived in the 4th century CE, cf. WILLIAMS 1998, but the synopsis is probably even later, cf. MIGNE 1887, 281–284. Manuscript 248 is also a part of G-I which includes additions to the G-I text in ZIEGLER 1980, cf. KEARNS 2011, 51. On G-I and G-II see Chapter 1.2.1.

62   3. Greek Prologue to Ben Sira

It is usually accepted that the "I" in the Prologue is in fact both the grandson of Ben Sira and the translator of the Book of Ben Sira into Greek.[10] This is also the main reason for dating the Greek translation of the Book of Ben Sira, like its Prologue, to the late 2nd century BCE.[11]

The Prologue is usually dated to the late 2nd century BCE. This date is based on the mention of the 38th year of the King Euergetes in Egypt in l. 27–28 of the Prologue.[12] King Ptolemy VIII Euergetes II was the only "Euergetes" to reign in Egypt for more than 38 years:[13] from 170 to 116 BCE, Euergetes II reigned for a total of 54 years (though for a part of this time his rule was shared with others).[14] Taking the 38th year from 170 BCE, it is usually deduced that the grandson came to Egypt[15] in 132 BCE and subsequently translated the book of Ben Sira into Greek.[16] It is disputed at which point after 132 BCE the Prologue could have been written. First, it is sometimes argued that the preposition ἐπί "at" in ἐπὶ τοῦ Εὐεργέτου βασιλέως "at (the time) of the King Euergetes" (l. 27) points towards a date after the king's death in 116 BCE for the Prologue (and according to the Prologue also the completion of the translation).[17] However, the same preposition can also be used to refer to living kings.[18] Second, it is argued that the

---

[10] Cf. MARBÖCK 2010, 39, 41, against DIEBNER 1982, 18–19, 28–29 (see Note 38). Also cf. EGO 2001, 591.

[11] Thus SKEHAN/DI LELLA 1987, 49; SAUER 1981, 486; WISCHMEYER 1994, 2; WAGNER 1999, 30–31; SAUER 2000, 22; MARBÖCK 2003, 112; UEBERSCHAER 2007, 29, 34; KREUZER 2009, 136; REITEMEYER 2011, 2162–2163; WITTE 2012a, 235–236; WITTE 2012b, 728, 737; UEBERSCHAER 2016, 446; SIEGERT 2019, 146, 155; WITTE 2015b, 19; WITTE 2017b, 30; CORLEY 2019, 219.

[12] FORSTER 1959, 6–7, argues that l. 27 could refer to the translator's 38th year rather than that of the king, but does not give other examples for such phrases, and as noted by FORSTER Hag 1:1; 2:1; Zech 1:1 also refer to the year of a king's reign.

[13] Cf. the list of Egyptian rulers in EDER/QUACK 2004. The other "Euergetes" in this list, Ptolemaios III Euergetes I, reigned for 25 years (264–221 BCE).

[14] Cf. AMELING 2001a.

[15] Αἴγυπτος "Egypt" is mentioned explicitly in l. 28 of the Prologue. There is no mention of Alexandria, and a restriction to Egypt as Alexandria is unnecessary, cf. AITKEN 2011, 98.

[16] Thus MARBÖCK 2003, 107; CRENSHAW 1997a, 610; SKEHAN/DI LELLA 1987, 134; WRIGHT 2003b, 634; GRABBE 2008, 101; HAMP 1951, 5, who give the end date of Euergetes' reign as 117 BCE, as 116 BCE SAUER 2000, 40. 116 BCE is correct, cf. AMELING 2001b.

[17] Thus WILCKEN 1906, 320–321; PETERS 1913, XXXII–XXXIII (referring to WILCKEN); KAHLE 1959, 216 (referring to WILCKEN); MARBÖCK 2003, 107 (referring to PETERS); SAUER 2000, 40, n. 9 (without a reference).

[18] SMEND 1906, 3 and SKEHAN/DI LELLA 1987, 134 (referring to SMEND) note (against WILCKEN 1906, 320–321) that texts such as Hag 1:1, 15; 2:10^{LXX}; Zech 1:1, 7; 7:1^{LXX} and 1 Macc 13:42; 14:27^{LXX} (which may be based on a lost Hebrew original, cf. ENGEL 2016, 391) use the same construction of designating a year (ἐπί "at" followed by a genitive) for a king who is alive at the time of the event described. WILCKEN 1906, 321–322, also notes Zech 1:7^{LXX} but as non-living "translation Greek" (German original: "Übersetzungsgriechisch") in contrast to the Prologue's "living Greek of Egypt" ("lebendig[e] Sprache Ägyptens"). However, WILCKEN 1906, 320–321, mainly bases his argument (which forms part of a review) on a single occurrence of ἐπί "at" followed by a genitive on one papyrus rather than all "living Greek of Egypt". Furthermore, WILCKEN himself argues that the translator himself shows the use of both possible types of

3.3 Analysis

participle συγχρονίσας "having spent some time" (l. 28) could point to a date of the Prologue after Euergetes' death since συγχρονίζω usually means "to be contemporary with".[19] Even if the author of the Prologue regards himself as a contemporary of Euergetes, it does not necessarily mean that he stayed in Egypt for the entire time of Euergetes' reign. He could also have completed the translation and Prologue during this reign, not immediately after arrival but συγχρονίσας "having spent some time".[20] The Prologue also mentions τῷ διαστήματι τοῦ χρόνου "the interval of time" (l. 32). Thus, the translation is described as taking some time.[21] The Prologue neither mentions nor excludes a date after Euergetes' death, but in both cases, the Prologue is dated to the late 2nd century BCE some time after 132 BCE.

However, it is possible that the "I" of the Prologue is not who he says he is, and that the date given in the Prologue is not the date at which the Prologue was written. This possibility has to be considered due to the phenomenon of ancient pseudepigraphy.[22] In research on the Second Temple Period, the term "pseudepigraphic" is often used specifically for a text attributed to an important figure (such as Enoch or Moses) which is not the actual author of the text.[23] In research on ancient texts across other disciplines, "pseudepigraphic" is often used more broadly for an ancient text giving information about its author (with or without a specific name) or its time of origin which are not the actual author or time of origin of the text.[24] In the present study, the term "pseudepigraphic" is used in this broader sense. There are some characteristics which are common in ancient pseudepigraphic texts and which can be indications of pseudepigraphy: specific names, first-person statements about the author's experience, references to other sources, and precise information about dates and places.[25] The Pro-

---

Greek within his own work (Prologue and translated book). Thus, with one and the same author thought to be using different types of Greek, a strict distinction cannot be drawn.

[19] Thus SMEND 1906, 3–4 (συγχρονίζω usually means "to be contemporary with"); SKEHAN/ DI LELLA 1987, 134 (referring to SMEND); WAGNER 1999, 130 (referring to SMEND); CRENSHAW 1997a, 610, 643 (referring to SMEND); CORLEY 2019, 221. This is indeed the usual meaning, cf. LIDDELL/SCOTT/JONES [1940], s. v. συγχρονέω, s. v. συγχρονίζω.

[20] Thus also SAUER 2000, 40.

[21] Although σπουδή can also mean "speed", cf. LIDDELL/SCOTT/JONES [1940], s. v. σπουδή, here in l. 30 it more likely means "effort".

[22] For the distinction between the terms "pseudepigraphy" and "Pseudepigrapha" cf. MROCZEK 2020, 637; on "Pseudepigrapha" cf. REED 2020, 634–637.

[23] Cf. on this use of the term "pseudepigraphy" (also called "pseudonymous attribution") MROCZEK 2020, 637–639; WRIGHT/MROCZEK 2021, 213–218, 220–222.

[24] Cf. on this as well as further uses of the term "pseudepigraphy" MARSHALL 2016 (Classics, Second Temple Studies, New Testament Studies); PEIRANO 2012, 2–6, esp. 3 (Classics); JANßEN 2011 (Classics, New Testament Studies).

[25] SPEYER 1971, 45–84, based on numerous examples from different periods in antiquity and later periods of time, lists as characteristics of pseudepigraphic texts amongst others a false author's name, first-person statements (e. g. about this author's own experience, identity, or trustworthiness), references to other sources (e. g. visions, texts and translated texts, witnesses

64   *3. Greek Prologue to Ben Sira*

logue shows precisely such characteristics of ancient pseudepigraphic texts. The Prologue mentions the name of an author: the nameless "I" who identifies himself as the author of the Prologue and translator of the following book calls the author of the book "grandfather Jesus". The Prologue also contains first-person statements about the author's own experience (coming to Egypt and translating his grandfather's book), references to other sources such as texts (the three categories of books), translated texts (the translation of the three categories of books), a reference to a person of old age (the grandfather), and precise information about dates and places (the 38th year of the King Euergetes in Egypt). Given these similarities with pseudepigraphic ancient texts, it is possible that the Prologue is also pseudepigraphic. However, further characteristics often used for a more certain detection of pseudepigraphy – such as contradictions in the use of names, places, and times, and demonstrably anachronistic terms and statements[26] – cannot be found in the Prologue.[27] For example, while euergetism was common in Hellenistic times,[28] the title "Euergetes" was indeed used for Ptolemy VIII from 164 BCE.[29] It is therefore not possible to determine with certainty if the Prologue is pseudepigraphic, or at which time other than the one mentioned in the Prologue itself it could have been written.[30] The use of the word Ἑβραϊστί "Hebrew" may point towards the 1st century CE or later since apart from the Prologue it only appears in texts from the 1st century CE onwards,[31] but it is also possible that the Prologue indeed predates all these other texts and is the earliest extant evidence for this word.

The possibility of the Prologue being pseudepigraphic is rarely considered in scholarship on Ben Sira. For example, MARTTILA/PAJUNEN note that most

---

who often are persons of old age), and further statements (e.g. precise information about dates and places). SPEYER 1971 is still the most comprehensive study available (cf. PEIRANO 2012, 1 n. 1), and the characteristics for pseudepigraphic texts mentioned there are similarly found in more recent publications, cf. JANßEN 2011. SPEYER 1971 includes statements on forgery as an unethical lie (e.g. SPEYER 1971, 13–15), and his work has been criticized as ahistorical (cf. MARSHALL 2016). Many studies of pseudepigraphy are connected with issues in the New Testament, cf. for an overview AUNE 2012, 792–793. Recent studies point out that the issue of pseudepigraphy is sometimes anachronistically connected with biblical canons, cf. MARSHALL 2016 (e.g. criticizing BAUM 2001), or academic canons (see Chapter 1 Note 86), cf. e.g. for Classics FRANKLINOS/FULKERSON 2020, 1–6. Recent studies of pseudepigraphic texts move away from a focus on forgery and canon, cf. e.g. for Classics PEIRANO 2012, 1–35, esp. 7–9, 31. A new comparative study of ancient sources regarding the characteristics of pseudepigraphic texts would be desirable.

[26] Cf. SPEYER 1971, 99–105.

[27] In contrast, explicit anachronisms are found, for example, in the Letter of Aristeas, cf. TILLY 2007.

[28] Cf. MEIER 1998; GEHRKE 2008, 50–51, 185–186; CHANIOTIS 2018, 318–322.

[29] Cf. AMELING 2001b.

[30] For the example of Plato, LIATSI 2017, 55, states that the burden of proof lies with those arguing against authenticity.

[31] Cf. a word search on Ἑβραϊστί sorted by date in PANTELIA 2014 [TLG].

scholars consider it "trustworthy" that the author of the Prologue was indeed the grandson of Ben Sira, and add in a footnote:

"Of course, it is worth seriously considering that the whole prologue is fictitious: there was no familial relationship between Ben Sira and the later translator. Such a reference in the prologue has only been composed to gain more prestige for the translated text. In any case, the translator had to convince his audience of his own trustworthiness, and this explains why the prologue was composed."[32]

The identification of the author of the Prologue with the translator of the Book of Ben Sira could also be pseudepigraphic. For example, many scholars have noted that the Greek of the Prologue is much more complicated in its grammar and style compared to the Greek translation of the Book of Ben Sira.[33] The Prologue also contains a number of *hapax legomena* within the Septuagint.[34] VELTRI also considers the Prologue's language to include words not regularly used before the 1st century CE, but this can be substantiated only for Ἑβραϊστί "Hebrew".[35] Even if the identification as the grandson and/or translator is pseudepigraphic, the Prologue could still be a product of the place and time it mentions. For example, VOITILA analyzes rhetoric strategies for trustworthiness in the Prologue and concludes:

"As an outsider in the Greek-speaking Jewish community in Egypt, the author had to convince his audience of his own trustworthiness as a translator of these traditions and of the value of his grandfather's work for the community. [...] He depicted himself as having family connection to the author of the source text, that is, his grandson, and then described both Ben Sira and himself as scribes, transmitters of the ancient Jewish traditions."[36]

However, it is also possible that the Prologue was written much later, at some time more than two generations after Ben Sira and before the 4th century CE (possibly also in a different place though with some knowledge of Egyptian history).

Whether or not it is pseudepigraphic, the Prologue must be dated between 132 BCE (the date mentioned in the Prologue itself as the 38th year of Euergetes) at the earliest and the 4th century CE (the date of its oldest extant manuscripts) at the latest, possibly to the 1st century CE (the date of other occurrences of the word Ἑβραϊστί "Hebrew"). This means that the Maccabean revolts around 167 BCE lie

---

[32] MARTTILA/PAJUNEN 2013, 9 n. 21.

[33] Cf. WRIGHT 2003b, 634. UEBERSCHAER 2016, 453, argues that this difference is due to the stichic style of the Book of Ben Sira. Also see Notes 18 and 277.

[34] Cf. for a full list with details WAGNER 1999, 117–134.

[35] Cf. VELTRI 1994, 139; VELTRI 2006, 196. Against VELTRI, CORLEY 2019, 219, states that "in fact a few of the translator's neologisms do not occur anywhere else in all of Greek literature". However, according to word searches sorted by date in PANTELIA 2014 [TLG], VELTRI also includes words which are used before the 1st century CE, and CORLEY's statement does not apply to the Prologue. Also see Note 31.

[36] VOITILA 2008, 460.

66   *3. Greek Prologue to Ben Sira*

in between the times of Ben Sira and the Prologue,[37] but no reference is made to this in the Prologue.

The place of the Prologue in the history of the canon of the Hebrew Bible also plays a role in answer to the question whether or not the Prologue dates to the time mentioned in it.[38] If a 1st century CE date for the tripartite canon is reconstructed,[39] this could also be taken as an indication of a pseudepigraphic character and a 1st century date of the Prologue, although this would be in danger of circular reasoning. In any case, the Prologue contains many more references to reading, writing, and books than the Book of Ben Sira itself (see Chapter 2.3.3).[40]

3.3.2 Context

The Greek Prologue to Ben Sira is placed before the beginning of the Greek translation of the Book of Ben Sira, which in its first chapter begins with God's creation of wisdom, and the giving of wisdom to those who fear God. The Prologue addresses the readers of the Greek Book of Ben Sira, as made explicit in l. 15–17: Παρακέκλησθε οὖν [...] τὴν ἀνάγνωσιν ποιεῖσθαι "You are therefore urged [...] to do for yourselves the reading". These readers probably live in Egypt (l. 28 mentions Αἴγυπτος "Egypt"), are educated (l. 29 mentions οὐ μικρᾶς παιδείας ἀφόμοιον "a likeness of no little education" in Egypt, l. 34 addresses the translation to τοῖς ἐν τῇ παροικίᾳ βουλομένοις φιλομαθεῖν "those wanting

---

[37] Thus SAUER 2000, 22, 30; HAYWARD 1996, 40; MITCHELL 2011, 3.

[38] DIEBNER 1982, 16–17, 27, argues that the Prologue must have its origins in the Christian era, in the early 2nd century CE. However, this is based on two arguments which can be questioned. First, DIEBNER 1982, 8–11, argues that the name Ἰησοῦς "Jesus" in l. 7 shows that the Prologue's author is not really the grandson of Ben Sira, as he does not know his grandfathers real first name "Simon" (as in the Hebrew tradition) but calls him "Jesus" (found as the first name in the Greek = Christian tradition only). However – as DIEBNER himself notes –, Ben Sira was not necessarily called by his own first name (as shown, in fact, by "Ben Sira"), and the Hebrew name ישוע "Jesus" does appear in all Genizah manuscripts (see Chapter 1.1). Even if different names are used, this may simply indicate a difference between Hebrew and Greek naming traditions at the time of the Prologue, which, as it is written in Greek, would use the name familiar to its readers. Second, DIEBNER 1982, 16–18, uses a reconstructed history of the canon for the argument that the Prologue must be later than the tripartite canon (rather than taking the Prologue as the earliest evidence for a tripartite canon) and argues for a Christian origin of the Prologue. While claiming that the history of the canon is unimportant to him personally (DIEBNER 1982, 26), he argues that the purpose of the Prologue was to include Sir in the Christian Old Testament (DIEBNER 1982, 18, 28), thus revealing an interest in questions of canon. Finally, DIEBNER 1982, 20–25, argues that based on modern fairy tales "grandfather" is a literary topos used to evoke credibility.

[39] See Chapter 1.3.7.

[40] In the Septuagint, the Prologue is also the only text using the term "prophets" for books rather than persons, see Chapter 3.4.2.

3.3 Analysis

to love learning in the foreign country"),[41] and live according to Israel's law (l. 3 mentions Ισραηλ "Israel", l. 36 ἐννόμως βιοτεύειν "live lawfully").[42]

3.3.3 Genre

The Prologue to Ben Sira is unique in the Greek Septuagint: no other book in it begins with a prologue by the translator.[43] In the Septuagint translation of Esther, there is a short Greek epilogue in Esther 10:3[ILXX] which also mentions the translator (in the third person). In 2 Maccabees – an originally Greek text rather than a translation into Greek – a prologue and epilogue by a compiler (in the first person) about his summary of a longer story are found in 2 Macc 2:19–32; 15:37–39[LXX].[44] Generally, the Prologue to Ben Sira belongs to a genre of prologues which is common in ancient Greek texts.[45] In ancient rhetorics in general and prologues in particular, apology is a common literary device to highlight achievements.[46] The Prologue to Ben Sira also uses this literary device.[47] The overall aim of the Prologue is to draw the readers into a favourable reading of the translated book of Ben Sira.

3.3.4 Structure

The Prologue to Ben Sira consists of three long sentences with several subordinate clauses as shown in Table 3–1.

---

[41] The expression ἐν τῇ παροικίᾳ "in the foreign country" in l. 34 probably refers to Egypt because the translation of the Book of Ben Sira is needed, made, and published there according to l. 30 and l. 33. Generally, παροικία "foreign country" can refer to different places (for example Babylon in Ezr 8:35[LXX]; Egypt in Wis 19:10[LXX]) as well as communities of persons rather than places, cf. BAUER/ALAND/ALAND 1988, s.v. παροικία. In the Greek Book of Ben Sira, παροικία is used twice, for the place of Lot in Sir 16:8[LXX], and for contemporary communities in Sir 41:5[LXX].

[42] Ισραηλ "Israel" refers to a people rather than a place, cf. BAUER/ALAND/ALAND 1988, s.v. Ἰσραήλ.

[43] This uniqueness is also noted by WRIGHT 2011, 75.

[44] Thus WAGNER 1999, 21–23; MARBÖCK 2003, 102–105; KREUZER 2009, 136; MARBÖCK 2010, 38; AITKEN 2011, 97 (only Esther). In the New Testament, Luke 1:1–4 contains a prologue by the author (in the first person), thus SKEHAN/DI LELLA 1987, 132; CRENSHAW 1997a, 642.

[45] Thus SKEHAN/DI LELLA 1987, 132; CRENSHAW 1997a, 642; WAGNER 1999, 25–27. Cf. on ancient prologues and prefaces in general MÄNNLEIN-ROBERT 1992; GÄRTNER 2001, 409–412. Also see Note 7.

[46] Cf. for the use of apologies in ancient rhetorics in general CURTIUS 1984, 93–95, specifically in ancient prefaces HAGENBICHLER (PAUL) 1992, 1491–1492; MÄNNLEIN-ROBERT 1992, 250.

[47] Thus with respect to the Prologue ALEXANDER 1993, 152–153; VOITILA 2008, 456–457; KREUZER 2009, 145–146, 150–151 (comparison with Isokrates); AITKEN 2011, 105–108 (comparison with Hellenistic texts); LAUBER 2013, 319–320. BECKER/FABRY/REITEMEYER 2011, 2172, note a parallel in content with an apology for translation issues: the epilogue in the 4th century CE Latin translation of Athanasius' Vita Antonii, cf. for this text BERTRAND/GANDT 2018, 42*, 204*–208*, 218*–219*, 177. Further comparisons of the Greek Prologue to the Book of Ben Sira with prologues and epilogues of texts in different periods between the 2nd century BCE and the 4th century CE (see Chapter 3.3.1) would be desirable.

68 *3. Greek Prologue to Ben Sira*

Table 3-1: Prologue to Ben Sira: Sentence Structure

l. 1–14	*Sentence 1: Book of the grandfather*
l. 1–2	Genitive absolute[48]
l. 3	Relative clause introduced by ὑπὲρ ὧν "because of which"
l. 4–6	Causal clause introduced by ὡς "since"
l. 7–12	Main clause (subject: ὁ πάππος μου Ἰησοῦς "my grandfather Jesus" l. 7, verb: προήχθη "was himself led" l. 12)
l. 13–14	Final clause introduced by ὅπως "in order that"

l. 15–26	*Sentence 2: Translation of the grandson*
l. 15–18	First main clause (subject: readers of the translation of the grandson, implied by verb: παρακέκλησθε "you are urged" l. 15) with participial clause
l. 19–20	Relative clause introduced by ἐφ' οἷς "in those things in which" with participial clause
l. 21–22	Second main clause connected through γάρ "for" (subject: αὐτά "they" l. 22, verb: ἰσοδυναμεῖ "do not have equal power" l. 21)
l. 23–26	Third main clause connected through δέ "for" (subject: ταῦτα "these" + law + prophets + remaining books l. 23–25, verb: ἔχει "have" l. 26)

l. 27–36	*Sentence 3: Translation of the grandson*
l. 27–28	Genitive absolute
l. 29	Participial clause
l. 30	Main clause (subject: grandson, implied by verb ἐθήμην "I set myself" l. 30)
l. 31–34	Participial clause
l. 35–36	Accusative and infinitive

The first sentence praises the book of the grandfather, i.e. the Hebrew Book of Ben Sira. The second and third sentences praise the translation of the grandson, i.e. the Greek Book of Ben Sira as – according to the Prologue – translated by the author of the Prologue. The three sentences deal with four different bodies of literature: a body of literature with three categories called law, prophets/prophecies, and other books (l. 1–2, 8–10) of which translations exist (l. 24–25), the original book of the grandfather (l. 7, 12), and the book's Greek translation made by the grandson (l. 30, 33). These four bodies of literature are clearly distinguished, but at the same time, they are connected through a number of repeated words as shown in Table 3-2.

---

[48] Cf. SMYTH/MESSING 1956, § 2070.

3.4 Key Terms: Law, Prophets, and Writings 69

Table 3–2: Prologue to Ben Sira: Repeated Words

l. 1–14	*Sentence 1: Book of the Grandfather (= Ben Sira's book)*
l. 1–2	τοῦ νόμου καὶ τῶν προφητῶν καὶ τῶν ἄλλων τῶν κατ᾽ αὐτοὺς ἠκολουθηκότων "[through] the law and the prophets and the others which followed in accordance with them" (= the *three categories*)
l. 3	παιδεία καὶ σοφία "wisdom and education" (in the *three categories*)
l. 4	ἀναγιγνώσκω "to read" (the *three categories*)
l. 4	ἐπιστήμων "understanding" (readers of the *three categories*)
l. 5	φιλομαθέω "to love learning" (readers of the *three categories*)
l. 8–10	τοῦ νόμου καὶ τῶν προφητῶν καὶ τῶν ἄλλων πατρίων βιβλίων "of the law and the prophets and the other ancestral books" (Ben Sira reading the *three categories*)
l. 10	ἀνάγνωσις "reading" (the *three categories*)
l. 12	παιδεία "education" + σοφία "wisdom" (in Ben Sira's book)
l. 13	φιλομαθής "lover of learning" (readers of Ben Sira's Hebrew book)
l. 14	ἔννομος "lawful" + βίωσις "life" (aim of living lawfully)

l. 15–26	*Sentence 2: Translation of the grandson (= Greek translation of Ben Sira)*
l. 17	ἀνάγνωσις "reading" (the Greek translation of Ben Sira)
l. 24–25	αὐτὸς ὁ νόμος καὶ αἱ προφητεῖαι καὶ τὰ λοιπὰ τῶν βιβλίων "the law itself and the prophecies and the remaining ones of the books" (original and translation of the *three categories*)

l. 27–36	*Sentence 3: Translation of the grandson (= Greek translation of Ben Sira)*
l. 29	παιδεία "education" (in Egypt)
l. 31	ἐπιστήμη "understanding" (grandson)
l. 34	φιλομαθέω "to love learning" (readers of the Greek translation of Ben Sira)
l. 36	ἐννόμως "lawfully" + βιοτεύω "to live" (aim of living lawfully)

The relation between the three categories, their translation, and Ben Sira's book and its translation according to the Prologue is debated in connection with the question of canon (see Chapter 3.5).

3.4 Key Terms: Law, Prophets, and Writings

3.4.1 Greek Prologue to Ben Sira

The Greek Prologue to Ben Sira mentions three categories of books (on the material forms of ancient books see Chapter 2.2.2). According to the Prologue, great things are given to Israel through τοῦ νόμου καὶ τῶν προφητῶν καὶ τῶν ἄλλων τῶν κατ᾽ αὐτοὺς ἠκολουθηκότων "the law and the prophets and the others which followed in accordance with them" (l. 1–2). The translator's grandfather gave himself to the reading of τοῦ νόμου καὶ τῶν προφητῶν καὶ τῶν ἄλλων πατρίων βιβλίων "the law and the prophets and the other ancestral books"

70   3. Greek Prologue to Ben Sira

(l. 8–10). Different in Hebrew as compared to their Greek translations are even αὐτὸς ὁ νόμος καὶ αἱ προφητεῖαι καὶ τὰ λοιπὰ τῶν βιβλίων "the law itself and the prophecies and the remaining ones of the books" (l. 24–25). Only the third category is described as βιβλία "books" (l. 10 and l. 25). Its designations as καὶ τῶν ἄλλων πατρίων βιβλίων "and the other of the ancestral books" (l. 10) and καὶ τὰ λοιπὰ τῶν βιβλίων "and the remaining ones of the books" (l. 25) imply that the first two categories are also ancestral books.[49] They also imply that the third category in the first list, τῶν ἄλλων τῶν κατ᾽ αὐτοὺς ἠκολουθηκότων "and the others which followed in accordance with them" (l. 2), also refers to books. According to l. 21–26, these books existed Ἑβραϊστί "in Hebrew" (l. 22) and in translations εἰς ἑτέραν γλῶσσαν "into another language" (l. 22). The other language is probably Greek because the book mentioned as the translator's own work compared to these books in l. 15–26 is a Greek book, and because the Prologue's readers must know Greek as they are reading a Greek text.

From today's point of view, three categories of books of Israel called "law", "prophets", and "others" written in Hebrew and translated into Greek strongly lend themselves to identification with items familiar today: the three parts of the Hebrew Bible, "Law", "Prophets", and "Writings",[50] and the Greek translation of the Hebrew Bible known as Septuagint.[51] Some manuscripts and versions of the Prologue contain variants which seem to reflect such an identification.[52] For example, in l. 24, some Greek manuscripts (mostly minuscules) and versions read οἱ προφῆται "the prophets" instead of the *lectio difficilior* αἱ προφητεῖαι "the prophecies".[53] However, in Hebrew and Greek texts earlier than or contemporary to Ben Sira, neither the terms for "law" nor those for "prophets" clearly refer to collections of books.

3.4.2 Hebrew and Greek Terms

The Hebrew word תורה "law" can refer to a broad range of human and divine rules, written and unwritten, and a written law of Moses is usually identified with the whole or parts of the Pentateuch.[54] However, ancient sources do not explicitly contain such an identification.[55] For the Second Temple Period, תורה "law" can-

---

[49] SWANSON 1970, 128, concludes that therefore ὁ νόμος "the law" refers "to the books of the Pentateuch, and not just to the legal material contained therein".

[50] See Chapter 1 Note 2.

[51] On the evidence for the LXX canon in the 4th century CE cf. SIEGERT 2001, 42–47, 101–103.

[52] See Notes 3–6.

[53] See Note 5. HENGEL 1994, 257 n. 214, takes this as the original reading. SAUER 2000, 36, n. 4, translates προφητεῖαι "prophecies" in l. 24 as "prophets" due to the other two mentions of the three categories.

[54] Cf. GESENIUS 2013, s. v. תּוֹרָה.

[55] Cf. FINSTERBUSCH 2011, 27–28; FINSTERBUSCH 2016, 1112–1118.

3.4 Key Terms: Law, Prophets, and Writings

not simply be equated with the Pentateuch now in the Hebrew Bible.[56] In texts among the Dead Sea Scrolls, the term תורה "law" is sometimes thought to refer to a form of the written Pentateuch,[57] but also to divine rules rather than any form of the written Pentateuch.[58] There are passages in the Dead Sea Scrolls where תורה "law" – even in connection with divine law given to Moses – is explicitly used for written texts which are not the Pentateuch but the Temple Scroll or Jubilees.[59] In addition to such uses of the term תורה "law" for texts not now included in the Pentateuch, texts now included in the Pentateuch are not fixed and are found in various text forms in the Second Temple Period.[60] Overall, in the Second Temple Period the term תורה "law" does not simply refer to the Pentateuch as it is found today in the Masoretic Text of the Hebrew Bible.

The word νόμος "law" in Ancient Greek refers to law or custom in general.[61] In Septuagint and New Testament texts, it can also refer specifically to the law of God.[62] In New Testament texts, νόμος "law" can also – amongst other meanings – refer to the Pentateuch or parts of the same, especially when collocated with words for books or writing or explicit quotations, and ὁ νόμος "the law" in combination with οἱ προφῆται "the prophets" usually refers to all of the texts seen as authoritative in the New Testament.[63] However, the texts in the New Testament were not written before the 1st century CE. The adjective ἔννομος "lawful" and the adverb ἐννόμως "lawfully" also refer to law in general in Ancient Greek.[64] In the Septuagint, the adverb ἐννόμως "lawfully" is used only once outside the Prologue to Ben Sira with no clear reference to the Pentateuch (Prov 31:25[LXX]).[65] In the New Testament, ἔννομος "lawful" is used twice and refers to the order of an assembly (Acts 19:39) and to the law of Christ (1 Cor 9:21).[66]

The Hebrew word נביא "prophet" describes persons who act as divine messengers rather than texts.[67]

---

[56] Cf. BARTON 2019, 222; ZAHN 2020c, 805–806; ZAHN 2021, 85–90.

[57] Cf. FINSTERBUSCH 2016, 1113–1116.

[58] Cf. MANDEL 2017, 90–92; STUCKENBRUCK 2020, 6–7.

[59] Cf. FABRY 1999, 265 (Temple Scroll); FINSTERBUSCH 2016, 1117 (Temple Scroll), 1118 (Jubilees).

[60] Cf. on this textual fluidity ZAHN 2020b, 410–420; ZAHN 2021, 80–85.

[61] Cf. LIDDELL/SCOTT/JONES [1940], s. v. νόμος.

[62] Cf. LUST/EYNIKEL/HAUSPIE 2003, s. v. νόμος.

[63] Cf. BAUER/ALAND/ALAND 1988, s. v. νόμος.

[64] Cf. LIDDELL/SCOTT/JONES [1940], s. v. ἔννομος.

[65] Cf. WAGNER 1999, 123; LUST/EYNIKEL/HAUSPIE 2003, s. v. ἐννόμως.

[66] Cf. BAUER/ALAND/ALAND 1988, s. v. ἔννομος. The adverb ἐννόμως "lawfully" only appears in a variant reading for ἐν νόμῳ "in law" in Rom 2:12, cf. BAUER/ALAND/ALAND 1988, s. v. ἐννόμως. For variants in the Prologue see Notes 4 and 6.

[67] Cf. GESENIUS 2013, s. v. נָבִיא. There are three examples in Dead Sea Scrolls for נביא "prophet" with references to books given in XERAVITS 2013, 849, but these are immediately preceded by a construct form of ספר "book", thus the Damascus Document (CD) Column 7 Line 17 (ספרי הנביאים "the books of the prophets", cf. BAUMGARTEN/SCHWARTZ 1995, 26–27) and the parallel 4Q266 (4QDᵃ, Fragment 3 iii Line 18 [ים]ספ[רי] הנביא "the book[s] of the proph[ets]",

72   3. Greek Prologue to Ben Sira

The Greek word προφήτης "prophet" refers to persons who act as divine messengers,[68] προφητεία "prophecy" to the gift or office of prophecy as well as individual prophecies.[69] In the Septuagint, the Prologue to Ben Sira is the only place where προφήτης "prophet" refers to written books,[70] a phenomenon more common in the New Testament.[71] However, even if the reference is to written texts, these could be texts outside the later "Prophets" section of the Hebrew Bible. For example, David is said to have composed songs through prophecy in the Dead Sea Psalms Scroll 11Q5 (11QPsᵃ),[72] and in the Hebrew Book of Ben Sira the person Job is called a prophet (see Chapter 6.5).

The Hebrew word כתובים "writings" is used as a reference to texts now in the Hebrew Bible only in the Common Era.[73] The Greek word βιβλίον "book" is a general term for written texts.[74]

Even where they refer to categories of books, the mere use of the terms "law", "prophets", and "writings" does not say which books these categories contain. Their combination, especially that of "law" and "prophets", is more specific, especially in the New Testament in the 1ˢᵗ century CE. In the late 1ˢᵗ century CE, Josephus (Ag. Ap. 1.37–45) explicitly mentions a tripartite division of twenty-two books.[75] However, it is not clear if these can be identified with the books now in the Hebrew Bible.[76]

3.4.3 Hebrew Book of Ben Sira

In the Hebrew Book of Ben Sira, the equivalent for the Greek νόμος "law" (see Chapter 3.4.4) is usually תורה "law" (Sir 15:1; 32:15, 24; 33:2, 3),[77] specifically תורת עליון "law of the Most High" (Sir 41:8; 42:2; 49:4) and תורת חיים ותבונה "law of life and understanding" (Sir 45:5, in a parallel with מצוה "commandment"). Other equivalents to νόμος "law" in Ben Sira are מצוה "commandment", specifically מצות עליון "commandment of the Most High" (Sir 44:20), and משפט "judgment"

---

cf. BAUMGARTEN et al. 1996, 43–45) as well as 4Q397 (4QMMTᵈ, see Chapter 2.2.3). The third example "4Q379 4,10.15" in XERAVITS 2013, 849, may be an error since 4Q379 (4QapocrJoshᵇ) Fragment 36 contains נביאים "prophets" without context, cf. NEWSOM 1996, 287, and no mention of prophets is found on Fragment 4 which contains 6 lines, cf. NEWSOM 1996, 266–267.

[68] Cf. LIDDELL/SCOTT/JONES [1940], s. v. προφήτης.

[69] Cf. LIDDELL/SCOTT/JONES [1940], s. v. προφητεία.

[70] Cf. LUST/EYNIKEL/HAUSPIE 2003, s. v. προφήτης.

[71] Cf. BAUER/ALAND/ALAND 1988, s. v. προφήτης.

[72] Cf. XERAVITS 2013, 850 (David's Compositions).

[73] See Chapter 1 Note 2. For the term הכתוב "the one written" see Chapter 5.5.2.

[74] Cf. LIDDELL/SCOTT/JONES [1940], s. v. βιβλίον.

[75] For the Greek text and an English translation of Josephus, Ag. Ap. 1.37–45, cf. THACKERAY 1926, 176–181. On Josephus in general see Chapter 2 Note 88.

[76] Cf. OSSÁNDON WIDOW 2019, 40–46, 67–82.

[77] The verse Sir 33:3 is missing on Manuscript E I recto but present on Manuscript B V verso, cf. RENDSBURG/BINSTEIN 2013.

3.4 Key Terms: Law, Prophets, and Writings

(Sir 45:17). No equivalent to νόμος "law" is found in the Hebrew text of Sir 9:15 or Sir 51:19. The other passages with νόμος "law" are not preserved in Hebrew, especially not Sir 24:23[LXX] identifying the law with a book (see Chapter 3.4.4), or Sir 38:34[LXX] and Sir 39:8[LXX] associating it with the profession of a scribe though not explicitly with writing (see Chapter 4). In addition to these equivalences for νόμος "law", תורה "law" occurs in Sir 32:17 (Greek equivalent σύγκριμα "interpretation"), Sir 32:18 (no Greek equivalent for this part of the verse),[78] and Sir 41:4 as תורת עליון "law of the Most High" (Greek equivalent εὐδοκία "goodwill").[79] In the Hebrew Book of Ben Sira, all occurrences of תורה "law" refer to God's law. However, nowhere is תורה "law" equated with the Pentateuch, although this is often assumed.[80] Scholars such as MARBÖCK have noted that in the Book of Ben Sira "law" even repeatedly refers to content not found in the Pentateuch, and creation, priesthood, and wisdom play a much more important role than "law".[81] Similarly, WISCHMEYER notes differences to the Pentateuch in the content of Ben Sira[82] and the universal meaning of "Torah" in Ben Sira.[83] She explicitly states that for Ben Sira experience plays a much more important role than "Torah":

"He [Ben Sira] formulates norms and models out of experienced reality, not as an interpretation of the Torah."[84]

In the Hebrew Book of Ben Sira, equivalents for προφήτης "prophet" also all refer to persons. נביא "prophet" in Sir 36:21 as the equivalent of Sir 36:15[LXX] refers to God's prophets,[85] in Sir 48:1 to Elijah who is mentioned in Sir 48:4, in Sir 48:8 to Elijah's successor, in Sir 49:7 to Jeremiah, and in Sir 49:10 to the twelve prophets (see Chapter 6.6 for the latter). חזה "seer" in Sir 46:15 refers to Samuel (Sir 46:13 on Manuscript B XVI recto uses as an equivalent נזיר ייי בנבואה "a consecrated one of YYY in prophecy" for Samuel). Sir 49:9 is damaged in Manuscript B but is likely to describe Job as a prophet: איוב נ[ב]יֹאֹ "Job, a p[roph]et" (see Chapter 6.5.1). The equivalent for προφήτης "prophet" in Sir 48:22[LXX] is not preserved in Hebrew. The verb נבא "to prophesy" as the equivalent of προφετεύω "to prophesy" is not used (Sir 46:20 on Manuscript B XVI verso uses [ה]נבוא

---

[78] תורה "law" is found in Sir 32:18 on Manuscript B V verso only, while marginal readings on Manuscript B as well as Manuscript E I recto and Manuscript F I verso read מצוה "commandment", cf. RENDSBURG/BINSTEIN 2013.

[79] תורת עליון "law of the Most High" is preserved, with damages in different places, on Manuscript B X verso and Masada Manuscript III, cf. RENDSBURG/BINSTEIN 2013.

[80] Thus SCHNABEL 1985, 42; BEENTJES 2006a, 170. Also see Chapter 3.4.4 on Sir 24:23[LXX].

[81] Cf. MARBÖCK 1995b, 60–63. Similarly SCHRADER 1994, 123, 130.

[82] Cf. WISCHMEYER 1994, 113 (topic of washing and purity almost entirely missing), 115 (feasts almost entirely missing), but differently 198–199 (all main topics of Pentateuch covered in Sir).

[83] Cf. WISCHMEYER 1994, 270–271 (Torah Pentateuch but also and more importantly for Ben Sira universal cosmic order), 295 (Torah both written book and living will of God).

[84] WISCHMEYER 1994, 82 (German original: "Er formuliert Wertmaßstäbe und Leitbilder aus der Erfahrungswirklichkeit heraus, nicht als Auslegung der Tora.").

[85] Sir 36:21 in RENDSBURG/BINSTEIN 2013 equals Sir 36:16 in BEENTJES 1997, 62.

74   *3. Greek Prologue to Ben Sira*

"prophecy", no word related to prophecy appears in Sir 47:1, and Sir 48:13 uses
נברא "it was created").[86] Hebrew equivalents for προφητεία "prophecy" in Ben
Sira are נבואה "prophecy" in Sir 44:3 referring to ancestors, in Sir 46:1 to Joshua,
and in Sir 46:20 to the deceased Samuel (the word also refers to the living Samuel
in Sir 46:13). חזון "vision" in Sir 36:20 as the equivalent of Sir 36:14[LXX] refers to
God's prophets.[87] Sir 24:33[LXX] and Sir 39:1[LXX] are not preserved in Hebrew.

"Writings" is not used as a specific term in Ben Sira (for the general use of
words related to writing and books see Chapter 3.3.2.).

3.4.4 Greek Book of Ben Sira

In the Greek Prologue to Ben Sira, ὁ νόμος "the law" appears three times (l. 1,
l. 8, l. 24), always in lists of three categories of books, and is implied to be a book
by l. 10 and l. 25. However, it is unclear if this book can be identified with the
Pentateuch.

In the Greek Book of Ben Sira, νόμος "law" only refers to the law of God.
In no occurrence is the word used for any general law or custom. Rather, in its
26 occurrences outside the Prologue, it is designated as νόμος θεοῦ ὑψίστου
"law of the Most High God" (Sir 41:8[LXX]) or νόμος ὑψίστου "law of the Most
High" (Sir 9:15; 19:17; 23:23; 38:34;[88] 42:2; 44:20[LXX]; with the article νόμος τοῦ
ὑψίστου "law of the Most High" Sir 49:4[LXX]), νόμος κυρίου "law of the Lord"
(Sir 46:14[LXX]), and νόμος διαθήκης κυρίου "law of the covenant of the Lord"
(Sir 39:8[LXX]). The "law" is explicitly kept by a figure prior to Moses, namely
Abraham in Sir 44:20[LXX]. "Law" is connected with life (νόμος ζωῆς "law of
life" Sir 17:11[LXX], νόμον ζωῆς καὶ ἐπιστήμης "law of life and understanding" Sir
45:5[LXX]), Israel (Sir 45:17[LXX], also Jacob and Israel in Sir 45:5[LXX]), love and fear of
God (Sir 2:16; 19:24; 32:1; 35:15, 24[LXX]),[89] and wisdom (Sir 15:1; 19:20; 21:11; 31:8;
36:2–3; 51:19[LXX]).[90] It is also associated with the profession of a scribe (Sir 38:34;
39:8[LXX]),[91] but only once, in Sir 24:23[LXX], with a book. Many scholars argue that
Sir 24:23[LXX] refers to the whole written Pentateuch.[92] There are also more re-

---

[86] This is also noted by Beentjes 2021, 70–74.

[87] Sir 36:20 in Rendsburg/Binstein 2013 equals Sir 36:15 in Beentjes 1997, 62.

[88] The last two lines of Sir 38:34[LXX] in Ziegler 1980, 305, equal the first two lines of Sir
39:1[LXX] in Rahlfs/Hanhart 2006, Vol. II 444. See Chapter 4.3.

[89] Sir 32:1; 35:15, 24[LXX] in Ziegler 1980, 276, 286, equal Sir 32:15, 24; 35:1[LXX] in Rahlfs/
Hanhart 2006, Vol. II 432, 436.

[90] Sir 31:8; 36:2–3[LXX] in Ziegler 1980, 277, 282, equal Sir 34:8; 33:2–3[LXX] in Rahlfs/Han-
hart 2006, Vol. II 433, 435.

[91] The last two lines of Sir 38:34[LXX] in Ziegler 1980, 305, equal the first two lines of Sir
39:1[LXX] in Rahlfs/Hanhart 2006, Vol. II 444. See Chapters 4.3 and 4.4.

[92] Thus Sheppard 1980, 68; Schnabel 1985, 42; Ego 1999, 207; Schreiner 2002, 132;
Grabbe 2004, 343 ; Carr 2005, 210–211; Veijola 2006, 434–435; Ueberschaer 2007, 220–
221, 249 (Pentateuch only, however, Torah may also comprise oral traditions), 357 (Pentateuch);
Liesen 2008, 200; Reiterer 2008a, 133 (for the grandson of Ben Sira law is the Pentateuch);

3.4 Key Terms: Law, Prophets, and Writings

strictive views – that the verse refers to the legislative parts of the Pentateuch,[93] or to only a version of Deuteronomy[94] – and more expansive views – that it refers to the Pentateuch and other texts in the Hebrew Bible.[95] Views which note that the Pentateuch may not be meant here at all are rare. Some scholars argue that the meaning of law in the Book of Ben Sira is too broad to identify such a specific reference here,[96] for example because law encompasses the whole order of creation.[97] Many scholars also note that the Book of Ben Sira does not quote the Pentateuch at all and often differs from its content.[98] For example, WRIGHT notes that Ben Sira never quotes the Pentateuch and sometimes does not follow its content,[99] and that the Pentateuch may only have become dominant after Ben Sira's time.[100] WRIGHT argues that Sir 24:23[LXX] could refer to oral traditions or written texts, including texts similar to but not identical with the Pentateuch found among the Dead Sea Scrolls.[101] Nevertheless, WRIGHT presumes that Ben Sira "knew something like our Pentateuch",[102] states "[t]hat Ben Sira knew texts that we now find in the Pentateuch is beyond doubt",[103] and compares Ben Sira to the Pentateuch in the Hebrew Bible.[104] Often, Sir 24:23[LXX] is also thought to contain a quotation of Deut 33:4[LXX].[105] Following Sir 24:1–22[LXX] where σοφία "wisdom" appears as a personified figure and is quoted in direct speech, Sir 24:23[LXX] reads:[106]

GOERING 2009, 101 (differently 95 n. 80); NISSINEN 2009, 387; REY 2016, 261; SCHMIDT 2019, 269–270. Thus also implicitly MARBÖCK 1995c, 83; KRAFT 1996, 211 (see Chapter 1 Note 255); LIM 2013, 106; MERMELSTEIN 2014, 20.

[93] Thus BURNS 2016, 244 (Pentateuch or legislative parts of the Pentateuch).

[94] Thus HORSLEY 2007, 120.

[95] Thus LIESEN 2000, 49–53, esp. 53; GOERING 2009, 95 n. 80 (differently 101).

[96] Thus BOX/OESTERLEY 1913, 305.

[97] Thus MARBÖCK 1995b, 59.

[98] ROGERS 2004, 117–119, notes that laws included in the Pentateuch play a very minor role in the Book of Ben Sira overall.

[99] Cf. WRIGHT 2013a, 166. Cf. similarly MARBÖCK 1995b, 62.

[100] Cf. WRIGHT 2013a, 186.

[101] Thus WRIGHT 2013a, 164–165.

[102] Cf. WRIGHT 2013a, 157. Cf. similarly MACK 1985, 100–101. REITEMEYER 2000, 167, 177, also argues for a broad meaning of law but still identifies the mention in Sir 24:23[LXX] with the Pentateuch.

[103] WRIGHT 2013a, 175.

[104] Thus WRIGHT 2013a, 165 (see Note 101), 175 (see Note 103).

[105] Thus PETERS 1913, 202; SHEPPARD 1980, 61–63; STADELMANN 1980, 250; SKEHAN/DI LELLA 1987, 336; MARBÖCK 1995c, 83; UEBERSCHAER 2007, 220–221, 356–358; GOERING 2009, 94; SCHMIDT 2019, 146.

[106] Cf. ZIEGLER 1980, 240.

| Sir 24:23[LXX] | Ταῦτα πάντα βίβλος διαθήκης θεοῦ ὑψίστου, νόμον[107] ὃν ἐνετείλατο ἡμῖν Μωυσῆς κληρονομίαν συναγωγαῖς[108] Ιακωβ. | These all: the book of the covenant of God the Most High, a law which Moses commanded to us, an inheritance for the congregations of Jacob. |

Deut 33:4[LXX] is identical with the second half of Sir 24:23[LXX]:[109]

| Deut 33:4[LXX] | νόμον, ὃν ἐνετείλατο ἡμῖν Μωυσῆς, κληρονομίαν συναγωγαῖς Ιακωβ. | A law which Moses commanded to us, an inheritance for the congregations of Jacob. |

The lexical and syntactial similarity of these eight words in the same forms and order indeed indicates an intertextual reference between Sir 24:23[LXX] and Deut 33:4[LXX]. Taking aside wider debates on the identification of wisdom and law in Sir 24,[110] or on the role of Israel's law compared to other sources of wisdom,[111] there are two issues with this reference. First, Sir 24:23[LXX] (like the entire chapter Sir 24[LXX]) is not extant in Hebrew.[112] Some scholars argue that the first half of the verse never existed in Hebrew,[113] giving as reasons that it is longer than most other verses,[114] that it contains a connection of law and book not found anywhere else in the whole book of Ben Sira,[115] or that it fits well into an Egyptian context in the late 2nd century BCE.[116] It is also thought that the verse could have second-arily been assimilated to the Septuagint text.[117] The lack of a Hebrew text makes it difficult to decide whether the verse contains secondary elements. Second, even

---

[107] Some Greek manuscripts and a version here read a nominative rather than an accusative form, cf. ZIEGLER 1980, 240. The accusative is also found in Deut 33:4[LXX] which can point to either a strong quotation or a secondary assimilation, see Note 108.

[108] Some Greek manuscripts and some versions including the Syriac Peshitta here read a singular rather than a plural form, cf. ZIEGLER 1980, 240. This singular form is also found in MT. The difference is argued to point to a diaspora situation at the time of translation (thus MARBÖCK 1971, 40; RICKENBACHER 1973, 167) or later (thus SAUER 2000, 178), to a clear quotation of the Septuagint in the original Greek translation (thus GILBERT 1974, 337), or to a secondary assimilation to the Septuagint in the transmission of the translation (thus UEBERSCHAER 2007, 357 Note 56).

[109] Cf. RAHLFS/HANHART 2006, Vol. I 351.

[110] Cf. the summary in WRIGHT 2013a, 157–159. For example, the identification of wisdom and law is questioned by ROGERS 2004; REITERER 2008a.

[111] Cf. the summary in WRIGHT 2013a, 169–178. Also cf. ADAMS 2008, 198–204.

[112] See Chapter 1.2.1. On the general problem of retroversions from Greek into Hebrew cf. CALDUCH-BENAGES 2016, 60.

[113] Thus MARBÖCK 1993, 186.

[114] Thus PETERS 1913, 203; RICKENBACHER 1973, 126–127; GILBERT 1974, 336–338.

[115] Thus RICKENBACHER 1973, 126–127. Against this, SCHMIDT 2019, 246, implies that a statement can be made only once. ADAMS 2008, 201 (similarly ADAMS 2017, 55), notes that there is no connection of wisdom and a book elsewhere in the Book of Ben Sira, and that Deut 33:4 does not mention a written text.

[116] Thus NEWMAN 2017, 157, 159.

[117] See Note 108.

3.4 Key Terms: Law, Prophets, and Writings

if the reference did exist in Hebrew,[118] it does not necessarily support a reference to the whole Pentateuch, as Deut 33:4 itself may not refer to the Pentateuch but to specific laws in the Book of Deuteronomy only.[119] It is also possible that there is no direct connection but an oral or written third source for both texts. Overall, in the Greek text, a reference to the Pentateuch in Sir 24:23^{LXX} is uncertain. In Hebrew, the verse is not preserved.

In the Greek Prologue to Ben Sira, the word προφήτης "prophet" appears twice (l. 1, l. 9), always in lists of three categories of writings, and refers to books (τῶν ἄλλων πατρίων βιβλίων "the other ancestral books" in l. 10 implies that the law and the prophets are also books, see Chapter 3.5.2). It is used synonymously with προφητεία "prophecy" in l. 24 which also refers to books (implied in l. 25).[120]

Outside the Prologue in the Greek Book of Ben Sira, προφήτης "prophet" always refers to persons, not to books: God's prophets in Sir 36:21^{LXX},[121] Samuel in Sir 46:13, 15^{LXX}, Elijah in Sir 48:1^{LXX}, prophets succeeding Elijah in Sir 48:8^{LXX}, Isaiah in Sir 48:22^{LXX}, Jeremiah in Sir 49:7^{LXX}, and the twelve prophets in Sir 49:10^{LXX} (see Chapter 6.6). The verb προφητεύω "to prophecy" also refers to living or dead persons (Samuel after his death in Sir 46:20^{LXX}, Nathan in Sir 47:1^{LXX}, Elisha after his death in Sir 48:13^{LXX}). The term προφητεία "prophecy" in the Greek Book of Ben Sira refers to words spoken by specific persons (Joshua in Sir 46:1^{LXX}, Samuel after his death in Sir 46:20^{LXX}, ancestors announcing prophecies in Sir 44:3^{LXX}) or God's prophets in general (Sir 36:20^{LXX}).[122] In Sir 24:33^{LXX}, Ben Sira's own teaching is compared to prophecy (διδασκαλίαν ὡς προφητείαν "teaching like prophecy"), although writing is not mentioned. According to Sir 39:1^{LXX}, a scribe studies prophecies, although it is not mentioned if this study consists of reading.

"Writings" is not used as a specific term in the Greek translation of Ben Sira (for the general use of words related to writing and books see Chapter 3.3.2).

3.4.5 Summary of Uses

The general use of the Hebrew and Greek terms for "law", "prophets" and "writings" in antiquity does not allow for a precise identification with the three parts of today's Hebrew Bible. In Hebrew in general, "law" is not explicitly identified with the Pentateuch but explicitly used for texts outside the Penta-

---

[118] For example, Sir 24:23^{LXX} is preserved in the Syriac Peshitta, but its Hebrew original cannot be reconstructed, see Chapter 1.2.1, esp. Note 54.

[119] Cf. FINSTERBUSCH 2011, 16–19. Also cf. ADAMS 2008, 201; ADAMS 2017, 55.

[120] See Chapter 3.4.1.

[121] Sir 36:21^{LXX} in ZIEGLER 1980, 276, 292, equals Sir 36:15^{LXX} in RAHLFS/HANHART 2006, Vol. II 439.

[122] Sir 36:20^{LXX} in ZIEGLER 1980, 276, 291–292, equals Sir 36:14^{LXX} in RAHLFS/HANHART 2006, Vol. II 438.

78   *3. Greek Prologue to Ben Sira*

teuch, and "prophets" refers to persons rather than books. In Greek, "law" and "prophets" refer to books in the New Testament, but not usually in earlier texts.

In the Hebrew Book of Ben Sira, "law" always refers to God's law, and "prophets" to persons. None of the passages connecting either law or prophecies to written texts in the Book of Ben Sira are preserved in Hebrew. In the Greek Book of Ben Sira only the "law" is once explicitly designated as a book, while the "prophets" always refers to persons rather than texts, although "prophecies" may imply written texts including those written by Ben Sira. Only in the Greek Prologue to Ben Sira, "law" and "prophets/prophecies" appear in combination and refer to categories of books.

3.5 The Prologue and the Question of Canon

3.5.1 Canonical References?

The Greek Prologue to Ben Sira is often regarded as the first mention of a tripartite biblical canon.[123] In a commentary in 1913, PETERS writes:

"On the prologue's importance for the history of the canon (three times ὁ νόμος, οἱ προφῆται καὶ τὰ λοιπά i.e. כְּתוּבִים – נְבִיאִים – תּוֹרָה) cf. the introductory handbooks to the Old Testament."[124]

More than a century after PETERS' commentary, introductory textbooks still point out the importance of the Greek Prologue to Ben Sira as the oldest extant mention of the Hebrew Bible's tripartite canon.[125]

3.5.2 Tripartite Canon?

The Prologue to Ben Sira is seen not just in textbooks but also by various commentators as the earliest extant evidence for a clearly defined tripartite canon.[126] For example, HAMP writes in 1951:

---

[123] Cf. BECKER 1998, 1409.

[124] PETERS 1913, 3, German original: "Über die Bedeutung des Prologs für die Geschichte des Kanons (dreimal ὁ νόμος, οἱ προφῆται καὶ τὰ λοιπά d.i. כְּתוּבִים – נְבִיאִים – תּוֹרָה) vgl. die Handbücher der Einleitung ins A. T.".

[125] Thus DIETRICH et al. 2014, 19–20. For further examples from textbooks see Chapter 1 Notes 25 and 26.

[126] Cf. esp. RYLE 1892, 10; WANKE 1980, 3–4, on the history of the biblical canon; cf. also on the Prologue BOX/OESTERLEY 1913, 304 (law with definite article); LEBRAM 1968, 175 (Prologue: law superior), 184 (generally: law equal to other parts); BECKWITH 1985, 17, 110–111 (repeated in BECKWITH 1988, 51–52, cf. also 59), 385; HANHART 1994, 2–3; WISCHMEYER 1994, 185 n. 46; STEMBERGER 2001, 636; SCHNIEDEWIND 2004, 195, 200; COLPE/HANHART 2005, 499; KAISER 2005, 157; *Stuttgarter Erklärungsbibel* 2005, 1226; REITERER 2008b, 210–211; REITERER 2008c, 224–225.

3.5 The Prologue and the Question of Canon

"In the prologue, the division of the Holy Scripture into three parts is attested for the first time".[127]

SKEHAN/DI LELLA note in 1987:

"Here for the first time mention is made of the threefold division of the OT".[128]

And in his 2012 introduction to Ben Sira, CORLEY writes:

"In the first paragraph, the grandson adopts a division of the Hebrew Bible into three parts, matching the subsequent rabbinic classification of law, prophets, and writings".[129]

Arguments brought forward for this view of a tripartite canon in the Prologue include the following:

(1) In the Prologue, there are three rather than two categories in every one of the three instances where categories of books are mentioned.[130]

(2) The third category is always designated with "other" (τῶν ἄλλων "of the other" l. 2, l. 10; τὰ λοιπά "the remaining ones" l. 25).[131] – The argument that the second category is always designated with something pertaining to prophecy could also be added here.

(3) The third category is, like the other two, always introduced with definite articles and is thus likely to be a defined category.[132]

(4) The designation τῶν ἄλλων πατρίων βιβλίων "the other ancestral books" in l. 10 implies that the law and the prophets are also ancestral books, and that all three categories belong to the same ancestral collection.[133] Similarly, in l. 25 τὰ λοιπὰ τῶν βιβλίων "the remaining ones of the books" implies that the law and the prophecies are also books which are different in their Greek translations, and that thus all three categories of books belong together.

---

[127] HAMP 1951, 7, German original: "Im Prolog ist zum ersten Mal die Dreiteilung der Heiligen Schrift bezeugt". HAMP also uses prophets in the translation of l. 24 despite noting that Greek manuscripts use prophecies.

[128] SKEHAN/DI LELLA 1987, 133. SKEHAN/DI LELLA 1987, 132–133, speak of the three parts of "the Sacred Scriptures, which are inspired by God".

[129] CORLEY 2013, 9.

[130] Thus BECKWITH 1991, 388–389; STEINS 1995, 512.

[131] Cf. BURKHARDT 1992, 138–139 (third part refers to biblical books even if the presence of a tripartite division does not necessarily include the concept of canonization).

[132] Cf. BECKWITH 1985, 111 (repeated in BECKWITH 1988, 52), 166 n. 2 (number of books complete); VAN DER KOOIJ 1998, 23; VAN DER KOOIJ 2003, 31 (tripartite canon specifically with a defined but not definitive or closed third section).

[133] Cf. VAN DER KOOIJ 1998, 23; VAN DER KOOIJ 2003, 32.

80   *3. Greek Prologue to Ben Sira*

(5) The third category is described with the adjective πάτριος "ancestral" in l. 10 and its translation exists according to l. 25, pointing towards a category which has existed for some time,[134] and ancestral authority.[135]

(6) Just as the later term כְּתוּבִים "writings", the different designations for the third category could point towards its less unified character rather than its openness at the time of the Prologue.[136]

Arguments based on sources outside the Prologue include the mention of a tripartite division in Luke 24:44,[137] and the use of definite articles for the third category of books by Josephus (Ag. Ap. 1.38–40).[138] However, both of these texts have their origin in the late 1st century CE.

Some scholars regard the third category of the tripartite canon as not closed at the time of the Prologue,[139] either as simply not yet including all the books included in it today,[140] or as open to including further books at the time.[141] Arguments for this view of the Prologue as referring to a tripartite canon whose third part is open include the following:

(1) The Prologue contains three different designations for the third group[142] despite the definite articles. – However, the designations for the second category

---

[134] Cf. BECKWITH 1985, 111 (repeated in BECKWITH 1988, 52), 166 n. 2. According to BECKWITH 1988, 53, 57, the different designations and lack of a title for the third category possibly points to a recent separation from the category "prophets".

[135] Cf. VAN DER KOOIJ 1998, 31 (the books are ancestral, kept in the temple, and studied). However, there is no mention of books being kept in the temple in the Prologue.

[136] Cf. STEINS 1995, 512.

[137] Thus SKEHAN/DI LELLA 1987, 133; CORLEY 2013, 9. On the date of Luke (around 80–90 CE) cf. RADL 2002, 550.

[138] Thus VAN DER KOOIJ 2003, 31. For the Greek text and an English translation of Josephus, Ag. Ap. 1.37–45, cf. THACKERAY 1926, 176–181. On Josephus in general see Chapter 2 Note 88.

[139] Thus ASLANOFF 1998, 172–173 (first and second section closed); COLLINS 2004, 582 (only Law and Prophets closed); SCHMITT 2011, 160.

[140] Thus even before the rediscovery of the Hebrew text FRITZSCHE 1859, 2 (also possible that there were books not included today); then BOX/OESTERLEY 1913, 316 (may still have been incomplete); EISSFELDT 1964, 765–768 (third category not closed, prophets possibly also not fixed, but only Daniel came later and into the Writings); SNAITH 1974, 8 (some books still contested); REITEMEYER 2000, 133 (Tora and Prophets closed, some of the Writings existed); TREBOLLE BARRERA 2002, 129 (excluding the possibility that the openness extended to books not later included in the Writings), 132–133 (Prologue evidence for the existence of a tripartite canon in the 2nd century).

[141] Thus BOX/OESTERLEY 1913, 316; LEIMAN 1976, 29, 149–151; MACKENZIE 1983, 20–21; STECK 1991, 139–140; HENGEL 1994, 256–258; CRENSHAW 1997a, 642; SCHREINER 2002, 15; SUNDBERG 2002, 81 (may have included books not later included in the Writings); FLINT 2003, 280 (third section "not as authoritative"); CARR 2005, 261, 265; MARBÖCK 2003, 109, n. 42; MARBÖCK 2010, 40; SCHMID/SCHRÖTER 2019, 199–200.

[142] Thus BOX/OESTERLEY 1913, 316; RÜGER 1984, 66–67; STECK 1992, 22 (referring to Rüger); SCHIFFMAN 1995, 164 (at the time of the Prologue, also seen in later rabbinic discussions); CRENSHAW 1997a, 642; BECKER 1998, 1409; FABRY 1999, 266; SCHREINER 2002, 15; FLINT 2003, 280; MARBÖCK 2003, 109, n. 42; CARR 2005, 261, 265 (not noting the variation of pro-

3.5 The Prologue and the Question of Canon

81

also vary: τῶν προφητῶν "of the prophets" in l. 1 and l. 9 but αἱ προφητεῖαι "the prophecies" in l. 24.

(2) The definite articles do not necessarily point to a closed group of books.[143] – Grammatically, definite articles point to something definite and known.[144] Here, the definite articles are likely to refer to particular things (rather than entire classes of things).[145] Thus, they indeed do not necessarily refer to groups which are defined in the sense of closed, but they do refer to known entities. This is true for all three categories, not just the third.

(3) The participle perfect ἠκολουθηκότων "which followed" in l. 2 may refer to writers rather than books.[146] – However, since a very similar threefold list is then twice designated as ending with books in l. 10 and l. 25, it is unlikely that when first mentioned it refers to writers.[147]

(4) The participle perfect ἠκολουθηκότων "which followed" in l. 2 could point to a lower status rather than a later origin of the third category.[148] – However, this argument is based on assumptions outside the Prologue: for example, TREBOLLE BARRERA argues that while the third category is merely ancestral, "law and prophecy were given to Moses and the prophets by God".[149] However, the Prologue itself implies that the first two categories are also ancestral books (l. 8–10). In κατ᾽ αὐτοὺς ἠκολουθηκότων "which followed in accordance with them", "them" most likely refers to the law and the prophets mentioned in the same genitive construction. The verb ἀκολουθέω "to follow" when referring to things may mean both "to follow" and "to be consistent with", and is usually constructed with a dative.[150] The preposition κατά with an accusative can refer to the directions of "down" or "towards", or to a time "at", but here it most likely refers to conformity "in accordance with".[151] A participle perfect usually refers to a past event which is completed in the present.[152] Thus, the construction probably expresses the conformity of the third group with the first two, rather than pointing to a lower status of the third group.

Based on sources outside the Prologue, some commentators doubt if the author of the Prologue knew all of the Writings as this part of the later canon

---

phets/prophecies); MARBÖCK 2010, 40; WITTE 2012a, 238 (translating prophets in l. 24 despite noting that the majority of Greek manuscripts uses prophecies); STÖKL BEN EZRA 2016, 181.

[143] Thus TREBOLLE BARRERA 2002, 129 (without reasons).

[144] Cf. SMYTH/MESSING 1956, § 1118.

[145] Cf. SMYTH/MESSING 1956, § 1119–1120, 1122.

[146] Thus MARBÖCK 2010, 40; arguing for a bipartite canon also CARR 1996, 43–44.

[147] Thus also ORLINSKY 1991, 486.

[148] Cf. TREBOLLE BARRERA 2002, 129.

[149] TREBOLLE BARRERA 2002, 129.

[150] Cf. LIDDELL/SCOTT/JONES [1940], s.v. ἀκολουθέω; LUST/EYNIKEL/HAUSPIE 2003, s.v. ἀκολουθέω.

[151] Cf. LIDDELL/SCOTT/JONES [1940], s.v. κατά ; LUST/EYNIKEL/HAUSPIE 2003, s.v. κατά.

[152] Cf. SMYTH/MESSING 1956, § 1872.

82   *3. Greek Prologue to Ben Sira*

may still have been incomplete.[153] A general tripartite division is sometimes seen as likely (e. g. on the basis of Sir 38:24–39:11) although the specific books in all three parts remain unclear.[154]

Regarding the distinction between grandfather and grandson, it is sometimes argued that the tripartite canon existed at both the time of Ben Sira and of his grandson, thus showing a continuity of tradition.[155] Arguments for this view include Sir 38:24–39:11 (see Chapter 4).[156] The opposite argument that the tripartite canon only existed at the time of the grandson, not the grandfather, is given by other scholars, often also based on a comparison with Sir 38:24–39:11,[157] and on the occurrence of the Maccabean revolts in between the generations.[158]

3.5.3 Bipartite Canon?

Some commentators argue that for both the grandfather and the grandson there was only a bipartite canon, Law and Prophets, with some additional undefined books.[159] Law and Prophets are sometimes seen as scriptures – with Prophets being a broad category including some of the later Writings – and the other books as all other literature.[160] Arguments for this view of a bipartite canon in the Prologue include the following:

(1) The term ὁ νόμος "the law" is the only one which appears in all three mentions of the categories, and the category of prophets is quite stable.[161] – However, the variation "prophets/prophecies" (l. 1 and l. 9 vs. l. 24) could be used both as a further argument in favour of a broad category of prophets and as a counterargument for the bipartite view.

(2) The grandfather is described as reading not only the "Law" and the "Prophets" but all literature.[162] – However, this is a circular argument: the Prologue

---

[153] Thus FRITZSCHE 1859, 2 (also possible that there were books not included today); BOX/ OESTERLEY 1913, 316 (may still have been incomplete); ORLINSKY 1991, 489 (later rabbinic debates).

[154] Cf. BRANDT 2001, 69–70 n. 234, 121.

[155] Thus BECKWITH 1985, 111 (repeated in BECKWITH 1988, 52), 166 n. 3; SAUER 2000, 38.

[156] SCHIFFMAN 1995, 164 (using Qumran manuscripts, 2 Macc 2:2–3, 13[LXX], and Luke 24:32, 44–45, and 4QMMT[d] as points of comparison).

[157] Cf. FABRY 1999, 252 (although Sir itself may be seen as canonical) (see Note 195); VAN DER KOOIJ 1998, 35–36; VAN DER KOOIJ 2003, 33–38 (Prologue reflects a higher value of the ancestral books than the book of Ben Sira itself); BEENTJES 2006a, 170; BEENTJES 2006d, 221; MAIER 2007, 183–185. On Sir 38:24–39:11 see Chapter 4.

[158] Cf. VAN DER KOOIJ 1998, 35–37; VAN DER KOOIJ 2003, 36–38.

[159] Cf. HART 1909, 231–232, 239; STEINMANN 1999, 53–54; CHAPMAN 2000, 258–261; GRABBE 2000, 153; GUILLAUME 2005, 22.

[160] Cf. BARTON 1986, 47–48; CAMPBELL 2000, 187–189 (following BARTON); ULRICH 2003b, 213 (although noting the possibility of a tripartite division, cf. ULRICH 2003a, 71, 77; ULRICH 2003b, 214).

[161] Cf. CARR 1996, 43–44; LIM 2013, 94, 101–102.

[162] BARTON 1986, 47.

3.5 The Prologue and the Question of Canon

does not mention the grandfather reading books other than those in the three categories (l. 1–14). The argument presupposes that the third category refers to all literature.

(3) The Prologue regards all translations as unequal to the originals, not only the "Law" and the "Prophets" but all other books.[163] – However, the only specific books that are mentioned are the translation of Ben Sira and the three categories in l. 23–26 (for the statement about translations see Chapter 3.5.6). Rather than placing himself within literature in general, according to the Prologue the translator compares his own work to the three categories only rather than to all other books.[164]

Based on sources outside the Prologue, arguments brought forward for a bipartite canon include the following:

(1) Both Law and Prophets occur in passages in the book of Ben Sira (Law: Sir 2:16; 9:15[LXX]; Prophets: Sir 36:21[LXX]).[165] – However, the two do not occur together in the Book of Ben Sira (see Chapter 3.4.3 and 3.4.4).

(2) Sir 44–49 (in Ben Sira's "Praise of the Ancestors" Sir 44–50) refer to Law and Prophets.[166] – However, Sir 44–50 do not contain a distinction between figures in the Law and in the Prophets[167] (see Chapter 5.4.3).

(3) That the third category refers to all other but only Israelite literature is argued with reference to Sir 38:34–39:1[LXX]. These sections are seen as linked through the use of δίδωμι "give" to express devotion and the use of adjectives noting that the third category of books is old. – However, this presupposes that Sir 38:34–39:1[LXX] refers to the same three categories as the Prologue (for an analysis see Chapter 4.5), and that everything mentioned in Sir 39:1–3[LXX] is Israelite literature only. The link between the Prologue and Sir 38:34–39:1[LXX] is also weak: ἐπιδίδωμι "to devote" with ψυχή "soul" is used Sir 38:34[LXX] while the Prologue in l. 7 uses δίδωμι "give" with a reflexive pronoun. For devotion both ἐπιδίδωμι "to devote" (Sir 38:30, 34; 39:5[LXX]) and δίδωμι "give" (Sir 38:26–28[LXX]) are used in the immediate context as well. The word ἀρχαῖος "ancient" is used for Israelite ancestors (Sir 2:10[LXX]) but also an old friend (Sir 9:10[LXX]) and giants (Sir 16:7[LXX]), whereas πάτριος "ancestral" only appears in the Prologue l. 10.[168]

(4) Apart from the Prologue no other attestation of a tripartite canon is seen by some scholars until the 1st century CE,[169] whereas the bipartite designation of

---

[163] Cf. BARTON 1986, 47.

[164] Thus BORCHARDT 2014, 69.

[165] Cf. CAMPBELL 2000, 187–189. Sir 36:21[LXX] in ZIEGLER 1980, 276, 292, equals Sir 36:15[LXX] in RAHLFS/HANHART 2006, Vol. II 439.

[166] Cf. ORLINSKY 1991, 486–490; CORLEY 2019, 228.

[167] Cf. BRANDT 2001, 102 (against BARTON 1986, 47).

[168] VAN KOOTEN 2010, 274, argues that the books mentioned in the Prologue are ancestral and thus authoritative.

[169] Cf. ULRICH 2003b, 214; ULRICH 2003a, 77; ULRICH 2000, 118.

84 *3. Greek Prologue to Ben Sira*

scriptures as Law and Prophets is regarded as known contemporarily to the Prologue.[170] Other early sources are seen as mentioning bipartite canons.[171]

(5) The third category does not have authority since it consists of "post-Prophetic books" (CARR) including the Book of Ben Sira.[172] – However, this argument uses a category ("post-Prophetic") which does not appear in the Prologue: the third category is always connected with both of the first two categories, not just the second.

3.5.4 One-Part Canon?

Some commentators argue for a one-part canon consisting of the Law only: The "law" is equated with the Pentateuch,[173] "prophets" may include those writings later included in the Hebrew prophetic canon, but also others,[174] possibly from among the later Writings,[175] and the third category is unclear.[176] The "law" is also sometimes seen to hold more authority than the prophets and the other books and Ben Sira's book, with only the Pentateuch being "scripture", and the Prophets having secondary authority.[177] Reasons for a one-part canon include the following:

(1) Only the category ὁ νόμος "the law" is always designated with the same word,[178] while there are varying designations for the second[179] and third categories.[180]

(2) The law is singled out with αὐτός "itself" in the third mention (l. 24).[181] – However, it is not mentioned without the other two categories.

(3) The law indirectly appears twice in the ultimate goal of a lawful life (ἔννομος "lawful" l. 14, 36).[182] It is thus mentioned first and last, forming an in-

---

[170] Cf. CARR 1996, 43–44; ULRICH 2003b, 212.

[171] Cf. ORLINSKY 1991, 486–490; CAMPBELL 2000, 187–189. For sources before the Common Era see Chapter 2.2.3 (4QMMT^d) and Chapter 2.2.2 (2 Macc 2:13–15^{LXX}).

[172] Cf. CARR 1996, 43–44 (referring to SWANSON 1970, 125–130, 248–250; BARTON 1986, 47, 50). However, SWANSON 1970, 126, argues that the Prologue equates Ben Sira with all other categories, not just the third. BARTON 1986, 47–48, argues that the category prophets was broad.

[173] Cf. SWANSON 1970, 126–128; COLLINS 1997, 18; WITTE 2012a, 237 (though also noting that the terms תּוֹרָה „law" and νόμος "law" may have different meanings not limited to the Pentateuch) against LANGE 2008, 55–80; ARNETH 2015, 46 (though not necessarily limited to the Pentateuch).

[174] Thus COLLINS 1997, 18; WITTE 2012a, 237–239; ARNETH 2015, 46–47.

[175] Cf. SWANSON 1970, 128–129.

[176] Thus COLLINS 1997, 18; WITTE 2012a, 237–239.

[177] Cf. SWANSON 1970, 125–131, 372.

[178] Cf. SWANSON 1970, 126–127.

[179] Cf. SWANSON 1970, 128–129.

[180] Cf. SWANSON 1970, 129–130; WITTE 2012a, 238; ARNETH 2015, 47 (at most bipartite canon).

[181] Cf. SWANSON 1970, 126–127.

[182] Cf. KOOLE 1965, 379; SWANSON 1970, 126–127. Cf. for similar observations on law MARBÖCK 2010, 39.

clusio.[183] – However, the explicit noun ὁ νόμος "the law" does not appear in l. 14 or l. 36.

Based on sources outside the Prologue, arguments for the openness of the category "prophets" are sometimes based on the mention of Job among the prophets in Sir 49:9 (see Chapter 6.5)[184] and the broad understanding of prophecy in Ben Sira especially in Sir 38:24–39:11 (see Chapter 4).[185]

3.5.5 No Canon?

It is sometimes argued that the Prologue does not refer to any canon at all.[186] Rather, the three categories of books are seen to represent Jewish literature in general.[187] Within the Prologue, this view of no canon in the Prologue is based on the following reasons:

(1) There are different wordings for the three categories.[188] – However, this does not apply to ὁ νόμος "the law".

(2) All translations are seen as inadequate in the Prologue.[189] – However, in the Prologue the author compares his own work to three categories of books only rather than to all other books.[190] If no special status is ascribed to the translation of the three categories, it is more difficult to explain why the author chooses these three in order to praise his own work.[191]

(3) The phrase τῶν ἄλλων τῶν κατ' αὐτοὺς ἠκολουθηκότων "the others which followed in accordance with them" is a non-exclusive way of referring to all Jewish books written later than the Law and the Prophets.[192] – However, this argument implies that the Law and the Prophets are different to and earlier than the other books.

Overall, even without a canon, three specific categories of books are described as authoritative in the Prologue.[193]

---

[183] Cf. SKEHAN/DI LELLA 1987, 135.

[184] Cf. SWANSON 1970, 128–129.

[185] Cf. WITTE 2012a, 238–239.

[186] Thus MROCZEK 2016, 12.

[187] Cf. KRAFT 1996, 211; LANGE 2008, 70; WRIGHT 2012, 364–365 (also referring to KRAFT 1996).

[188] Cf. LANGE 2008, 67–68.

[189] Cf. LANGE 2008, 68.

[190] See Note 164.

[191] On the rhetorical device of apology for self-praise see Chapter 3.3.3.

[192] Cf. LANGE 2008, 70.

[193] Cf. WRIGHT 2011, 83–84, esp. 84 n. 22 (referring to BARTON 1986).

86   *3. Greek Prologue to Ben Sira*

3.5.6 Open Canon including Ben Sira?

Yet other scholars argue that according to the Prologue there is a tripartite canon but it is still open[194] since the Prologue sees Ben Sira's book as canonical itself,[195] as a part of the third category,[196] or at least as having the same value as the three categories of books.[197] This view of an open canon including Ben Sira is based on the following arguments within the Prologue:

(1) Parallel expressions using the same words equate the Book of Ben Sira with the three categories: παιδεία καὶ σοφία "education and wisdom" in l. 3 and l. 12,[198] φιλομαθέω "to love learning" in l. 5 and φιλομαθής "lover of learning" in l. 13.[199] – Indeed, Ben Sira's book is described with the same characteristics as the three categories (see Chapter 3.3.4).

(2) The translation of Ben Sira's book is compared to those of the three categories, thus equating Ben Sira's value with those of the three categories in l. 15–26[200] (this also applies to the translation of Ben Sira)[201].

(3) The Septuagint *hapax legomenon* συγγράφω "to write down" in l. 12 is sometimes seen to imply the equal status of Ben Sira's work.[202] – However, συγγράφω "to write down" in Ancient Greek usually simply refers to the composition of a written work.[203]

(4) A divine passive pointing towards Ben Sira's divine inspiration is seen in the aorist passive προήχθη "was led" in l. 12 since the same verb is used in 2 Macc 10:1[LXX].[204] – However, in 2 Macc 10:1[LXX] the verb προάγω "to lead" appears in an active participle with God as its explicit subject, while in Greek in general, the verb is frequently used in the passive form.[205] The verb is not used in a

---

[194] Cf. BOCCACCINI 2012, 45.

[195] Thus PETERS 1913, 3 (open canon); FABRY 1999, 252 (Ben Sira's book according to the Prologue at least valuable and important); implicitly MARBÖCK 2003, 111, n. 49 (referring to PRATO 2000, 86). MARBÖCK speaks of the generative impulse of the three categories in the context of a living tradition, cf. MARBÖCK 2003, 110–113. Cf. also MARBÖCK 2010, 41 (generative process).

[196] Thus BUHL 1891, 13–14; SCHMID 2012b, 298 (referring to BUHL 1891).

[197] Thus SCHRADER 1994, 84; VOITILA 2008, 456, 460; LIM 2013, 101–102; BORCHARDT 2014, 69.

[198] Cf. SWANSON 1970, 125–126; MARBÖCK 2003, 109, n. 42; WRIGHT 2013b, 2213; BORCHARDT 2014, 69.

[199] Cf. WRIGHT 2011, 84–85.

[200] Thus JONES 1995, 65; BORCHARDT 2014, 69.

[201] Thus VOITILA 2008, 457, 460; BORCHARDT 2014, 70. See 3.5.7.

[202] Thus MARBÖCK 2010, 41.

[203] Cf. LIDDELL/SCOTT/JONES [1940], s. v. συγγράφω. According to WAGNER 1999, 129–130, it here stresses the individual authorship of a literary work in general. The verb may also stress the educative purpose of Ben Sira's composition, or refer to Thucydides as an important author, thus AITKEN 2011, 104.

[204] Thus PERDUE 2004, 135; LANGE 2008, 69 (following PERDUE 2004).

[205] Cf. LIDDELL/SCOTT/JONES [1940], s. v. προάγω.

3.5 The Prologue and the Question of Canon

divine context in any other occurrence within the Septuagint.[206] In the Greek Septuagint text of the Book of Ben Sira, προάγω "to lead" only appears once in Sir 20:27[LXX] where the subject is a wise man promoting himself through words. The grandfather may also have led himself to writing (as in a medium form).[207]

The participle perfect δεδομένων "have been given" in l. 2 is also sometimes seen as a divine passive with no subject.[208] – However, the three categories of books in l. 1–2, introduced by διά "through", may form a logical subject for the participle.[209] Grammatically, both options are possible since διά "through" with genitive can refer to an instrument or means, but also to an agent.[210]

Overall, impersonal constructions with a third person singular passive form are frequent in the Septuagint as in the New Testament, and do not necessarily imply God as an agent.[211] Whether or not the implicit agent is God (and thus the passive form is a divine passive) has to be determined by the context. Since God is not mentioned anywhere in the Prologue, the context does not suggest a divine passive in l. 2 or l. 12 of the Prologue.[212]

(5) The very first words of the Prologue, πολλῶν καὶ μεγάλων "many and great things", could be used as a further argument for an open canon, as HART observes:

"The many things and great are given *through the Law and the Prophets and the others who have followed after them*. The Scriptures, therefore, contain and do not constitute this treasure."[213]

(6) The argument that ἔνοχος "connected with" in l. 13 implies a sense of authority could be added, since the adjective usually appears in legal contexts meaning "bound by, liable, guilty".[214]

---

[206] Cf. LUST/EYNIKEL/HAUSPIE 2003, s. v. προάγω. The same applies to the New Testament, cf. BAUER/ALAND/ALAND 1988, s. v. προάγω.

[207] Passive forms in the Septuagint are frequently used like middle forms (and the other way round), cf. CONYBEARE/ST. STOCK 1995, 75–76; MURAOKA 2016, § 27db. Also cf. SMYTH/MESSING 1956, § 1736.

[208] Thus REITERER 2008b, 211; PERDUE 2004, 135.

[209] Thus LANGE 2008, 69 n. 54 (against PERDUE 2004, 135).

[210] Cf. LIDDELL/SCOTT/JONES [1940], s. v. διά. While usually ὑπό "by" with genitive is used to express the agent of the passive, διά "through" with genitive is also possible, cf. MURAOKA 2016, § 63e; SMYTH/MESSING 1956, § 1755.

[211] Cf. for the Septuagint MURAOKA 2016, § 87a (without mentioning a divine passive); for the New Testament WALLACE 1996, 436–438 (noting several options for agentless passive forms in addition to a divine passive, such as a focus on other aspects).

[212] In contrast, a divine passive is possible in Sir 51:11[LXX], where God is explicitly mentioned in the preceding verse (and also is the explicit subject in Hebrew), cf. BECKER/FABRY/REITEMEYER 2011, 2267.

[213] HART 1909, 238–239 (emphasis in original). On HART's view of a one-part or bipartite canon see Note 159. Cf. similarly PRATO 2000, 97.

[214] Cf. LIDDELL/SCOTT/JONES [1940], s. v. ἔνοχος; LUST/EYNIKEL/HAUSPIE 2003, s. v. ἔνοχος.

88 3. *Greek Prologue to Ben Sira*

(7) The introduction καὶ αὐτὸς "also himself" in l. 12 implies an equal status.[215]

Based on sources outside the Prologue, the value of Ben Sira's book being equal to that of at least the prophets and other books is sometimes based on Sir 24:33[LXX].[216] According to CARR, the Prologue's implication of an equal status of Ben Sira shows both the knowledge and rejection of a tripartite canon, and that the Prologue is an endorsement of Ben Sira against the endorsement of a tripartite canon.[217] The two endorsements are linked not only in CARR's argument, but also in the Prologue itself: if the translator is endorsing Ben Sira as of the same value as the three categories, he also has to value the three categories. CARR's argument rests on the historical hypothesis of an emergent bipartite canon in Hasmonean times that excluded postprophetic writings (on the history of the canon see Chapter 1.3.7). However, no such antagony can be seen in the Prologue.

In contrast, other scholars argue that the Book of Ben Sira is not seen as of the same value.[218] Reasons for this view of the Book of Ben Sira not having the same value are the following:

(1) Ben Sira is distinguished from the three categories as something additional (l. 12) rather than πάτριος "ancestral" (l. 10).[219] While a πάππος "grandfather" (l. 7) is also an ancestor,[220] his book is not included in the same three categories of books.

(2) In l. 23, ταῦτα "this" is distinguished from the translations of the three categories in l. 24–25.[221] – However, at the same time, it is equated with them (οὐ μόνον "not only" l. 23 – ἀλλὰ καί "but also" l. 24). The neuter plural demonstrative pronoun ταῦτα "these"[222] in l. 23 could refer to the Greek translation of Ben Sira which the readers are called to read in l. 17,[223] or to the specific difficult cases introduced with the neuter plural relative pronoun[224] οἷς "those" in l. 19.

---

[215] Thus SCHRADER 1994, 84.

[216] Thus KOOLE 1977, 229 (Ben Sira on the same level as prophets and wise teachers). On prophecy in Sir 24:33[LXX] see Chapter 3.4.4.

[217] Cf. CARR 2005, 265.125

[218] Cf. HANHART 1994, 2–3 (canonical vs. apocryphal); HENGEL 1994, 256–258 (Ben Sira as a manual for living according to the three categories).

[219] Cf. BECKWITH 1991, 389; VAN DER KOOIJ 2003, 30.

[220] The word πάππος can mean "grandfather" or "ancestor", cf. LIDDELL/SCOTT/JONES [1940], s. v. πάππος, cf. also VELTRI 1994, 134 n. 75.

[221] Thus BECKWITH 1985, 111 (repeated in BECKWITH 1988, 52). Cf. also BECKWITH 1985, 385.

[222] The demonstrative pronoun generally refers to what precedes, cf. SMYTH/MESSING 1956, § 1245, and the neuter form can refer to an idea not expressed in a neuter form, cf. SMYTH/MESSING 1956, § 1253. Neuter plural forms are often used to express the entirety of an idea, cf. SMYTH/MESSING 1956, § 1003.

[223] NRSV translates l. 23 with "not only this book", NETS (= WRIGHT 2007b, 719) with "not only in this case".

[224] There is no antecedent to the relative pronoun, it may be used like a conjunction "where", cf. SMYTH/MESSING 1956, § 2511.

3.5 The Prologue and the Question of Canon

The neuter plural personal pronoun αὐτά "they"[225] in l. 22 refers to the cases in l. 19–22 introduced by the relative pronoun οἷς "which" ("for they – the cases just mentioned – do not have equal power"). The pronoun αὐτά "they" is connected to the specific cases through γάρ "for" in l. 21. The pronoun ταῦτα "these" in l. 23 then refers back to the cases mentioned in l. 19 and again in l. 22,[226] though given the comparison with whole books in l. 23–26 it may indeed encompass the entire translated book.[227] If αὐτά "they" in l. 22 was preceded by an article, l. 21–22 would contain a general statement about translations ("for the same does not have equal power"),[228] but such an article is not found in even a single Septuagint manuscript.[229] The only language mentioned explicitly in the Prologue is Hebrew (Ἑβραϊστί "in Hebrew" l. 22). It could thus be asked if the Prologue refers specifically to translations from Hebrew but in a general statement, e.g. because Hebrew is regarded as a special, holy language.[230] However, the adverb Ἑβραϊστί simply means "in Hebrew",[231] with no further qualification. The phrase εἰς ἑτέραν γλῶσσαν "into another language" again points in the direction of a general statement; Greek is not explicitly mentioned. However, since the following book is translated into Greek and the Prologue is in Greek, the translations mentioned in l. 24–26 are likely to also be Greek translations, and thus l. 21–22 probably also refer to Greek (also see Chapter 3.4.1). The Septuagint *hapax legomena* ἀδυναμέω "to lack power" in l. 20 and ἰσοδυναμέω "to have equal power" may refer to the meaning (in which case a comparison to the Hebrew is necessary),[232] or to the expression in Greek (in which case monolingual Greek-speaking readers could note the lack of power as inelegant Greek),[233] or both.[234]

---

[225] αὐτός on its own usually takes up a preceding idea, cf. SMYTH/MESSING 1956, § 1212–1214. A neuter plural form often has its verb in a singular form, cf. SMYTH/MESSING 1956, § 958.

[226] Thus also VELTRI 1994, 142.

[227] NRSV translates l. 23 with "not only this book", NETS (= WRIGHT 2007b, 719) with "not only in this case".

[228] Thus translated by FABRY 2009, 1091. Cf. on the combination of αὐτός with an article expressing identity SMYTH/MESSING 1956, § 1204, 1210–1211 (only in Homeric Greek the meaning "same" is found without an article); for the LXX MURAOKA 2016, § 14.

[229] Cf. ZIEGLER 1980, 125: one majuscule even reads ταῦτα "those" which would refer to something near, cf. SMYTH/MESSING 1956, § 1240. In addition, αὐτός with a following article is used in l. 24 to single out the law.

[230] Thus VELTRI 1994, 145. However, VELTRI uses examples from CE centuries. For the use of Hebrew, Aramaic, and Greek at Ben Sira's time in general cf. WISCHMEYER 1994, 136–140.

[231] Cf. LIDDELL/SCOTT/JONES [1940], s.v. Ἑβραῖος; BAUER/ALAND/ALAND 1988, s.v. Ἑβραϊστί.

[232] Thus VELTRI 1994, 143.

[233] Thus WRIGHT 2003a, 15–20; WRIGHT 2003b, 638, 640–641; WRIGHT 2011, 76–77.

[234] Thus WAGNER 1999, 118, 125.

90   *3. Greek Prologue to Ben Sira*

Some scholars state that while there is continuity between the three categories and Ben Sira's book, the question whether the latter is at the same level or an addition cannot be decided.[235]

It is debated whether the Prologue includes explicit references to writings other than the three categories and Ben Sira's book. A reference to a literary work other than the three categories is sometimes found in the word ἀφόμοιον "likeness" in l. 29. ἀφόμοιον "likeness" is a substantivized adjective.[236] In the Prologue, the word is sometimes translated as "copy"[237] or "exemplar" in the sense of an instructive book which the translator found in Egypt.[238] However, other scholars translate the word as "likeness", or "alike", pointing to an education in Egypt like the one the translator knew before, as flattery to his readers.[239] Given the general meaning of ἀφόμοιος "like" and the context of the Prologue which does not say anything else about another book, ἀφόμοιον "likeness" is the most likely interpretation. That the education in Egypt is compared to that of Israel may point towards an Israelite or Israelite-friendly audience in Egypt.

The verb ἐπιπροστίθημι "to add" (literally maybe "to put on towards") in l. 14 is a rare word in Greek generally,[240] and a *hapax legomenon* in the Greek Book of Ben Sira and the Septuagint.[241] In the Prologue of Ben Sira in l. 14, it is sometimes translated as "to add",[242] implying the addition of many oral traditions or written texts other than the Book of Ben Sira, especially since l. 6 addresses those who are writing.[243] The verb ἐπιπροστίθημι is also sometimes translated as "to gain",[244] or as "to make progress",[245] implying progress concerning a lawful

---

[235] Cf. Aslanoff 1998, 175.

[236] Against Voitila 2008, 458 n. 22, adjectives can be substantivized without an article, cf. Smyth/Messing 1956, § 1021–1023, and the word cannot be a predicative adjective to the genitive παιδείας "of education" as it appears in an accusative form, cf. Smyth/Messing 1956, § 1020. While ἀφόμοιος can in another case also mean "unlike", the verb ἀφομοιόω means "to make like", cf. Liddell/Scott/Jones [1940], s.v. ἀφόμοιος, s.v. ἀφομοιόω, a translation as "unlikeness" – thus Zöckler 1891, 262; Zenner 1896, 573; MacKenzie 1983, 21 – is therefore unlikely, cf. Wagner 1999, 119–120.

[237] Thus also Liddell/Scott/Jones [1940], s.v. ἀφόμοιος.

[238] Thus Hart 1907, 295 (corpus of Greek wisdom-literature); Skehan/Di Lella 1987, 134 (written copies of Jewish teachings); Wright 2003a, 14 (copies of instructive literature); Wright 2011, 85 (instructive book or books); Wright 2013b, 2214 (written material); Corley 2019, 221 ("biblical books in Greek" or "other instructive writings"). Peters 1913, 4, argues that it points to the Septuagint, but this is unlikely according to Auvray 1957, 286, since the Septuagint was known rather than found.

[239] Thus Auvray 1957, 286–287; Böhmisch 1997, 102–105; Wagner 1999, 119–120; Voitila 2008, 458, esp. n. 22; Marböck 2010, 37, 43.

[240] Cf. Liddell/Scott/Jones [1940], s.v. ἐπιπροστίθημι ("to add besides").

[241] Cf. Lust/Eynikel/Hauspie 2003, s.v. ἐπιπροστίθημι.

[242] Thus e.g. LXX.D (= Fabry 2009, 1091).

[243] Thus Wagner 1999, 124.

[244] Thus NETS (= Wright 2007b, 719).

[245] Thus NRSV, thus also Zöckler 1891, 261; Ryssel 1900, 260; Fritzsche 1859, 3 (though only if a similar meaning is attributed to ἐπιπροστίθημι as to the similar verb ἐπιδίδωμι which

3.5 The Prologue and the Question of Canon

way of life.[246] The verb form used in l. 14, ἐπιπροσθῶσιν "they might add", is an active form (in the aorist subjunctive), which makes the active meaning "to add" most likely. However, there is no object. The implied object of "to add" could be other oral traditions or written texts, or other rules[247] or activities,[248] or – closer to a middle voice meaning – an advancement through lawful life ("to gain" or "to make progress"). This last option seems most plausible: βίωσις "way of life" refers to a manner of life rather than a time span,[249] which indicates that the preposition διά "through"[250] refers to this way of life as a means ("through") rather than a time span ("throughout"). In addition, a parallel in content to l. 13–14 can be found within the Prologue itself, in a structurally similar place at the end of the two sentences about the Greek translation of Ben Sira: according to l. 34 and l. 36, the Greek translation of Ben Sira has the aim that those loving learning abroad (l. 34 uses φιλομαθέω "to love learning", just as l. 13) live lawfully (l. 36 uses ἐννόμως "lawfully" + βιοτεύω "to live" similar to l. 14 which uses ἔννομος "lawful" + βίωσις "life"). No other texts or a call for their production are mentioned. In addition, the overall aim of the Prologue is a praise of Ben Sira's book and its translation. Given the parallel in l. 36 and the overall aim of the Prologue, it seems more likely that l. 14 asks lovers of learning to use Ben Sira's book (as mentioned in l. 13) and further their own lawful life than to compose many new texts themselves, and πολλῷ μᾶλλον "much more" in l. 14 is more likely to refer to the impact of Ben Sira's book on advancement through a lawful life rather than the extent of new texts. Even if l. 14 should ask for the composition of new texts, l. 13 underlines the importance of studying the Book of Ben Sira. An intransitive translation of ἐπιπροστίθημι as "to gain" best expresses the furthering of those loving learning through a lawful life.

Overall, no references to books other than the three categories and Ben Sira's book and their respective translations are made explicit in the Prologue. This suggests a special connection between the three categories and Ben Sira's book.

---

may mean "to advance"); SKEHAN/DI LELLA 1987, 131, 133; CRENSHAW 1997a, 641; SAUER 2000, 36, 39; CORLEY 2013, 9; WRIGHT 2013b, 2214.

[246] Thus ZÖCKLER 1891, 261; RYSSEL 1900, 260; FRITZSCHE 1859, 3; SKEHAN/DI LELLA 1987, 131, 133; CRENSHAW 1997a, 641; SAUER 2000, 36, 39; CORLEY 2013, 9; WRIGHT 2013b, 2214.

[247] Cf. PETERS 1913, 3, who sees a reference to the addition of wise rules as in Sir 21:15[LXX] without specifying if they are written down.

[248] Thus MARBÖCK 2010, 37 (German "beitragen"/"to contribute"), 41 (activities of those reading).

[249] Cf. LIDDELL/SCOTT/JONES [1940], s. v. βίωσις.

[250] Cf. LIDDELL/SCOTT/JONES [1940], s. v. διά. Against FRITZSCHE 1859, 3; PETERS 1913, 3; WRIGHT 2013b, 2214.

3.5.7 Greek Canon?

The Prologue is sometimes seen as the first evidence not only of the Hebrew but also the Greek canon. Reasons for this view include the following:

(1) To the readers of the Prologue, the canon must have been accessible in Greek only[251] or at least primarily, otherwise the translation of Ben Sira's book into Greek would be unnecessary.

(2) The translator is aware of previously existing Greek translations of the Hebrew Bible later included in the Septuagint,[252] or even the entire Septuagint translation.[253] – However, while the Septuagint Pentateuch may have been translated in the 3rd century BCE, various books of the later Prophets and Writings were only translated later, and there was no fixed Septuagint translation in antiquity.[254] The Prologue mentions translations of the three categories of books from Hebrew, but it is unclear whether these are Spetuagint books. Some scholars also note that the Prologue mentions categories of books similar to the order of the later Hebrew Bible (Law – Prophets – Writings) rather than the Greek Septuagint (Historical – Didactic – Prophetic Books).[255] However, the prophetic books are only sometimes and not consistently placed at the end of the Septuagint.[256]

Beyond the Prologue, it is sometimes argued that the Greek translation of Ben Sira draws on the Septuagint,[257] but also that the translator of Ben Sira may hardly draw on Septuagint texts[258] while adopting a very literary style of trans-

---

[251] Cf. KREUZER 2009, 135–137, 139–140.

[252] Thus SWETE 1900, 24 (including translations of the Pentateuch and all prophets, former and latter); CADBURY 1955, 219–220, 223 (some books); SWANSON 1970, 79–83, 131 n. 2 (Pentateuch and some or all of the former and latter prophets); CAIRD 1982, 96, 100 (Pentateuch and some other books); MACKENZIE 1983, 21 (all books but open third part); SKEHAN/DI LELLA 1987, 134 (almost all books); WRIGHT 1989, 9, 119, 138 (definitely Pentateuch); MARBÖCK 2003, 110 (existing parts); SCHMITT 2011, 165 (some parts); WRIGHT 2011, 82 (existing parts); CORLEY 2013, 11 (existing parts); BERLEJUNG 2019, 30 (existing parts); CORLEY 2019, 220 (existing parts); BOYD-TAYLOR 2021, 19.

[253] Thus JELLICOE 1968, 60 (against KAHLE 1959, 217); SAUER 2000, 39. NESTLE 1897, 123–124, even suggests that the grandfather may have been one of the 72 translators of the Septuagint called Jesus. However, this view is based on sources many centuries younger than the Prologue, which includes no indications for this.

[254] See Chapter 2 Notes 100–101.

[255] Thus LEIMAN 1976, 150 n. 135; SCHMITT 2011, 159–160.

[256] Cf. BRANDT 2001, 172–217. For example, in the 4th century CE Codex Vaticanus (B), the prophetic books are placed at the end of the Old Testament, while this is not the case in the 4th century Codex Sinaiticus (S) and the 5th century Codex Alexandrinus (A), cf. BRANDT 2001, 183–192; GALLAGHER/MEADE 2017, 245–249.

[257] Thus CADBURY 1955, 223–225 (some books); CAIRD 1982, 96, 100 (Pentateuch and some other books); MACKENZIE 1983, 21 (all books but open third part); WRIGHT 1989, 9, 119, 138 (definitely Pentateuch); CORLEY 2019, 220, 225–226 (existing parts).

[258] Cf. REITERER 1980, 242–249; WRIGHT 1989, 9, 229, 265 n. 25 (referring to Reiterer); WAGNER 1999, 30. As WRIGHT 1989, 140–141, notes, CAIRD's comparison (see Note 252) is based on the assumption that non-parallel translations mean non-existence of the respective LXX books, while other reasons (choice of non-use of LXX, use of other material or trans-

3.5 The Prologue and the Question of Canon

lation similar to that of the Septuagint.[259] WRIGHT in his 1989 monographic study comparing the Greek translation of Ben Sira with the Septuagint concludes that while the Prologue probably refers to the Septuagint Pentateuch,[260] the Greek translation hardly depends on the Septuagint (including the Septuagint Pentateuch) at all, and it is unclear which Greek translations the translator might have known.[261]

Another area of dispute is whether the translator also sees his own Greek translation of Ben Sira as authoritative: Some scholars argue that according to the Prologue the Greek translation of Ben Sira is equal to both its Hebrew original and the three categories of Hebrew books.[262] Arguments brought forward for this view are the following:

(1) The Greek translation of Ben Sira and those of the three categories are compared and equated in l. 15–26.[263]

(2) Several Greek words are repeated in the description of the three categories of Hebrew books, Ben Sira's Hebrew book, and the Greek translations of the Hebrew books and Ben Sira's book. The combination παιδεία καὶ σοφία "wisdom and education" appears in l. 3 as a quality of the Hebrew books, in l. 12 as quality of Ben Sira's Hebrew book. The term παιδεία "education" also appears in l. 29 for a quality found in Egypt.[264] The verb ἀναγιγνώσκω "to read" in l. 4 (reading the Hebrew books) and the related noun ἀνάγνωσις "reading" in l. 10 (Ben Sira reading the Hebrew books) and l. 17 (reading the Greek Book of Ben Sira) connect the Hebrew books with the Greek Book of Ben Sira.[265] Following ἐπιστήμων "understanding" in l. 4 for those reading Hebrew books, ἐπιστήμη "understanding" in l. 31 is brought by the grandson to the task of translating.[266] The verb φιλομαθέω "to love learning" connects readers of the Hebrew books in l. 5 with readers of the Greek Book of Ben Sira in l. 34[267] and readers of the He-

---

lations including non-written materials, non-recognition of allusions in Hebrew) are not taken into account.

[259] Cf. WRIGHT 2011, 88–89.

[260] Thus WRIGHT 1989, 138.

[261] Thus WRIGHT 1989, 229. On the difficulties of a comparison of the unknown Hebrew and Greek originals cf. also CADBURY 1955, 219–220, 223.

[262] Thus PRATO 2000, 86; AITKEN 2011, 101, 104, 106. It is doubtful if the translator of the Book of Ben Sira equates himself with the LXX translators, since he only mentions the importance of his grandfather's work but does not refer to any authorization of LXX translations, thus KREUZER 2009, 138. According to LANGE 2008, 72, the Letter of Aristeas alludes to the Prologue and thus compares the LXX translators with Ben Sira (not the other way round). However, the shared two-word combination appears in many texts as noted by LANGE 2008, 71, which, even apart from questions of absolute dates, makes an intertextual reference from the Letter of Aristeas to the Prologue unlikely. For intertextual criteria see Chapter 1.4.4.

[263] Thus VOITILA 2008, 457.

[264] Cf. AITKEN 2011, 105; BORCHARDT 2014, 68–70.

[265] Cf. AITKEN 2011, 104–105.

[266] Cf. AITKEN 2011, 105.

[267] Cf. AITKEN 2011, 101, 105.

94   *3. Greek Prologue to Ben Sira*

brew Book of Ben Sira through the related noun φιλομαθής "lover of learning" in l. 13. The grandfather's effort in l. 7 and the grandson's effort in l. 31 can also be seen as parallel in content.[268] Both his grandfather's work and the translator's work have the aim of helping to live lawfully, using the same word ἔννομος "lawful" in l. 14 (adjective ἔννομος "lawful" with βίωσις "life") and l. 36 (adverb ἐννόμως "lawfully" with βιοτεύω "to live").[269] – Indeed, repeated words are an important feature of the Prologue (see Chapter 3.3.4).

In contrast, it is sometimes argued that the author of the Prologue did not attribute the same authority to the three categories of books in Hebrew as in their Greek translations because both his own Greek translation and the Septuagint are very close to the Hebrew, resulting in unidiomatic Greek.[270] While this argument rests on observations outside the Prologue, the Prologue does explicitly say that the Hebrew originals and the Greek translations do not have equal power (l. 21), even if this serves to highlight the translator's achievement.[271]

In between these two opposites, yet other scholars argue that the author of the Prologue stresses both the general difficulties of translation and his valuable contribution to a living tradition.[272] Thus, both the Hebrew and the Greek version, while connected through the aim of lawful living, have to be taken at their own weight – even in modern interpretations.[273]

Tied in with the question of the canonicity of the Greek text is the question whether the translator apologizes for the insufficient quality of his translation[274] or even criticizes the Septuagint translation.[275] Reasons for the former include the comparison with the equally fallible translations of the three categories,[276] and the difference of the Greek employed in the Prologue (idiomatic) versus the translation (very literal, like the Septuagint),[277] even though the translator may not draw on the Septuagint.[278] Against this, scholars point out that the translator does not criticize the previous translations but instead equals his translation to those. The main reason given is that the translator points out difficulties in order

---

[268] Cf. AITKEN 2011, 105.

[269] Cf. AITKEN 2011, 105; BORCHARDT 2014, 70.

[270] WRIGHT 2011, 94.

[271] On the rhetorical device of apology for self-praise see Chapter 3.3.3.

[272] Cf. MARBÖCK 2010, 41.

[273] Cf. MARBÖCK 2003, 112. Cf. WITTE 2015a, 28, 37, on the necessity of a separate exegesis of the Hebrew and Greek versions.

[274] Thus WAGNER 1999, 28–29 (despite ancient genre 25–27); WRIGHT 2003b, 637–638; WRIGHT 2011, 82.

[275] Thus SMEND 1906, 3; SKEHAN/DI LELLA 1987, 134; WAGNER 1999, 28–29; MARBÖCK 2010, 38.

[276] WRIGHT 2011, 82.

[277] Cf. WRIGHT 2003a, 16–19.

[278] Thus WRIGHT 2003a, 26, esp. n. 48 (referring to WRIGHT 1989).

3.6 Conclusion

to highlight his own achievement as common in ancient prologues.[279] Further reasons are that a criticism of the Septuagint would offend his audience,[280] that in order to praise his own translation he is unlikely to criticize those translations to which he compares his own,[281] or that he points out his achievement while none of his Greek-speaking audience could actually have compared the translation with the Hebrew original.[282] Overall, the apology used to highlight the translator's achievement points towards an equal status of his translation to the other translations.

3.6 Conclusion

Views of the Prologue's relation to a biblical canon are often influenced by modern reconstructions of the history of the canon. For example, BECKWITH, who argues that the words of the Prologue reflect a closed tripartite canon,[283] states:

"The words of the prologue are often interpreted much more loosely, to make them harmonize better with the current critical hypothesis about the history of the canon; but there is no good reason why evidence should be tailored to fit a hypothesis, which is a reversal of proper historical procedure."[284]

However, BECKWITH does not discuss any arguments against this view at all.[285] In contrast, BORCHARDT, who argues for an open canon including Ben Sira,[286] states that his article "relies only on the evidence provided from within the prologue, and makes no conjectures based on later reception".[287] However, BORCHARDT's article does include statements about the development of the later tripartite canon:

"Though it does appear that the beginnings of a tripartite division of valued books exists in the mind of the translator, it is plain that these corpora are not closed".[288]

In a hermeneutical circle from the Prologue's text to historical information and the other way around, no interpretation can rely solely on the Prologue. For ex-

---

[279] Thus ALEXANDER 1993, 152–153; VOITILA 2008, 456–457; KREUZER 2009, 145–146, 150–151; AITKEN 2011, 107; LAUBER 2013, 319–320; see also Note 47, and see 3.3.3 on the genre of the Prologue.

[280] Thus WRIGHT 2003a, 15; WRIGHT 2003b, 637–638; VOITILA 2008, 457.

[281] Thus WRIGHT 2003b, 637–638.

[282] Thus SAUER 2000, 39.

[283] See Note 126.

[284] BECKWITH 1985, 111, 166 n. 3.

[285] Cf. the criticisms in BARTON 1987; BRANDT 2001, 98.

[286] See Note 197.

[287] Cf. BORCHARDT 2014, 65.

[288] Cf. BORCHARDT 2014, 71.

96   *3. Greek Prologue to Ben Sira*

ample, the Greek words used in the Prologue and the concepts known at its time (such as a bipartite canon, or features of pseudepigraphy) can only be understood by using other sources outside the Prologue. However, in analyzing the Prologue it can be helpful to distinguish arguments resting mainly on observations within the Prologue from those requiring significant external information as in the following summary.

The Prologue refers to three categories of books of Israel called "law", "prophets", and "others" written in Hebrew and translated into Greek. The Prologue describes these books as ancestral and as containing Israel's wisdom and education wherefore they are likely to be authoritative books of Israel. The grouping of these authoritative books is most likely tripartite based on the threefold mention of three categories of ancestral and already translated books with the same or very similar names and definite articles. However, the definite articles do not necessarily point to categories which are "defined" in the sense of "closed". While the designations of the third category differ, this is also true for the second one, and the Prologue does not suggest a lower status of the third category. Evidence outside the Prologue for a tripartite canon is drawn from later centuries. The strongest arguments for the reference to a bipartite canon also rest on sources outside the Prologue. Regarding a one-part canon of the law, within the Prologue only this first category is always designated with the same word "the law", it is once singled out, and it also appears twice indirectly in the ultimate goal of all the books mentioned. However, it never appears directly without the other two categories, which may imply that they are equally authoritative. While there is no explicit mention of God anywhere in the Prologue, prophets and prophecies imply a divine connection in which the law – in line with the use of the word in the Greek Book of Ben Sira in general – is God's law. The law is not explicitly identified with the Pentateuch, and the likelihood of such an identification is debated. As for a Greek canon, the Prologue mentions translations of the three categories of books and addresses Greek-speaking readers. It is unclear if the Prologue refers to any Septuagint books. Based on external evidence, at least the Septuagint's Pentateuch is usually seen to be much older than the Prologue, but this is not the case for all Septuagint books.

The Prologue uses a number of repeated words for both the Book of Ben Sira and the three categories of books. The Hebrew Book of Ben Sira is connected with the authority of the three categories through repeated words, and is explicitly attributed the same status as connected with education and wisdom. The Prologue also directly compares the Greek translation of the Book of Ben Sira with the translations of the three categories, and closely connects it with the Hebrew three categories and the Hebrew Book of Ben Sira through repeated words. While still distinguishing between Hebrew and Greek versions and highlighting his achievement of a translation, the Prologue claims the same quality for the

Greek translation of Ben Sira as for the translation of the three categories. And both Ben Sira's book and its translation direct towards a lawful life.

Taken together, arguments resting on observations within the Prologue point towards a tripartite group of ancestral authoritative books. The Book of Ben Sira and its Greek translation are distinguished from this group but claim at least some of the same authority as they are also connected with education and wisdom. This authority is connected with the goal of living lawfully. Whether "books" in the Prologue refers to texts written on scrolls or in codices depends on the date of the Prologue (for the shift from scrolls to codices around the 2nd to 4th centuries CE see Chapter 2.2.2). The content of the three categories of books is not mentioned at all in the Prologue. It is unclear if they contain books now in the Hebrew Bible.[289] Depending on the date of the Prologue, external sources may make this likely – the oldest preserved manuscripts of the Prologue are 4th century CE codices containing the whole Septuagint translation of the Hebrew Bible. However, the Prologue itself – which may be earlier and dates itself to the late 2nd century BCE – does not refer to any specific contents of the three categories of books.

If it is compared to the canon of the Hebrew Bible only, the Prologue is most similar to a tripartite but open canon allowing authority to be held by books such as Ben Sira's. If general criteria for ancient authoritative texts are applied (see Chapter 1.3.6), the Prologue explicitly refers to three categories of books, their translations, and the importance of their study (criteria 2 and 3: fact and way of the use in other ancient texts) as well as their ancestral origin (criterion 4: presumed antiquity). However, the very same aspects are also explicitly mentioned for the Book of Ben Sira: written by an ancestor (criterion 4: presumed antiquity), the book receives a translation, and the importance of its study is highlighted (criteria 2 and 3: fact and way of the use in other ancient texts). Both the three categories of books and the Book of Ben Sira are explicitly connected with education and wisdom.

---

[289] Thus regarding the "prophets" also MCDONALD 2007, 227–228.

4. Ben Sira 38:24–39:11

4.1 Introduction

Like the Greek Prologue, Sir 38:34–39:1^{LXX}, a part of the passage Sir 38:24–39:11, is often seen as referring to a biblical canon.[1] Sir 38:24–39:11 is partly extant in Hebrew and fully in Greek. This chapter provides a comparative analysis of the text in both languages and a systematic assessment of possible canonical references in Sir 38:24–39:11.

4.2 Hebrew Text and Translation

Sir 38:24–39:11 is not fully preserved on any Hebrew manuscript. Manuscript B VIII verso contains parts of Sir 38:24–27 and the extant texts then continues with Sir 39:15 on Manuscript B IX recto.[2] The Hebrew text here follows the transcription presented by Martin G. ABEGG in RENDSBURG/BINSTEIN 2013 (www.bensira.org).[3] Following this transcription, superlinear additions in the manuscript are marked with ^^, marginal additions with ><, and small dots or circles ° above letters indicate that these letters are only partly or hardly preserved on the manuscript.[4] Letters not preserved on the manuscript are represented here by [...].[5]

---

[1] See Chapter 4.5 for details.

[2] Cf. BLACHORSKY [2014], 23–23.

[3] Cf. RENDSBURG/BINSTEIN 2013, Manuscript B VIII verso, IX recto.

[4] Some of these letters are not reconstructed in BEENTJES 1997, 67.

[5] ABEGG in RENDSBURG/BINSTEIN 2013 uses [–] or [ ] to indicate missing letters, but there is often space for many more than one or two letters in a gap. Here, [...] represents a gap of any length. Spaces between phrases in the middle of each line – indicated with [[ ]] by ABEGG in RENDSBURG/BINSTEIN 2013 – are not represented here.

100   *4. Ben Sira 38:24–39:11*

Sir 38:24	חכמת סופר תרבה חכמה וחֹסֵ֯ר עסק הוא :יתחֹכֹּם	The wisdom of a scribe will make much[6] wisdom, and someone lacking[7] labour will show himself as wise.[8]
38:25	מה יתחכם תומך מלמד ומתפאר בחנית מרעיד: באלוף ינהג ישובב ^לשדד^ בשור <וישובב בשיר> ושעיותיו עֹד בֹּ[ני...]	How will someone holding a goad show himself as wise, and someone glorifying himself with a spear, someone making shake[9]? A bull he will lead, he will bring back ^to plow^[10] an ox, >and he will bring back with a song< and his plans[11] to son[s ...]
38:26	ושקידתו לכלות מרבק לֵב יָשִׁית לשֹד[ד ...]	And his focus (is) to finish[12] the binding,[13] he will set the heart to plo[w ...]
38:27	אף עשה חֹרֹשֹ וחֹושב אשר לילֹהֹ[...] >ינהג<	Also someone doing, someone crafting, and someone engraving, who by night [...] >will lead<

4.3 Greek Text and Translation

The Greek text of Sir 38:24–39:11[LXX] presented here follows the Göttingen Septuagint edited by ZIEGLER.[14]

Sir 38:24[LXX]	Σοφία γραμματέως ἐν εὐκαιρίᾳ σχολῆς, καὶ ὁ ἐλασσούμενος πράξει αὐτοῦ σοφισθήσεται.	The wisdom of a scribe (is) in the opportunity of leisure, and the one reducing his business will be made wise.
38:25[LXX]	τί σοφισθήσεται ὁ κρατῶν ἀρότρου καὶ καυχώμενος ἐν δόρατι κέντρου, βόας ἐλαύνων καὶ ἀναστρεφόμενος ἐν ἔργοις αὐτῶν, καὶ ἡ διήγησις αὐτοῦ ἐν υἱοῖς ταύρων;	How will be made wise the one ruling a plow and boasting about a shaft of a goad, the one driving oxen and being engagaged in their works, and his narration (is) on sons of bulls?

---

[6] Hiphil imperfect תַּרְבֶּה "will make much" (thus also translated by REITERER 2008c, 224), cf. GESENIUS 2013, s. v. רבה, though qal תִּרְבֶּה "will be much" is also possible. This intransitive aspect "to become greater, to increase" in addition to the transitive aspect "to increase something" is also noted by REITERER 2008c, 225.

[7] Verbal noun = qal participle חָסֵר "lacking", cf. GESENIUS 2013, s. v. חסר, חָסֵר.

[8] Hithpael imperfect, cf. GESENIUS 2013, s. v. חכם.

[9] Hiphil participle, cf. GESENIUS 2013, s. v. רעד.

[10] Cf. GESENIUS 2013, s. v. שדד.

[11] Cf. GESENIUS 2013, s. v. שעיה*.

[12] Piel infinitive, cf. GESENIUS 2013, s. v. כלה.

[13] This refers to the binding of calfs to cows in order to prevent them from drinking milk which can then be consumed by humans, cf. GESENIUS 2013, s. v. מַרְבֵּק.

[14] Cf. ZIEGLER 1980, 303–307.

4.3 Greek Text and Translation

38:26[LXX]	καρδίαν αὐτοῦ δώσει ἐκδοῦναι αὔλακας, καὶ ἡ ἀγρυπνία αὐτοῦ εἰς χορτάσματα δαμάλεων.	He will give his heart to make furrows, and his sleeplessness (is) over the fodder of young cows.
38:27[LXX]	οὕτως πᾶς τέκτων καὶ ἀρχιτέκτων, ὅστις νύκτωρ ὡς ἡμέρας διάγει· οἱ γλύφοντες γλύμματα σφραγίδων, καὶ ἡ ἐπιμονὴ αὐτοῦ ἀλλοιῶσαι ποικιλίαν· καρδίαν αὐτοῦ δώσει εἰς ὁμοιῶσαι ζωγραφίαν, καὶ ἡ ἀγρυπνία αὐτοῦ τελέσαι ἔργον.	So (is) every craftsman and master-craftsman whoever lives by night as by day, the ones engraving engravings of seals, and his steadfastness (is) to change variety, he will give his heart to making a picture alike, and his sleeplessness (is) to finish a work.
38:28[LXX]	οὕτως χαλκεὺς καθήμενος ἐγγὺς ἄκμονος καὶ καταμανθάνων ἔργα σιδήρου· ἀτμὶς πυρὸς τήξει σάρκας αὐτοῦ, καὶ ἐν θέρμῃ καμίνου διαμαχήσεται· φωνὴ σφύρης καινιεῖ[15] τὸ οὖς αὐτοῦ, καὶ κατέναντι ὁμοιώματος σκεύους οἱ ὀφθαλμοὶ αὐτοῦ· καρδίαν αὐτοῦ δώσει εἰς συντέλειαν ἔργων, καὶ ἡ ἀγρυπνία αὐτοῦ κοσμῆσαι ἐπὶ συντελείας.	So (is) the smith, sitting by an anvil, and observing works of iron, vapour of fire will melt his flesh, and in the heat of a furnace he will struggle, the voice of a hammer will make strange his ear, and opposite the image of an object (are) his eyes, he will give his heart to the completion of works, and his sleeplessness (is) to adorn at the time of completion.
38:29[LXX]	οὕτως κεραμεὺς καθήμενος ἐν ἔργῳ αὐτοῦ καὶ συστρέφων ἐν ποσὶν αὐτοῦ τροχόν, ὃς ἐν μερίμνῃ κεῖται διὰ παντὸς ἐπὶ τὸ ἔργον αὐτοῦ, καὶ ἐνάριθμιος πᾶσα ἡ ἐργασία αὐτοῦ·	So (is) the potter sitting at his work and turning at his foots a wheel, who lies down in worry because of everything at his work, and in quantity (is) all his production.
38:30[LXX]	ἐν βραχίονι αὐτοῦ τυπώσει πηλὸν καὶ πρὸ ποδῶν κάμψει ἰσχὺν αὐτοῦ· καρδίαν ἐπιδώσει συντελέσαι τὸ χρῖσμα, καὶ ἡ ἀγρυπνία αὐτοῦ καθαρίσαι κάμινον.	With his arm he will form clay and before the feet he will bend his strength, he will devote the heart to finish the glazing, and his sleeplessness (is) to clean the furnace.
38:31[LXX]	Πάντες οὗτοι εἰς χεῖρας αὐτῶν ἐνεπίστευσαν, καὶ ἕκαστος ἐν τῷ ἔργῳ αὐτοῦ σοφίζεται·	All these have trusted in their hands, and each one is wise in his work.
38:32[LXX]	ἄνευ αὐτῶν οὐκ οἰκισθήσεται πόλις, καὶ οὐ παροικήσουσιν οὐδὲ περιπατήσουσιν.[16] ἀλλ᾽ εἰς βουλὴν λαοῦ οὐ ζητηθήσονται	Without them, a city will not be built, and they will neither live as foreigners nor wander around. But for the counsel of a people they will not be sought out,

---

[15] Future indicative of καινίζω "to make strange", cf. LIDDELL/SCOTT/JONES [1940], s.v. καινίζω. RAHLFS/HANHART 2006, Vol. II 443, instead read φωνῇ σφύρης κλινεῖ τὸ οὖς αὐτοῦ "to a voice of a hammer he will incline his ear" following the emendation κλινεῖ "he will incline" by SMEND 1906, 350, but this reading is not preserved on any manuscripts, cf. ZIEGLER 1980, 32–33, 304.

[16] In RAHLFS/HANHART 2006, Vol. II 444, Sir 38:32[LXX] ends here and Sir 38:33[LXX] begins.

102   4. Ben Sira 38:24–39:11

38:33^LXX καὶ ἐν ἐκκλησίᾳ οὐχ ὑπεραλοῦνται· ἐπὶ δίφρον δικαστοῦ οὐ καθιοῦνται καὶ διαθήκην κρίματος οὐ διανοηθήσονται.[17] οὐδὲ μὴ ἐκφάνωσιν παιδείαν καὶ κρίμα καὶ ἐν παραβολαῖς οὐχ εὑρεθήσονται,

and in the assembly they will not rise high, on the seat of a judge they will not sit, and the will of judgment they will not understand. And not at all will they reveal education and judgment, and in proverbs they will not be found,

38:34^LXX ἀλλὰ κτίσμα αἰῶνος στηρίσουσιν, καὶ ἡ δέησις αὐτῶν ἐν ἐργασίᾳ τέχνης.[18] Πλὴν τοῦ ἐπιδιδόντος τὴν ψυχὴν αὐτοῦ καὶ διανοουμένου ἐν νόμῳ ὑψίστου,

but they support the foundation of the world, and their petition (is) in the production of craft. Except for the one devoting his soul, and thinking in the law of the Most High,

39:1^LXX σοφίαν πάντων ἀρχαίων[19] ἐκζητήσει καὶ ἐν προφητείαις[20] ἀσχοληθήσεται,

the wisdom of all ancients he will seek out, and with prophecies he will be occupied,

39:2^LXX διήγησιν ἀνδρῶν ὀνομαστῶν συντηρήσει καὶ ἐν στροφαῖς παραβολῶν συνεισελεύσεται,

the narration of famous men he will preserve, and in twists of parables he will enter along,

39:3^LXX ἀπόκρυφα παροιμιῶν ἐκζητήσει καὶ ἐν αἰνίγμασιν[21] παραβολῶν ἀναστραφήσεται.

the hidden things of sayings he will seek out, and in the riddles of parables he will be engaged.

39:4^LXX ἀνὰ μέσον μεγιστάνων ὑπηρετήσει καὶ ἔναντι ἡγουμένων ὀφθήσεται· ἐν γῇ ἀλλοτρίων ἐθνῶν διελεύσεται, ἀγαθὰ γὰρ καὶ κακὰ ἐν ἀνθρώποις ἐπείρασεν.

In the middle of the great he will serve, and before leading ones he will appear, in the land of foreign nations he will pass through, for good and bad things among humans he has tested.

39:5^LXX τὴν καρδίαν αὐτοῦ ἐπιδώσει ὀρθρίσαι πρὸς κύριον τὸν ποιήσαντα αὐτὸν καὶ ἔναντι ὑψίστου δεηθήσεται· καὶ ἀνοίξει στόμα αὐτοῦ ἐν προσευχῇ καὶ περὶ τῶν ἁμαρτιῶν αὐτοῦ δεηθήσεται.

He will devote his heart to rise early to the Lord who has made him, and before the Most High he will beg; and he will open his mouth in prayer, and about his sins he will beg.

39:6^LXX ἐὰν κύριος ὁ μέγας θελήσῃ, πνεύματι συνέσεως ἐμπλησθήσεται· αὐτὸς ἀνομβρήσει ῥήματα σοφίας αὐτοῦ καὶ ἐν προσευχῇ ἐξομολογήσεται κυρίῳ·

If the great Lord is willing, he will be filled with the spirit of understanding, he himself will pour forth words of his wisdom, and in prayer he will sing praises to the Lord.

---

[17] In RAHLFS/HANHART 2006, Vol. II 444, Sir 38:33^LXX ends here and Sir 38:34^LXX begins.

[18] In RAHLFS/HANHART 2006, Vol. II 444, Sir 38:34^LXX ends here and Sir 39:1^LXX begins.

[19] Some Greek manuscripts read ἀνθρώπων "humans" instead, cf. ZIEGLER 1980, 305.

[20] Some Greek manuscripts, some manuscripts of the Latin Vulgate, and the Syriac Peshitta read a form of "prophets" instead of "prophecies", cf. ZIEGLER 1980, 305.

[21] RAHLFS/HANHART 2006, Vol. II 444, read αἰνίγμασι without the final ν, but this is only a variant in spelling, not in meaning.

39:7[LXX]	αὐτὸς κατευθυνεῖ βουλὴν[22] καὶ ἐπιστήμην καὶ ἐν τοῖς ἀποκρύφοις αὐτοῦ διανοηθήσεται·	He himself[23] will make straight counsel and knowledge, and in his hidden things he will think.
39:8[LXX]	αὐτὸς ἐκφανεῖ παιδείαν διδασκαλίας αὐτοῦ καὶ ἐν νόμῳ διαθήκης κυρίου καυχήσεται.	He himself will reveal the education of his teaching, and about the law of the covenant of the Lord he will boast.
39:9[LXX]	αἰνέσουσιν τὴν σύνεσιν αὐτοῦ πολλοί, καὶ ἕως τοῦ αἰῶνος οὐκ ἐξαλειφθήσεται· οὐκ ἀποστήσεται τὸ μνημόσυνον αὐτοῦ, καὶ τὸ ὄνομα αὐτοῦ ζήσεται εἰς γενεὰς γενεῶν·	Many will praise his understanding, and until the age it will not be wiped out: his remembrance will not de- part, and his name will live to the generations of generations.
39:10[LXX]	τὴν σοφίαν αὐτοῦ διηγήσονται ἔθνη, καὶ τὸν ἔπαινον αὐτοῦ ἐξαγγελεῖ ἐκκλησία·	Nations will describe his wisdom, and the assembly will proclaim his praise.
39:11[LXX]	ἐὰν ἐμμείνῃ, ὄνομα καταλείψει ἢ χίλιοι, καὶ ἐὰν ἀναπαύσηται ἐκποιεῖ αὐτῷ.	If he abides, he will leave a name (better) than a thousand, and if he takes rest, it is enough for him.

4.4 Comparative Analysis

4.4.1 Manuscripts and Date

In Hebrew, parts of Sir 38:24–27 are preserved on Manuscript B (dated to the turn of the 10th and 11th centuries CE) only.[24] Older Greek manuscripts preserving the full passage Sir 38:24–39:11[LXX] exist from the 4th century CE, especially Codices Vaticanus (B) and Sinaiticus (S).[25] The passage Sir 38:24–39:11, like the Hebrew Book of Ben Sira overall (see Chapter 2.1), probably dates to the much earlier time of the early 2nd century BCE.[26]

Sir 38:24 is preceded on Manuscript B VIII verso by an empty line which marks a new topic.[27] In the Hebrew text of Manuscript B, both superlinear and marginal additions are visible. In Sir 38:25 לשדד "to plow" is written above ישוב "he will bring back", while the right hand margin contains וישובב בשיר "and he

---

[22] RAHLFS/HANHART 2006, Vol. II 444, read βουλὴν αὐτοῦ "his counsel".

[23] Some translations (e. g. NRSV) regard αὐτός "he himself" here as referring to God, but given the use of the same pronoun in Sir 39:6[LXX] it is more likely to refer to the scribe (thus e. g. NETS = WRIGHT 2007b, 751).

[24] Cf. BLACHORSKY [2014], 22–23. For the date of Manuscript B see Chapter 1.2.1.

[25] Cf. ZIEGLER 1980, 303–307, in combination with SEPTUAGINTA-UNTERNEHMEN 2012, 1.

[26] Cf. WRIGHT 2013b, 2309 (early 2nd century BCE). Also implied by SKEHAN/DI LELLA 1987, 450 ("Ben Sira's time"); SAUER 2000, 266 (Hellenistic times).

[27] Cf. REY/DHONT 2018, 103–104.

104   *4. Ben Sira 38:24–39:11*

will bring back with a song".[28] The left hand margin contains ינהג "will lead" in
Sir 38:27. The first two additions are also found in the Greek text, whereas the
last one could be equated with διάγει "spends" in Sir 38:27[LXX]. Overall, the Hebrew and Greek texts show various small differences (starting with the Greek ἐν
εὐκαιρίᾳ σχολῆς "in the opportunity of leisure" in Sir 38:24[LXX] for the Hebrew
תרבה חכמה "will make much wisdom" in Sir 38:24), but most of the phrases and
the overall content of a scribe contrasted with a farmer and craftsman are the
same in Hebrew (as far as it is preserved) as in Greek.

4.4.2 Context

In Hebrew, Sir 38:24 marks the beginning of a new passage through a new topic:
rather than dealing with death and grief, the topic of Sir 38:16–23, Sir 38:24 introduces the topic of wisdom and different professions. Manuscript B marks this
new topic with an empty line preceding it (see Chapter 4.4.1). The only preserved
Hebrew text of this passage is its beginning, Sir 38:24–27. The end of the passage on wisdom and different professions, found in Sir 39:11[LXX], is not preserved
on Manuscript B, but the manuscript contains parts of the following passage Sir
39:15–35 in which Ben Sira praises God's creation.

In Greek, Sir 38:24–39:11[LXX] also forms a passage on the topic of wisdom and
different professions following the topic of grief (Sir 38:16–23[LXX]) and preceding
the topic of creation (Sir 39:12–35[LXX]).

4.4.3 Genre

In both Hebrew and Greek, the passage Sir 38:24–39:11[LXX] is not addressed to
anyone in particular. In the wider context of the Book of Ben Sira as advice used
in teaching – διδασκαλία "teaching" is also explicitly mentioned in Sir 39:8[LXX] –[29]
the passage functions as an depiction of the wise scribe to which the students are
meant to aspire.[30] The passage begins and ends with the scribe, the other professions provide a contrast.[31]

Some scholars state that Sir 38:24–39:11[LXX] refers to an Egyptian text called
"Satire on the Trades",[32] while others argue against a direct literary dependency,[33]
noting that in contrast to the Egyptian text Ben Sira's view of the other professions is not entirely negative,[34] and that the topic of praising the scribe above

---

[28] Cf. Rey/Dhont 2018, 122.

[29] Cf. Sauer 2000, 270. For the teaching setting see Chapter 2.3.1.

[30] Cf. Corley 2013, 106. On the term סופר "scribe" cf. Mandel 2017, 1–4, 68, who argues that
the term in the Second Temple Period refers to instruction rather than textual interpretation.

[31] Cf. Sauer 2000, 266; Becker/Fabry/Reitemeyer 2011, 2229; Wright 2013b, 2309.

[32] Cf. Corley 2013, 106. A translation of the "Satire on the Trades" can be found in
Pritchard 1969, 432–434. Also see Chapter 1.4.5.

[33] Cf. Zapff 2010, 261 (remote similarity).

[34] Cf. Wischmeyer 1994, 126–128; Crenshaw 1997a, 812; Wright 2013b, 2309.

different professions is a common in Egyptian texts.[35] Rather than depending on a specific Egyptian text, Ben Sira may have known an Egyptian genre of texts praising the scribe.[36]

4.4.4 Structure

Sir 38:24–39:11[LXX] describes how those working in different professions (farmer, craftsman, smith, and potter)[37] cannot acquire wisdom because they are occupied with their work (Sir 38:24–34[LXX]), in contrast to the scribe who is occupied with wisdom and God (Sir 38:34–39:11[LXX]).

In Hebrew, only Sir 38:24–27 is preserved, which can be structured as shown in Table 4–1:

Table 4–1: Sir 38:24–27: Structure

Verse	Introductory Words	Content
Sir 38:24		Scribe
Sir 38:25–26	מה "how?"	Farmer
Sir 38:27	אף "also"	Craftsman

Imperfect forms are used in the descriptions of all three professions. In the Hebrew Sir 38:24–27, חכמה "wisdom" begins and ends the first sentence, and הכם "to be wise" is used in hithpael forms "to show oneself as wise" at the end of Sir 38:24 and, in a contrasting rhetorical question about a farmer, at the beginning of Sir 38:25. The description of the craftsman is connected to that of the farmer (the end of which is not preserved on Manuscript B) through אף "also". The expression לב ישית "he will set the heart" is only preserved in the description of the farmer in Sir 38:26.

In Greek, Sir 38:24–39:11[LXX] can be structured as shown in Table 4–2:

Table 4–2: Sir 38:24–39:11[LXX]: Structure

Verse	Introductory Words	Content
Sir 38:24[LXX]		Scribe
Sir 38:25–26[LXX]	τί "how?"	Farmer

---

[35] Cf. ROLLSTON 2001, 132–133 (topic attested more widely in Egyptian literature); REY 2016, 261 (referring to ROLLSTON 2001).

[36] Cf. ROLLSTON 2001, 136.

[37] There is a wide consensus regarding the identification of the professions of a farmer (Sir 38:25–26), smith (Sir 38:28[LXX]), and potter (Sir 38:29–30[LXX]), whereas the second profession is sometimes interpreted as craftsman or artisan (thus CRENSHAW 1997a, 812; WRIGHT 2013b, 2309; BECKER/FABRY/REITEMEYER 2011, 2229), sometimes with different sub-professions (such sealmaker/tailor/painter, thus SAUER 2000, 266, similarly HAMP 1951, 102), sometimes more specifically as seal maker (thus CORLEY 2013, 106–107; SKEHAN/DI LELLA 1987, 450). A variety of translations for the different professions is discussed by MARBÖCK 2008, 48–52.

106   *4. Ben Sira 38:24–39:11*

Verse	Introductory Words	Content
Sir 38:27[LXX]	οὕτως "so"	Craftsman
Sir 38:28[LXX]	οὕτως "so"	Smith
Sir 38:29–30[LXX]	οὕτως "so"	Potter
Sir 38:31–34[LXX]	πάντες οὗτοι "all these"	The four previous professions
Sir 38:34–39:11[LXX]	πλήν "except for"	Scribe

Future forms (probably translating Hebrew imperfect forms) are used in all de-scriptions. Σοφία "wisdom" is only mentioned at the beginning and not the end of the first sentence, but as in Hebrew, σοφισθήσεται "will be made wise" is used both at the end of Sir 38:24[LXX] and in a contrasting rhetorical question about a farmer at the beginning of Sir 38:25[LXX]. The descriptions of craftsman, smith, and potter are each connected with that of the farmer through οὕτως "so". In addition, all four descriptions share the expressions καρδίαν αὐτοῦ δώσει "he will give his heart" (with the variation καρδίαν ἐπιδώσει "he will devote the heart" in the final description in Sir 38:30[LXX]) and καὶ ἡ ἀγρυπνία αὐτοῦ "and his sleeplessness". The four professions are explicitly summarized in Sir 38:31–34[LXX] with the introduction πάντες οὗτοι "all these", and the scribe is then con-trasted with them with πλήν "except for" in Sir 38:34[LXX]. Σοφία "wisdom" does not appear again before the description of the scribe where it is mentioned twice in Sir 39:1[LXX] and Sir 39:10[LXX].

The description of the scribe in Sir 38:34–39:11[LXX] is approximately as long as that of the other four professions together, and can further be subdivided along syntactical changes as shown in Table 4–3:

Table 4–3: Sir 38:34–39:11[LXX]: Syntax

Verse	Syntax	Content
Sir 38:34–39:3[LXX]	Participles, Future forms	Learning
Sir 39:4[LXX]	Future forms, Aorist form	Public and international ac-tivities
Sir 39:5[LXX]	Future forms	Prayer, also about own sins
Sir 39:6[LXX]	New subject: κύριος "Lord", Future forms	Inspiration
Sir 39:7–8[LXX]	Future forms	Learning and teaching
Sir 39:9–11[LXX]	New subjects: πολλοί "many", ἔθνη "nations", ἐκκλησία "assembly", Future forms	Eternal international fame

There are no introductory words which mark clear distinctions between the dif-ferent activities of the scribe. The implicit subject is almost always the scribe. However, an aorist form in Sir 39:4[LXX] and new subjects other than the scribe in Sir 39:6[LXX] and Sir 39:9–10[LXX] interrupt a long line of future forms with the scribe as their implicit subject. The distinctions between "learning" and "public and international activities" and that between "inspiration" and "learning and teaching" are not explicitly marked and can only be deducted from the content of the text. The expression "to give his heart" appears in two variations: τοῦ ἐπιδιδόντος τὴν ψυχὴν αὐτοῦ "the one devoting his soul" in Sir 38:34[LXX] and καρδίαν αὐτου ἐπιδώσει "he will devote his heart" in Sir 39:5[LXX]. The repetition of καυχάομαι "to boast" contrasts the farmer in Sir 38:25[LXX] who boasts about a shaft of a goad with the scribe who boasts about the law of the covenant of the Lord in Sir 39:8[LXX]. Nowhere in the passage are writing or reading explicitly mentioned as the scribe's activities. In contrast, the scribe's divine inspiration is explicitly mentioned in Sir 39:6[LXX].[38]

4.5 Sir 38:24–39:11 and the Question of Canon

4.5.1 Canonical References?

Sir 38:34–39:1[LXX] is not preserved in Hebrew at all, but Sir 38:34–39:1[LXX] mentions νόμος ὑψίστου "the law of the Most High", σοφία πάντων ἀρχαίων "the wisdom of all ancients" and προφητεῖαι "prophecies" in this order.[39] Like the Greek Prologue, Sir 38:34–39:1[LXX] is often used to argue for Ben Sira's knowledge of a biblical canon.[40] For example, ZENGER writes about the canon of the Hebrew Bible:

"The *fundamental* division into three parts is first indicated in Sir 38:34b–39:1 (around 190 BCE)".[41]

Similarly, SKEHAN/DI LELLA note:

"Ben Sira alludes to the threefold division of the OT in a manner similar to that of his grandson's Prologue: 'the Law of the Most High' (38:34d), 'the wisdom of the ancients' (39:1a), and 'the prophecies' (39:1b)."[42]

In contrast, SWANSON argues against a tripartite canon in Sir 38:34–39:1[LXX]:

"To make such a claim, however, does violence to the natural sense of the passage, and appears to be the result of approaching the passage with preconceived notions of the existence of a tri-partite collection of Hebrew Scriptures in Ben Sira's day."[43]

---

[38] The scribe's divine inspiration is also highlighted by HORSLEY/TILLER 2002, 99–103.

[39] Textual variants make these terms both more and less similar to terms for a tripartite canon, see Notes 19–20.

[40] Sir 38:34d[LXX] is sometimes designated with Sir 38:34b[LXX] or Sir 38:34bβ[LXX]. There are four lines for Sir 38:34[LXX] in ZIEGLER 1980, 305, which can be counted as a, b, c, and d (since the number of lines per verse varies in the surrounding verses, e.g. in Sir 39:5[LXX] with five lines, it seems best to simply count the lines using letters). The final line (d) is most relevant for the question of canon. See Chapter 4.3.

[41] ZENGER 2008, 23 (emphasis in original, see Chapter 1 Note 26).

[42] SKEHAN/DI LELLA 1987, 452.

[43] SWANSON 1970, 99.

108   *4. Ben Sira 38:24–39:11*

Thus, just as for the Greek Prologue, suggestions regarding the relation of Sir 38:34–39:1^{LXX} to the question of canon range from a clear reference of this passage to the full tripartite canon of the Hebrew Bible to no reference to any canon.

4.5.2 Tripartite Canon?

That the passage refers to a tripartite canon or the three parts of the later tripartite canon is often stated without giving further arguments.[44] Sometimes, the third canonical section of the Writings is seen as open.[45] Where arguments for a reference to a tripartite canon in Sir 38:34–39:1^{LXX} are given, they include the following:

(1) The passage has to refer to written works since in Sir 24:23^{LXX} the law is a book.[46] – However, it is unclear which book is meant there (see Chapter 3.4.4). Sir 24:23^{LXX} also does not refer to any more than one book and is thus a weak argument for a tripartite canon.

(2) The Prologue also knows a tripartite canon.[47] – However, as some scholars note, this argument applies preconceived notions about the Prologue (see Chapter 3) to Sir 38:34–39:1^{LXX}.[48]

(3) The "Praise of the Ancestors" also refers to canonical texts.[49] – However, this argument needs further assessment (see Chapter 5).

(4) Some scholars refer to Ezr 7:10 as a similar text,[50] as there Ezra only reads the law rather than a tripartite canon.[51] However, Ezra is not mentioned anywhere in Ben Sira (see Chapter 5.5.1).

---

[44] Cf. SMEND 1906, 353; PETERS 1913, 324; EBERHARTER 1925, 129–130; KOOLE 1965, 379; MACK 1982, 311; PRATO 1987, 171–172; SKEHAN/DI LELLA 1987, 451–452, esp. 452 (see Notes 42, 78); STADELMANN 1980, 223–225; SAUER 2000, 38, 269; SCHIFFMAN 1995, 164; VOS 2006, 48; MARBÖCK 2008, 53; UEBERSCHAER 2007, 218–221, 368; ZAPFF 2010, 264; CORLEY 2013, 107; REITERER 2013, 145; STEMBERGER 2019, 36.

[45] Cf. FOULKES 1994, 79 n. 11; Ueberschaer 2007, 369; MARBÖCK 1995e, 45 (wisdom may include writings not included in the later Hebrew Bible); REITEMEYER 2000, 305 (wisdom of "all" the ancients may include writings not included in the later Hebrew Bible), 308 (prophets in Ben Sira always refer to canonical figures); BECKER/FABRY/REITEMEYER 2011, 2231 (prophecies refers to Former and Latter Prophets, prophets in Ben Sira always refer to canonical figures).

[46] Cf. LIESEN 2000, 49–53. On Sir 24:23^{LXX} see Chapter 3.4.4 .

[47] Cf. HAMP 1951, 103; FRUHSTORFER 1941, 142; FOULKES 1994, 79 n. 11; *Stuttgarter Erklärungsbibel* 2005, 1262.

[48] This is also noted by BRANDT 2001, 70 n. 234.

[49] Cf. LEBRAM 1968, 180; MARBÖCK 1995e, 45–46 (not just the Pentateuch books but also prophets, cf. Sir 48:24 for Third Isaiah, Sir 49:10 for the Twelve Prophets, Sir 48:10–11 for the end of Mal 3:23).

[50] Cf. SMEND 1906, 353; BOX/OESTERLEY 1913, 455; HAMP 1951, 103; VOS 2006, 48.

[51] Cf. SKEHAN/DI LELLA 1987, 451; STADELMANN 1980, 224; MARBÖCK 1995e, 44; UEBERSCHAER 2007, 227 (also mentioning Neh 8:8–9).

4.5 Sir 38:24–39:11 and the Question of Canon

It is often argued that in addition to the tripartite canon the passage refers to many other sources of wisdom.[52] Sometimes, partly retrospectively from later traditions, oral tradition is seen to be complementing the tripartite written canon in Sir 39:2–3[LXX].[53]

Overall, all arguments for a tripartite canon rely on texts outside the passage Sir 38:24–39:11[LXX], and all of these texts are subject to debates.

4.5.3 Bipartite Canon?

Some scholars state that Sir 38:34–39:1[LXX] only refers to Law and Prophets.[54] The following reasons are given:

(1) The terms νόμος "law" and προφητεῖαι "prophecies" are close to the later designations "Law" and "Prophets" of these two parts of the canon of the Hebrew Bible, while the middle term σοφία πάντων ἀρχαίων "the wisdom of all the ancients" is too specific to correspond to "Writings".[55] – However, this argument presupposes the later designations of the three parts of the canon of the Hebrew Bible.[56]

(2) προφητεῖαι "prophecies" in Sir 39:1b[LXX] and διήγησις ἀνδρῶν ὀνομαστῶν "the narration of famous men" in Sir 39:2a[LXX] both refer to prophetic books since these books contain stories about famous people, and the Prologue equates prophecies with prophetic books.[57] – However, there is no indication in the passage itself that these two terms but not those following in Sir 39:2b[LXX] or preceding in Sir 39:1a[LXX] refer to prophetic books, and no indication of references to written texts at all.

Overall, all arguments for a bipartite canon cannot be verified in the passage Sir 38:24–39:11[LXX] itself.

---

[52] Cf. MACK 1982, 311 (wide and international literature and experience); ZAPFF 2010, 264–265 (beyond biblical texts, Hellenistic education).

[53] Cf. SMEND 1906. 353; BOX/OESTERLEY 1913, 455; SNAITH 1974, 192.

[54] Cf. HENGEL 1988, 247–248; TREBOLLE BARRERA 2002, 129. RICKENBACHER 1973, 184–185, also implies a bipartite canon (Sir 39:1ab[LXX] refers to prophets only under a wisdom lense).

[55] Cf. RÜGER 1984, 66.

[56] See Chapter 1 Note 2.

[57] Cf. VAN DER KOOIJ 1998, 35 ≈ VAN DER KOOIJ 2003, 36.

110   *4. Ben Sira 38:24–39:11*

4.5.4 One-Part Canon?

Some scholars state that there is a clear reference only to the Law,[58] whereas references to any other categories (of Israelite or non-Israelite literature)[59] are unclear. Reasons given for this view include the following:

(1) Ps 1:2[LXX] also includes thinking about the law.[60] – However, there is no intertextual link to Ps 1[LXX].

(2) Sir 24:23[LXX] refers to the written Pentateuch.[61] – However, while Sir 24:23[LXX] (not preserved in Hebrew) does refer to a book, it is unclear if this book can be equated with the Pentateuch (see Chapter 3.4.4).

(3) The law is mentioned first,[62] and it is the object of the participles forming the subject of all the following future forms.[63] – In contrast, some scholars note that the mention of the law is followed by many other sources of wisdom, and it is only one of many objects of study of the wise.[64]

(4) There is a lack of evidence for a tripartite canon at the time of this passage.[65] – However, this argument relies on sources outside Sir 38:24–39:11[LXX], namely the history of the canon which is subject to debate (see Chapter 1.3.1).

Overall, most arguments for a one-part canon rely on texts outside Sir 38:24–39:11[LXX]. The mention of νόμος "law" is indeed emphasized in the structure of

---

[58] Cf. SWANSON 1970, 103–104; CRENSHAW 1997a, 813 (law plus various sources of wisdom); BRANDT 2001, 70, n. 234 (law = Pentateuch, identification of Prophets and Writings speculative); SCHRADER 1998, 131 (law = written Pentateuch though the version may differ from the later MT, other categories may refer to things beyond or different to the canonical writings).

[59] Cf. MACK 1985, 95; LIM 2013, 98–99. According to VAN DER KOOIJ 1998, 34 ≈ VAN DER KOOIJ 2003, 35, σοφία πάντων ἀρχαίων "the wisdom of all ancients" in Sir 39:1[LXX] implies wide, international literature because in 1 Kgs 5:10[LXX] Solomon is said to be wiser than all ancient humans including non-Israelites (ὑπὲρ τὴν φρόνησιν πάντων ἀρχαίων ἀνθρώπων "above the intelligence of all ancient humans" as well as the wise of Egypt in 1 Kgs 5:10[LXX]). Against this, it is noted that in Sir 2:10[LXX] the adjective ἀρχαῖος "ancient" only refers to Israelite ancestors. However, the same adjective is also used in general meanings two more times in Sir[LXX] (see 3.5.3). The adjective itself neither implies a restriction to Israelites nor a necessary universality. The textual variant ἀνθρώπων "humans" in Sir 39:1[LXX] (see Note 19) points into a universal direction. Furthermore, according to VAN DER KOOIJ 1998, 35 ≈ VAN DER KOOIJ 2003, 36, Sir 39:2b–3[LXX] refers to Jewish wisdom literature since αἰνίγματα "riddles" and παραβολαί "parables" are also used regarding Solomon in Sir 47:15, 17[LXX]. Indeed, αἰνίγματα "riddles" only appears in Sir 39:3[LXX] and Sir 47:15[LXX], whereas παραβολαί "parables" is used more frequently in connection with wise people in Sir[LXX], e.g. in in Sir 3:29[LXX].

[60] Cf. EGO 2009, 206–207 (Law = Pentateuch while other categories may go beyond the later canon, Law = Pentateuch due to μελετάω "to meditate" in Ps 1:2[LXX] being a synonym for διανοέομαι "to think" which is used for the law in Sir 38:34[LXX]).

[61] Cf. REY 2016, 261 (see Chapter 3 Note 92).

[62] Cf. EBERHARTER 1925, 129; CARR 2005, 209, 211, 225, 261; UEBERSCHAER 2007, 220 (law mentioned first).

[63] Cf. SWANSON 1970, 102.

[64] Cf. MACK 1985, 94–95; FOULKES 1994, 81–82; UEBERSCHAER 2007, 220–221, 226.

[65] Cf. WRIGHT 2013b, 2310 (lack of contemporary evidence for canonical categories of Prophets and Writings).

4.5 Sir 38:24–39:11 and the Question of Canon

Sir 38:34–39:3^{LXX} by being mentioned first and as the object of the participles ἐπιδιδόντος τὴν ψυχὴν αὐτοῦ καὶ διανοουμένου "the one devoting his soul and thinking" which designate the subject of the following future forms. Nevertheless, the law does not necessarily refer to the Pentateuch (see Chapter 3.4.4).

4.5.5 No Canon?

Some scholars state that Sir 38:34–39:3^{LXX} is unlikely to refer to a tripartite canon.[66] Arguments against a reference to a tripartite canon include the following:

(1) The content of Sir 39:2–3^{LXX} makes it unlikely that Sir 39:1^{LXX} could refer to a tripartite canon since Sir 39:2–3^{LXX} include many sources of wisdom.[67] A wide education is emphasized in the context of the wider passage,[68] while texts are not explicitly mentioned.[69]

(2) A *parallelismus membrorum* is found in Sir 39:2–5^{LXX}. This makes it unlikely that there is no such parallelism in Sir 39:1^{LXX}.[70]

(3) It is unlikely that Ben Sira would write one colon each about the Law and the Prophets, but five cola (Sir 39:1a, 2–3^{LXX}) about the Writings.[71] – However, there may not be any reference to such canonical categories in the passage at all.

(4) The passage contrasts the wise with other professions[72] using the same words: in Sir 38:24^{LXX} σοφία "wisdom" and ἀσχολέω "to occupy oneself" are found, in Sir 39:1^{LXX} also σοφία "wisdom" and the related σχολή "leisure". This is seen to indicate that the point of the passage is not to enumerate a canon but to explain the activities of a scribe.[73] At the beginning of the "Praise of the Ancestors", Sir 44:3–4^{LXX} shares many words with Sir 39:1–8^{LXX}, for example προφητεῖαι "prophecies" in Sir 39:1^{LXX} and Sir 44:3^{LXX}, and ἄνδρες ὀνομαστοί "famous men" in Sir 39:3^{LXX} and Sir 44:3^{LXX}.[74] These shared words are seen to put the scribe on the same level of importance as the ancestors.[75] Indeed, the

---

[66] Cf. Beentjes 2006d, 221 ≈ Beentjes 2006f, 119. However, Beentjes still assumes the identification of the three categories in Sir 38:34–39:1^{LXX}: for example, he argues that wisdom is identified with Torah, whereas prophecy is seen as an interpretation of Torah, cf. Beentjes 2006d, 222 ≈ Beentjes 2006f, 120.

[67] Cf. Fabry 1999, 252; Steinmann 1999, 36; Flint 2003, 279; Lange 2004, 75 ("Ben Sira recommends the study of authoritative literature as such, rather than specifying a list of authoritative texts."); Beentjes 2006a, 170 n. 3 ≈ Beentjes 2006d, 221 n. 48; Lange 2008, 67.

[68] Cf. Maier 2007, 184 ("law" = Torah is not limited to the Pentateuch, the rest refers to literature in general).

[69] Thus Mandel 2017, 68 ("Ben Sira's *sofer* is not one who is involved with texts.", emphasis in original). Mandel's view is criticized by Stemberger 2019, 36, who argues that Ben Sira knew and used the Hebrew Bible but did not quote it due to the genre of wisdom literature.

[70] Cf. Beentjes 2006d, 221–222 ≈ Beentjes 2006f, 119–120.

[71] Cf. Beentjes 2006d, 221 ≈ Beentjes 2006f, 119.

[72] Cf. Maier 2007, 183–184.

[73] Cf. Beentjes 2006d, 222 ≈ Beentjes 2006f, 119–120.

[74] Cf. van der Kooij 1998, 35; Beentjes 2006d, 223 ≈ Beentjes 2006f, 120–122.

[75] Cf. Beentjes 2006d, 223 ≈ Beentjes 2006f, 120–122.

112   *4. Ben Sira 38:24–39:11*

shared words emphasize the importance of the profession of the scribe and do
not point towards any canon.

Overall – in contrast to arguments for a tripartite, bipartite, or one-part
canon – most arguments for the lack of any canon rely on the context within
the passage Sir 38:24–39:11[LXX]: this context includes many sources of wisdom
and points out the importance of the profession of a scribe rather than the
importance of a particular canon.

4.5.6 Open Canon including Ben Sira?

Some scholars argue for a reference to an open canon.[76] In particular, it is noted
that in Sir 39:6[LXX] the wise is described as inspired and as pouring forth his own
words of wisdom rather than simply interpreting tradition.[77] Indeed, Sir 39:6[LXX]
explicitly mentions the scribe's divinely inspired words: πνεύματι συνέσεως
ἐμπλησθήσεται· αὐτὸς ἀνομβρήσει ῥήματα σοφίας αὐτοῦ "he will be filled with
the spirit of understanding, he himself will pour forth words of his wisdom". Furthermore, the scribe's teaching is set in parallel with the law in Sir 39:8[LXX]. At the
same time, the whole passage does not explicitly refer to any written texts or the
activities of writing or reading.

4.5.7 Greek Canon?

Within the view that Sir 38:34–39:1[LXX] refers to a tripartite canon, several scholars
note that the order indicates a reference to the Greek Septuagint (Historical –
Didactic – Prophetic Books) rather than the Hebrew Bible (Law – Prophets –
Writings) – in contrast to the Prologue.[78] Some take this as an indication for the
early existence of the order of the Septuagint division of the canon,[79] while others
refute this,[80] sometimes arguing that the order is due to Ben Sira's emphasis on

---

[76] Cf. MACK 1985, 94–95.

[77] Cf. BOX/OESTERLEY 1913, 456; ZAPFF 2010, 265–266 (inspired wise does not simply
receive and interpret scripture but creates his own words, almost prophetic); WRIGHT 2013b,
2311 (as in Sir 24:33[LXX]).

[78] Cf. SKEHAN/DI LELLA 1987, 452; BURKHARDT 1992, 139; CRENSHAW 1997a, 813; VOS 2006,
48 n. 46; ZAPFF 2010, 264.

[79] Cf. LEBRAM 1968, 183–184 (LXX division older); KOOLE 1977, 235 (division similar to
LXX); MARBÖCK 1995e, 46–47 (may indicate LXX division); UEBERSCHAER 2007, 220–221,
n. 142 (νόμος "law", σοφία "wisdom", and προφητεῖαι "prophecies" could reflect the LXX
order and may be its first known mention; νόμος "law", προφητεῖαι "prophecies", and στροφαί
παραβολῶν "twists of parables" could reflect the MT order, but the third expression is unlikely
to describe the "Writings"); KREUZER 2015, 453–455 (LXX division existed in the 2nd century
BCE for Hebrew canon).

[80] Cf. LEIMAN 1976, 150–151 n. 135; RICKENBACHER 1973, 184–185 (prophets cannot come
last in the canon, Sir 39:1ab[LXX] refers to prophets only); EGO 2009, 207, n. 14 (reference to LXX
canon unlikely).

wisdom.[81] However, all of these arguments presuppose that the passage refers to parts of a canon, and do not take variant orders within the Septuagint into account.[82]

4.6 Conclusion

The passage Sir 38:24–39:11[LXX] of which only the beginning, Sir 38:24–27, is partly preserved in Hebrew, presents a comprehensive picture of the scribe in contrast to other professions, stresses the international breadth of his study, and his own inspired words. Divine law is an important source of wisdom, and there are also other sources of wisdom. The scribe may himself produce divinely inspired words. Written texts are not explicitly mentioned anywhere in the passage, and neither are the activities of writing or reading. The term νόμος "law" is mentioned both at the beginning of the description of the scribe's activities and at its end: the scribe thinks ἐν νόμῳ ὑψίστου "in the law of the Most High" (Sir 38:34[LXX]) and boasts ἐν νόμῳ διαθήκης κυρίου "in the law of the covenant of the Lord" (Sir 39:8[LXX]). However, νόμος "law" does not necessarily refer to the Pentateuch (see Chapter 3.4.4).

If Sir 38:24–39:11[LXX] is compared to the canon of the Hebrew Bible only, the emphasis on the law is most similar to a one-part but open canon in which the "Law" and other sources of wisdom hold authority which is complemented by divine inspiration. Sir 38:34–39:1[LXX] is unlikely to refer to a tripartite or bipartite canon, including a Greek tripartite canon. But if general criteria for ancient authoritative texts are applied (see Chapter 1.3.6), Sir 38:34–39:1[LXX] does not explicitly refer to any written texts at all.

---

[81] Cf. SNAITH 1974, 191.
[82] See Chapter 3 Note 256.

5. Ben Sira 44–50: Survey

5.1 Introduction

Sir 44–50 is often called "Praise of the Ancestors"[1] or "Praise of the Fathers".[2] These designations are based on the superscriptions at the beginning of Sir 44:1, in Hebrew שבח אבות עולם "Praise of fathers of duration" and in Greek Πατέρων ὕμνος "Song of praise of fathers". Since Sir 44–50 mentions many generations, the broader English term "Praise of the Ancestors" is used here for Sir 44–50.[3] Apart from the High Priest Simon in Sir 50, Sir 44–50 praises figures also found in the Hebrew Bible, and the "Praise of the Ancestors" is often seen as referring to a biblical canon.[4] This chapter provides a comparative survey of Sir 44–50 in Hebrew and Greek and a systematic assessment of possible canonical references in Sir 44–50 as a whole, including discussions of the order of figures and possible quotations.

5.2 Textual Basis

The seven chapters Sir 44–50 are partly extant in Hebrew and fully in Greek (for details see Chapter 5.3.1). The Hebrew transcription in RENDSBURG/BINSTEIN 2013 and the Greek text in ZIEGLER 1980 (see Chapter 1.2) are used here as the textual basis for the analysis of Sir 44–50.

The preserved Hebrew parts of Sir 44–50 with transcriptions and photographs of the manuscripts as well as English translations can be found in RENDSBURG/BINSTEIN 2013 (www.bensira.org).[5] The full Greek text of Sir 44–50[LXX] can be found in the Göttingen Septuagint edited in ZIEGLER 1980,[6] a full English trans-

---

[1] Cf. e.g. WRIGHT 2008; CALDUCH-BENAGES 2011.
[2] Cf. e.g. GOSHEN-GOTTSTEIN 2002.
[3] On the issue of female ancestors see Chapter 5.5.1.
[4] See Chapter 5.4 for details.
[5] Cf. RENDSBURG/BINSTEIN 2013, Masada Manuscript (transcriptions and translations by Eric REYMOND) and Manuscript B (transcriptions by Martin G. ABEGG, translations by Martin G. ABEGG and Benjamin H. PARKER).
[6] Cf. ZIEGLER 1980, 331–362.

116   *5. Ben Sira 44–50: Survey*

lation by WRIGHT in "A New English Translation of the Septuagint" (NETS) which is also available online (http://ccat.sas.upenn.edu/nets/edition).[7]

5.3 Comparative Analysis

5.3.1 Manuscripts and Date

In Hebrew, the beginning of the "Praise of the Ancestors" with parts of Sir 44:1–15, 17 is preserved on the oldest extant Ben Sira manuscript, the Masada Manuscript (Mas1h; 1st century BCE), in Column VII. Sir 44–50 is fully preserved on Manuscript B (turn of the 10th and 11th centuries CE), XIIIv to XXr (although there are no equivalents to the seven verses Sir 44:12; 46:18; 47:16, 25; 49:11; 50:15, 29LXX).[8] Greek manuscripts for Sir 44–50LXX exist from the 4th century CE, especially Codices Vaticanus (B) and Sinaiticus (S).[9] Sir 44–50 as a literary unit can be dated to the early 2nd century BCE like the Hebrew Book of Ben Sira (see Chapter 2.1).[10]

The two Hebrew manuscripts, more than a millennium apart, only differ from each other regarding individual words (the Masada Manuscript sometimes agreeing with the main text of Manuscript B, sometimes with the additions in B, and sometimes with neither).[11] For Sir 44–50, in the Hebrew Manuscript B, mostly marginal and a few superlinear additions are visible.[12] The Greek text in its overall content of praising famous ancestors agrees with the Hebrew texts. Only the following few passages where famous ancestors are mentioned show significant differences between the two Hebrew manuscripts or between the Hebrew and Greek texts. In the Masada Manuscript, Enoch may be left out and Noah the first figure mentioned in the "Praise of the Ancestors", but the fragmentary state of the manuscript does not allow for certainty (see Chapter 6.2.1). In Sir 44:23 in Manuscript B, ישראל "Israel" is used rather than Ιακωβ "Jacob" in Sir 44:23LXX. Where Ελισαιε "Elisha" is mentioned in Sir 48:12LXX, Manuscript B is damaged, only a part of a ל "l" is visible.[13] Sir 49:9 in Manuscript B mentions איוב "Job" between Ezekiel and the twelve prophets, while Sir 49:9LXX

---

[7] Cf. WRIGHT 2007b.

[8] Cf. BLACHORSKY [2014], 28–34. For the dates of the Masada Manuscript and Manuscript B see Chapter 1.2.1.

[9] Cf. ZIEGLER 1980, 331–362, in combination with SEPTUAGINTA-UNTERNEHMEN 2012, 1.

[10] In Sir 44–50, only a few individual phrases are sometimes argued to be later additions as they show differences in their content to the rest of Ben Sira, thus SAUER 2000, 313, 318, 327. It is also sometimes argued that existing traditions were used in the composition of Sir 44–50, thus WITTE 2020, 398–399, but Sir 44–50 then still forms a part of the Book of Ben Sira, cf. UEBERSCHAER 2007, 34.

[11] For a discussion and tables listing the differences cf. YADIN 1999, 157–169.

[12] For these additions cf. REY/DHONT 2018, esp. 107–108, 119–121.

[13] Cf. the photograph of Manuscript B XVII verso in RENDSBURG/BINSTEIN 2013. BEENTJES

5.3 Comparative Analysis

does not mention Job but enemies (probably translating a plural form of the Hebrew אויב "enemy" instead of איוב "Job", see Chapter 6.5.1). Where Ζοροβαβελ "Zerubbabel" is mentioned in Sir 49:11[LXX], Manuscript B is damaged, only a ל "l" may be reconstructed.[14] Where Ἰησοῦς "Jeshua" is mentioned in Sir 49:12[LXX], Manuscript B is not preserved. Sir 49:16 in Manuscript B mentions שם "Shem" and שת "Seth" and אנוש "Enosh", whereas Sir 49:16[LXX] only mentions Σημ "Shem" and Σηθ "Seth". Sir 50:24 in Hebrew mentions שמעון "Simon" whereas Sir 50:24[LXX] does not.

5.3.2 Context

In the larger context of the Book of Ben Sira in both Hebrew and Greek, Chapters 44–50 stand at the end of the book, only followed by a prayer in the first person in Sir 51. Sir 50 is sometimes not seen as a part of the "Praise of the Ancestors"[15] since Simon as a contemporary of Ben Sira is not counted among the ancestors.[16] However, the connections with the preceding praise, particularly with Aaron, make this unlikely,[17] and the passage may have been written after Simon's death.[18]

In Hebrew, the very beginning of Sir 44 is not extant in the Masada Manuscript (Mas1h), and the manuscript does not contain Sir 45–50. In Manuscript B, the beginning of a new passage in Sir 44 it is clearly marked with the superscription שבח אבות עולם "Praise of fathers of duration" at the top of a new page.[19] The passage also introduces a new topic, moving on from the praise of God's works in nature in Sir 43.[20] The end of Sir 44–50 is marked less clearly in Hebrew: in Manuscript B, Sir 50:29 continues with Sir 51:1 on the same line. In content, the praise of Simon in Sir 50:1–21 is followed by a benediction in Sir 50:22–23 with another mention of Simon in Sir 50:24, a note in the first person singular about two nations in Sir 50:25–26, and the reference to Ben Sira as the author and a blessing in Sir 50:27–29. In contrast, Sir 51 opens with a prayer in the first person. Thus, the "Praise of the Ancestors" in Hebrew probably ends with Sir 50:29.

In Greek, Sir 44–50[LXX] is introduced by the superscription Πατέρων ὕμνος "Song of praise of fathers", and the end could be marked with the benediction in

---

1997, 86, reconstructs only ל "l", ABEGG in RENDSBURG/BINSTEIN 2013, Manuscript B XVII verso, reconstructs [...יהו]ל[א] "[E]l[ijah ...]".

[14] Thus both BEENTJES 1997, 88, and ABEGG in RENDSBURG/BINSTEIN 2013, Manuscript B XVIII verso.

[15] Thus HAMP 1951, 136; SMEND 1906, 412; GOSHEN-GOTTSTEIN 2002, 236.

[16] Thus BOX/OESTERLEY 1913, 479; SKEHAN/DI LELLA 1987, 499; DI LELLA 2006, 152.

[17] Thus MARBÖCK 1993, 181; HAYWARD 1996, 41; CORLEY 2008b, 151; BEENTJES 2006h, 130; MITCHELL 2011, 13; MULDER 2011, 274–276.

[18] See Chapter 2 Note 19.

[19] Cf. REY/DHONT 2018, 103.

[20] The preceding praise of nature in Sir 43 is still connected to Sir 44–50 by the overall topic of praise and shared words, cf. ZAPFF 2010, 315.

118   *5. Ben Sira 44–50: Survey*

Sir 50:22–24^{LXX} as there is no further mention of Simon in Sir 50:24^{LXX}. Thus, the "Praise of the Ancestors" in Greek could already end with the praise of Simon in Sir 50:21^{LXX}, but also, as in Hebrew, with Sir 50:29^{LXX}.

5.3.3 Genre

In both Hebrew and Greek, Sir 44–50 is not addressed to anyone in particular. It stands in the wider context of the Book of Ben Sira as advice used in teaching.[21] It is likely that Sir 44–50 represents a praise of persons who serve as examples for Ben Sira's students.[22] Different genres have been suggested for Sir 44–50.[23] Summaries of deeds of ancestors are also found in earlier texts in the Hebrew Bible, e.g. Ps 68, 77–78, 105–106, 135–136, or Ezek 20, but these praise God or all of Israel rather than individual human figures.[24] Similar surveys of figures which are praised are found in texts such as 1 Macc 2:49–68^{LXX}, Wis 10–19^{LXX}, and in the New Testament in Heb 11,[25] summaries of Israel's history for example in 1 En 85–90 (Book of Dream Visions).[26] ZAHN notes that that information about ancestors in such summaries may have been known from sources other than texts later included in the Hebrew Bible, but still argues for references to texts in the Hebrew Bible in Sir 44–50.[27]

While it is sometimes argued that Sir 44–50 is based on the genre of an *encomium* and meant to praise Simon,[28] the differences in the content of Sir 44–50 when compared to Greek and Latin *encomia* – especially the lack of any mention of Simon himself before Sir 50, and the much longer praise of ancestors which are not only Simon's – seem too great to place Sir 44–50 within the genre of *encomia*.[29] However, encomiastic features may still be present in the description of all figures and in the overall structure of Sir 44–50.[30] It is sometimes argued that the purpose of Sir 44–50 is to highlight figures in the history of Israel in implicit contrast to Hellenistic heroes,[31] e.g. Enoch who was taken up just

---

[21] Thus UEBERSCHAER 2007, 235–236 n. 214. For the teaching setting see Chapter 2.3.1.

[22] Cf. WISCHMEYER 1994, 116.

[23] Cf. for an overview HILDESHEIM 1996, 38–53.

[24] Thus MARTIN 1986, 143; SAUER 2000, 302; CRENSHAW 1997a, 619, 638; BEENTJES 2017c, 90.

[25] Thus SAUER 2000, 302; ZAPFF 2010, 315; CALDUCH-BENAGES 2011, 303; GILBERT 2011, 322; CORLEY 2013, 123. CORLEY 2008b, 181, argues that 1 Macc 2 imitates Sir 44–50.

[26] Cf. GILBERT 2011, 322; ZAHN 2020a, 181–186.

[27] Thus ZAHN 2020a, 181–186.

[28] Thus LEE 1986, 241–245; CORLEY 2008b, 152–154; KAISER 2005, 152–153; WITTE 2006, 144 (referring to LEE 1986); CORLEY 2013, 123; WRIGHT 2013b, 2326 (referring to LEE 1986).

[29] Thus ROLLSTON 1992, 39, 59, 61 (against LEE 1986, referring to MACK 1985); CRENSHAW 1997a, 631–632 (referring to ROLLSTON 1992); DI LELLA 2006, 151–152 (against LEE 1986, referring to MACK 1985).

[30] Thus MACK 1985, 134–136 (discussing LEE 1986).

[31] Thus ZAPFF 2010, 315

like Heracles.[32] But against a significant influence of Greek genres, other scholars focus on the Hebrew Bible, for example DI LELLA:

"Indeed, for the source of Ben Sira's many references to Israel's history we need look no farther than the earlier books of the OT."[33]

Other scholars see Sir 44–50 as an early form of Midrash,[34] i.e. a form of literature with explicit references to the Hebrew Bible.[35] However, Sir 44–50 does not contain any such explicit references.

5.3.4 Structure

Sir 44–50, the "Praise of the Ancestors", mentions many figures by name. In Hebrew, Sir 44–50 can be structured as shown in Table 5–1:

Table 5–1: Sir 44–50: Structure

Verse	Main Words Hebrew	Main Words Greek	Content
Sir 44:1–15	Superscription, 1st person singular + plural 44:1	Superscription, 1st person plural 44:1^{LXX}	Introduction: General praise of ancestors
Sir 44:16	– 44:16 Maslh, חנוך 44:16 B	Ενωχ 44:16^{LXX}	Enoch (B and LXX only)
Sir 44:17–18	ח[נ] 44:17 B, [נוח] 44:17 Maslh	Νωε 44:17^{LXX}	Noah
Sir 44:19–21	אברהם 44:19	Αβρααμ 44:19^{LXX}	Abraham
Sir 44:22–23	יצחק 44:22	Ισαακ 44:22^{LXX}	Isaac
Sir 44:23	ישראל 44:23	Ιακωβ 44:23^{LXX}	Jacob
Sir 44:23–45:5	משה 45:1	Μωυσῆς 45:1^{LXX}	Moses
Sir 45:6–22	אהרן 45:6	Ααρων 45:6^{LXX}	Aaron
Sir 45:23–24	פינחס 45:23	Φινεες 45:23^{LXX}	Phineas
Sir 45:25	דוד 45:25	Δαυιδ 45:25^{LXX}	David
Sir 45:25–26/ 45:26^{LXX}	2nd person plural	2nd person plural	Blessing
Sir 46:1–7	יהושע 46:1	Ἰησοῦς 46:1^{LXX}	Joshua
Sir 46:7–10	כלב 46:7	Χαλεβ 46:7^{LXX}	Caleb
Sir 46:11–12	והשופטים איש בשמו 46:11	οἱ κριταί, ἕκαστος τῷ αὐτοῦ ὀνόματι 46:11^{LXX}	The judges by their names
Sir 46:13–20	שמואל 46:13	Σαμουηλ 46:13^{LXX}	Samuel
Sir 47:1	נתן 47:1	Ναθαν 47:1^{LXX}	Nathan

---

[32] Thus WITTE 2006, 147 (Heracles' ascension e.g. in Hesiod's Theogony, 954); ZAPFF 2010, 373 (referring to WITTE).

[33] DI LELLA 2006, 152.

[34] Thus LEE 1986, 48–54; HILDESHEIM 1996, 38–39; ZAPFF 2010, 315 (referring to HILDESHEIM 1996).

[35] Cf. TALABARDON 2012.

120   5. Ben Sira 44–50: Survey

Verse	Main Words Hebrew	Main Words Greek	Content
Sir 47:1–11	דוד 47:1, דויד 47:2	Δαυιδ 47:1–2[LXX]	David
Sir 47:12–23	שלמה 47:13	Σαλωμων 47:13[LXX]	Solomon
Sir 47:23–24 / 47:23–25[LXX]	רחבעם 47:23	Ροβοαμ 47:23[LXX]	Rehoboam
	ירבעם 47:24	Ιεροβοαμ 47:23[LXX]	Jeroboam
Sir 47:24– 48:11[12] / 48:1– 12[LXX]	אליהו 48:4	Ηλίας 48:1, 4[LXX] + 1st person plural 48:11[LXX]	Elijah
Sir 48:12	[...]ל[...] 48:12	Ελισαιε 48:12[LXX]	Elisha (Greek only, Hebrew damaged)
Sir 48:17–22	יחזקיהו 48:17	Εζεκίας 48:17[LXX]	Hezekiah
Sir 48:22–25	[...] 48:22	Ησαίας 48:20, 22[LXX]	Isaiah (Greek only, Hebrew damaged)
Sir 49:1–6	יאשיהו 49:1	Ιωσίας 49:1[LXX]	Josiah
Sir 49:7	ירמיהו 49:7	Ιερεμίας 49:7[LXX]	Jeremiah
Sir 49:8	יחזקאל 49:8	Ιεζεκιηλ 49:8[LXX]	Ezekiel
Sir 49:9	איוב 49:9	–	Job (Hebrew only)[36]
Sir 49:10	עשר שנים הנביאים 49:10	οἵ δώδεκα προφῆται 49:10[LXX]	The twelve prophets
Sir 49:11	[...]ל[...] 49:11	Ζοροβαβελ 49:11[LXX]	Zerubbabel (Greek only, Hebrew damaged)
Sir 49:12	[...]	Ἰησοῦς 49:12[LXX]	Jeshua (Greek only, Hebrew damaged)
Sir 49:13	נחמיה 49:13 + 1st person plural	Νεεμίας 49:13[LXX] + 1st person plural	Nehemiah
Sir 49:14	הניך 49:14	Ενωχ 49:14[LXX]	Enoch
Sir 49:15	יוסף 49:15	Ιωσηφ 49:15[LXX]	Joseph
Sir 49:16	שם 49:16	Σημ 49:16[LXX]	Shem
	שת 49:16	Σηθ 49:16[LXX]	Seth
	אנוש 49:16	–	Enosh (Hebrew only)
	אדם 49:16	Αδαμ 49:16[LXX]	Adam
Sir 50:1–21	שמעון 50:1	Σιμων 50:1[LXX]	Simon
Sir 50:22–24	2nd person plural 50:22–23	2nd + 1st person plural 50:22–24[LXX]	Blessing
	שמעון 50:24		Simon (Hebrew only)
	פינחס 50:24		Phineas (Hebrew only)[37]

---

[36] See Chapter 6.5.1.
[37] See Chapter 2 Note 4.

5.3 Comparative Analysis

Verse	Main Words Hebrew	Main Words Greek	Content
Sir 50:25–26	1st person singular 50:25	1st person singular 50:25^{LXX}	Unwelcome people
Sir 50:27–29	שמעון בן ישוע בן אלעזר בן סירא 50:27	Ἰησοῦς υἱὸς Σιραχ Ελεαζαρ ὁ Ἱεροσολυμίτης 50:27^{LXX}	Author Ben Sira
	3rd person singular Sir 50:28	3rd person singular Sir 50:28–29^{LXX}	Blessing

Sir 40–55 mostly contains verb forms referring to the past. This includes Sir 50 with the praise of Simon the High Priest, which supports the view that Ben Sira composed the book after Simon's death.[38]

Sir 40–55 is mostly written as a description in the third person, the subjects being God (e. g. Sir 45:19) and different figures.[39] In addition to being described in the third person, two figures are also addressed in the second person singular: Elijah (Sir 48:4, 11 / Sir 48:4, 11^{LXX}) and Solomon (Sir 47:14–15, 17–20 / Sir 47:14–20^{LXX}). One figure, Samuel, is also quoted in a direct speech in the first person singular (Sir 46:19 / Sir 46:19^{LXX}). The author is explicitly named in the third person (Sir 50:27 / Sir 50:27^{LXX}), as is a follower of his wisdom (Sir 50:28 / Sir 50:28–29^{LXX}). A first person singular probably referring to the author is found in Sir 50:25 / Sir 50:25^{LXX}. Further subjects, probably people in Israel and Jerusalem, appear in first and second person plural forms. In Hebrew, Sir 44:1 contains a call to praise in the first person singular (possibly corresponding to Sir 50:25 which also uses the first person singular probably for the author) which continues with a pronoun in the first person plural, while in Greek in Sir 44:1^{LXX} the call to praise is wholly found in the first person plural (possibly corresponding to Sir 50:22–24^{LXX} which also uses the first person plural, implicitly referring to people in Israel including the author). Three passages mention a first person plural "we" (Sir 48:11^{LXX} in Greek only as the verse is damaged in in Manuscript B; Sir 49:13 / Sir 49:13^{LXX}; Sir 50:22–24^{LXX} in Greek where the Hebrew uses the second person plural), of which the second passage implicitly refers to people in Jerusalem (as the city restored by Nehemiah) and the third passage implicitly refers to people in Israel including the author (as Sir 50:23^{LXX} mentions ἐν ἡμέραις ἡμῶν ἐν Ισραηλ "in our days in Israel"). Two passages address a group in the second person plural, asking this group to bless the God of Israel and be blessed by him (Sir 45:25–26 / Sir 45:26^{LXX}; Sir 50:22–23 / Sir 50:22^{LXX}; Sir 50:22–24^{LXX} continues in the first person plural).

---

[38] See Chapter 2 Note 19.

[39] Against GOSHEN-GOTTSTEIN 2002, 248, who argues that the "linguistic subject" of the first large section is God and that of the second part is not, cf. DI LELLA 2006, 153.

Mostly based on the concept of a bipartite canon, the "Praise of the Ancestors" is often seen as consisting of four sections: (1) Introduction (Sir 44:1–15); (2) Figures from the Pentateuch (Sir 44:16–45:26) ending with a blessing (Sir 45:25–26); (3) Figures from the Prophets (Sir 46:1–49:16); (4) Simon (Sir 50:1–24) ending with another blessing (Sir 50:23–24).[40] Sometimes, an additional section is seen in Sir 49:14–16 where figures appear outside the previous ascending chronological order,[41] and other subdivisions of the third part are also suggested.[42] However, there are only two blessings within Sir 44–50. This points to the "Praise of the Ancestors" as consisting of two parts, Sir 44–45 and Sir 46–50, with the second part including the praise of the High Priest Simon.[43]

5.4 Sir 44–50 and the Question of Canon

5.4.1 Canonical References?

Like the Greek Prologue and Sir 38:34–39:1^{LXX}, the "Praise of the Ancestors" in Sir 44–50 is often used to argue for Ben Sira's references to a biblical canon.

5.4.2 Tripartite Canon?

Sir 44–50 is sometimes argued to refer to the tripartite canon of the Hebrew Bible. For example, CRENSHAW writes:

"The sequence of heroes follows the canonical divisions, first those characters whose lives are recorded in the Pentateuch; then prophets, including Job; and finally Nehemiah, from the writings."[44]

Although CRENSHAW also notes that Job is not included in the "Prophets" section of the Hebrew Bible,[45] he still argues that Ben Sira means "to embrace the whole Hebrew canon"[46] and wants "to achieve canonical coverage"[47] in the "Praise of the Ancestors". Other scholars also argue for references from Sir 44–50 to almost all books in all three parts of the tripartite canon of the Hebrew Bible.[48] For example, SKEHAN/DI LELLA note:

---

[40] Cf. ZAPFF 2010, 315; CORLEY 2013, 123.

[41] Thus BECKER/FABRY/REITEMEYER 2011, 2248.

[42] Thus MULDER 2003, 52; MULDER 2011, 274–276.

[43] Thus BEENTJES 2006h, 128–130.

[44] CRENSHAW 1997a, 620.

[45] Thus CRENSHAW 1997a, 634 n. 86.

[46] CRENSHAW 1997a, 620.

[47] CRENSHAW 1997a, 631.

[48] Cf. BOX/OESTERLEY 1913, 479; PETERS 1913, XLVII; MACK 1985, 81, 91; VAN DER KOOIJ 2003, 33–34; CARR 2005, 209; CORLEY/VAN GROL 2011, v–vi; VAN DER KOOIJ 2012, 33; CORLEY 2013, 7.

5.4 Sir 44–50 and the Question of Canon 123

"Throughout these chapters, Ben Sira manifests an easy and thorough familiarity with the earlier Scriptures – the Pentateuch (the Law), Deuteronomy, Joshua, Judges, Samuel and Kings, Chronicles, Nehemiah, Psalms, Proverbs, and Job. Following the basic narrative contained in these sources, he attempts to show how Israel's ancestors have something significant to say to believers of his day."[49]

Arguments for the "Praise of the Ancestors" as referring to all or almost all of the tripartite canon most frequently include the following:

(1) The overall order of figures mentioned in Sir 44–50 is similar to the Hebrew Bible (see Chapter 5.5.1).

(2) Sir 48:10 contains a quotation of Mal 3:23–24 (see Chapter 5.5.2).

(3) There are allusions to texts in the Hebrew Bible in Sir 44–50 (see Chapter 6).[50]

(4) Sir 46:11–12 mentions "the judges" (see Chapter 6.3).

(5) Sir 49:10 mentions "the twelve prophets" (see Chapter 6.6).

(6) Sir 47:9 is argued to mention "the Psalms as compositions of David" and Sir 47:14–17 is argued to mention "Proverbs as the work of Solomon".[51] – However, both passages do not refer to books at all.

(7) The evidence of the Prologue for a tripartite canon is thought to be supported by Sir 44–50.[52] – However, this argument is opposite to the chronological sequence of Sir 44–50 and the Prologue to the translation of Ben Sira's book, and based on a text outside Sir 44–50.

5.4.3 Bipartite Canon?

Sir 44–50 is also sometimes seen as the earliest evidence for a bipartite canon, with a third part not yet developed.[53] For example, GOSHEN-GOTTSTEIN argues that Sir 44–49 is "reflecting a bipartite division of scriptural canon".[54] GUILLAUME counts Sir 44–49 among the earliest evidence for the "Prophets":

"the so-called Praise of the fathers (Ben Sira 44–49) names in the correct order the title of each book of the *Nebiim*."[55]

But rather than any book titles, only figures are named in Sir 44–49, figures which also are named in some parts of the "Prophets" section now in the Hebrew

---

[49] SKEHAN/DI LELLA 1987, 500.

[50] Cf. GRABBE 2004, 340 = GRABBE 2006, 326 = GRABBE 2008, 102 ("He gives a close paraphrase – almost a quote – from a number of passages"). Also see Note 48.

[51] SKEHAN/DI LELLA 1987, 41. Thus also MOPSIK 2003, 48.

[52] Thus CRENSHAW 1997a, 633–634.

[53] Thus STADELMANN 1980, 190–191; SAUER 1981, 492 (Sir 42:15–49:16 based on Pentateuch and most of the Former and Latter Prophets); STECK 1991, 138–140, 144 (Tora and Prophets two closed parts of a canon); WISCHMEYER 1994, 185; GUILLAUME 2005, 17; SKA 2009, 187, 195 (with STECK 1991 against CARR 1996); CARR 2011, 163, 192–193, 344–345; SCHMITT 2011, 160.

[54] GOSHEN-GOTTSTEIN 2002, 261.

[55] GUILLAUME 2005, 4.

124 5. Ben Sira 44–50: Survey

Bible.[56] The lack of references to books is also noted by SKA, who nevertheless argues that Ben Sira uses a bipartite canon.[57]

Arguments for the "Praise of the Ancestors" as referring to a bipartite canon of "Law" and "Prophets" include the following:

(1) A blessing in Sir 45:25–26 divides the Law and Prophets summaries in Sir 44–50.[58] For example, according to SKA Sir 44–50 is divided into three parts, Sir "44:1–45:28 [sic] (from Noah to Phinehas), 46:1–49:10 (from Joshua to the twelve minor prophets), and 49:11–50:21 (rebuilding the temple)".[59] SKA concludes:

> "Sirach is hardly interested in the biblical books as such. His first aim was to run through the history of his people [...] However, Ben Sirach introduces a periodization principle into this reconstruction, a principle that was to be found, in large part, in the first two parts of the Hebrew canon."[60]

Indeed, there is a clear division in Sir 45:25–26 with a call to praise in the second person plural before the introduction of Joshua. However, no such clear division exists between SKA's second and third part, and it seems that the second division is lead by previous knowledge of today's canon.[61] In addition, other divisions of Sir 44–50 have been suggested (see Chapter 5.3.4). In no possible division, Sir 44–49 or Sir 44–50 end with the Writings like the canon of the Hebrew Bible or with the Twelve Prophets like the Old Testament canon.[62]

(2) Sir 44–50 only uses the word "prophet" and related words for figures between Joshua and the twelve prophets.[63] Joshua is not called a "prophet" in the Hebrew Bible, wherefore the word signals the beginning of a summary of the "Prophets" section of the Hebrew Bible.[64] – However, if according to Sir 46:1[LXX] Joshua is διάδοχος Μωυσῆ ἐν προφητείαις "successor of Moses in prophecies" (in Hebrew משרת משה בנבואה "a ministering one of Moses in prophecy" in Sir 46:1), Moses is implied to also be a prophet. The use of the Hebrew term נביא "prophet" for Job[65] is a further argument against the alignment of the Former and Latter Prophets of the Hebrew Bible with figures called prophets in Sir 44–50. Furthermore, the term נביא "prophet" is not limited in ancient texts outside the Book of Ben Sira to referring to figures or books of the Prophets section of the later Hebrew Bible.[66] For example, the word נביא "prophet" is used outside

---

[56] GUILLAUME 2005, 9, states regarding the prophets that "each book is alluded to in almost perfect order".

[57] Cf. SKA 2009, 187, 195. Thus also STECK 1991, 136–139.

[58] Thus GUILLAUME 2005, 9.

[59] Thus SKA 2009, 187 [45:28 probably refers to 45:26]. Similarly GUILLAUME 2005, 14.

[60] SKA 2009, 195.

[61] GUILLAUME 2005, 14, also refers to "the canon".

[62] Thus CARR 1996, 39. See Chapter 1 Notes 2–3.

[63] Thus STECK 1991, 137–138; GUILLAUME 2005, 10; SKA 2009, 187.

[64] Cf. GUILLAUME 2005, 9.

[65] See Chapter 6.5.

[66] Thus BARTON 1986, 44, 48; CARR 1996, 39–41. See Chapter 3.4.2.

the "Prophets" section of the Hebrew Bible for Moses in Deut 34:10, for Aaron in Exod 7:1, and for Daniel in 4Q174 (4QFlor) Column 2 Line 3.[67] At the same time, many figures now in the "Prophets" section are not labelled as "prophets" in Sir 44–50.[68]

(3) The twelve prophets mentioned in Sir 49:10 are often seen to refer to a literary entity (see Chapter 6.6).

(4) Sir 48:10 quotes the end of Malachi and thus the end of the Former and Latter Prophets (see Chapter 5.5.2).

(5) Sir 44–50 is based on the "Former Prophets" rather than Chronicles (which form a part of the "Writings" section of the Hebrew Bible). According to SKA, Sir 44–50 relies more on 1 Samuel to 2 Kings than on 1–2 Chronicles.[69] – However, the opposite statement that Chronicles is more important than 1 Samuel to 2 Kings is also found, for example by CARR:

> "Ben Sira's praise is thoroughly informed by texts such as Chronicles, which are now in the Writings section of the Tanakh. [...] Rather than focusing exclusively on what he understood to be prophetic figures or material from a defined 'prophetic' corpus, Ben Sira in chs. 44–49 gives a historical overview extending from the creation to Nehemiah, an overview which draws freely on a number of non-Torah authoritative writings, writings now found both inside and outside the Prophets section of the later Jewish canon. Such data militate against an assumption that Ben Sira had before him any circumscribed, 'canonical' collection of prophets."[70]

CARR here also argues that Ben Sira draws on material not included in any part of the Hebrew Bible today.

(6) The Prologue also mentions two categories together with a rather vague third category.[71] – However, this argument is not based on Sir 44–50 itself (for the Prologue see Chapter 3).

5.4.4 One-Part Canon?

That Sir 44–50 points to a one-part canon consisting of the Law only, with all other texts merely illuminating the Law, is stated by some scholars without giving further arguments.[72] In contrast, other scholars note that the Pentateuch is – if at all – only briefly and indirectly alluded to in Sir 44–50, and is unlikely to be its

---

[67] Cf. ALLEGRO 1968, 4.

[68] Thus CARR 1996, 39. Cf. also CARR 1996, 28.

[69] Thus SKA 2009, 187.

[70] CARR 1996, 39.

[71] Thus STECK 1991, 137; SKA 2009, 194.

[72] Thus KOOLE 1965, 379. However, KOOLE 1965, 378–379, 396, also states that Ben Sira regarded as authoritative the whole Hebrew Bible except for Esther and Daniel. KOOLE 1965, 392, notes both that canonisation would have required a decision by "the leaders of the Jewish Church administration" (sic, German original "Leitung der jüdischen Kirchenbehörde"), and that there is no evidence for such a decision.

126 *5. Ben Sira 44–50: Survey*

main source.[73] With respect to the Pentateuch, SKA notes that "Sirach knows of no division into five books, or he is not interested in it."[74]

5.4.5 No Canon?

Arguments for no canon at all are not usually made on the basis of Sir 44–50. Even scholars who note that Ben Sira may have had many different sources still assume the canon of the Hebrew Bible as his main source.[75]

5.4.6 Open Canon including Ben Sira?

As for an open canon including Ben Sira, some of the same adjectives are used to describe a scribe in Sir 38:24–39:11[LXX] and the praiseworthy ancestors in Sir 44[LXX], which may serve to highlight Ben Sira's own authority as a scribe.[76]

5.4.7 Greek Canon?

A Greek canon is not seen as related to Sir 44–50. Instead, Sir 44–50 is seen to reflect the order of "Former Prophets" and "Latter Prophets" in the Hebrew Bible.[77]

5.4.8 Summary of Arguments

Arguments for an at least bipartite if not tripartite canon of the Hebrew Bible in Sir 44–50 are mostly based on the overall order of figures, a possible quotation of Mal 3:23–24 in Sir 48:10, and intertextual references to the Hebrew Bible, especially to the Book of Judges in Sir 46:11–12 and to the Book of the Twelve Prophets in Sir 49:10. In the following sections of the present study, the order of figures (Chapter 5.5.1) and the possible quotation of Mal 3:23–24 in Sir 48:10 (Chapter 5.5.2) are discussed. Possible intertextual references to texts in the Hebrew Bible are then assessed in detailed case studies (Chapter 6), including the judges in Sir 46:11–12 (Chapter 6.3) and the twelve prophets in Sir 49:10 (Chapter 6.6).

---

[73] Thus REITERER 2011b, 45–46, 61–63. Nevertheless, REITERER 2011d, 82, argues for "the Bible" as the basis of Ben Sira's work.

[74] SKA 2009, 191.

[75] Cf. MACK 1985, 15, 112.

[76] Thus LIESEN 2000, 57; BEENTJES 2006f, 121–122. See Chapter 4.5.5.

[77] Thus LEIMAN 1976, 150 n. 135.

5.5 Figures and the Question of Quotation

5.5.1 Order of Figures in Sir 44–50

The order of figures mentioned in Sir 44–50 is often argued to prove the existence of not just authoritative texts but a canon of books in the Masoretic order of books in the Hebrew Bible. Amongst others,[78] LEIMAN states:

"Ben Sira's tripartite canon shows greater affinity to the talmudic order and division of canonical books. Note especially Ben Sira 46:1–49:10, which reflects the Masoretic sequence of books".[79]

Similarly, CHILDS argues:

"Moreover, that Ben Sira knows all the prophetic books in a canonical order (46.1–49.13) and even the title of the Book of the Twelve, appears to be strong evidence for a fixed canonical unit of prophets by the beginning of the second century."[80]

Using the superscription "Ben Sira's References to Hebrew Bible Passages", GRABBE places a list of figures in the Hebrew Bible next to the list of figures in Ben Sira's "Praise of the Ancestors".[81] This comparison of lists puts an emphasis on similarities in the order of appearance of these figures. For example, passages such as the mention of Adam in Sir 49:16 where Ben Sira shows differences are set in brackets. From this comparison of lists, GRABBE draws the following conclusion:

"The most significant conclusion is that Ben Sira is more than just a collection of oral traditions or material derived from several sources. For the most part he follows the order of the biblical contents."[82]

Despite the fact that the whole books of Leviticus and Deuteronomy are missing in his list, GRABBE also concludes:

"The most reasonable conclusion from these considerations is that Ben Sira had essentially the present biblical text of the Pentateuch, Joshua to 2 Kings, 1–2 Chronicles, the Prophets, and the book of Job in front of him. [...] the sections of the Hebrew Bible that we now call the Torah and both the Former and Latter Prophets were evidently authoritative for him."[83]

However, such a conclusion is not obvious. The lists compiled by GRABBE are based solely on the Hebrew Bible, and passages in Ben Sira are included only

---

[78] Cf. CRENSHAW 1997a, 631; LIM 2013, 105.

[79] LEIMAN 1976, 150–151 n. 135. Also cf. LEIMAN 1976, 27.

[80] CHILDS 1979, 64.

[81] Cf. GRABBE 2004, 338–340 and GRABBE 2006, 324–326.

[82] GRABBE 2006, 323. Also cf. GRABBE 2006, 322–323, 326–327.

[83] GRABBE 2004, 341, who also notes that "one must keep in mind that slightly different versions of some parts of the Old Testament circulated in Hebrew until at least the first century CE" but that "the many 'parabiblical' traditions known to us from Second Temple Jewish literature are not found in Ben Sira's account." Also cf. GRABBE 2004, 343; GRABBE 2008, 102.

128   *5. Ben Sira 44–50: Survey*

where they are similar to the Hebrew Bible. But what happens if we take such a list which, rather than taking the Hebrew Bible as given in the 2nd century BCE, we take Ben Sira as given, and compare the later Hebrew Bible to it?

In such an opposite approach, the differences between Ben Sira and the Hebrew Bible become much more visible, even though the very same sources are used. The list presented in Table 5–2 does not aim at comprehensiveness, but provides a survey of figures in Sir 44–50 compared to the Hebrew Bible – rather than the other way round. Included in this list are in the first column all figures appearing in Ben Sira, even if they only play a minor role in the Hebrew Bible. The second column lists the main passages in the Hebrew Bible describing these figures, with the addition of a few figures (in brackets) who appear in major roles in the Hebrew Bible but not in Ben Sira. The third column gives an overview of the books in the Hebrew Bible in which the figures mainly appear, on the basis of the order of books in the Hebrew Bible. Even though the focus on figures mentioned in Sir 44–50 still highlights similarities, and no texts beyond the Hebrew Bible are included, a list oriented on Ben Sira rather than the Hebrew Bible shows remarkable differences, as Table 5–2 illustrates:

Table 5–2: List of Figures in Sir 44–50 compared to the Hebrew Bible

Figures in Sir 44–50	*Main Hebrew Bible passages describing these figures*	*Books in the Hebrew Bible*
Enoch Noah Abraham Isaac Jacob	Gen 5–9; 12–36 (also Ishmael)	Gen
Moses Aaron Phineas	Exod (also Golden Calf Exod 32) / Lev / Num / Deut Num 25	Exod Lev Num Deut
David	1 Sam 17, 2 Sam 7 / 1 Chr	1+2 Sam / 1 Chr
Joshua	Josh	Josh
Caleb	Num 14 / Josh 14–15	Num / Josh
Judges	Judg	Judg
Samuel Nathan David	1 Sam 1 (also Saul) 2 Sam / 1 Chr 11–29	1+2 Sam / 1 Chr

5.5 Figures and the Question of Quotation

Figures in Sir 44–50	Main Hebrew Bible passages describing these figures	Books in the Hebrew Bible
Solomon Rehoboam Jeroboam Elijah Elisha	1 Kgs 1 – 2 Kgs 9 / 2 Chr 1–12	1+2 Kgs / 2 Chr
Hezekiah Isaiah	2 Kgs 18–20 / Isa 1–39 / 2 Chr 29–32	2 Kgs / Isa / 2 Chr
Josiah	2 Kgs 22–23 / 2 Chr 34–35	2 Kgs / 2 Chr
Jeremiah	Jer	Jer
Ezekiel Job	Ezek Ezek 10; 14; Job	Ezek / Job
12 Prophets	12 Prophets	12 Proph
		Ps
		Prov
		Ruth
		Song
		Eccl
		Lam
		Esth
		Dan
Zerubbabel Jeshua	Hag / Zech / Ezr+Neh	12 Proph / Ezr+Neh
Nehemiah	Neh (also Ezra)	Ezr+Neh
Enoch Joseph Shem Seth Enosh Adam	Gen 5 Gen 37–50 / Josh 24 Gen 5 Gen 2–3	Gen / Josh
Simon		
Phineas	Num 25	Num

The survey in Table 5–2 highlights the following main differences between Sir 44–50 and the Hebrew Bible:

(1) Figures corresponding to the books in the "Writings" part of the Hebrew Bible are largely missing in Sir 44–50. For example, Ruth, Esther, and Daniel are missing entirely in Sir 44–50. Only Nehemiah but not Ezra is mentioned. Job

appears only in the Hebrew text of Sir 44–50 and as a prophet (see Chapter 6.5). This points against a reference to a tripartite canon of the Hebrew Bible in Sir 44–50.[84]

(2) The order of figures also shows differences between the Hebrew Bible and Ben Sira, for example in the double mention of Enoch, David and Phineas, the different place of Job, and the arrangement of figures also appearing in Genesis at the end.[85]

(3) The Hebrew Bible mentions many more female figures than Ben Sira, for example in the whole books of Ruth and Esther. This may be explained by the genre of praising "fathers",[86] or by the focus on priests and those leading temple cult,[87] but it still indicates that Ben Sira does not seem to be concerned with a full description of figures of the canon of the Hebrew Bible.

(4) There are also substantial differences in the mention and description of male figures: major events and figures in the Hebrew Bible such as Cain and Abel (Gen 3–4), Ishmael (Gen 16, 21), Aaron's building of the Golden Calf (Exod 32), King Saul (1–2 Sam), and Ezra (Ezr) are missing entirely, while Simon the High Priest plays a very prominent role. Specifically for Ezra, there is a debate about the reasons why he is not mentioned in the Book of Ben Sira,[88] with explanations including an anti-Levitical stance of Ben Sira,[89] or a focus on building works which are connected with Nehemiah but not Ezra.[90] In contrast, ADAMS argues that the figure of Ezra was simply not important enough at the time.[91] Indeed, the non-mention of Ezra may even more simply be due to a lack of knowledge or importance of texts now in the Hebrew Bible at Ben Sira's time.[92] The need for explanations regarding the non-mention of Ezra seems to be based on the canon of the Hebrew Bible.

In more detail, there are differences between the extant Hebrew and Greek manuscripts in the sequence of figures in Sir 44–50 as summarized in Table 5–3:

---

[84] Against LEIMAN 1976, 150–151 n. 135 (see Note 79).

[85] Additional differences regarding Joshua and Caleb in first Joshua and then Numbers are listed in GRABBE 2004, 339.

[86] Cf. CALDUCH-BENAGES 2011, 313.

[87] Thus CRENSHAW 1997a, 631.

[88] Cf. BEGG 1988, 14; BERGREN 1998, 355–356; DUGGAN 2004, 201–202; ADAMS 2021, 155–162.

[89] Thus HÖFFKEN 1975, 200–201.

[90] Thus BEGG 1988, 18.

[91] Thus ADAMS 2021, 154. ADAMS also notes other dissimilarities between Sir 44–50 and the Hebrew Bible, cf. ADAMS 2021, 155.

[92] This possibility is rejected by HÖFFKEN 1975, 201; BEGG 1988, 17.

5.5 Figures and the Question of Quotation

Table 5–3: Sequence of Figures in Sir 44–50 (Hebrew and Greek)

Sir 44 Enoch (Hebrew Manuscript B and Greek LXX only, not on Hebrew Masada Manuscript Mas1h), Noah (Manuscript B and LXX only, reconstructed for Mas1h), Abraham, Isaac, Jacob, Moses
Sir 45 Aaron, Phineas, David
Sir 46 Joshua, Caleb, "the judges", Samuel
Sir 47 Nathan, David, Solomon, Rehoboam, Jeroboam
Sir 48 Elijah, Elisha (LXX only, B damaged, Mas1h not extant), Hezekiah, Isaiah (LXX only, B damaged, Mas1h not extant)
Sir 49 Josiah, Jeremiah, Ezekiel, Job (B only, not in LXX, Mas1h not extant), "the twelve prophets", Zerubbabel (LXX only, B damaged, Mas1h not extant), Jeshua (LXX only, B damaged, Mas1h not extant), Nehemiah, Enoch, Joseph, Shem, Seth, Enosh (B only, not in LXX, Mas1h not extant), Adam
Sir 50 Simon the Priest, Phineas (Hebrew only, not in LXX)

Enoch is mentioned twice in Sir 44 and Sir 49 in the Hebrew Manuscript B and the Greek Septuagint, in both cases as the very first figure mentioned in the "Praise of the Ancestors", while the first mention of Enoch is missing in the Hebrew Masada Manuscript (Mas1h) which is damaged there (see Chapter 6.2.1 for details). Where Elisha, Isaiah, Zerubbabel, and Jeshua are mentioned in the Septuagint of Sir 48–49^{LXX}, the Hebrew Manuscript B is damaged and the Masada Manuscript is not extant. Unlike the Septuagint, the Hebrew Manuscript B mentions Job and Enosh, placing Job between Ezekiel and the twelve prophets (see Chapter 6.5.1 for details).

All differences between Sir 44–50 and the Hebrew Bible are usually explained as Ben Sira's intentional deviations from the Hebrew Bible.[93] Even scholars arguing for a chronological rather than canonical order of figures in Ben Sira's "Praise of the Ancestors" still refer to Ben Sira's knowledge of the canon[94] or most books included in it.[95] Explanations about intentional deviations are usually based on a comparison of the Hebrew Bible with Ben Sira (rather than the other way round). Any similarities are then explained through Ben Sira's knowledge of the Hebrew Bible, whereas differences are explained through Ben Sira's own thinking. For example, BEENTJES writes on Sir 50:24:

"This unique word combination which occurs nowhere else in the entire Old Testament is a creation of Ben Sira himself."[96]

On Sir 44:20, BEENTJES' reference point also is the Hebrew Bible only:

---

[93] Thus e.g. CRENSHAW 1997a, 631. The differences are also sometimes explained through secondary insertions of passages such as Sir 49:14–16, cf. LIM 2013, 104–105, but there is no manuscript evidence for this. On LIM's appendix 5, a list of "Scriptural References in Sirach 44–50", see Chapter 1 Note 211.

[94] Cf. STEINMANN 1999, 38–39; CHAPMAN 2000, 260.

[95] Cf. CARR 2011, 163, 192–193, 344–345.

[96] BEENTJES 2006h, 129.

132   *5. Ben Sira 44–50: Survey*

"That this must be a *deliberate* reference appears from the fact that the collocation [...] is found nowhere in the Hebrew Bible".[97]

Similarly, REITERER writes on the mention of Aaron in Sir 45:

"it is particularly interesting when Ben Sira leaves the firmly established paths and creates new emphases. In order to collect these elements specific to Ben Sira, the statements in Sir 45:6–22 will here be compared with the references from the TaNaK."[98]

BEENTJES and REITERER thus compare Ben Sira only with today's Hebrew Bible, arguing that he knew the Hebrew Bible and added his own creation to it.[99] However, arguments that Ben Sira's description of figures is based on the Hebrew Bible only while every difference is Ben Sira's own creation are in danger of circular reasoning. Such circular reasoning is sometimes rather explicit. In Sir 45:25–26, a blessing in the second person plural is found which seems to mark a division in the "Praise of the Ancestors". GOSHEN-GOTTSTEIN, having stated that Sir 50 is not a part of the "Praise of the Ancestors",[100] interprets this blessing as a break between references to the two canonical parts "Torah" and "Prophets":

"An examination of what precedes this transition point and of what follows it reveals an obvious fact: the transition occurs at the point at which Ben Sira concludes his reference to personalities of whom we hear in the Torah, and before he embarks on a description of personalities of whom we hear in the prophetic corpus. The transition point thus reflects the transition from Torah to Prophets, the two parts of the canon, known to have existed in Ben Sira's times. Once we become aware of the canonical dimension of the arrangement of the Praise, many other facts corroborate the canonical concerns of the Praise."[101]

Here, the assumption of a bipartite canon "known to have existed in Ben Sira's times" explicitly forms the basis of noticing a canon in Ben Sira as an "obvious fact".[102] While GOSHEN-GOTTSTEIN also explicitly mentions similarities between Sir 44–49 and Sir 50,[103] he does not see the description of Simon in Sir 50 as a part of the "Praise of the Ancestors", but as a reflection of a closed canon.[104] This seems to be a form of circular reasoning, presupposing a closed bipartite

---

[97] BEENTJES 2008, 222. Cf. for another example BEENTJES 2008, 214–215, on the mention of Abraham in Sir 44:19–20: "In a rather creative way, Ben Sira has deviated from the 'canonical' order in which major themes of the Abraham cycle are found in the Book of Genesis and has rearranged them in a quite surprising new composition. [...] The lines referring to Genesis 17, in fact, enclose two cola which can by no means be traced back to specific biblical passages and therefore should be considered Ben Sira's own creation". This restriction to the Hebrew Bible also applies to BEENTJES' concept of a "structural use of scripture", cf. BEENTJES 2008, 214–215.

[98] REITERER 2011a, 29.

[99] Cf. also VAN DER KOOIJ 2010, 59–60.

[100] Cf. GOSHEN-GOTTSTEIN 2002, 236.

[101] GOSHEN-GOTTSTEIN 2002, 241.

[102] Cf. also GOSHEN-GOTTSTEIN 2002, 250.

[103] Cf. GOSHEN-GOTTSTEIN 2002, 262–263.

[104] Cf. GOSHEN-GOTTSTEIN 2002, 260–261; GUILLAUME 2005, 18 (referring to GOSHEN-GOTTSTEIN 2002).

5.5 Figures and the Question of Quotation

133

canon of Law and Prophets and then finding it in Sir 44–49 excluding Sir 50. GOSHEN-GOTTSTEIN himself criticizes such a circular approach.[105] On the one hand, GOSHEN-GOTTSTEIN states that "Ben Sira describes the contents of the entire prophetic corpus",[106] implying the corpus of today's Hebrew Bible. But at the same time, GOSHEN-GOTTSTEIN notes:

"Once it is recognized that Ben Sira's interests focus on a description of the canon, it is possible to view the mention of Job in this section as indication that the book of Job was part of the prophetic corpus, possibly even in the location assigned by Ben Sira. [...] I prefer to understand the reference to Job as growing out of its canonical context, rather than out of his mention in Ezek 14."[107]

The contradictory statements show the difficulty of applying the concept of "canon" (see Chapter 1.3) to Ben Sira: according to GOSHEN-GOTTSTEIN, the closed canon of the Hebrew Bible underlies Sir 44–49, but at the same time this canon may have been different at the time of Ben Sira and thus not closed.

Such problems of anachronisms have been noted, for example, by GRABBE who points out that assuming a canon at Ben Sira's time is problematic:

"The variety of Israelite and Judaic traditions needs to be recognized and not seen as if they derived from the Bible. Traditions parallel to the biblical ones – but independent – existed, but did not happen to become canonical or even survive."[108]

According to GRABBE, in Sir 44–50 "Ben Sira's aim was not to demonstrate which books or writings were authoritative for him."[109] Yet nevertheless, GRABBE concludes regarding the "Praise of the Ancestors":

"Ben Sira has listed, paraphrased, and quoted material too parallel to our present canonical text to be coincidental."[110]

However, Ben Sira does not actually quote any material at all. At least some of the same figures are also described in ancient texts not now included in the Hebrew Bible (for example Enoch and the judges, see Chapter 6.2.4 and Chapter 6.3.5). While figures known to us from today's Hebrew Bible do appear in the Book of Ben Sira, there are no lists of books and no explicit quotations at all in the entire book. The one possible exception is Sir 48:10 which is discussed in the following section.

---

[105] Thus GOSHEN-GOTTSTEIN 2002, 240 n. 14.
[106] GOSHEN-GOTTSTEIN 2002, 251.
[107] GOSHEN-GOTTSTEIN 2002, 242.
[108] GRABBE 2006, 321.
[109] GRABBE 2006, 321.
[110] GRABBE 2006, 327.

134   *5. Ben Sira 44–50: Survey*

5.5.2 Question of Quotation in Sir 48:10

Sir 48:10 is the only verse in the Book of Ben Sira which at first sight seems to contain an explicit quotation. With reference to אליהו "Elijah" who is mentioned in Sir 48:4, Sir 48:10 begins with הכתוב "the one written". In Hebrew on Manuscript B, Sir 48:10 reads:[111]

Sir 48:10	הכתוב נכון לעת להשבית אף	The one written as set for a time to make
	לפנ[י...] להשיב לב אבות על	quiet the anger befo[re ...], to turn back a
	בנים ולהכין ש]בטי ישרא[ל:	heart of fathers to sons, and to set up the tr[ibes of Israe]l.

In Greek, Sir 48:10[LXX] reads with reference to Ηλίας "Elijah" mentioned in Sir 48:1, 4[LXX].[112]

Sir 48:10[LXX]	ὁ καταγραφεὶς ἕτοιμος[113]	The one written ready at appointed times
	εἰς καιροὺς κοπάσαι ὀργὴν	to stop the anger before the wrath, to turn
	πρὸ θυμοῦ, ἐπιστρέψαι	a heart of a father to a son and to restore
	καρδίαν πατρὸς πρὸς υἱὸν καὶ	the tribes of Jacob.
	καταστῆσαι φυλὰς Ιακωβ.	

Usually, by commentators of both Ben Sira[114] and Malachi,[115] this verse in Ben Sira is taken to be a quotation of the end of the Book of Malachi in the Hebrew Bible, Mal 3:23–24 – even though the name Malachi does not appear in the Book of Ben Sira. For example, CRENSHAW writes on Ben Sira:

"In v. 10, Ben Sira uses the formula for citing Scripture, 'it is written,' with reference to Mal 3:23–24".[116]

In the Hebrew Bible, Mal 3:23–24 (Mal 4:5–6 in the numbering of the NRSV) reads as follows:[117]

Mal 3:23	הִנֵּה אָנֹכִי שֹׁלֵחַ לָכֶם אֵת אֵלִיָּה	Look, I, I (am) sending for you the
	הַנָּבִיא לִפְנֵי בּוֹא יוֹם יְהוָה הַגָּדוֹל	prophet Elijah before the coming of the
	וְהַנּוֹרָא:	day of the Lord, the great and feared one.

---

[111] Cf. the transcription by ABEGG in RENDSBURG/BINSTEIN 2013, Manuscript B XVII verso.

[112] Cf. ZIEGLER 1980, 351.

[113] ZIEGLER 1980, 351, here reads ἕτοιμος "ready". RAHLFS/HANHART 2006, Vol. II 468, instead follow manuscripts reading ἐν ἐλεγμοῖς "in punishments".

[114] Cf. PETERS 1913, 412; EBERHARTER 1925, 154; MIDDENDORP 1973, 134; STADELMANN 1980, 200; BEENTJES 1981, 39–40; BEENTJES 1984, 150; SCHRADER 1994, 84, 95; CHAPMAN 2000, 260; SAUER 2000, 327; KAISER 2005, 187; BEENTJES 2006a, 174; WRIGHT 2006a, 320; MCDONALD 2007, 82 n. 27; ZAPFF 2010, 359; KOET 2011, 183; CORLEY 2013, 137; BEENTJES 2017c, 93; STEMBERGER 2019, 36.

[115] Cf. STECK 1991, 140–142; KESSLER 2011, 314; KELLERMANN 2017, 54.

[116] CRENSHAW 1997a, 846.

[117] Cf. ELLIGER/RUDOLPH 1997 [BHS], 1086; GELSTON 2010 [BHQ], 155. The Masoretic accents are not reproduced here.

5.5 Figures and the Question of Quotation

3:24 וְהֵשִׁיב לֵב־אָבוֹת עַל־בָּנִים וְלֵב And he will turn back a heart of fathers to
בָּנִים עַל־אֲבוֹתָם פֶּן־אָבוֹא וְהִכֵּיתִי sons, and a heart of sons to their fathers,
אֶת־הָאָרֶץ חֵרֶם: so that I do not come and strike the earth
(with) destruction.

The Greek verses equivalent to Mal 3:23–24, Mal 3:22–23[LXX], read as follows:[118]

Mal 3:22[LXX]	καὶ ἰδοὺ ἐγὼ ἀποστέλλω ὑμῖν Ηλιαν τὸν Θεσβίτην πρὶν ἐλθεῖν ἡμέραν κυρίου τὴν μεγάλην καὶ ἐπιφανῆ,	And look, I, I send for you Elijah the Tishbite before the coming of the day of the Lord, the great and notable [day],
3:23[LXX]	ὃς ἀποκαταστήσει καρδίαν πατρὸς πρὸς υἱὸν καὶ καρδίαν ἀνθρώπου πρὸς τὸν πλησίον αὐτοῦ μὴ ἔλθω καὶ πατάξω τὴν γῆν ἄρδην.	who will bring back a heart of a father to a son and a heart of a human to his neighbour, so that I do not come and strike the earth completely.

In Hebrew, Mal 3:23–24 and Sir 48:10 share the word לפני "before" and the phrase השיב לב אבות על בנים "turn back a heart of fathers to sons". Different forms of the name "Elijah" are used, אליהו "Elijah" in Sir 48:4 (a form also used in 1–2 Kgs and in 2 Chr in the Hebrew Bible) and אליה "Elijah" in Mal 3:23. Parts of Malachi 3:23–24 are preserved on a manuscript dating to the 2nd half of the 2nd century BCE, 4Q76 (4QXII[a]), in Column IV Lines 16–20. Of the words shared with Sir 48:10, in 4Q76 (4QXII[a]) Column IV only אליהו "Elijah" (in the same form of the name as in Sir 48:4 in contrast to MT) in Line 16 and אבות "fathers" in Line 19 are extant, as well as some rests of לפני "before" in Line 17.[119] In Greek, Mal 3:22–23[LXX] shares with Sir 48:10[LXX] the phrase καρδίαν πατρὸς πρὸς υἱὸν "a heart of a father to a son" (preceded by a different verb)[120] with reference to Ηλιας "Elijah" in Sir 48:1, 4[LXX] and Mal 3:22[LXX].[121]

In terms of content, according to Sir 48:10 Elijah has three tasks: to stop the anger, to turn back a heart of fathers to sons, and to set up the tribes of Israel. Only the second task, to turn back a heart of fathers to sons, appears in Mal 3:23–24.[122] The first and third task do not appear in Mal 3:23–24. The Book of Malachi does not even use the words שבת "to quiet", אף "anger, שבט "tribe", or the verb כון "to set" anywhere at all. As it is not found in Mal 3:23–24, the third task is frequently explained as a reference to Isa 49:6.[123]

---

[118] Cf. RAHLFS/HANHART 2006, Vol. II 565.

[119] Cf. FULLER 1997, 228. 4Q76 (4QXII[a]) is dated to around 150–125 BCE, cf. FULLER 1997, 221.

[120] Due to the different verb, BEENTJES 2017c, 98, and KELLERMANN 2017, 55, regard a reference in Greek from Sir 48:10[LXX] the Mal 3:22–23[LXX] as unlikely.

[121] Θεσβείτης "Tishbite" in Mal 3:22[LXX] is not shared with Sir 48:10[LXX].

[122] This is also noted by BEENTJES 2006d, 215 (see Note 131); KOET 2011, 183.

[123] Cf. PETERS 1913, 412; MIDDENDORP 1973, 135; STADELMANN 1980, 200; BEENTJES 1984, 152; STECK 1991, 140–142; SCHRADER 1994, 83; ÖHLER 1997, 7; KAISER 2005, 187; ZAPFF 2010,

136   *5. Ben Sira 44–50: Survey*

In Isa 49:6, the word שֵׁבֶט "tribe" appears in the servant's task of raising up the tribes of Jacob. Again, the similarities between Sir 48:10 and Isa 49:6 are not actually that many. In Hebrew, Isa 49:6 contains as the servant's task לְהָקִים אֶת־שִׁבְטֵי יַעֲקֹב "to raise up the tribes of Jacob". This shares with Sir 48:10 the word שֵׁבֶט "tribe" (partly reconstructed in Sir 48:10 and followed by the recon-structed word יִשְׂרָאֵל "Israel") as well as a hiphil infinitive (להכין "to set up" in Sir 48:10 and להקים "to raise up" in Isa 49:6). כון "to set" and שֵׁבֶט "tribe" are not combined anywhere in the Hebrew Bible. In Hebrew in the Dead Sea Scrolls, Isa 49:6 is preserved on 1QIsaᵃ, 1Q8 (1QIsaᵇ), and 4Q58 (4QIsaᵈ).[124] In 1QIsaᵃ, the task in Isa 49:6 is להקים את שבטי ישראל "to raise up the tribes of Israel",[125] sharing שֹׁ[בטי ישרא]ל "tribes of Israel" but not כון "to set up" with Sir 48:10. In 1Q8 (1QIsaᵇ), the expression reads ב[...] ב את שבטי יעקב "[...] the tribes of Jacob".[126] In 4Q58 (4QIsaᵈ), only להקים את "to raise up the" is preserved in Column 4, Line 12.[127] In Greek in Isa 49:6ᴸˣˣ, the equivalent is στῆσαι τὰς φυλὰς Ιακωβ "to put up the tribes of Jacob". This shares φυλὰς Ιακωβ "tribes of Jacob" and a verb related to στῆσαι "to put up" with Sir 48:10ᴸˣˣ. The Book of Ben Sira itself con-tains the task of setting up the tribes of Jacob as God's task: in Hebrew, Sir 36:13 asks of God: אסוף כל שבטי יעקב "gather all tribes of Jacob!".[128] The equivalent in the Greek Sir 36:10ᴸˣˣ reads συνάγαγε πάσας φυλὰς Ιακωβ "gather all tribes of Jacob!". In the Greek Septuagint, the combination φυλὰς Ιακωβ "tribes of Jacob" only appears in Isa 49:6ᴸˣˣ and in Sir 36:10; 48:10ᴸˣˣ. Sometimes, the third task is seen as a refence to this earlier passage in the Book of Ben Sira.[129] But mostly, a reference is seen to Isa 49:6. This is then sometimes taken to prove Ben Sira's knowledge of the Hebrew Bible. For example, GUILLAUME writes on Sir 48:10:

"this [...] has a canonical explanation: it combines oracles from Isa. 49:10 [sic, meaning Isa 49:6] and Mal. 3:23–24 and applies them to Elijah in order to tie up the last book of the Former Prophets (Kings) with the first and the last of the Latter Prophets (Isaiah and Malachi). This *inclusio* suggests that the juxtaposition of the prophetic books and the 'his-torical' ones into one collection is recent".[130]

359; KESSLER 2011, 314; KOET 2011, 183; CORLEY 2013, 137; BEENTJES 2017c, 94; KELLERMANN 2017, 56, 58.

[124] Cf. ULRICH 2002a, 193.

[125] Cf. BURROWS 1950, Plate XLI, Line 3. 1QIsaᵃ is dated to around 125–100 BCE, cf. WEB-STER 2002, 365.

[126] Cf. SUKENIK 1955, Pl. 8. The letter ב points to neither כון "to set up" nor קום "to raise up". 1Q8 (1QIsaᵇ) is dated to around 50–25 BCE, cf. WEBSTER 2002, 402.

[127] Cf. SKEHAN/ULRICH 1997b, 80. The manuscript 4Q58 (4QIsaᵈ) is dated to the middle of the 1ˢᵗ century CE, cf. SKEHAN/ULRICH 1997b, 76.

[128] Sir 36:13 in RENDSBURG/BINSTEIN 2013, Manuscript B VI verso, equals Sir 36:11 in BEENTJES 1997, 62.

[129] Cf. WRIGHT 2006a, 320. In contrast, BEENTJES 2006d, 215, notes the occurrence in Ben Sira, but argues for a reference to Isa 49:6 (see Note 131).

[130] GUILLAUME 2005, 9–10 (emphasis in original).

5.5 Figures and the Question of Quotation

Here, Sir 48:10 is compared by GUILLAUME with today's Hebrew Bible only, not even with the other passages in the Book of Ben Sira itself. This limited comparison is then taken as a proof that Ben Sira knew the whole Former and Latter Prophets of today's Hebrew Bible in their canonical order. There is a danger of circular reasoning here, which can also be found in the argument presented by BEENTJES:

"At the end of the Elijah pericope, Ben Sira surprisingly adds another interesting perspective of his own. For in 48:10c he quotes only the *first half* of Mal 3:24a ('to turn the hearts of the fathers to their children'). The remainder from this verse in Malachi ('and the children to their parents') is left out; instead of it we find: 'and to restore the tribes of Israel' (48:10d), a phrase that is still dependent on *hakkatub* ('it is written') in 48:10a. To what biblical passage, however, does Ben Sira refer? For nowhere in the Hebrew Bible it is said that it is *Elijah* who will restore the tribes of Israel! No doubt Ben Sira hints at Isa 49:6, a line that belongs to the Second Song of the Servant. However, what could be the reason that Ben Sira does not quote Isa 49:6 just *literally?* And this is the more remarkable, since the collocation 'the tribes of Jacob' is found elsewhere in his book (36: 11 [33: 13a Gr.])!"[131]

Here, BEENTJES uses as the basis for his argument of a reference to Isa 49:6 the assumption that הכתוב "the one written" has to refer to a "biblical passage", a text "in the Hebrew Bible". Even though BEENTJES notes that the Book of Ben Sira itself includes the same phrase, the possibility that the reference is to a text outside the Hebrew Bible, such as the Book of Ben Sira itself, is not considered.[132]

When looking beyond the Hebrew Bible, Mal 3:23–24 is far from the only text sharing a number of words in the same forms and order as well as some content with Sir 48:10. Shared with Sir 48:10, the combination אבות על בנים "fathers to sons" also appears in 4Q521 (4QMessianic Apocalypse) on Fragment 2, Column III, Line 2, preceded in the same line by נכון "set", and followed in Line 6 by a partly reconstructed singular form of [ו]שבט "[his] sceptre" or "[his] tribe".[133] It is sometimes argued that this passage also refers to Elijah, but this name is not actually mentioned on the preserved parts of 4Q521.[134] The manuscript 4Q521 is dated to the first quarter of the 1st century BCE around 100–80 BCE, its content to the second half of the 2nd century BCE.[135] In addition, there are other texts about Elijah. The name אליה "Elijah" appears on 4Q558 (4QpapVision^b ar) on Fragment 51, Column II, Line 4, where Elijah is sent, possibly "before" something, but the end of the line is not preserved, and the context does not include any of

---

[131] BEENTJES 2006d, 215 (emphases in original). The same argument is found in BEENTJES 1984, 152.

[132] Cf. similarly BEENTJES 2017c, 97.

[133] Cf. PUECH 1998, 18–19. SCARSO 2020, 242, states based on this expression that "there is an indubitable reference with Malachi 3:24". שבט in 4Q521 (4QMessianic Apocalypse) is sometimes translated as "tribe" due to Sir 48:10, cf. SCARSO 2020, 238–239.

[134] Cf. PUECH 1998, 19–20 (Elijah, Moses, or another figure); SCARSO 2020, 237 (Elijah).

[135] Cf. PUECH 1998, 5, 37.

138 *5. Ben Sira 44–50: Survey*

the tasks in Sir 48:10.[136] The manuscript 4Q558 is dated around the middle of the 1st century BCE.[137] אליה "Elijah" also appears on 4Q382 (4Qpap paraKings et al.), a manuscript dated to around 75 BCE, in a fragmentary context mentioning kings which does not include any of the tasks in Sir 48:10.[138] In the later New Testament, Luke 1:17 contains a tradition about Elijah which is similar to Sir 48:10.[139] In Luke 1:17, the angel Gabriel tells Zechariah that he will have a son and call him John. Gabriel then says about John (the Baptist):[140]

| Luke 1:17 | καὶ αὐτὸς προελεύσεται ἐνώπιον αὐτοῦ ἐν πνεύματι καὶ δυνάμει Ἡλίου, ἐπιστρέψαι καρδίας πατέρων ἐπὶ τέκνα καὶ ἀπειθεῖς ἐν φρονήσει δικαίων, ἑτοιμάσαι κυρίῳ λαὸν κατεσκευασμένον. | And he will go ahead before him in the spirit and power of Elijah, to turn back hearts of fathers to children and disobedient ones to the understanding of righteous ones, to make ready for the Lord a prepared people. |

Luke 1:17 shares with Sir 48:10^{LXX} the form ἐπιστρέψαι "to turn back", while καρδίας πατέρων ἐπὶ τέκνα "hearts of fathers to children" uses plural forms for fathers and children like the Hebrew Sir 48:10.[141] It is also sometimes argued that the task of gathering the tribes of Jacob in Sir 48:10 also appears in the Mishnah in Eduyyot 8:7.[142] However, Eduyyot 8:7 does not explicitly mention tribes of Israel or Jacob, and may refer to other groups such as families.[143]

The participle הכתוב "the one written" in Sir 48:10 is usually seen as proof for a quotation.[144] However, WRIGHT points out that the participle הכתוב "the one written" stands in a row of participles all referring to Elijah.[145] WRIGHT then argues that this participle also refers to Elijah as a person and can be translated as follows:

"The one who is certainly appointed (or enrolled) for the time".[146]

---

[136] Cf. PUECH 2009a, 215–218. SCARSO 2020, 246, states that "there is a mention of Malachi 3:23 in which Elijah will be sent before the 'Day of the Lord.'". However, such a text is not extant in 4Q558 (4QpapVision^b ar), cf. PUECH 2009a, 215–220.

[137] Cf. PUECH 2009a, 181.

[138] Cf. OLYAN 1994, 363, 365.

[139] Thus WRIGHT 1989, 210–211, 303 n. 183 (Sir 48:10 depends on a variant of Mal 3:23–24); KOET 2011, 185, 187 (both Sir 48:10 and Luke 1:17 depend on Mal 3:23–24). The passage is also noted by KAISER 2005, 187.

[140] Cf. NESTLE-ALAND 2012, 178.

[141] This is also noted by WRIGHT 1989, 303 n. 183; KOET 2011, 185.

[142] Thus SNAITH 1974, 240.

[143] Thus MÜLLER 2005, 90 n. 59.

[144] Thus BEENTJES 1984, 152; SCHRADER 1994, 82–84 (the quotation is an exception in Sir and does not indicate the existence of a canon).

[145] Thus WRIGHT 1989, 210, 302 n. 181–182 (referring to BEENTJES 1981, 39–40, who argues for a double function of the participle including a scriptural reference); WRIGHT 2006a, 320 (in addition arguing for "practically a citation" of Mal 3:24); WRIGHT 2013b, 2340 (in addition arguing for Mal 3:23–24 as the "biblical background" of Sir 48:10).

[146] WRIGHT 2006a, 320. Cf. similarly WRIGHT 2013b, 2340.

5.5 Figures and the Question of Quotation

Indeed, כתב "to write" can also mean "to record", "to enrol", "to register" with reference to persons.[147] While in the Dead Sea Scrolls כתוב "written" in combinations such as כאשר כתוב "as what is written" or ככתוב "as written" is used to mark quotations,[148] with an article הכתוב "the one written" it most often refers to records of persons.[149] The Rule of the Community 1QS uses כתב "to write" in 1QS 5:23 for the process of recording community members in the order of their ranks.[150] 1QS 6:10–11 then forbids every man to speak לפני תכונו הכתוב לפניו "before his rank, the one recorded before him".[151] 1QS 6:26 lines out punishment for a man's wrong behaviour against רעהו הכתוב לפניהו "his companion recorded before him".[152] 1QS 7:2 mentions הכוהנים הכתובים בספר "the priests recorded in the book".[153] Similarly, 4Q265 (4QMiscellaneous Rules) Fragment 4 Column I Line 7 contains רעהו הכתוב לפניו "his companion recorded before him" in the context of punishments for persons.[154] 4Q265 (4QMiscellaneous Rules) even uses כתוב "written" on Fragment 1 Line 3 in כתוב בס]פר[ישעיה הנביא "written in the bo[ok] of Isaiah the prophet",[155] but הכתוב "the one written" for the rank of a person on Fragment 4 Column I Line 7.[156] 4Q279 (4QFour Lots) Fragment 5 Line 2 reads ר]עֵֹהֹוּ הכתוֹב אחרי]וֹ["his [com]panion recorded after [him]".[157] Two further occurrences of הכתוב "the one written" in Dead Sea Scrolls refer to promises of life for persons: 4Q504 (4QDibHam^a) Fragment 1–2 recto Column VI Line 14 mentions persons recorded in the "book of life", שם כול הכתוב בספר החֹיֹֹּים "the name of everyone that is written in the book of li[fe]".[158] 1QIsa^a with Isa 4:3 also refers to persons, כל הכתוב לחיים "everyone written for life".[159] References to documents rather than persons using הכתוב "the one written" are less frequent

---

[147] Cf. CLINES 1998, s. v. כתב.

[148] Cf. METZENTHIN 2013, 457–458.

[149] Cf. *Accordance 13* 2020, words search on ה "the" followed by a form of כתב "to write" in "Qumran Non-biblical Manuscripts" (QUMRAN), "Judean Desert Manuscripts" (JUDEAN-T, Version 3.3), and "Dead Sea Scrolls Biblical Corpus (Manuscript order)" (DSSB-M, Version 3.5).

[150] Cf. QIMRON/CHARLESWORTH 1994, 24–25 (1QS), 74–75 (4Q258 = 4QS^d = 4QS MS D).

[151] Cf. QIMRON/CHARLESWORTH 1994, 28–29. METSO 2019, 34, sees this as part of "an intentional addition", but the manuscript itself does not indicate this, cf. BURROWS 1951, Plate VI.

[152] Cf. QIMRON/CHARLESWORTH 1994, 30–31 (לפנוהי is a misprint there for לפניהו, cf. the photograph and transcription in BURROWS 1951, Plate VI). The Rule of the Community 1QS is dated to around 100–75 BCE, its content to the middle of the 2nd century BCE, cf. QIMRON/ CHARLESWORTH 1994, 2.

[153] Cf. QIMRON/CHARLESWORTH 1994, 30–31.

[154] Cf. BAUMGARTEN 1999, 64–65. No date is given there for the manuscript 4Q265 (4QMiscellaneous Rules).

[155] Cf. BAUMGARTEN 1999, 61–62.

[156] See Note 154.

[157] Cf. ALEXANDER/VERMES 1998, 221. The manuscript 4Q279 (4QFour Lots) is dated to around 30–1 BCE, cf. ALEXANDER/VERMES 1998, 218.

[158] Cf. BAILLET 1982b, 148–149. The manuscript 4Q504 (4QDibHam^a) is dated around 150 BCE, cf. BAILLET 1982b, 137.

[159] Cf. BURROWS 1950, Pl. IV, Line 7–8.

140   5. Ben Sira 44–50: Survey

in the Dead Sea Scrolls: 3Q15 (3QCopper Scroll) Column 12 Line 11, refers to a
copy of itself, a written list of hidden treasures, as משנה הכתוב הזא "a duplicate of
this written one".[160] 4Q29 (4QDeut^b) Fragment 3 Line 14 which contains parts of
Deut 30:10 uses the plural הכּתוּבים "the written ones" for laws which are written
rather than for persons.[161] And in only one text, 11Q13 (11QMelch) Column 2
Line 19, הכתוב "the one written" refers to a person and a written text, but this
is made explicit by the combination הואה הכתוב עליו אשר "he the one written
about him as follows".[162] Overall, in the Dead Sea Scrolls, הכתוב "the one written"
without explicit mentions of written texts refers to records of persons.[163] The
Greek equivalent ὁ καταγραφείς "the one written" can also refer to a person recorded.[164] The verb καταγράφω "to write" in Ancient Greek generally[165] and in
the Septuagint can mean "to record" referring to persons, for example in Num
11:26^LXX.[166] Thus, in both Hebrew and Greek, what at first sight seems to be an
explicit quotation formula is more likely to describe a person as recorded.

Overall, there are five shared words in the same forms and order with Mal
3:24 in Sir 48:10 in Hebrew, three of which also appear in 4Q521 (4QMessianic
Apocalypse) in the same order. There are four shared words in the same forms
and order in Mal 3:23^LXX and Sir 48:10^LXX. The contents differ significantly in
both Hebrew and Greek: only one of Elijah's three tasks is shared between
Mal 3:23–24 in Sir 48:10. The supposed quotation formula refers to a person
as "recorded" rather than a text as "written". Sir 48:10 does not contain a quotation of Mal 3:23–24 combined with a reference to Isa 49:6, proving the textual
authority of Malachi and thus the whole Prophets section of the Hebrew Bible.
Even scholars rejecting an explicit quotation still assume an allusion to Mal
3:23–24 in Sir 48:10.[167] But instead, Sir 48:10 seems to relate to a wider tradition
about Elijah,[168] parts of which such as 4Q558 (4QpapVision^b ar), 4Q382 (4Qpap

---

[160] Cf. MILIK 1962a, 298. The Copper Scroll 3Q15 (3QCopper Scroll) is dated to around 25–75
CE, cf. the excursus by F. M. CROSS in MILIK 1962a, 217.

[161] Cf. DUNCAN 1995, 10–11. The manuscript 4Q29 (4QDeut^b) is dated to around 150–100
BCE, cf. DUNCAN 1995, 9. The MT of Deut 30:10 contains a feminine singular form הכתבה "the
written one".

[162] Cf. GARCÍA MARTÍNEZ/TIGCHELAAR/VAN DER WOUDE 1998c, 224–233, esp. 225.
The manuscript 11Q13 (11QMelch) is dated to around 75–50 BCE, cf. GARCÍA MARTÍNEZ/
TIGCHELAAR/VAN DER WOUDE 1998c, 223.

[163] Similarly, in the Hebrew Bible, ה "the" followed by a form of כתוב "written" is combined
with ספר "book" in 17 out of 20 occurrences (Deut 28:58; 29:19–20, 26; 30:10; Josh 1:8; 8:34;
23:6; 2 Kgs 22:13; 23:3, 24; Jer 25:13; 32:12; 51:60; 2 Chr 34:21, 24, 31), in 1 Chr 16:40 it is
combined with תורה "law". In contrast, without explicit mentions of books, it refers to persons
in Isa 4:3 כל הכתוב לחיים "everyone written for life" and in 1 Chr 4:41 to persons who are named.

[164] Thus WRIGHT 1989, 210; WRIGHT 2006a, 320; PIETERSMA/WRIGHT 2007 (NETS), 759.

[165] Cf. LIDDELL/SCOTT/JONES [1940], s. v. καταγράφω ("to register", "to record", "to enroll").

[166] Cf. LUST/EYNIKEL/HAUSPIE 2003, s. v. καταγράφω ("to enroll").

[167] Thus WRIGHT 1989, 210–211; ÖHLER 1997,7–8.

[168] Cf. similarly HORSLEY 2007, 107 (oral tradition).

paraKings et al.), and Luke 1:17 are still extant today. This wider tradition may also have included Mal 3:23–24 as it is partly preserved on 4Q76 (4QXII^a), but this is neither clearly nor necessarily the case. Mal 3:23–24 only shares a small part of the content of Sir 48:10, and both words and contents shared between Mal 3:23–24 and Sir 48:10 are also shared between Sir 48:10 and other extant texts. In any case, Mal 3:23–24 is not quoted in Sir 48:10 or referred to as an authoritative text in any way.

5.5.3 Beyond the Hebrew Bible

The problem underlying the supposed quotation in Sir 48:10 and the supposed references based on the order of figures in Sir 44–50 is pointed out by HORSLEY:

"The problem may be rooted in the limitations of established biblical studies. Given its root in modern print culture and its dedication to the interpretation of the Scriptures (sacred *writings*), biblical studies tends to focus almost exclusively on written texts. We have tended to assume that Judean culture was virtually identical with the books of the Hebrew Bible. Unable to imagine a figure or a motif or a story that we know in a given book as having existed independently of that book (such as the legend of the giants in Gen. 6:1–4), we assume that its presence in a 'later' text (such as *1 Enoch*) must be a reference to or an interpretation of the 'earlier' or 'biblical' text (such as Genesis). The appearance of figures such as Abraham, Aaron, Solomon, Elijah, and the Twelve Prophets, and so forth, in the praise of the ancestors in Sirach 44–50 must mean that Ben Sira knew most of the books of the Hebrew Bible. [...] Despite the concerns of modern biblical scholars to find stable, precisely definable writings, the realities of ancient cultural practices were evidently more fluid in their mixture of media, oral and written, and in the definition of what constituted texts, oral and written. We may approach ancient scribal practice more appropriately if we think in terms of a rich repertoire of traditional culture of various distinctive forms that was cultivated (learned and recited and written) in transgenerational scribal circles. [...] Extant written texts constitute our only sources. Yet they are sources for the broader cultural repertory that was not confined to written texts".[169]

Indeed, oral tradition is explicitly mentioned as important in the Book of Ben Sira (see Chapter 2.2.3), and there are extant written texts providing evidence for traditions not included in the Hebrew Bible (see Chapters and 2.2 and 5.5.2).

5.6 Conclusion

The "Praise of the Ancestors" is a praise of figures, not a praise of texts. No reference to any textual authority is found in Sir 44–50. Sir 44–50 once implicitly refers to written texts by introducing the ancestors as readers and writers (see Chapter 2.3.2). The only text explicitly mentioned at all and in the Greek version only is Ben Sira's own book in Sir 50:27^{LXX}. Rather, important figures and

---

[169] HORSLEY 2007, 110–111 (emphases in original).

142   5. *Ben Sira 44–50: Survey*

their deeds are praised, possibly as examples for teaching. While these figures also appear in parts of the Hebrew Bible, their sequence and descriptions show significant differences. Sir 44–50 does not indicate whether knowledge about these figures comes from any texts at all, or oral traditions, or other sources. Using the modern canon of the Hebrew Bible as the only point of comparison leads to circular reasoning: the conclusion that the Hebrew Bible was authoritative for Ben Sira is based on the presupposition that the Hebrew Bible was authoritative for Ben Sira. Instead, the question of textual authority needs to be reassessed on the background of orality and literacy in Ben Sira's times, without limiting the search for possible intertextual references to the Hebrew Bible.

Sir 48:10, rather than quoting an authoritative text, uses the meaning "record" of כתב "to write" to refer to the record of a person, a meaning common in the Dead Sea Scrolls. The words shares some words and one part of its contents with Mal 3:23–24, but also shares words and contents with texts outside the Hebrew Bible, namely 4Q521 (4QMessianic Apocalypse), 4Q558 (4QpapVision^b ar), 4Q382 (4Qpap paraKings et al.), and Luke 1:17.

If Sir 44–50 is compared to the canon of the Hebrew Bible only, figures appearing in the two parts of "Law" and "Prophets" also appear in Sir 44–50, with significant differences, while figures appearing in the "Writings" are much less present in Sir 44–50. But if general criteria for ancient authoritative texts are applied (see Chapter 1.3.6), Sir 44–50 does not explicitly refer to any written texts at all except to itself (Sir 50:27^{LXX}).

6. Ben Sira 44–50: Case Studies

6.1 Selection of Case Studies

Sir 44–50 is often seen to contain intertextual references to the canon of the Hebrew Bible (see Chapter 5.4). This chapter presents five case studies of passages in Sir 44–50 which are are particularly frequently used to argue for canonical references in Sir 44–50: Sir 44:16 and 49:14 (Enoch), Sir 46:11–12 (the judges), Sir 48:17–25 (Isaiah), Sir 49:9 (Job), and Sir 49:10 (the twelve prophets). These five passages are not only argued to contain intertextual references to individual passages now in the Hebrew Bible, but to contain references to whole canonical books. These references to whole canonical books are then used to argue for Ben Sira as referring to a biblical canon: Sir 46:11–12 and Sir 49:10 are highlighted as referring to the whole Books of Judges and the Twelve Prophets.[1] Sir 48:17–25 is seen to contain a reference to the whole Book of Isaiah.[2] Sir 49:9 is argued to refer to the whole Book of Job, although this is debated since the Book of Job its not part of the "Prophets" section in the Hebrew Bible.[3] And, in contrast, Sir 44:16 and 49:14 are usually argued to refer to a particular short passage in Genesis rather than any whole Book of Enoch.[4] The selected five case studies also cover examples regarding all parts of the canon of the Hebrew Bible – Law (Enoch), Prophets (Former Prophets: Judges; Latter Prophets: Isaiah, Twelve Prophets) and Writings (Job) – as well as extant literature outside the Hebrew Bible (Enoch).

In both Hebrew and Greek, the five passages are compared to texts both in and beyond the Hebrew Bible in order to assess possible intertextual references (see Chapter 1.4). While a similar analysis of many more case studies and ultimately all of Sir 44–50 would be desirable in future research, the five case studies selected here serve to answer the main question of the present study: whether Ben Sira refers to a canon of the Hebrew Bible. This chapter provides a comparative analysis of the passages Sir 44:16 and 49:14, Sir 46:11–12, Sir 48:17–25, Sir

---

[1] See Chapter 4.5. For further references see Chapter 6.3.2 on the Book of Judges and Chapter 6.6.2 on the Book of the Twelve Prophets.

[2] For references see Chapter 6.4.2 on the Book of Isaiah.

[3] For references see Chapter 6.5.2 on the Book of Job.

[4] For references see Chapter 6.2.2 on Genesis 5:21–24.

144 6. *Ben Sira 44–50: Case Studies*

49:9, and Sir 49:10 in Hebrew and Greek, and a detailed assessment of previously assumed canonical references with systematic comparisons of each passage with the Hebrew Bible, the Greek Septuagint, the Dead Sea Scrolls, and the Book of Ben Sira itself, using equal standards for all of these comparisons.

6.2 Enoch (Sir 44:16; 49:14)

6.2.1 Hebrew and Greek Text

In the Hebrew Manuscript B and the Greek Septuagint, Enoch appears twice in the Book of Ben Sira. In Manuscript B, the two verses on Enoch read:[5]

Sir 44:16	חנוך נִמְצָא תמים והתהלך עם ייי וְלֻקח אות דעת לדור ודור:	Enoch was found blameless, and he was walking with YYY, and he was taken as a sign of knowledge from generation to generation.
Sir 49:14	מעט נוצר על הארץ כהניך וגם הוא נלקח פנים:	Little was created on the earth like [E]n[o]ch and also he was taken up regarding the face.

The Greek version of the same verses reads:[6]

Sir 44:16[LXX]	Ενωχ εὐηρέστησεν κυρίῳ καὶ μετετέθη[7] ὑπόδειγμα μετανοίας ταῖς γενεαῖς.	Enoch was pleasing to the Lord and was transferred, an example of repentance for the generations.
Sir 49:14[LXX]	Οὐδεὶς ἐκτίσθη ἐπὶ τῆς γῆς τοιοῦτος οἷος Ενωχ· καὶ γὰρ αὐτὸς ἀνελήμφθη ἀπὸ τῆς γῆς.	No one was created on the earth such as one of the sort of Enoch, for he himself was taken up from the earth.

In Hebrew, the Masada Manuscript (Mas1h) differs from Manuscript B. In the Masada Manuscript which preserves only parts of Sir 44, the first of the two mentions of Enoch is missing. Where Sir 44:16 could follow Sir 44:15, a fragmentary empty line (Column VII Line 23) is found, followed by one more fragmentary line (Column VII Line 24) starting with נִמְצָא תמים "was found blameless". The reconstruction of the Masada Manuscript Column VII Line 24 by Reymond in Rendsburg/Binstein 2013 reads [...]נח צדיק נמצא תמים ב "righteous Noah was found innocent in [...]", including the name of Noah.[8]

---

[5] Cf. the transcription by Abegg in Rendsburg/Binstein 2013, Manuscript B XIII verso, XIX recto.

[6] Cf. Ziegler 1980, 333, 356.

[7] The Latin version adds *in paradiso* "in paradise", cf. Ziegler 1980, 333; *Biblia Sacra* 1964, 340; Weber/Gryson 2007, 1085.

[8] Cf. the transcription by Reymond in Rendsburg/Binstein 2013, Masada Manuscript VII.

6.2 Enoch (Sir 44:16; 49:14)   145

However, on the infrared image of the Masada Manuscript Column VII supplied there, the two first words צדיק נוח "righteous Noah" are not actually preserved.[9] The same applies to the colour photograph in the Leon Levy Dead Sea Scrolls Library.[10] The name Noah is only preserved on a separate small fragment placed at the beginning of Line 24 in the edition by YADIN.[11] If the fragment was placed elsewhere, נמצא תמים "was found blameless" could refer to Enoch as well as Noah: in Manuscript B, נמצא תמים "was found blameless" is used for Enoch in Sir 44:16 as well as for Noah in Sir 44:17.[12] The following letter ב is an argument for a reference to Noah only if the marginal correction בעת "in the time" after the mention of Noah in Manuscript B is read instead of the manuscript's main text לעת "at the time".[13] The Masada Manuscript breaks off after Column VII Line 24 or 25.[14] Some scholars take the lack of a first mention of Enoch in the Masada Manuscript and a double mention of Enoch in Sir 44:16 and 49:14 as an indication that the first mention may not be original at all,[15] or was originally placed with Sir 49:14.[16] The first person mentioned in the "Praise of the Ancestors" would then be Noah rather than Enoch.[17] But the fragmentary evidence of the Masada Manuscript does not suffice to prove an intentional omission of Enoch.[18] The empty line could simply result from a copying error.[19] A double mention of figures appears elsewhere in Sir 44–50: other figures, especially David[20] but also Phineas, are mentioned twice.[21]

In the Hebrew Manuscript B, חנוך "Enoch" is mentioned in Sir 44:16. In Sir 49:14, Manuscript B reads כהניך. This is usually translated as "like Enoch", conjecturally taking הניך as an alternative spelling of חנוך "Enoch"[22] combined with

---

[9] Cf. the infrared image of Maslh VII by the Israel Antiquities Authority (Leon Levy Dead Sea Scrolls Digital Library) in RENDSBURG/BINSTEIN 2013, Masada Manuscript VII.

[10] Cf. ISRAEL ANTIQUITIES AUTHORITY 2013.

[11] Cf. YADIN 1999, 208 (= Plate 7), 210 (= Plate 8).

[12] Cf. the transcription by ABEGG in RENDSBURG/BINSTEIN 2013, Manuscript B XIV recto.

[13] This is also noted by LÜHRMANN 1975, 108–109. KVANVIG 1988, 121–123, argues that there must have been two Hebrew versions, one without and one with Enoch.

[14] Cf. YADIN 1999, 208 (= Plate 7); RENDSBURG/BINSTEIN 2013, Masada Manuscript VII.

[15] Thus SKEHAN/DI LELLA 1987, 499 (possibly later expansion due to the popularity of Enoch); BEENTJES 2006h, 130–132; CORLEY 2013, 125 (possibly not original), 141. SKEHAN/DI LELLA and BEENTJES also note that this verse with the first mention of Enoch is missing in Syriac, but it is present in both Greek (cf. ZIEGLER 1980, 333) and Latin (cf. Biblia Sacra 1964, 340; WEBER/GRYSON 2007, 1085).

[16] Thus YADIN 1999, 196 (sign for generations originally in Sir 49); against this view cf. ARGALL 1995, 10.

[17] Thus BEENTJES 2006h, 132.

[18] Thus also LARSON 2005, 85.

[19] Thus VanderKam 1995, 105–106; WRIGHT 1997, 215; WRIGHT 2013b, 2328.

[20] This is also noted by MARBÖCK 1995d, 134.

[21] See Chapter 5.3.4.

[22] Cf. GESENIUS 2013, s. v. חֲנוֹךְ.

146　　　　　　　　　　6. Ben Sira 44–50: Case Studies

the preposition כ "like". However, it could also be read as כהניך "your priests"[23] (a plural form of כהן "priest" with a second person singular suffix).[24] MULDER translates it as "your priesthood", taking the plural form as a "plural of abstraction".[25] However, a "plural of abstraction" is not found elsewhere for כהן "priest".[26] Further, it is unclear to whom a second person singular suffix could refer as Ben Sira's audience is elsewhere addressed in the second person plural (for example in Sir 45:25–26),[27] and to whom הוא "he" as someone who is נלקח "taken" (a niphal form of לקח "to take" used in Manuscript B for Enoch in Sir 44:16 and for Elijah in Sir 48:9) then refers. Grammatically, the last figure mentioned prior to the pronoun הוא "he", Nehemiah, could be adressed with "you" in the second person suffix and then immediately referred to with הוא "he". However, no other sources about Nehemiah exist where he is "taken".[28] Overall, the explanation of הניך as representing חנוך "Enoch" seems most plausible.[29]

The "Praise of the Ancestors" Sir 44–50 thus begins, in Hebrew at least on Manuscript B as in Greek, with Enoch as its first named figure in Sir 44:16. Enoch is mentioned again in Sir 49:14 after Nehemiah (Sir 49:13), followed by Joseph, Shem, Seth, Enosh (in Hebrew only), and Adam (Sir 49:15–16), and finally the High Priest Simon (Sir 50:1). The mention of Enoch in Sir 44:16 and Sir 49:14 is frequently interpreted as forming a frame around the "Praise of the Ancestors", with the second mention placed at the beginning of a passage outside a previous chronological order to mark the transition to the praise of the High Priest Simon.[30]

6.2.2 References to Genesis 5:21–24?

Sir 44:16 and Sir 49:14 are usually seen to refer to Gen 5:21–24.[31] Few scholars note that aspects such as the "sign" are not found in Genesis but other ancient texts about Enoch such as 1 Enoch,[32] and that references to such texts are also

---

[23] Cf. MULDER 2003, 93.

[24] Cf. GESENIUS 2013, s. v. כֹּהֵן.

[25] Thus MULDER 2003, 93.

[26] Cf. for "plural of abstraction" GESENIUS/KAUTZSCH 1909, § 124a–f; JOÜON/MURAOKA 2011, § 136g–i.

[27] See Chapter 5.3.4. MULDER 2003, 94, nevertheless takes the singular suffix as referring to the audience.

[28] Cf. TÅNGBERG 1994, 245.

[29] Thus also RYSSEL 1900, 467; VANDERKAM 1995, 107; WITTE 2006, 142.

[30] Thus BOX/OESTERLEY 1913, 506; ZAPFF 2010, 373; BECKER/FABRY/REITEMEYER 2011, 2262

[31] Thus BOX/OESTERLEY 1913, 482, 506; SKEHAN/DI LELLA 1987, 499, 545; WRIGHT 1997, 215–217; KAISER 2005, 185, 188; GRABBE 2006, 327 ("Ben Sira seems to know about Enoch through the biblical text."); ZAPFF 2010, 320, 373; CORLEY 2013, 12, 141. GOFF 2018, 185, argues that the Greek text is more similar to Gen 5:24 than the Hebrew, in a "secondary biblicization".

[32] Thus VANDERKAM 1995, 107. Others scholars such as also note a similarity between Sir 16:7 and 1 En 6–11 (Book of Watchers) against Genesis 6 regarding the punishment of leaders

possible.[33] However, even where similarities with Enochic literature are noted, the similarities with Genesis are still thought to be the only direct references,[34] or at least the stronger ones.[35] This is the case even where the anachronism of a biblical canon is explicitly acknowledged.[36] Only rarely is 1 Enoch seen as authoritative for Ben Sira.[37] However, it seems that a double standard is applied to texts now in the Hebrew Bible or outside it. The following section of the present study compares possible references to texts both in and beyond the Hebrew Bible.

6.2.3 Comparison with the Hebrew Bible and the Greek Septuagint

Gen 5:21–24 is the only place in the Hebrew Bible where both Enoch's name[38] and a description of his actions are found:[39]

Gen 5:21	וַיְחִי חֲנוֹךְ חָמֵשׁ וְשִׁשִּׁים שָׁנָה וַיּוֹלֶד אֶת־מְתוּשָׁלַח:	And Enoch lived sixty-five years, and he fathered Methuselah.
5:22	וַיִּתְהַלֵּךְ חֲנוֹךְ אֶת־הָאֱלֹהִים אַחֲרֵי הוֹלִידוֹ אֶת־מְתוּשֶׁלַח שְׁלֹשׁ מֵאוֹת שָׁנָה וַיּוֹלֶד בָּנִים וּבָנוֹת:	And Enoch walked with God after his fathering of Methuselah three hundred years, and he fathered sons and daughters.
5:23	וַיְהִי כָּל־יְמֵי חֲנוֹךְ חָמֵשׁ וְשִׁשִּׁים שָׁנָה וּשְׁלֹשׁ מֵאוֹת שָׁנָה:	And all the days of Enoch were[40] three hundred and sixty-five years.
5:24	וַיִּתְהַלֵּךְ חֲנוֹךְ אֶת־הָאֱלֹהִים וְאֵינֶנּוּ כִּי־לָקַח אֹתוֹ אֱלֹהִים:	And Enoch walked with God, and he was not, because God took him.

(Hebrew Sir 16:7) or giants (Greek Sir 16:7[LXX]), cf. WRIGHT 2012, 376, 385 (also see Chapter 1 Note 210); assuming an allusion to 1 Enoch in Sir 16:7 KVANVIG 2011, 336–338; with a negative view of Enochic literature by SKEHAN/DI LELLA 1987, 270 and VANDERKAM 1995, 107; assuming a a more general knowledge of "early Jewish traditions" GOFF 2010, 655. For 1 En 6–11 cf. the translation NICKELSBURG/VANDERKAM 2012b, 23–31.

[33] Thus SNAITH 1974, 217; MARBÖCK 1995d, 135–137; KVANVIG 2011, 339. Also cf. WRIGHT 2012, 385 (see Chapter 1 Note 210).

[34] Thus HAMP 1951, 120–121; BECKER/FABRY/REITEMEYER 2011, 2251; WITTE 2006, 142–143.

[35] Thus VANDERKAM 1995, 104–105; CRENSHAW 1997a, 842; WRIGHT 1997, 215–217; KVANVIG 2011, 330; CORLEY 2013, 141; WRIGHT 2013b, 2328. ARGALL 1995, 10–11, also notes references to Gen 5:24.

[36] Cf. VANDERKAM 1995, 107, 183. On Enochic literature and its ancient authoritative status cf. VANDERKAM 1995, 183–185.

[37] Thus WITTE 2012a, 247 (Enochic writings possibly authoritative); POPOVIĆ 2010, 8 (1 Enoch authoritative); KNIBB 2010, 145 (Hebrew Bible and 1 Enoch authoritative).

[38] Wis 4:10–11[LXX] (mentioned by CORLEY 2013, 125) does not mention Enoch's name but describes a person being taken up, 1 Chr 1:3 mentions Enoch's name but no actions. The name Enoch is also used in the Hebrew Bible for other figures who are not taken up, e.g. a son of Cain in Gen 4:17–18, cf. HERRMANN 2000, 1626.

[39] Cf. ELLIGER/RUDOLPH 1997 [BHS], 8; TAL 2015 [BHQ], 14. The Masoretic accents are not reproduced here.

[40] The singular form of the verb is sometimes used in Hebrew for a following plural noun, cf. JOÜON/MURAOKA 2011, § 150b. Many Hebrew manuscripts and versions here use a plural verb form, cf. ELLIGER/RUDOLPH 1997 [BHS], 8; TAL 2015 [BHQ], 14, 91*.

148   6. Ben Sira 44–50: Case Studies

In the Greek Septuagint, the same verses read:[41]

Gen 5:21[LXX]   Καὶ ἔζησεν Ενωχ ἑκατὸν   And Enoch lived one hundred and sixty-
                καὶ ἑξήκοντα πέντε ἔτη καὶ   five years[42] and he fathered Methuselah.
                ἐγέννησεν τὸν Μαθουσαλα.

5:22[LXX]   εὐηρέστησεν δὲ Ενωχ τῷ   And Enoch pleased God after he fathered
                θεῷ μετὰ τὸ γεννῆσαι αὐτὸν   Methuselah two hundred years and he
                τὸν Μαθουσαλα διακόσια   fathered sons and daughters.
                ἔτη καὶ ἐγέννησεν υἱοὺς καὶ
                θυγατέρας.

5:23[LXX]   καὶ ἐγένοντο πᾶσαι αἱ ἡμέραι   And all the days of Enoch were three hun-
                Ενωχ τριακόσια ἑξήκοντα   dred and sixty-five years.
                πέντε ἔτη.

5:24[LXX]   καὶ εὐηρέστησεν Ενωχ τῷ   And Enoch pleased God and he was not
                θεῷ καὶ οὐχ ηὑρίσκετο, ὅτι   found, because God transferred him.
                μετέθηκεν αὐτὸν ὁ θεός.

The descriptions of Enoch in Ben Sira and Genesis share two aspects of content: that Enoch walked with or pleased God, and that he was taken by God. In Hebrew, these two aspects also include three shared words: חנוך "Enoch", הלך "to walk" in hithpael forms, and לקח "to take". In Greek, Ενωχ "Enoch" (repeated in every verse of Gen 5:21–24[LXX]) and εὐαρεστέω "to please" are shared. The shared word μετατίθημι "to transfer" is used in Gen 5:24[LXX] and Sir 44:16[LXX], but not in Sir 49:14[LXX] where ἀναλαμβάνω "to take up" is used. In Hebrew, syntactical similarity is limited to the use of the הלך "to walk" in hithpael forms in Sir 44:16 and Gen 5:22, 24 combined with a word for God (יי in Sir 44:16 and אלהים in Gen 5:22, 24). In Greek, forms of εὐαρεστέω "to please" are combined with words for God (κύριος in Sir 44:16, missing in Sir 49:14[LXX]; θεός "God" in Gen 5:22, 24[LXX]). Such combinations are also used in the Hebrew and Greek Book of Genesis in Gen 6:9 for Noah, in Gen 17:1 and Gen 24:40 for Abraham, and in Gen 48:15 for Abraham and Isaac.

   In both words and content, all other aspects of the descriptions of Enoch in Ben Sira differ from Genesis. In Sir 44:16, Enoch is also described as blameless (Hebrew תמים "blameless", missing in Greek), as unique (Hebrew מעט נוצר "little was created", Greek οὐδεὶς ἐκτίσθη "no one was created"),[43] and as a sign of knowledge (Hebrew אות דעת "sign of knowledge") or repentance (Greek ὑπόδειγμα μετανοίας "example of repentance") for generations. All these aspects

        ───────────
        [41] Cf. RAHLFS/HANHART 2006, Vol. I 7.
        [42] On the recurring plus of one hundred years compared to MT cf. PRESTEL/SCHORCH 2011, 165–166.
        [43] Elijah is also taken up in Ben Sira (and in the Hebrew Bible), which leads some commentators, e.g. BOX/OESTERLEY 1913, 506, to see a problem in Enoch's uniqueness here. However, the conjunction connecting Enoch's uniqueness with his being taken could point to his uniqueness as a separate point from his being taken: Enoch was unique and he was taken, not because he was taken.

are not mentioned at all in Genesis. Mentioned in Genesis but not at all in Ben Sira are the 365 years of Enoch's life – counted differently in the Hebrew and Greek versions of Genesis but appearing in both – and Enoch's son Methuselah and other sons and daughters. תמים "blameless" is used in the Hebrew Book of Genesis in Gen 6:9 for Noah and in Gen 17:1 for Abraham, but not for Enoch. Collocations of אות "sign" and דעת "knowledge" or of יצר "to create" and מעט "little" are not used anywhere in the Hebrew Bible, nor a collocation of לקח "to take" and פנה "face". The combination לדור ודור "from generation to generation" is only used regarding the inhabitance of the promised land in Isa 34:17 and Joel 4:20. Similarly, in Greek collocations of ὑπόδειγμα "example" and μετάνοια "repentance", or of οὐδείς "no one" and κτίζω "to create", or ἀναλαμβάνω "to take up" and γῆ "earth" are not used in the Septuagint. Plural forms of γενεά "generation" are used in the passages equivalent to the Hebrew Bible as well as in other passages.

Overall, in Hebrew three individual words and two out of six aspects of content are shared between Sir 44:16; 49:14 and Gen 5:21–24. Most words and contents are not shared with the Hebrew Bible at all, and the case is similar in the Greek Septuagint.

6.2.4 Comparison with the Dead Sea Scrolls

Gen 5:21–24 is not preserved on any of the Dead Sea Scrolls.[44] Rather, the name חנוך "Enoch" is mentioned several times in 1 Enoch and Jubilees (see Chapter 2.2.4) and in other texts among the Dead Sea Scrolls.[45] Words other than the name "Enoch" are also shared between Sir 44:16; 49:14 and the Dead Sea Scrolls generally: for example, combinations of תמים "blameless" and הלך "to walk" in a hithpael form are frequent in the Dead Sea Scrolls.[46]

1 Enoch (for its date and sources see Chapter 2.2.4) shows similarities with Sir 44:16; 49:14 in the parts dated prior or contemporary to Ben Sira: the Book of Watchers (1 En 1–36), the Astronomical Book (1 En 72–82), and the Epistle of Enoch (1 En 91–105).[47] For 1 Enoch, the Dead Sea Scrolls are fragmentary and written in Aramaic rather than Hebrew or Greek, which limits the possibility of

---

[44] Cf. ULRICH 2002a, 185. Only one fragment of a manuscript containing parts of Genesis may predate Ben Sira: 6Q1 (6QpaleoGen), dated to 250–150 BCE and containing parts of Gen 6:13–21 about Noah, cf. BAILLET 1962, 105–106; BAILLET et al. 1962, Pl. XX; WEBSTER 2002, 378. No manuscript among the Dead Sea Scrolls preserves the entire Book of Genesis, cf. ULRICH 2002a, 185–186. On the issue that the Pentateuch is not fixed in the Second Temple Period see Chapter 3 Note 60.

[45] For mentions of the personal name Enoch in the Dead Sea Scrolls cf. ABEGG 2002, 251; for a discussion cf. BAUTCH 2011, 1016–1021.

[46] Cf. STADEL 2011, 782; STRAWN 2016, 1137, 1140–1141.

[47] For other similarities between 1 Enoch and Ben Sira which are not shared with the Hebrew Bible cf. e.g. ARGALL 1995, 230, on Sir 15–16. Also see Chapter 1.4.5.

150   6. Ben Sira 44–50: Case Studies

a comparison of shared words with Ben Sira. However, the ancient Greek translation of 1 Enoch can be compared with that of Ben Sira. Additionally, a comparison of contents is possible in all extant versions. Such a comparison of contents has to be taken with caution as later translations may differ from Aramaic originals which are not extant.[48] The following comparison is based on the ancient Aramaic fragments of 1 Enoch whereever they are available. Where the ancient Greek translation or modern English translations of 1 Enoch (for details see Chapter 2.2.4) are used for additional comparisons, this is explicitly noted.

A direct mention of the name חנוך "Enoch" in 1 En 1:1 is preserved on the Aramaic manuscript 4Q201 (4QEnᵃ ar), Fragment 1, Line 1.[49] This manuscript is dated to the end of the 3ʳᵈ or beginning of the 2ⁿᵈ century BCE and thus into Ben Sira's time.[50] The Greek name Ἐνώχ "Enoch" also appears in the Greek text of 1 En 1:1.[51]

In content, the very same aspects present in Ben Sira but not in Genesis – righteousness, uniqueness, sign of knowledge or repentance for generations – as well the lack of aspects present only in Genesis – Enoch's 365 years and his daughters – are also found 1 Enoch.

Enoch's righteousness is a topic expressed at the very beginning of 1 Enoch (Book of Watchers): in 1 En 1:2, Enoch is described as "righteous",[52] in Greek using the word δίκαιός "righteous".[53] Enoch is also described as "righteous" in 1 En 12:4; 15:1 (Book of Watchers),[54] in Greek using the words τῆς δικαιοσύνης "of righteousness" in 1 En 12:4 and ἀληθινός "truthful" and τῆς ἀληθείας "of truth" in 1 En 15:1.[55]

Enoch's uniqueness is highlighted in 1 En 19:3 (Book of Watchers): "I, Enoch, alone saw the visions, the extremities of all things. And no one among humans has seen as I saw."[56] The Greek text of 1 En 19:3 uses the word μόνος

---

[48] See Chapter 2 Note 160.

[49] Cf. DRAWNEL 2019, 74–75 (waw superlinear).

[50] Cf. DRAWNEL 2019, 70–71. Also see Chapter 2.2.3.

[51] Cf. BLACK 1970, 19. Also cf. 1 En 1:1 in the translations NICKELSBURG/VANDERKAM 2012b, 19; STUCKENBRUCK 2016, 32.

[52] 1 En 1:2 in the translation NICKELSBURG/VANDERKAM 2012b, 19. Also cf. the translation STUCKENBRUCK 2016, 33.

[53] Cf. BLACK 1970, 19. This verse is damaged in Aramaic, cf. DRAWNEL 2019, 16–19, 74–77.

[54] Cf. NICKELSBURG/VANDERKAM 2012b, 31, 36. Enoch's "righteousness" is also highlighted in a later part of 1 Enoch, 1 En 71:14 (Parables of Enoch), cf. 1 En 71:14 in the translation NICKELSBURG/VANDERKAM 2012b, 95.

[55] Cf. BLACK 1970, 27, 29. These verses are not extant (1 En 15:1) or damaged (1 En 12:4) in Aramaic, cf. MILIK 1976, 162–163, 365–366; DRAWNEL 2019, 16–19. For 1 En 15:1 BOKHORST 2021, 79–80, 86, 117, 135, 147, additionally notes the variant spelling ἀληθεινός "truthful" for ἀληθινός "truthful", and that righteousness rather than truthfulness is found only in the Ancient Ethiopic version of 1 En 15:1.

[56] 1 En 19:3 in the translation NICKELSBURG/VANDERKAM 2012b, 40. Enoch's uniqueness is also highlighted in 1 En 37:4 (Parables of Enoch): "Until now there had not been given from the presence of the Lord of Spirits such wisdom as I have received according to my insight, by

6.2 Enoch (Sir 44:16; 49:14)   151

"alone".[57] Enoch's uniqueness also appears in 1 En 92:1 (Epistle of Enoch). 1 En 92:1 reads: "Written by Enoch the scribe (this complete sign of wisdom) (who is) praised by all people and a leader of the whole earth, to all my sons who will dwell on the earth, and to the last generations who will observe truth and peace."[58] The verse 1 En 92:1 is partly extant in the Aramaic fragment 4Q212 (En^g ar) 1 II 11, a manuscript dated to the middle of the 1st century BCE, where Enoch is described as [ח]ﬞכ֗ים אנושא "wisest of the humanity" and [ר]ﬞבחי "chosen".[59]

Similar to Enoch's description in the Hebrew Sir 44:16 אות דעת לדור ודור "sign of knowledge from generation to generation", in 1 En 92:1 (Epistle of Enoch) Enoch's writing is described as a "sign of wisdom".[60] The Greek Sir 44:16^{LXX} which mentions ὑπόδειγμα μετανοίας "example of repentance" for generations is also sometimes seen as similar to 1 Enoch generally in its emphasis of repentance.[61] 1 En 92:1 (Epistle of Enoch) also describes Enoch's passing on of wisdom "to the last generations",[62] in Aramaic in 4Q212 1 II 12 לדריא אחריא "to the later generations".[63] It is sometimes argued that Ben Sira knew such passages.[64]

Aspects included in the Hebrew Bible but not in Ben Sira are also not at all or not fully mentioned in 1 Enoch. In 1 En 72:32; 74:10, 12; 82:6 (Astronomical

---

whom the lot of everlasting life was given to me." (1 En 37:4 in the translation NICKELSBURG/VANDERKAM 2012b, 50). The similarity between Sir 44:16 and 1 En 37:4 is also noted by PETERS 1913, 378.

[57] Cf. BLACK 1970, 32. The verse is not extant in Aramaic, cf. MILIK 1976, 365–366; DRAWNEL 2019, 16–19.

[58] 1 En 92:1 in the translation NICKELSBURG/VANDERKAM 2012b, 138; cf. the translation STUCKENBRUCK 2007, 217: "That which was written by Enoch the scribe (which is a complete sign of wisdom), praised by all men, and judge of all the earth: 'To all my sons who will dwell upon the earth and to the last generations who will do uprightness and peace.'".

[59] Cf. DRAWNEL 2019, 404–405, 409–410. The similarity of the Aramaic version of 1 En 92:1 with Enoch's uniqueness in Sir 49:14 is also pointed out by STUCKENBRUCK 2007, 222. The verse is not extant in Greek, cf. BLACK 1970, 37.

[60] See Note 58. This expression is not extant in Hebrew or Greek, see Note 59. For a commentary on 1 En 92:1 cf. NICKELSBURG 2001, 430–431. The similarity of Ben Sira's description with 1 En 92:1 is noted by ARGALL 1995, 11; ARGALL 2002, 170; CORLEY 2013, 125. MILIK 1976, 11, argues for a general reference to 1 Enoch (Book of Watchers and Astronomical Book).

[61] Cf. KVANVIG 1988, 125; KVANVIG 2011, 332.

[62] See Note 58. In addition, 1 En 82:1–3 (Astronomical Book; possibly a later addition, see Chapter 2 Note 154) also describes Enoch as passing on wisdom to later generations, cf. the translation NICKELSBURG/VANDERKAM 2012b, 112. 1 En 82:1–3 is not extant in Aramaic, cf. MILIK 1976, 365–366; DRAWNEL 2019, 16–19; or in Greek, cf. BLACK 1970, 36. A similarity between Ben Sira and 1 En 82:1–2 is also noted by KVANVIG 1988, 124; KVANVIG 2011, 334. 1 En 92:1 is partly extant in Aramaic, cf. DRAWNEL 2019, 409–410 (also see Note 59), but not in Greek, cf. BLACK 1970, 37. Enoch's passing on of wisdom is also highlighted in 1 En 37:1–5 (Parables of Enoch), cf. the translation NICKELSBURG/VANDERKAM 2012b, 50.

[63] Cf. DRAWNEL 2019, 409–410.

[64] Thus MOPSIK 2003, 278–279 (1 En 92:2 [probably meaning 1 En 92:1]; 1 En 82). KVANVIG 2011, 332–335, concludes that not necessarily 1 En 92:1 but oral and written traditions about Enochic wisdom lie behind Sir 44:16.

152   *6. Ben Sira 44–50: Case Studies*

Book),[65] the number of days in a year is 364 – not 365, Enoch's age in years in Gen 5:23. Enoch's son Methuselah and other sons are mentioned in 1 En 92:1 (Epistle of Enoch) in the Aramaic fragment 4Q212 1 II 11, 13,[66] but daughters are not mentioned in 1 Enoch.

Aspects found in the Hebrew Bible as well as in Ben Sira are also covered by 1 Enoch. The use of הלך "to walk" in a hithpael form in Sir 44:16 is often taken as a direct reference to Gen 5:22.[67] However, for example in 1 En 92:3; 94:1–4; 99:10 (Epistle of Enoch), walking in righteousness also plays a role.[68] In Aramaic, [א]ארחת קשט "ways of righteousness" are mentioned in 4Q212 3 III 15 (1 En 94:1).[69] 1 En 99:10 in Greek reads καί πορεύσονται ἐν ὁδοῖς δικαιοσύνης αὐτοῦ [τοῦ ὑψίστου] "and they will walk in the paths of his [the Most High's] righteousness".[70] In the Hebrew Bible, Enoch is taken instead of dying (Gen 5:24 וְאֵינֶנּוּ כִּי־לָקַח אֹתוֹ אֱלֹהִים "and he was not, because God took him"). In Ben Sira, the Hebrew verb לקח "to take" in a niphal stem (Sir 44:16; 49:14 Hebrew) is only used for one other person, Elijah, who is "taken" in a firestorm (Sir 48:9). The same is true for the Greek verb ἀναλαμβάνω "to take up" in a passive voice (Sir 48:9; 49:14[LXX]). This similarity between Enoch and Elijah in Sir 44–50 may point towards Enoch being taken up instead of dying.[71] However, there is no clear reference to Enoch's ascension rather than death in Ben Sira.[72] According to Sir 44:16, Enoch נלקח אות דעת לדור ודור "was taken as a sign of knowledge from generation to generation", and according to Sir 49:14 נלקח פנים "was taken up regarding the face" – with the latter expression being less specific than the Greek ἀνελήμφθη ἀπὸ τῆς γῆς "was taken up from the earth" (Sir 49:14[LXX]), but probably still meaning "from the face [of the earth]".[73] These descriptions

---

[65] Cf. the translation NICKELSBURG/VANDERKAM 2012b, 99, 102, 113. These verses are not extant in Aramaic, cf. MILIK 1976, 365–366; DRAWNEL 2019, 16–19; or in Greek, cf. BLACK 1970, 36.

[66] Cf. DRAWNEL 2019, 409–410. Both Enoch's son Methuselah and his brothers are mentioned in 1 En 91:1–2 (Epistle of Enoch), cf. the translations NICKELSBURG/VANDERKAM 2012b, 136; STUCKENBRUCK 2007, 157, although this passage may be later than Ben Sira, see Chapter 2 Note 154. 1 En 91:1–2 is not extant in Greek, cf. BLACK 1970, 37.

[67] Thus MOPSIK 2003, 278–279; BECKER/FABRY/REITEMEYER 2011, 2251.

[68] Cf. the translations NICKELSBURG/VANDERKAM 2012b, 138, 143, 151; STUCKENBRUCK 2007, 223, 243, 407.

[69] Cf. DRAWNEL 2019, 438–439. 1 En 92:3 and 1 En 99:10 are not extant in Aramaic, cf. MILIK 1976, 365–366; DRAWNEL 2019, 16–19.

[70] Cf. BLACK 1970, 39. 1 En 92:3 and 1 En 94:1–4 are not extant in Greek, cf. BLACK 1970, 37.

[71] Cf. e.g. SKEHAN/DI LELLA 1987, 545; WRIGHT 2013b, 2344.

[72] Such a clear reference to a non-death is mentioned e.g. by SAUER 2000, 304, 335.

[73] Thus KVANVIG 1988, 121. ARGALL 1995, 12, implies God's face, and translates "to the heavenly sanctuary" due to the mention of Ezekiel in Sir 49:8 and the similar imagery in 1 En 14 (however, Ezekiel ist not mentioned there). Against this, WRIGHT 1997 and KVANVIG 2011, 335–336, translate, less specifically, "into the presence [of God]", and conclude that "there is no specific reference to Enoch traditions outside the Hebrew Bible in Ben Sira 49:14" (KVANVIG 2011, 336). God's face is mentioned as something that not even angels can see in 1 En 14:21 (Book

6.2 *Enoch (Sir 44:16; 49:14)* 153

of Enoch being taken in the Book of Ben Sira contain similarities with 1 Enoch. Enoch is "taken" – in Greek using the word λαμβάνω "to take"[74] – in 1 En 12:1–2 (Book of Watchers): "Before these things, Enoch was taken; and no human being knew where he had been taken, or where he was, or what had happened to him. His works were with the watchers, and with the holy ones were his days."[75] Here, Enoch seems to be taken up during his lifetime to receive revelations.[76] This could also be the case in Ben Sira.[77]

References to Enoch's being taken in Ben Sira and 1 Enoch are sometimes both seen as an expansion of Gen 5:24,[78] but such an expansion is debated for 1 Enoch.[79] In any case, Ben Sira and 1 Enoch share many similarities which are not shared with Genesis 5:21–24.[80]

The same applies to Jubilees. Many passages in Jubilees (see Chapter 2.2.4 for details on its date and sources) are not extant in Hebrew,[81] but later translations contain shared content with Ben Sira. According to Jub 4:18, Enoch "was the first to write a testimony. He testified to humanity in the generations of the

---

of Watchers, translation NICKELSBURG/VANDERKAM 2012b, 35, also cf. the editions and translations of 1 En 14:21 in Greek and Ancient Ethiopic in BOKHORST 2021, 79, 85, 116, 124, 134, 146), and Enoch is also brought "from the face of the earth" to heaven by a whirlwind in 1 En 39:3 (Parables of Enoch, translation NICKELSBURG/VANDERKAM 2012b, 52).

[74] 1 En 12:1 in Greek, cf. BLACK 1970, 27. The similarity to ἀναλαμβάνω "to take up" in Sir 49:14[LXX] is noted by LARSON 2005, 88.

[75] 1 En 12:1–2 in the translation NICKELSBURG/VANDERKAM 2012b, 31. The verses are not extant in Aramaic, cf. MILIK 1976, 365–366; DRAWNEL 2019, 16–19. 1 En 39:3–4 (Parables of Enoch) also mentions that Enoch is taken up "from the face of the earth": "And in those days a whirlwind snatched me up from the face of the earth and set me down within the confines of the heavens. And there I saw another vision [...]" (1 En 39:3–4 in the translation NICKELSBURG/VANDERKAM 2012b, 52; cf. for a commentary NICKELSBURG/VANDERKAM 2012a, 109). In 1 En 70:1–2 (Parables of Enoch), Enoch is also taken up, cf. the translation NICKELSBURG/VANDERKAM 2012b, 92; similarly in 1 En 71:1, 5 (Parables of Enoch), cf. the translation NICKELSBURG/VANDERKAM 2012b, 93.

[76] According to NICKELSBURG 2001, 233, "this paraphrase of Gen 5:24 refers not to Enoch's disappearance at the end of his life, but to the beginning of a period of association with the angels". According to 1 En 81:5–6 (Astronomical Book; possibly a later addition, see Chapter 2 Note 154), Enoch is later (still during his lifetime) returned to his home to pass on revelations to others before being taken a second time, cf. 1 En 81:5–6 in the translation of NICKELSBURG/VANDERKAM 2012b, 111.

[77] Thus ARGALL 1995, 11. Against ARGALL, WRIGHT 1997, 216 n. 84, argues: "This latter claim seems to me to be based on *1 Enoch* 92,1, and I am not sure that a return from heaven is implied in Sirach." However, this argument applies a double standard to Genesis and 1 Enoch.

[78] Cf. ARGALL 1995, 11. Also see Notes 76, 77. BOKHORST 2021, 1, 18, 371, 373, also states that all of 1 Enoch is an interpretation of the text of Genesis 5:24, but at the same time notes that the Book of Watchers contains much material which is not covered by this explanation.

[79] Cf. STONE 1978, 484; DAVIES 2006, 100, 106–107. Cf. on 1 Enoch's lack of any explicit references in to what is now the Hebrew Bible and its notion of authority which is unrelated to now biblical texts NICKELSBURG 2001, 29, 50, 57, 66, 119–120, who, however, still argues for references to texts in the Hebrew Bible.

[80] This is also noted by DAVIES 2006, 101–102.

[81] Cf. VANDERKAM 2018, 4–8.

154   *6. Ben Sira 44–50: Case Studies*

earth".[82] Jub 4:18 thus mentions Enoch's uniqueness as well as his writing. According to Jub 4:23, Enoch "was taken from human society" into the garden of Eden. According to Jub 4:24, Enoch "was placed there as a sign and to testify against all people in order to tell all the deeds of history until the day of judgment".[83] Thus, in Jub 4:24, like in Ben Sira, Enoch is described as a "sign" for generations.[84] Jub 10:17 repeats the aspect of Enoch as a witness for generations as well as his connection with Noah and righteousness in a description of Noah: "[Noah] who lived longer on the earth than (other) people except Enoch because of his righteousness [...]; because Enoch's work was something created as a testimony for the generations of eternity so that he should report all deeds throughout generation after generation on the day of judgment."[85] Thus, Enoch is connected with righteousness and uniqueness and described as as a sign for generations in Jubilees as well as in Ben Sira, but not in the Hebrew Bible. All three share the aspects of Enoch being taken, while Enoch's walking with God is only implicit in Jubilees when Enoch is taken to the garden of Eden. 365 years are not mentioned in Jubilees,[86] and neither Enoch's daughters. Other mentions of Enoch in Jubilees also show additional overlaps with Ben Sira. In Jub 7, Enoch is mentioned by Noah, the figure following Enoch in Sir 44.[87] In Jub 7:38–39, Noah addresses his descendants: "For this is how Enoch, the ancestor of your father, commanded his son Methuselah; then Methuselah his son Lamech; and Lamech commanded me everything that his fathers had commanded him. Now I am commanding you, my children, as Enoch commanded his son in the first jubilees, while he was living in its seventh generation."[88] In Jub 19 and Jub 21, Enoch is mentioned by Abraham, the figure following Noah in Sir 44.[89] In Jub 19:23–24, Abraham adresses Rebecca: "May all the blessings with which the Lord blessed me and my descendants belong to Jacob and his descendants for

---

[82] Jub 4:18 as translated in VanderKam 2018, 235. These parts of Jub 4:18 are not extant in Hebrew, cf. García Martínez/Tigchelaar/van der Woude 1998b, 212–213.

[83] Jub 4:23–24 as translated in VanderKam 2018, 236. Jub 4:23–24 is not extant in Hebrew, cf. VanderKam 2018, 4–8. The garden of Eden in Jub 4:23 is similar to the Latin version of Sir 44:16 which mentions paradise (see Note 7), but Jub 4:23 is not extant in Latin, cf. VanderKam 2018, 14, and the background of the Latin version of Sir 44:16 would have to be studied in its own historical contexts (see Chapter 1.2).

[84] This is also noted by Taylor/Hart 1903, 591; Milik 1976, 11; Kvanvig 1988, 122–123; Marböck 1995d, 138; Kvanvig 2011, 334–335; VanderKam 2018, 260.

[85] Jub 10:17 as translated in VanderKam 2018, 394. VanderKam 2018, 411, explains that the long life of Enoch mentioned here refers to his being taken. Jub 10:17 is also mentioned as similar to Sir 44:16 by Milik 1976, 11. Jub 10:17 is not extant in Hebrew, cf. VanderKam 2018, 4–8.

[86] Cf. VanderKam 2018, 128, 256–257, 411.

[87] This is also true for 1 En 65:1–3, 9 (Book of Dream Visions), cf. the translation Nickelsburg/VanderKam 2012b, 84.

[88] Jub 7:38–39 as translated in VanderKam 2018, 331. Jub 7:38–39 is not extant in Hebrew, cf. VanderKam 2018, 4–8.

[89] See Chapter 6.2.1.

all time. Through his descendants may my name and the name of my ancestors Shem, Noah, Enoch, Malaleel, Enosh, Seth, and Adam be blessed."[90] In Jub 19:27, Abraham then addresses Jacob: "My dear son Jacob whom I myself love, may God bless you from above the firmament. May he give you all the blessings with which he blessed Adam, Enoch, Noah, and Shem."[91] Except for Malaleel (whose appearance in Jub 19 strikes commentators as difficult to explain),[92] all these figures also appear together (albeit it in slightly a different order) in Sir 44 and Sir 49 at the beginning and the end of the descriptions of ancestors.[93] Jubilees also describes priestly actions of Adam and other ancestors. This includes Enoch who according to Jub 4:25 "burned the evening incense of the sanctuary".[94] It has been suggested that, in line with the priestly actions mentioned in Jubilees, the placement of Adam in Sir 49:16 immediately before the High Priest Simon in Sir 50:1 forms a connection between Adam as the first and Simon as the current priest.[95] In Jub 21:10, Abraham explains to Isaac how sacrifices are to be made, saying: "because this is the way I found (it) written in the book of my ancestors, in the words of Enoch and the words of Noah."[96] Here, Abraham's ancestral book includes words of Enoch and Noah.[97]

Enoch also plays a prominent role in the Aramaic so-called Genesis Apocryphon (1Q20, 1QapGen ar), which is preserved on a manuscript dated to the late 1st century BCE with its content dated to the first half of the 2nd century BCE.[98] The text of 1Q20 is sometimes argued to be based on Genesis,[99] but a dependence on 1 Enoch is also possible,[100] and the text mentions written words of Noah which cannot be identified with any text extant today.[101] In any case, 1Q20 mentions Enoch by name and shows similarities in content with Ben Sira which are not shared with Genesis.[102] Enoch's righteousness appears in 1Q20, where יצבא

---

[90] Jub 19:23–24 as translated in VANDERKAM 2018, 583. Jub 19:23–24 is not extant in Hebrew, cf. VANDERKAM 2018, 4–8.

[91] Jub 19:27 as translated in VANDERKAM 2018, 584. Jub 19:27 is not extant in Hebrew, cf. VANDERKAM 2018, 4–8.

[92] Cf. VANDERKAM 2018, 598–601.

[93] This similarity is also noted by HAYWARD 1996, 46–47.

[94] Jub 4:25 as translated in VANDERKAM 2018, 235. Jub 4:25 is not extant in Hebrew, cf. VANDERKAM 2018, 4–8.

[95] Thus HAYWARD 1996, 46–47.

[96] Jub 21:10 as translated in VANDERKAM 2018, 620. This part of the verse is not contained in 4Q219 (4QJub[d]), cf. VANDERKAM/MILIK 1994a, 42, or 4Q220 (4QJub[e]), cf. VANDERKAM/MILIK 1994b, 57.

[97] Cf. VANDERKAM 2018, 633–635.

[98] Cf. MACHIELA 2009, 1, 137, 142. On the anachronism of the term "Apocryphon" cf. ZAHN 2011a, 105–106.

[99] Thus MACHIELA 2009, 131; ZAHN 2020a, 22–24, 164–167.

[100] Thus MACHIELA 2009, 13, 141; MROCZEK 2016, 124.

[101] On the possible existence of an ancient "Book of Noah" cf. MACHIELA 2009, 9–12; STONE 2010, 7, 20; MROCZEK 2016, 124, 147–149. Also see Note 110.

[102] Such similarities are also noted by MARBÖCK 1995d, 138 (with few details).

156   *6. Ben Sira 44–50: Case Studies*

"certainty"[103] (1Q20 II 20) and קושטא "the truth" (1Q20 II 22) are mentioned as something to be learned from Enoch.[104] Enoch's uniqueness is stressed by the participle רחים "beloved" (1Q20 II 20).[105] Enoch is also connected with knowledge, someone from whom one can ידע "to know" (1Q20 II 20, 22),[106] and ספרא "the art of letters", חכמתא "the wisdom", and קושטא "the truth" are found in ספר מלי חנוך "the book of the words of Enoch" (1Q20 XIX 25).[107] Enoch's son Methuselah is also mentioned in 1Q20 (מתושלח "Methuselah" in 1Q20 II 19; V 2, חנוך אבוהי "Enoch his father" in 1Q20 II 22, 24; Methuselah and Enoch also appear in a more fragmentary passage in 1Q20 V 2–3).[108] 365 years or Enoch's daughters are not mentioned in 1Q20. No passages in which Enoch walks with or is taken by God are preserved in 1Q20. Similar to Jub 21:10, 1Q20 in fragmentary lines mentions ספר מלי חנוך "the book of the words of Enoch" (1Q20 XIX 25) and מלי חנוך "the words of Enoch" (1Q20 XIX 29) in Abraham's speech,[109] as well as in a another context כתב מלי נוח "writing of the words of Noah" (1Q20 V 6).[110]

Overall, extant sources earlier than or contemporary to Ben Sira outside the Hebrew Bible share all aspects of content with Sir 44:16; 49:14, including several aspects which are not shared with Gen 5:21–24. The text of Gen 5:21–24 is not preserved among the Dead Sea Scrolls.

6.2.5 Comparison within the Book of Ben Sira

In the Hebrew Book of Ben Sira, נמצא תמים "was found blameless" is also used for a person not influenced by wealth in Sir 31:8 and for Noah in Sir 44:17.[111] נמצא combined with other qualities is used for Abraham in Sir 44:20 and for Samuel in Sir 46:20, a form of תמים "blameless" for an addressee of Ben Sira's advice in Sir 7:6. Hithpael forms of הלך "to walk" are used for an addressee of Ben Sira's advice in Sir 3:17[112] and Sir 9:13. A niphal form of לקח "to take" is used for Elijah in Sir 48:9, and also for a dead brother in Sir 14:14. לדר ודור "from generation to generation" also appears in Sir 44:14[113] for all those praised. Niphal forms of יצר "to create" are also used, for example, for Adam (or all humans) in Sir 33:10, Joshua in Sir 46:1, and Isaiah in Sir 49:7.

---

[103] MURAOKA 2011, 77 (§ 19l), translates יצבא as "assured".
[104] Cf. MACHIELA 2009, 36.
[105] Cf. MACHIELA 2009, 36.
[106] Cf. MACHIELA 2009, 36.
[107] Cf. MACHIELA 2009, 73.
[108] Cf. MACHIELA 2009, 36–37, 40.
[109] Cf. MACHIELA 2009, 73.
[110] Cf. MACHIELA 2009, 42.
[111] See Chapter 6.2.1.
[112] Manuscript A only, Manuscript C contains a qal form, cf. RENDSBURG/BINSTEIN 2013, Manuscript A I recto, Manuscript C I recto.
[113] Complete in the Masada Manuscript, the first word reconstructed in Manuscript B, cf. RENDSBURG/BINSTEIN 2013, Masada Manuscript VII, Manuscript B XIII verso.

In Greek, εὐαρεστέω "to please", ὑπόδειγμα "example", and μετάνοια "repentance" are not used anywhere else in the Book of Ben Sira. The verb μετατίθημι "to transfer" is used for a person's change in behaviour in Sir 6:9^{LXX}. Plural forms of γενεά "generations" are used frequently in the Book of Ben Sira, e. g. for Ben Sira in Sir 24:33^{LXX}, the wise in Sir 39:9^{LXX}, all ancestors in Sir 44:7, 14^{LXX}, and God's people in Sir 45:26^{LXX}. The verb κτίζω "to create" is used for Adam in Sir 36:10^{LXX},[114] but also, for example, wisdom in Sir 1:4^{LXX}, fire in Sir 39:29^{LXX}, or a physician in Sir 38:12^{LXX}. The verb ἀναλαμβάνω "to take up" is used for Elijah in Sir 48:9^{LXX}, also in a passive form, but also, in an active form, for the High Priest Simon putting on his garment in Sir 50:11^{LXX}.

Overall, in Hebrew more words are shared with other passages in the Book of Ben Sira than with Gen 5:21–24.

6.2.6 Conclusion

Only three individual words in Hebrew (two in Greek) and two out of six aspects of content – Enoch walking with and being taken by God – are shared between Sir 44:16; 49:14 and Gen 5:21–24. No intertextual reference can be substantiated. More words are shared between Sir 44:16; 49:14 and other passages in the Hebrew Book of Ben Sira itself than with Genesis 5:21–24, and shared words such as הלך "to walk" in a hithpael form are not unique to Genesis or the Hebrew Bible but frequent in the Dead Sea Scrolls. All other words and the other four aspects of content differ between Sir 44:16; 49:14 and Gen 5:21–24 in both Hebrew and Greek. At the same time, the very same aspects present in Ben Sira but not in Genesis – righteousness, uniqueness, sign of knowledge or repentance for generations – as well as the lack of aspects present only in Genesis – Enoch's 365 years and his daughters – are found in extant ancient literature outside the Hebrew Bible and older than Ben Sira, namely 1 Enoch, and in literature contemporary to Ben Sira, namely Jubilees and 1Q20 (1QapGen ar). All of this ancient literature about Enoch is often argued to have grown out of Gen 5:21–24.[115] Other explanations, for example that Gen 5:21–24 depends on 1 Enoch, or that both independently relate to other oral traditions or written texts about Enoch, are not usually considered. In any case, there is material proof that literature about Enoch other than Gen 5:21–24 existed during Ben Sira's time – Enoch is mentioned on 4Q201 (4QEn^a ar) – while there is no such material proof for the particular passage of Gen 5:21–24 which is not preserved at all in the Dead Sea Scrolls.

Where the Hebrew Bible is seen as Ben Sira's only source for the passages about Enoch, complicated explanations are necessary where Ben Sira differs from the

---

[114] Sir 36:10^{LXX} in ZIEGLER 1980, 278, equals Sir 33:10^{LXX} in RAHLFS/HANHART 2006, Vol. II 433.

[115] Cf. ALEXANDER 1998, 87, 90–91, 93, 97; BAUTCH 2011, 1021.

Hebrew Bible. For example, Enoch as a "sign" or "example" for generations is explained as an example for the lasting presence of famous and wise men in the Book of Ben Sira (Sir 44:10–15)[116] or as an example for Jewish rather than Hellenistic wisdom.[117] However, an easier explanation is that Ben Sira uses a range of contemporary traditions. It is unlikely that Ben Sira took texts which now are part of the Hebrew Bible as his only sources and invented everything deviating from these himself[118] while extant contemporary literature contains the very same ideas.

Using the standards often applied to texts in the Hebrew Bible in comparison with Ben Sira – some individual shared words and some shared content – it would be possible to argue on the basis of the "Praise of the Ancestors" that Ben Sira knew all three parts of 1 Enoch available at his time: the Book of Watchers, the Astronomical Book, and the Epistle of Enoch. Due to a lack of explicit inter-textual connections, this would be a rather weak argument. It would, however, not be weaker than the same claim often found about the whole Book of Isaiah (see Chapter 6.4). It could also be argued that Ben Sira did not even necessarily know Gen 5:21–24 as extant in the Hebrew Bible,[119] since Enoch's 365 years and his daughters play no role at all in Ben Sira, while all other aspects shared with Genesis are also found in 1 Enoch. But just as Ben Sira does not explicitly refer to any texts now in the Hebrew Bible, he also does not explicitly refer to texts now in 1 Enoch or other texts. Thus, it is not possible to argue for 1 Enoch or other texts being authoritative texts for Ben Sira. Sir 44:16; 49:14 do prove the authoritative status of Enochic literature for Ben Sira.[120] It may not even be possible to reconstruct whether or not Ben Sira in the "Praise of the Ancestors" knew and referred to Enochic literature since references to specific texts are simply absent.[121] Here, the point is not to argue for a literary dependance of Ben Sira on 1 Enoch or other texts, or vice versa, but to demonstrate that aspects preserved in 1 Enoch, Jubilees, and 1Q20 (1QapGen ar) show similarities with Ben Sira which are not shared with the Hebrew Bible, and that overall Ben Sira shares many more similarities with other texts about Enoch than with Gen 5:21–24.

---

[116] Thus ZAPFF 2010, 321.

[117] Thus DI LELLA 2006, 159.

[118] For this view see Chapter 5 Notes 93–99.

[119] Gen 5:21–24 could also itself refer to traditions outside it, cf. VANDERKAM 1984, 51.

[120] Against POPOVIĆ 2010, 8 (1 Enoch authoritative); KNIBB 2010, 145 (Hebrew Bible and 1 Enoch authoritative).

[121] For the more general argument by ARGALL and WRIGHT that Ben Sira and 1 Enoch show a common contemporary background see Chapter 1.4.5.

6.3 Judges (Sir 46:11–12)

6.3.1 Hebrew and Greek Text

"The judges" are mentioned in Sir 46:11–12. In Hebrew, these verses are not preserved in the Masada Manuscript (Mas1h). In Manuscript B, Sir 46:11–12 reads as follows:[122]

Sir 46:11	והשופטים איש בשמו כל אשר	And the judges, each one with his name,
	לא נשא לבו: ולא נסוג מאחרי אל	everyone for whom his heart was not
	יהי זכרם לברכה	carried away, and who did not turn back from after God: may their remembrance be for a blessing,
46:12	ושמם תחליף לבניהם:	and their name a continuation for their sons!

In the Greek Septuagint, Sir 46:11–12[LXX] reads as follows:[123]

Sir 46:11[LXX]	Καὶ οἱ κριταί, ἔκαστος τῷ αὐτοῦ ὀνόματι, ὅσων οὐκ ἐξεπόρνευσεν ἡ καρδία καὶ ὅσοι οὐκ ἀπεστράφησαν ἀπὸ κυρίου, εἴη τὸ μνημόσυνον αὐτῶν ἐν εὐλογίαις·	Also the judges, each one with his name, of as many as the heart did not commit fornication, and however many did not turn away from the Lord, may their remembrance be in blessings!
46:12[LXX]	τὰ ὀστᾶ αὐτῶν ἀναθάλοι ἐκ τοῦ τόπου αὐτῶν[124] καὶ τὸ ὄνομα αὐτῶν ἀντικαταλλασσόμενον ἐφ᾽ υἱοῖς δεδοξασμένος ἀνθρώπων.[125]	May their bones sprout again from their place,[126] and their name transferred to sons, someone glorified by humans.[127]

6.3.2 References to the Book of Judges?

This mention of "the judges" in Sir 46:11–12 is usually seen as a reference to judges mentioned in the Book of Judges now in the Hebrew Bible,[128] even by

---

[122] Cf. the transcription by ABEGG in RENDSBURG/BINSTEIN 2013, Manuscript B XVI recto.

[123] Cf. ZIEGLER 1980, 343.

[124] See Chapter 6.3.6 for this phrase.

[125] The last two words δεδοξασμένος ἀνθρώπων "someone glorified by humans" are a conjecture by ZIEGLER, cf. ZIEGLER 1980, 119, 343 (the Latin version reads *illorum sanctorum virorum gloria* "the glory of these holy men", cf. *Biblia Sacra* 1964, 349; WEBER/GRYSON 2007, 1088). CORLEY 2019, 224, explains them as translating the Hebrew words אוהב עמו "loving his people" at the beginning of Sir 46:13 which refer to the next figure, Samuel. Instead of these two words, RAHLFS/HANHART 2006, Vol. II 460 (like most Greek manuscripts, cf. ZIEGLER 1980, 343), read δεδοξασμένων αὐτῶν "as they have been glorified".

[126] See Note 124.

[127] See Note 125.

[128] Thus SKEHAN/DI LELLA 1987, 41; CRENSHAW 1997a, 631; GOSHEN-GOTTSTEIN 2002, 241–242; MOPSIK 2003, 47; CARR 2011, 192.

160 6. Ben Sira 44–50: Case Studies

scholars who note that it does not include any names of these judges.[129] There are two opposing views on how exactly Sir 46:11–12 refers to the Book of Judges. One view is that Sir 46:11–12 praises all of the judges in the Book of Judges, and paints a more positive picture of the judges than the Book of Judges itself,[130] where Gideon is involved in idol worship (Judg 8:27) and Samson is left by God (Judg 16:20). The more common view is that Sir 46:11–12 does not praise all of the judges in the Book of Judges, but excludes those judges who turned away from God[131] – thus excluding Samson,[132] or Gideon and Samson,[133] or Gideon, Abimelech, and Samson,[134] or Gideon, Jephtah, and Samson.[135] The female judge Deborah (Judg 4:4) is sometimes argued to be included,[136] sometimes excluded.[137]

Other references to texts in the Hebrew Bible are also sometimes seen. For example, the sprouting of bones in Sir 46:12[LXX] is thought to refer to a story about Elisha's grave in 2 Kgs 13:20–21.[138] It is also noted that the topic is used for the twelve prophets in Sir 49:10[LXX].[139] The combination of זכר "remembrance" and לברכה "for a blessing" is seen as a reference to Prov 10:7.[140]

6.3.3 Comparison with the Hebrew Bible

When Sir 46:11–12 is compared to the Book of Judges and other texts in the Hebrew Bible, there are more dissimilarities than similarities regarding shared words, syntax, and content. Regarding shared words, השפטים "the judges" (a qal plural participle of שפט "to judge") with a definite article is not used in the Book of Judges. It only appears in Deut 19:17–18 (referring to a future time period with judges after the conquest of the promised land), 2 Kgs 23:22 (referring to a past time period with judges and before the time of kings), Ruth 1:1 (referring to a past time period with judges), and 2 Chr 19:6 (referring to judges during the time of King Jehoshaphat of Judah). Without an article, forms of the plural participle שפטים "judges" are found three times in the Book of Judges, at its beginning in Judg 2:16–18, followed by the singular form השפט "the judge" with an article in Judg 2:19. In the Hebrew Bible in general, this participle is used for God and for

---

[129] Thus SAUER 2000, 316.
[130] Thus SKEHAN/DI LELLA 1987, 520; ZAPFF 2010, 340.
[131] Thus WRIGHT 2013b, 2335.
[132] Thus CORLEY 2013, 131.
[133] Thus SNAITH 1974, 230; CRENSHAW 1997a, 846; KAISER 2005, 186; CORLEY 2008b, 171.
[134] Thus HAMP 1951, 127.
[135] Thus BROWN 2002, 218–219; CORLEY 2008b, 172 (referring to BROWN 2002).
[136] Thus KAISER 2005, 186.
[137] Thus BROWN 2002, 218.
[138] Thus SKEHAN/DI LELLA 1987, 517, 520; ZAPFF 2010, 340 (referring to SKEHAN/DI LELLA 1987); BECKER/FABRY/REITEMEYER 2011, 2257.
[139] Thus KAISER 2005, 186; CORLEY 2013, 131; WRIGHT 2013b, 2335.
[140] Thus CORLEY 2008b, 171.

6.3 Judges (Sir 46:11–12)

humans.[141] The verb שׁפט "to judge" then appears as an activity of a number of figures mentioned by name, first Othniel in Judg 3:9–10 (who is there described as a nephew of Caleb, and as Caleb's nephew and son-in-law in Josh 15:17 and Judg 1:13). The names of figures in the Book of Judges are not combined with שׁם "name", with the exception of Samson who gets his name by his mother in Judg 13:24 (just as Abimelech by his father Gideon in Judg 8:31). No combination of נשׂא "to lift" and לב "heart" is used in the Book of Judges at all, neither the root סוג "to turn away". לברכה "for a blessing" is used in Prov 10:7 in combination with זכר "remembrance", but also in Ps 37:26 in combination with descendants. The noun תחליף "continuation" and the combination לבניהם "for their sons" are not used anywhere in the Hebrew Bible.

In content, there is a major similarity between Sir 46:11–12 and the Book of Judges: both mention a past time period with judges after Caleb (a figure described in Num, Josh, and Judg) and before Samuel (a figure described in 1 Sam). The Book of Judges describes a past time period with judges before the time of kings. A past time period of שׁפטים "judges" before a period of kings is also mentioned outside the Book of Judges but within the Hebrew Bible, for example in Isa 1:26; 1 Chr 17:10. However, judges also appear in the Hebrew Bible before and after the time covered by the Book of Judges. In Num 25:5, שׁפטי ישׂראל "the judges of Israel" are mentioned during the time of Phineas, and in 2 Chr 19:6 השׁפטים "the judges" during the time period of king Jehoshaphat. Even for the time period between Caleb and Samuel, mentions of judges are not restricted to the Book of Judges. Before Samuel, in 1 Sam 4:18 Eli (a priest according to 1 Sam 1:9) is mentioned by name as someone who "judged" (שָׁפַט) Israel for forty years. Thus, the similarity between Sir 46:11–12 and the Hebrew Bible is a time period with judges after Caleb and before Samuel, but this time period is not restricted to the Book of Judges. Names of judges are also found outside the Book of Judges, in 1 Sam 12:11 in the words of Samuel (Jerubbaal = Gideon, Barak, Jephthah, Samson).

The two opposing views regarding an inclusive versus restrictive praise of the judges (see Chapter 6.3.2) are based on an inclusive or restrictive reading of כל אשר "everyone for whom" in Sir 46:11. Grammatically, both views are possible.[142] If the phrase is read as inclusive, it refers to all of the judges who are therefore seen as positive examples of not turning away from God. If it is restrictive, only those judges who did not turn away from God are to be remembered, while others are excluded. In the restrictive view, there is a major difference in content between Sir 46:11–12 and the Book of Judges. In the Book of Judges, in a repeated pattern the judges save the people Israel who disregard God (Judg 2:16–19 explicitly mentions this pattern, and the first example is the judge Othniel in Judg

---

[141] Cf. Gesenius 2013, s. v. שׁפט.
[142] Cf. Joüon/Muraoka 2011, § 158a*, on limiting and non-limiting relative clauses.

162   6. *Ben Sira 44–50: Case Studies*

3:7–11).[143] The judges themselves do not turn away from God. The only possible exception is Gideon, who takes part in idol worship in Judg 8:27. In Judg 8:27, however, the people Israel still are the explicit main subject, with Gideon joining them. In an inclusive view, there is still a difference in content, as Gideon's involvement in idol worship is then missing in Sir 46:11–12.

Overall, the only significant shared word between Sir 46:11–12 and the Book of Judges is שפטים "judges", but this word also appears in many other contexts in the Hebrew Bible. There is no syntactical similarity. The main shared content is a time period between Caleb and Samuel, mentions of which are not limited to the Book of Judges in the Hebrew Bible. If Sir 46:11–12 is restricted to only some judges, those who did not turn away from God, there is also a major difference in content: the main pattern in the Book of Judges is that the people Israel, not the judges, turn away from God.

6.3.4 Comparison with the Greek Septuagint

In the Greek Septuagint, most occurences of shared words are parallel to the Hebrew Bible. There are a few differences: οἱ κριταί "the judges" in a plural form with a definite article is used in the Book of Judges once (in a genitive form, Judg 2:17[LXX]). Num 25:5[LXX] does not use κριταί "judges" but φυλαί "tribes", but κριταί "judges" is used for times without kings for the time of Ezra in 1 Esd 9:13[LXX]. In the Book of Judges in the Septuagint, ἐκπορνεύω "to commit fornication" (not combined with καρδία "heart") is used for the people Israel in Judg 2:17; 8:33[LXX], and for the people Israel together with the judge Gideon in Judg 8:27[LXX]. The verb ἀποστρέφω "to turn away" is used for the people Israel who turn away from God in Judg 2:19; 8:33[LXX], but not for any judges.

Outside the Book of Judges, Prov 10:7[LXX] uses μνήμη "memory" rather than μνημόσυνον "remembrance" and ἐγκώμιον "encomium" rather than εὐλογία "blessing" (the latter is used in Ps 36:26[LXX] = Ps 37:26[MT]). 1 Macc 3:7[LXX] uses the similar phrase τὸ μνημόσυνον αὐτοῦ εἰς εὐλογίαν "his remembrance for a blessing" for Judas Maccabaeus. Unlike the Hebrew Sir 46:11–12, Sir 46:12[LXX] mentions the sprouting of bones. 2 Kgs 13:20–21[LXX] only shares the word ὀστᾶ "bones" with Sir 46:12[LXX], and the content of the story also differs significantly: rather than Elisha's bones themselves, another dead man thrown into Elisha's grave comes back to life.

Overall, in the Septuagint, more words are shared with the Book of Judges, but these make the contrast in content even stronger. The use of ὅσων "of as many as" in a genitive form in Sir 46:11[LXX] points to a restrictive view of the judges praised.[144] This stands in contrast with the pattern in the Book of Judges in which the people, not the judges, turn away from God.

---

[143] Cf. GERTZ 2012, 361–362.
[144] Cf. LIDDELL/SCOTT/JONES [1940], s. v. ὅσος.

6.3.5 Comparison with the Dead Sea Scrolls

Fragments of texts now in the Book of Judges are preserved in Dead Sea Scrolls from 50 BCE onwards.[145] No fragments of texts in the Book of Judges among the Dead Sea Scrolls contain forms of שפט "to judge", while a mention of כלב "Caleb" is preserved.[146] In the Dead Sea Scrolls preserving texts not now in the Book of Judges, forms of שפט "to judge" in a qal participle mostly refer to contemporary human judges or to God as a judge.[147] Specific names of judges also found in the Book of Judges in the Hebrew Bible[148] are included in some fragments.[149] In particular, 4Q559 (4QpapBibChronology ar) in a fragmentary list of names and years mentions names of some figures also found in the Book of Judges. The manuscript 4Q559 is dated to the first half of the first century BCE,[150] its content to the 3rd century BCE.[151] Preserved on Fragment 4 are the names כוש רשעתים מלך "Cush-rishathaim, king" (כושן רשעתים "Cushan-rishathaim" as a king of Aram is mentioned in Judg 3:8, 10), עתניאל "Othniel" (the name Othniel referring to a judge is also used in Judg 1:13; 3:9, 11 as well as in Josh 15:17), עגלון מלך מואב "Eglon the king of Moab" (also mentioned in Judg 3:12, 14–15, 17), [אה]וד בר ג[רא] "[Eh]ud the son of Ge[ra]" (the name Ehud is also used for a judge in Judg 3:15–16, 20–21, 23, 26; 4:1), and שמ[גר] "Sham[gar]" (the name Shamgar also appears for a judge in Judg 3:31; 5:6) in this order, the same order as in Judg 3.[152] 4Q559 also includes the name חנו[ך] "Eno[ch]" on Fragments 2 and 3.[153] The list in 4Q559 could be based on texts now the Hebrew Bible, and is reconstructed using the Hebrew Bible,[154] but both points also apply to Enochic books.[155] In any case, 4Q559 proves that traditions with the names of figures existed outside texts now in the Hebrew Bible. Additionally, [ש]משון "Samson" may be mentioned in 4Q465 (4QpapText Mentioning Samson?) which can be dated around 75–50 BCE, but the text is too fragmentary to reconstruct its content.[156] The Dead Sea Scroll 4Q559 shows that names connected with judges were transmitted outside texts now the Hebrew Bible.

---

[145] Cf. Tov 2002, 171, 180; Ulrich 2002a, 191; Webster 2002, 402; Lange 2009, 203–209; Tov 2010, 118, 128.

[146] Cf. Ulrich 2010, 254.

[147] Cf. Paganini/Jöris 2016, 1045.

[148] Cf. for a list of the judges' names in the Book of Judges Scherer 2005.

[149] Cf. for a list of personal names in the Dead Sea Scrolls Abegg 2002. Names in scrolls published later, e. g. Enoch in 4Q559 (4QpapBibChronology ar) (see Note 153), are not yet included in this list.

[150] Cf. Puech 2009b, 266–267.

[151] Cf. Wise 1997; 50–51; Puech 2009b, 266–267.

[152] Cf. Puech 2009b, 278–279.

[153] Cf. Puech 2009b, 271, 273–274.

[154] Thus Puech 2009b, 264, 282.

[155] Thus Puech 2009b, 273.

[156] Cf. Larson 2000, 394–395; Webster 2002, 356, 358, 397.

164   6. Ben Sira 44–50: Case Studies

6.3.6 Comparison within the Book of Ben Sira

In the Hebrew Book of Ben Sira, the qal participle שׁפט "judge" is used for human judges at the time of Ben Sira (e.g. Sir 10:1–2, 24), for God (Sir 35:22), and for Samuel (Sir 46:13). זרכם "their remembrance" with a third person plural suffix is used nowhere in the Hebrew Bible, but in Sir 10:17, where it refers to the lack of remembrance of the proud, and in Sir 44:13,[157] where it refers to the ancestors to be praised. The noun תחליף "continuation" is not used anywhere in the Hebrew Bible, but in Sir 44:17[158] referring to Noah and in Sir 48:8 referring to Elijah's successor.

In the Greek Book of Ben Sira, κριτής "judge" is used for contemporary human judges (e.g. Sir 10:1–2, 24[LXX]) and God (Sir 32:15[LXX]),[159] and κρίνω "to judge" for Samuel in Sir 46:14[LXX]. The very same phrase τὸ μνημόσυνον (αὐτῶν Sir 46:12[LXX] only) ἐν εὐλογίαις is also used in Sir 45:1[LXX] for Moses. The combination of ὀστᾶ "bones" and ἀναθάλλω "to sprout again" is used nowhere else in the Septuagint, but in the same phrase τὰ ὀστᾶ (αὐτῶν Sir 46:12[LXX] only) ἀναθάλοι ἐκ τοῦ τόπου αὐτῶν "may (their) bones sprout again from their place" in Sir 49:10[LXX] for the twelve prophets. The content of bones sprouting again also appears in the Hebrew Sir 49:10 about the twelve prophets (see Chapter 6.6.6), but is missing in the Hebrew Sir 46:11–12.

Overall, there are some shared words and phrases within the Hebrew and Greek Book of Ben Sira which are not found in the Hebrew Bible or Septuagint. This highlights the coherence of the Book of Ben Sira itself rather than any references to the Hebrew Bible or Septuagint.

6.3.7 Conclusion

There is no material evidence for the Book of Judges during the time of Ben Sira. If Sir 46:11–12 is compared to the later Hebrew Bible and Septuagint, there are more dissimilarities than similarities with the Book of Judges, and no reference can be clearly identified. Sir 46:11–12 and the Book of Judges in both Hebrew and Greek contain very few shared words, mainly "judges", a word not restricted to the Book of Judges or the time period associated with it in the Hebrew Bible and Septuagint. Possibly in the Hebrew and probably in the Greek text of Sir 46:11–12, there is a major difference in content: in the Book of Judges, the judges save the people Israel who turn away from their God rather than turning away themselves. If Sir 46:11–12 was a reference to the Book of Judges, this reference would include

---

[157] Only in Manuscript B, the Masada Manuscript instead reads זרעם "their seed", cf. RENDSBURG/BINSTEIN 2013, Manuscript B XIII verso, Masada Manuscript VII.

[158] Only in Manuscript B, the Masada Manuscript is damaged there, cf. RENDSBURG/BINSTEIN 2013, Manuscript B XIV recto, Masada Manuscript VII.

[159] Sir 32:15[LXX] in ZIEGLER 1980, 288, equals Sir 35:12[LXX] in RAHLFS/HANHART 2006, Vol. II 437.

6.4 Isaiah (Sir 48:17–25)

Isaiah is praised in Sir 48:17–25, a passage about Hezekiah and Isaiah. In Hebrew, these verses are not extant in the Masada Manuscript (Mas1h). In Manuscript B, Sir 48:22–24 is damaged and the explicit mention of the name Isaiah is extant in Sir 48:20 only (not in Sir 48:22). Sir 48:17–25 reads as follows in Manuscript B:[160]

Sir 48:17	יחזקיהו חזק עירו בהטות אל תוכה מים: ויחצב כנחשת צורים ויחסום הרים מקוה:	Hezekiah strengthened his city by turning water into its midst. And he hew out rocks like bronze, and he blocked mountains for a reservoir.
48:18	בימיו עלה סנחריב וישלח את רב שקה: ויט ידו על ציון ויגדף אל בגאונו:	In his days, Sennacherib came up and he sent Rabshakeh. And he stretched out his hand against Zion and blasphemed God in his pride.
48:19	[ונ]מוגו בגאון לבם ויחילו כיולדה:	[And] their hearts melt[ed] before pride and they writhed like someone giving birth.
48:20	[ויקר]אֿו אל אל עליון ויפרשו אליו כפים: [וישמע] קול תפלתם ויושיעם ביד ישעיהו:	[And] they [cried out] to God Most High and they stretched out their palms toward him. [And he heard] the voice of their prayers and he saved them through the hand of Isaiah.
48:21	[...] [מ]חֿנה אשור ויהמם במגפה:	[... the c]amp of Assyria and he confused them with a plague.
48:22	וֿיֿחזק [יח[זֿ]קיהו את הטו]ב בדרכי דוד: [...]	[Heze]kiah the go[od] and he was strong in the ways of David. [...]
48:23	[...]	[...]
48:24	[...] ברוח גבורה חזה אחרית וינחם אבלי ציון:	[...] With a spirit of might he saw the end and he comforted the mourning ones of Zion.
48:25	עד עולם הגיד נהיות ונסתרות לפני בואן:	Until duration he declared happening things and hidden things before their coming.

---

[160] Cf. the transcription by ABEGG in RENDSBURG/BINSTEIN 2013, Manuscript B XVIII recto–verso. The letters in square brackets are not reconstructed in BEENTJES 1997, 86–87.

166   6. Ben Sira 44–50: Case Studies

In the Greek Septuagint, Isaiah is mentioned by name in Sir 48:20, 22[LXX] and described as follows:[161]

Sir 48:17[LXX] Ἐζεκίας ὠχύρωσεν τὴν πόλιν αὐτοῦ καὶ εἰσήγαγεν εἰς μέσον αὐτῆς ὕδωρ, ὤρυξεν σιδήρῳ ἀκρότομον καὶ ᾠκοδόμησεν κρήνας εἰς ὕδατα.

Hezekiah fortified his city, and he lead into its midst water, he dug with iron a sharp cut, and he built wells for the waters.

48:18[LXX] ἐν ἡμέραις αὐτοῦ ἀνέβη Σενναχηριμ καὶ ἀπέστειλεν Ραψάκην, καὶ ἀπῆρεν· καὶ ἐπῆρεν χεῖρα αὐτοῦ ἐπὶ Σιων καὶ ἐμεγαλαύχησεν ἐν ὑπερηφανίᾳ αὐτοῦ.

In his days went up Sennacherib and he sent Rabshakeh, and departed, and he lifted up his hand against Zion, and boasted highly in his arrogance.

48:19[LXX] τότε ἐσαλεύθησαν καρδίαι καὶ χεῖρες αὐτῶν, καὶ ὠδίνησαν ὡς αἱ τίκτουσαι·

Then their hearts and hands were shaken, and they were in pain like those giving birth.

48:20[LXX] καὶ ἐπεκαλέσαντο τὸν κύριον τὸν ἐλεήμονα ἐκπετάσαντες τὰς χεῖρας αὐτῶν πρὸς αὐτόν. καὶ ὁ ἅγιος ἐξ οὐρανοῦ ταχὺ ἐπήκουσεν αὐτῶν καὶ ἐλυτρώσατο αὐτοὺς ἐν χειρὶ Ησαίου·

And they called the merciful Lord, stretching out their hands to him. And the holy one from heaven heard them quickly, and he redeemed them through the hand of Isaiah.

48:21[LXX] ἐπάταξεν τὴν παρεμβολὴν τῶν Ἀσσυρίων, καὶ ἐξέτριψεν αὐτοὺς ὁ ἄγγελος αὐτοῦ.

He struck the camp of the Assyrians, and his angel destroyed them.

48:22[LXX] ἐποίησεν γὰρ Ἐζεκίας τὸ ἀρεστὸν κυρίῳ καὶ ἐνίσχυσεν ἐν ὁδοῖς Δαυιδ τοῦ πατρὸς αὐτοῦ, ἃς ἐνετείλατο Ησαίας ὁ προφήτης ὁ μέγας καὶ πιστὸς ἐν ὁράσει αὐτοῦ.

For Hezekiah did the pleasing thing for the Lord, and he was strong in the ways of David his ancestor, which Isaiah the prophet commanded, the one great and faithful in his vision.

48:23[LXX] ἐν ταῖς ἡμέραις αὐτοῦ ἀνεπόδισεν ὁ ἥλιος καὶ προσέθηκεν ζωὴν βασιλεῖ.

In his days the sun stepped back, and he/it added life for the king.

48:24[LXX] πνεύματι μεγάλῳ εἶδεν τὰ ἔσχατα καὶ παρεκάλεσεν τοὺς πενθοῦντας ἐν Σιων.

Through his great spirit he saw the last things, and he comforted the mourning ones in Zion.

48:25[LXX] ἕως τοῦ αἰῶνος ὑπέδειξεν τὰ ἐσόμενα καὶ τὰ ἀπόκρυφα πρὶν ἢ παραγενέσθαι αὐτά.

Until the age he showed the things going to be, and the hidden things before they arrived.

---

[161] Cf. ZIEGLER 1980, 352–354.

6.4.2 References to the Book of Isaiah?

The description of Isaiah in Sir 48:17–25 is usually seen as evidence that Ben Sira knew the entire Book of Isaiah with its 66 chapters now found in the Hebrew Bible. For example, SKEHAN/DI LELLA comment on Sir 48:

"From vv 24–25, which allude clearly to Second and Third Isaiah, it is obvious that Ben Sira attributed the whole Book of Isaiah to the eighth-century B.C. prophet."[162]

Similar views are expressed by many scholars: Ben Sira serves as evidence that in the 2nd century BCE, the whole of Isa 1–66 formed the Book of Isaiah,[163] that this Book of Isaiah existed in its current scope and sequence including Isa 40–66,[164] and was attributed to the 8th century BCE prophet Isaiah.[165] Even scholars who explicitly note that the "Praise of the Ancestors" refers to persons conclude that Ben Sira used books of the Hebrew Bible, such as all of Isaiah, as his only source.[166]

The 66 chapters now in the Book of Isaiah were most likely written at different times. By name, kings of Judah who reigned in the 8th century BCE ending with Hezekiah are mentioned in Isa 1:1, but in Isa 44:28; 45:1 the Persian king Cyrus, probably Cyrus II who reigned in the 6th century BCE, is named. The Book of Isaiah is thus often seen as a combination of Proto-Isaiah (First Isaiah: Isa 1–39), Deutero-Isaiah (Second Isaiah: Isa 40–55), and Trito-Isaiah (Third Isaiah: Isa 56–66), or, more recently, of Isa 1–39 and Isa 40–66.[167]

Ben Sira's description of Isaiah is often thought to refer to all of Isa 1–66. Differences between Ben Sira and the Hebrew Bible are then attributed to Ben Sira's creativity.[168] For example, regarding the passage about Hezekiah and Isaiah in Sir 48, BEENTJES writes:

"expressions which occur nowhere else in the entire Old Testament can be found here. The most plausible inference is that they reflect the author's own creative style."[169]

However, these assumptions are problematic, as the comparisons in the following sections of the present study show.

---

[162] SKEHAN/DI LELLA 1987, 539.

[163] Thus SCHILDENBERGER 1950, 204 (referring to Roman Catholic documents and inspiration of biblical texts); MIDDENDORP 1973, 65, 69; HILDESHEIM 1996, 157; MARBÖCK 2000, 314; MARTTILA 2008, 445; SKA 2009, 185 n. 8; SCHMITT 2011, 312; VAN WIERINGEN 2011, 191–192.

[164] Thus HAMP 1951, 134; SAUER 2000, 330.

[165] Thus PETERS 1913, 416; SNAITH 1974, 244; WRIGHT 2013b, 2342.

[166] Thus STECK 1991, 136–137 (excluding Job where Ben Sira differs from the sequence of the Hebrew Bible).

[167] Cf. SCHMID 2012a, 404–406, 426.

[168] Thus HILDESHEIM 1996, 158; REITERER 2011a, 29.

[169] BEENTJES 2006b, 149.

6.4.3 Comparison with the Hebrew Bible

For a comparison with the Hebrew Bible, in addition to the whole Book of Isaiah, the chapters 2 Kgs 18–20, Isa 36–39, and 2 Chr 29–32 are of particular importance as they describe events involving Hezekiah and Isaiah.[170] For example, Sir 48:18–21 describes the siege and delivery of Jerusalem led by the Assyrian king Sennacherib and his commander Rabshakeh. This content is also found in the Hebrew Bible in 2 Kgs 18–19, Isa 36–37, and 2 Chr 32.

Sir 48:17 describes Hezekiah's building activities regarding the fortification of his city, i. e. Jerusalem, and its supply with water. This content is also found in the Hebrew Bible: the fortification of Jerusalem is mentioned in 2 Chr 32:5 regarding walls, the city's water supply is mentioned in 2 Kgs 20:20 and in 2 Chr 32:30.[171] However, in this shared content there are hardly any shared words with 2 Kgs 18–20, and 2 Chr 29–32, or the Book of Isaiah. מים "water" and עיר "city" are used in 2 Kgs 20:20 and 2 Chr 32:30 for Hezekiah's building activities. These words also appear in regarding building activities in Jerusalem in Isa 22:9, 11, but without a mention of Hezekiah. חזק "to be strong", used in Sir 48:17 in a qal perfect form for Hezekiah strengthening his city, is used in 2 Chr 29:3 for Hezekiah strengthening the doors of the temple (in a piel imperfect form), and in 2 Chr 32:5 for Hezekiah strengthening incomplete walls and the Millo of the city of David (in a hithpael and in a piel imperfect form). It is not used for Hezekiah's building activities in either 2 Kgs 18–20 or Isa 36–39. For Hezekiah supplying water, the verb נטה "to stretch out" and תוך "midst" used in Sir 48:17 are not used in 2 Kgs 18–20, 2 Chr 29–32, or the Book of Isaiah. For Hezekiah's fortification of the city, the same applies to חצב "to hew out", נחשת "bronze", צור "rock", חסם "to block", and הר "mountain": these words appear in Sir 48:17 only and are not used for Hezekiah's building activities in 2 Kgs 18–20, or 2 Chr 29–32, or the Book of Isaiah. מקוה "reservoir" is used once in the Book of Isaiah, in Isa 22:11, in the context of fortfications and water supply for Jerusalem, but Hezekiah is not mentioned there.

Sir 48:18 uses עלה סנחריב "Sennacherib came up", two words also combined in this order in 2 Kgs 18:13 and the parallel verse Isa 36:1,[172] where, however, Sennacheribs successful conquest of Judaean cities rather than his unsuccesful siege of Jerusalem are described. שלח "to send" and רב שקה "Rabshakeh" appear in one verse regarding Sennacheribs sending of Rabshakeh to Jerusalem in 2 Kgs 18:17, 27; 19:4 and the parallel verses Isa 36:2, 12; 37:4. In 2 Kgs 18:17 the king also sends Tartan and Rab-saris, in Isa 36:2 Rabshakeh only.

---

[170] Parts of these chapters are listed by KAISER 2005, 188.

[171] On archaeological evidence regarding the Siloam tunnel cf. FREVEL 2018, 282–283.

[172] The two words are also preserved in Isa 36:1 on 1QIsaᵃ, cf. BURROWS 1950, Plate XXVIII, and on 4Q56 (4QIsaᵇ), cf. SKEHAN/ULRICH 1997a, 34.

6.4 Isaiah (Sir 48:17–25) 169

The verb נטה "to stretch out" is not used for Assyrians in 2 Kgs 18–20, 2 Chr 29–32, or the Book of Isaiah. Instead, נטה "to stretch out" combined with קו "measuring line" is used with God as the subject in 2 Kgs 21:13. The combination of נטה "to stretch out" and יד "hand" is used for God only in the Book of Isaiah, for example in Isa 5:25 for the punishment of his people, and in Isa 45:12 for the creation of heaven. The verb גדף "to blaspheme" is used for Assyrians in 2 Kgs 19:6, 22 and Isa 37:6, 23 in God's words against them, but God is there designated with יהוה "YHWH" rather than אל "God". The word גאון "pride" is not used for any Assyrians in 2 Kgs 18–19, Isa 36–37, or 2 Chr 32.

Sir 48:19 uses the verb מוג "to melt" which does not appear in 2 Kgs 18–19, Isa 36–37, or 2 Chr 32. A combination of מוג "to melt" and לב "heart" is found in the whole Hebrew Bible only in Ezek 20:21. חיל "to writhe" is not used at all in 2 Kgs 18–19, Isa 36–37, or 2 Chr 32. Combinations of חיל "to writhe" and כיולדה "like someone giving birth" are not restricted to the Book of Isaiah but also appear, for example, in Mi 4:10.

Sir 48:20 describes that the people in Jerusalem cry to אל עליון "God Most High", a title not used anywhere in 2 Kgs, Isa, or 2 Chr at all, and in the Hebrew Bible only in Gen 14:18–20, 22 and Ps 78:35.[173] עליון "Most High" is used in Isa 14:14 for God, and in 2 Chr 32:30 for the upper source of a stream of water rather than God. פרש "to stretch out" and כף "palm" are not used for the people in Jerusalem in 2 Kgs 18–19, Isa 36–37, or 2 Chr 32, and in the Book of Isaiah combined only in Isa 1:15. Instead, פרש "to stretch out" is used for an Assyrian letter which Hezekiah stretches out before God in 2 Kgs 19:14 and Isa 37:14, and כף "hand" for the hand of the king of Assyria in 2 Chr 32:11. תפלה "prayer" is asked only of Isaiah (rather than all people) in 2 Kgs 19:4 and Isa 37:4. A construct form of קול "voice" followed by תפלה "prayer" is used only in Ps 66:19 in the Hebrew Bible.[174] A combination of ישע "to save" and יד "hand" is used for saving from the hand of the king of Assyria through God (rather than through the hand of Isaiah) in 2 Kgs 19:19, Isa 37:20, and 2 Chr 32:22. יד ישעיהו "the hand of Isaiah" only appears in Isa 20:2 in the whole Hebrew Bible.[175] There are some differences in content. According to Sir 48:20, the people cry out to God, stretch out their hands, and pray, but in 2 Kgs 18:36; 19:1–4, 14–20 and Isa 36:21; 37:1–4, 14–21 and 2 Chr 32:20, only Hezekiah and Isaiah pray to God.[176] Isaiah's hand or a direct role of Isaiah in God's saving intervention are not mentioned.[177]

---

[173] According to ULRICH 2002a, 185, 196, Gen 14:18–20, 22 and Ps 78:35 are not extant in the Dead Sea Scrolls. 4Q482 (4Qpap Jubⁱ?) may be based on Gen 14:22–24 or Jub 13:29, and includes the word [ן]עליו "most high" on Fragment 1 Line 1, cf. BAILLET 1982a, 1.

[174] This part is not extant in Ps 66:19 in 4Q83 (4QPsª), cf. SKEHAN/ULRICH/FLINT 2000, 19.

[175] The two words are also preserved in Isa 20:2 on 1QIsaª, cf. BURROWS 1950, Plate XVI, and on 4Q56 (4QIsaᵇ), cf. SKEHAN/ULRICH 1997a, 30.

[176] This is also noted by HÖFFKEN 2000, 173.

[177] This is also noted by STADELMANN 1980, 205; HÖFFKEN 2000, 171; BEENTJES 2006b, 153.

170   6. *Ben Sira 44–50: Case Studies*

Sir 48:21 mentions מחנה אשור "the camp of Assyria" which also appears in 2 Kgs 19:35, Isa 37:36,[178] and 2 Chr 32:21. המם "to confuse" is not used in 2 Kgs 18–20, Isa 36–39, or 2 Chr 29–32, and in the Book of Isaiah only once, in Isa 28:28 regarding grain. מגפה "plague" does not appear in 2 Kgs 18–20, Isa 36–39, and 2 Chr 29–32, or the whole Book of Isaiah. Instead, in 2 Kgs 19:35 and Isa 37:36 and 2 Chr 32:21, God's מלאך "angel" strikes the Assyrian camp. This angel is not mentioned in the Hebrew Sir 48:21,[179] while in the Hebrew Bible neither Isaiah's hand nor a plague are mentioned.

Sir 48:22 mentions Hezekiah and הטוב "the good". According to 2 Kgs 20:3, Isa 38:3, and 2 Chr 31:20, Hezekiah also does הטוב "the good". However, combinations of דרך "way" and דוד "David" are not connected with Hezekiah in the Hebrew Bible. בדרכי דויד "in the ways of David" only appears in 2 Chr 17:3; 34:2 regarding Jehoshaphat and Josiah, דרך דויד "the way of David" in 2 Kgs 22:2 (with the spelling דוד "David") regarding Josiah and in 2 Chr 11:17 regarding the Levites and their followers under Rehoboam. That Isaiah commanded Hezekiah the ways of David is an aspect of content not mentioned in the Hebrew Bible.

Following a gap in the preserved manuscript, Sir 48:24 mentions רוח גבורה "spirit of might". In the Hebrew Bible, a construct form of רוח "spirit" combined with גבורה "strength" is found only in Isa 11:2 in the combination רוח עצה וגבורה "a spirit of counsel and might".[180] The mention of Isaiah's mighty spirit is sometimes seen as a reference to Isa 61:1, where רוח "spirit" is also mentioned,[181] but גבורה "might" does not appear there. The seeing of the end is sometimes thought to refer to Proto-Isaiah in Isa 2:2 for Isaiah,[182] or to Deutero-Isaiah, e. g. Isa 46:10 for God, or to both,[183] in each case based on the shared word אחרית "end". The combination חזה אחרית "he saw the end" does not appear anywhere in the Hebrew Bible. The comfort of the mourning ones of Zion is sometimes thought to refer to Isa 40:1 (with the shared word נחם "to comfort")[184] or Isa 61:2–3 (with the shared word נחם "to comfort" in Isa 61:2 and the shared combination אבלי ציון "mourning ones of Zion" in Isa 61:3),[185] or both.[186] The combination of Isa

---

[178] The two words are also preserved in Isa 37:36 on 1QIsaᵃ, cf. Burrows 1950, Plate XXXI.

[179] This is also noted by Höffken 2000, 173; Marböck 2000, 310; Becker/Fabry/Reitemeyer 2011, 2261; Corley 2013, 138–139. For the Greek Sir 48:21[LXX] see Chapter 6.4.4.

[180] The three words are also preserved in Isa 11:2 on 1QIsaᵃ, cf. Burrows 1950, Plate X.

[181] Thus Zapff 2010, 366.

[182] Thus Marböck 2000, 313; Zapff 2010, 366.

[183] Thus Marböck 2000, 313;

[184] Thus Snaith 1974, 244; Crenshaw 1997a, 853; Becker/Fabry/Reitemeyer 2011, 2261 (quotation of Isa 40:1).

[185] Thus Hamp 1951, 134; Middendorp 1973, 65; Marböck 1995a, 164; Hildesheim 1996, 154; Höffken 2000, 165 (Isa 60:3 there probably a typographical error for Isa 61:3, cf. Höffken 2000, 170); Marböck 2000, 313; Zapff 2010, 366; van Wieringen 2011, 201; Adams 2016, 102 (referring to Beentjes 2006e, 203).

[186] Thus Peters 1913, 416; Stadelmann 1980, 205–206; Skehan/Di Lella 1987, 539; Knibb 1997, 649; Sauer 2000, 330; Di Lella 2006, 165.

6.4 Isaiah (Sir 48:17–25)   171

40:1 and Isa 61:2–3 as proposed reference texts is criticized by BEENTJES,[187] who, however, argues for a "biblical quotation" of Isa 61:2–3 in Sir 48:24–25 based on a combination of words (נחם "to comfort" Isa 61:2, אבלי ציון "mourning ones of Zion" Isa 61:3).[188] Overall, other than אבלי ציון "mourning ones of Zion" which also appears in Isa 61:3,[189] only individual words are shared between Sir 48:24 and the Book of Isaiah.

Sir 48:25 mentions נהיות "happening things" and נסתרות "hidden things". The first form is not used anywhere in the Hebrew Bible, the niphal participle form נסתרות "hidden" of סתר "to hide" is used in Deut 29:28 and Ps 19:13 for things known to God only. לפני בואן "before their coming" is not used anywhere in the Hebrew Bible. The declaration of future and hidden things is sometimes seen as a reference to Deutero-Isaiah in general.[190] The declaration of future things is sometimes taken as a reference to Isa 42:9 with the shared word נגד "to declare".[191] The declaration of hidden things is sometimes thought to refer to Isaiah as an apocalyptic seer as an aspect not found in the Hebrew Bible but in later literature such as the 2nd century CE "Ascension of Isaiah".[192]

Overall, no intertextual references from Sir 48:17–25 to the Book of Isaiah or 2 Kgs 18–20 and 2 Chr 29–32 can be substantiated. The proposed references mostly rely on individual shared words, at most on combinations of two consecutive words in syntactical similarity. Shared combinations of two consecutive words are not limited to the Book of Isaiah or 2 Kgs 18–20 and 2 Chr 29–32, but also appear in other texts in the Hebrew Bible such as texts about Josiah or Rehoboam. The shared words are also not always combined with shared contents, and sometimes used for different subjects or in different meanings. While much content is shared overall, there are differences to the Book of Isaiah, 2 Kgs 18–20, and 2 Chr 29–32 in the prayer of the people and the role of Isaiah in Sir 48:20 and the plague in Sir 48:21.

Even if, for the sake of argument, individual shared words are taken as a basis for intertextual references, a reference to all 66 chapters of the Book of Isaiah is still questionable. No book written by Isaiah is mentioned at all in Ben Sira. In

---

[187] BEENTJES 2006b, 155: "Words [...] or combinations of words [...] are isolated from their context in order to prove that Ben Sira is quoting or alluding to all three parts of the Book of Isaiah in this passage. Such an approach can lead to strange and forced interpretations." Thus also BEENTJES 2006e, 203.

[188] BEENTJES 2006b, 156. Thus also BEENTJES 2006e, 202: "deliberate quotation from Is 61,3". That a reference to the exile is not necessarily implied here is noted by ZAPFF 2010, 366.

[189] The two words are also preserved in Isa 61:3 on 1QIsaᵃ, cf. BURROWS 1950, Plate XLIX (there spelled אבילי ציון "mourning ones of Zion"), but not on 4Q66 (4QIsaᵐ), cf. SKEHAN/ ULRICH 1997c, 132.

[190] Thus PETERS 1913, 416 (mentioning literal allusions without specific examples); DI LELLA 2006, 165 (mentioning "a clear allusion" to a whole list of verses in Isa 40–55).

[191] Thus ZAPFF 2010, 366;

[192] Thus BOX/OESTERLEY 1913, 503; KNIBB 1997, 650; ZAPFF 2010, 366. The "Ascension of Isaiah" is a composite apocalyptic work from the 2nd century CE, cf. KNIGHT 1995, 9–11.

172   *6. Ben Sira 44–50: Case Studies*

Sir 44–50, the figure of Isaiah is directly connected with Hezekiah, and followed by Josiah. The reign of Josiah of Judah can be dated to the first half of the 7th century BCE,[193] well before the 6th century BCE Persian king Cyrus mentioned in Isa 40–66. It is sometimes noted that Sir 48:22–25 could refer to parts of Isa 1–39 (Proto-Isaiah) only, but the conclusion that Ben Sira refers to the whole of Isa 1–66 is still upheld.[194] However, Isaiah is prominently connected with Hezekiah in Ben Sira, and this connection also appears in Isa 36–39 (First Isaiah), 2 Kgs 18–20, and 2 Chr 32, while there is no mention of Hezekiah in Isa 40–66. Sir 48:20–23 could, for example, refer to Isa 36–38 or the parallel text 2 Kgs 18–20. Sir 48:24 could refer to Isa 1–39 only, as the word רוח "spirit" used in Sir 48:24 appears several times in Isa 1–39, e.g. in Isa 11:2 and Isa 34:16.[195] אחרית "end" appears in Isa 2:2 just as in Isa 46:10. The word נחם "to comfort" appears in Isa 1:24 in connection with Zion (Isa 1:27) just as in Isa 40:1 or Isa 61:2 (though it could be argued that the overall frequency of the word is greater in Isa 40–66). אבלי ציון "mourning ones of Zion" only appears in Isa 61:3, but, as Isa 3:16, 26 and Isa 24:4, 7, 23 show, אבל "to mourn" (Isa 3:26; 24:4, 7) in the context of ציון "Zion" (Isa 3:16, 17; 24:23) also appears in Isa 1–39. A declaration with נגד "to declare" is also found in in Isa 21:10. Thus, all individual shared words can be found in Isa 1–39 only, as can similar combinations of two words. An intertextual reference to all of Isa 1–66 cannot be substantiated.

6.4.4 Comparison with the Greek Septuagint

In the Greek Septuagint, most occurences of shared words are parallel to the Hebrew Bible. There are a few differences:

In Sir 48:17[LXX], the verb ὀχυρόω "to fortify" is not shared with texts about Hezekiah (2 Kgs 18–19; Isa 36–37; 2 Chr 32[LXX]) in the Septuagint. The verb οἰκοδομέω "to build" appears for Hezekiah's fortifications rather than water supply in 2 Chr 32:5[LXX]. The word κρήνη "well" in a singular form for Hezekiah's water supply is used in 2 Kgs 20:20[LXX], but not in Isa 22:11[LXX].

In Sir 48:18[LXX], ἐπαίρω "to lift up" is not shared with 2 Kgs 21:13[LXX]. No combination of ἐπαίρω "to lift up" and χείρ "hand" is used at all in Isa[LXX]. μεγαλαυχέω "to boast" is not used in 2 Kgs[LXX] and Isa[LXX] at all.

In Sir 48:19[LXX], σαλεύω "to shake" is not shared with Ezek[LXX].

In Sir 48:20[LXX], ἐλεήμων "merciful" for God is not shared with Isa[LXX], 2 Kgs[LXX], or 2 Chr[LXX]. ἐκπετάννυμι "to stretch out" is not used in 2 Kgs[LXX] or Isa 1:15; 37:14[LXX], and in Isa[LXX] combined with χείρ "hand" only in Isa 65:2[LXX] for

---

[193] Cf. FREVEL 2018, 423.

[194] Thus SNAITH 1974, 244; SAUER 2000, 330; *Stuttgarter Erklärungsbibel* 2005, 1274.

[195] It could be argued that Isa 11:2 and Isa 34:16 do not explicitly refer to Isaiah, but this is not clear for Isa 61:1 either, cf. COGGINS 2007, 481. The word does not appear in 2 Kgs in connection with Isaiah.

6.4 Isaiah (Sir 48:17–25)

God's hands. λυτρόω "to redeem" is not used in 2 Kgs 19:19^{LXX}, Isa 37:20^{LXX}, or 2 Chr 32:22^{LXX}. χείρ "hand" is not followed by Ησαιας "Isaiah" anywhere in the Septuagint except in Sir 48:20^{LXX}.

In Sir 48:21^{LXX}, πατάσσω "to strike" is shared with 2 Kgs 19:35^{LXX}. In 2 Kgs 19:35^{LXX}, Isa 37:36^{LXX}, and 2 Chr 32:21^{LXX}, an ἄγγελος "angel" strikes the Assyrian camp, in 2 Chr 32:21^{LXX} even combined with ἐκτρίβω "to destroy". Here, the Greek Sir 48:21^{LXX} shares the angel as an agent which is missing in the Hebrew Sir 48:21 with texts in the Hebrew Bible and Greek Septuagint.[196]

Like Sir 48:22^{LXX}, Isa 38:3^{LXX} also uses ἀρεστός "pleasing", but 2 Kgs 20:3^{LXX} and 2 Chr 31:20^{LXX} do not. The exact phrase ἐν ὁδοῖς Δαυιδ τοῦ πατρὸς αὐτοῦ "in the ways of David his ancestor" is used in 2 Chr 34:2^{LXX} for Josiah. The verb ἐντέλλομαι "to command" is used in 2 Kgs 18:12; 20:1; 21:8^{LXX}, but in all cases connected with Moses rather than Isaiah.

According to Sir 48:23^{LXX}, a verse not preserved in Hebrew, the sun stepped back, and Isaiah (or the sun as the subject of the previous line) added life for Hezekiah. In the Hebrew Bible as well as the Greek Septuagint, a similar story is told in 2 Kgs 20:1–11, Isa 38:1–8, and 2 Chr 32:24–26. In 2 Kgs 20:8–11, the shadow rather than the sun steps back,[197] while in Isa 38:8 both the shadow and the sun move backwards, and neither are mentioned in 2 Chr 32:24–26 which only generally mentions a sign. The verb ἀναποδίζω "to step back" is not used in any of these texts in the Septuagint. In 2 Kgs 20:4–6 and Isa 38:4–6, God rather than Isaiah adds life for the king, with Isaiah merely being the messenger.[198]

Sir 48:24^{LXX} only shares πνεῦμα "spirit" with Isa 11:2^{LXX}. πενθέω "to mourn" and Σιων "Zion" are shared with Isa 61:3^{LXX}, but not in the same forms. Thus, this direct combination of two words shared in Sir 48:21 with the Book of Isaiah in Hebrew is not shared in Greek. The word παρακαλέω "to comfort" is also shared with Sir 49:10^{LXX} about the twelve prophets.

In Sir 48:25^{LXX}, τὰ ἐσόμενα "things going to be" is shared in the context of visions with Dan 2:45^{LXX}. ἀπόκρυφος "hidden" is not shared with Deut 29:28^{LXX} or Ps 18:13^{LXX} (= Ps 19:13^{MT}). ὑποδείκνυμι "to show" is not shared with Isa 42:9^{LXX}.

Overall, the Greek Septuagint version contains even fewer shared words with 2 Kgs 18–20^{LXX}, Isa 36–39^{LXX}, and 2 Chr 29–32^{LXX}, especially regarding combinations of two consecutive words, while the same time showing some additional similarities in content such as an angel striking the Assyrian camp.

---

[196] This is also noted by HILDESHEIM 1996, 148. HÖFFKEN 2000, 168–169, interprets this as an assimilation of the Greek Ben Sira to biblical texts.

[197] This is also noted by ZAPFF 2010, 365.

[198] This is also noted by ZAPFF 2010, 366.

174   *6. Ben Sira 44–50: Case Studies*

6.4.5 Comparison with the Dead Sea Scrolls

The Book of Isaiah is fully extant on 1QIsaᵃ, a manuscript dated to around 125–100 BCE.[199] Parts of Isa 36–39 (Isa 36:1–2; 37:8–12, 29–32; 38:12–22; 39:1–8) are additionally extant on 1Q8 (1QIsaᵇ) and 4Q56 (4QIsaᵇ), both dated to 50–25 BCE, while only a fragment of 2 Chr 29:1–3 is preserved on 4Q118 (4QChr), and 2 Kgs 18–20 are not extant in the Dead Sea Scrolls.[200] Many of the expressions which are not shared with these passages about Hezekiah and Isaiah now in the Hebrew Bible are expressions which are frequently attested in the Dead Sea Scrolls outside these passages.

אל עליון "God the Most High" in Sir 48:20 is an expression frequently found in the Dead Sea Scrolls,[201] for example in 1Q20 (1QapGen ar)[202] and in Jubilees.[203] ביד "through the hand" referring to the mediation of prophets or other figures in Sir 48:20 is frequently attested in the Dead Sea Scrolls.[204]

גבורה "might" used in Sir 48:24 is frequently used for might, mostly divine might, in the Dead Sea Scrolls.[205] Sir 48:24 mentions רוח גבורה "spirit of might", which does not appear in this combination in the Hebrew Bible (see Chapter 6.4.3). The very same combination רוח גבורה "spirit of might" appears in 4Q372 (4QapocrJosephᵇ) Fragment 16 Line 2.[206]

Sir 48:25 mentions נהיות "happening things" and נסתרות "hidden things". The first form is not used anywhere in the Hebrew Bible, the second one hardly (see Chapter 6.4.3). Niphal forms of היה "to be" are frequent in the Dead Sea Scrolls.[207] The same niphal participle feminine plural form נהיות "happening things" is preserved, for example, in 4Q268 (4QDᶜ) Fragment 1 Line 8.[208] Niphal forms of סתר "to hide" and the form נסתרות "hidden things" are also frequently used.[209] נסתרות "hidden things" appears, for example, in 4Q268 (4QDᶜ) Fragment 1 Line 7, one line before נהיות "happening things".[210]

---

[199] Cf. Tov 2002, 29–30; WEBSTER 2002, 365. For an edition of 1QIsaᵃ cf. BURROWS 1950.

[200] Cf. ULRICH 2002a, 192–193, 201. 1Q8 (1QIsaᵇ) and 4Q65 (4QIsaᵇ) are dated to 50–25 BCE, cf. WEBSTER 2002, 402. 5Q3 (5QIsa) preserves fragments of Isa 40, cf. MILIK 1962b, 173. For the fragment 4Q118 (4QChr) cf. TREBOLLE BARRERA 2000, 295–297.

[201] Cf. KUMPMANN 2016, 118–120.

[202] Cf. MACHIELA 2009, 293.

[203] Cf. VANDERKAM 2018, 41; for example in Jub 21:20, cf. VANDERKAM/MILIK 1994a, 47.

[204] Cf. FABRY 2013, 56, 62.

[205] Cf. REYMOND 2011, 568–570.

[206] Cf. SCHULLER/BERNSTEIN 2001, 192, Pl. XLIX. The manuscript 4Q372 (4QapocrJosephᵇ) can be dated around 50 BCE, cf. SCHULLER/BERNSTEIN 2001, 165.

[207] Cf. BARTELMUS 2011, 767.

[208] Cf. BAUMGARTEN et al. 1996, 119, Pl. XXII. The manuscript 4Q268 (4QDᶜ) can be dated to the early 1ˢᵗ century CE, cf. BAUMGARTEN et al. 1996, 116, 118. The Damascus Document (CD) which is preserved on multiple manuscripts can be dated to the last half of the 2ⁿᵈ century BCE, cf. BAUMGARTEN et al. 2006, 3.

[209] Cf. BECKER 2013, 1123–1126.

[210] Cf. BAUMGARTEN et al. 1996, 119, Pl. XXII.

6.4 Isaiah (Sir 48:17–25)

Overall, while no intertextual connections can be shown, Sir 48:17–25 and Dead Sea Scrolls texts share several words. These shared words include נהיות "happening things" as well as the expression רוח גבורה "spirit of might" (consisting of two consecutive words in the same forms), neither of which appear anywhere in the Hebrew Bible.

6.4.6 Comparison within the Book of Ben Sira

In Hebrew, following Sir 48:17, 22, יחזקיהו "Hezekiah" is mentioned again in Sir 49:4 together with David and Josiah as the only kings who kept תורת עליון "the law of the Most High".

As in Sir 48:17, חזק "to be strong" and עיר "city" are combined in Sir 50:4 for Simon strengthening Jerusalem. מקוה "reservoir" is also used in Sir 50:3 for Simon's building works in Jerusalem.

As in Sir 48:20, אל עליון "God Most High" is used in Sir 46:5 where Josiah calls God and in Sir 47:5, 8 where David does the same. תפלה "prayer" said by the people is shared with Sir 50:19. ביד "in the hand" followed by a person is also used in Sir 46:4 for Josiah and in Sir 49:7 for Jeremiah, in both cases seemingly not referring to a use of the person's "hand" but their "speech", which could also be the case in Sir 48:20.

As in Sir 48:25, נהיות "happening things" and נסתרות "hidden things" are both used in Sir 49:12 as those which God reveals.[211]

In Greek, Sir 48:17^{LXX} does not share ὀχυρόω "to fortify" and κρήνη "well" with any other texts in Sir^{LXX}.

In Sir 48:18^{LXX}, a shared combination of ἐπαίρω "to lift up" and χείρα "hands" connects Joshua in Sir 46:2^{LXX} and David in Sir 47:4^{LXX} who raise their hands against enemies with Sennacherib in Sir 48:18^{LXX} who is an enemy and with Simon in Sir 50:20^{LXX} who raises his hands to bless Israel. In Sir 33:3^{LXX},[212] God is called to raise his hands against foreigners.

In Sir 48:19^{LXX}, σαλεύω "to shake" regarding the people is shared with Sir 48:12^{LXX} where, in contrast, Elisha does not shake.

In Sir 48:20^{LXX}, ἐλεήμων "merciful" is used for God, as in Sir 2:11; 50:19^{LXX}. ἐκπετάννυμι "to spread out" is shared with the first person prayer in Sir 51:19^{LXX}. λυτρόω "to redeem" is shared with Sir 49:10^{LXX} through the twelve prophets as well as Sir 50:24; 51:2^{LXX} through God.

In Sir 48:21^{LXX}, ἐκτρίβω "to destroy" is shared with Sir 46:18, 47:7^{LXX} connecting Hezekiah with Samuel and David.

Sir 48:22^{LXX} uses πιστός "faithful" combined with ὅρασις "vision", two words also combined in Sir 46:15^{LXX} for Samuel and nowhere else in the Septuagint.

---

[211] This is noted by MARBÖCK 2000, 313; BEENTJES 2006b, 157.
[212] Sir 33:3^{LXX} in ZIEGLER 1980, 190, equals Sir 36:22^{LXX} in RAHLFS/HANHART 2006, Vol. II 438.

176 *6. Ben Sira 44–50: Case Studies*

ἐνισχύω "to strengthen" is shared with Sir 50:4^{LXX} connecting Isaiah and Simon. ἐντέλλομαι "to command" is also used in the "Praise of the Ancestors" for God in Sir 45:3^{LXX}. προφήτης "prophet", πιστός "faithful", and ὅρασις "vision" are all shared with Sir 46:15^{LXX} about Samuel. ὑποδείκνυμι "to show" is shared with Sir 46:20^{LXX} about Samuel and Sir 49:8^{LXX} about Ezekiel.

Sir 48:23^{LXX} with the mention of an unusual behaviour of ὁ ἥλιος "the sun" connects Isaiah with Joshua (Sir 46:4^{LXX}).[213]

Like Sir 48:25^{LXX}, Sir 42:19^{LXX} uses ἐσόμενα "things going to be" and ἀπόκρυφα "hidden things" as those which God reveals. The understanding of ἀπόκρυφα "hidden things" is also attributed to the wise person in Sir 14:21; 39:3, 7^{LXX}.

Overall, in both Hebrew and Greek, individual words are shared with other texts in the Book of Ben Sira, including words not shared with texts about Hezekiah and Isaiah in the Hebrew Bible or Septuagint. Some shared words connect Hezekiah and Isaiah with other figures mentioned in the "Praise of the Ancestors".

6.4.7 Conclusion

In Ben Sira's description of Isaiah, there are no explicit references to any texts. There are similarities in Sir 48:17–25 with the Book of Isaiah, 2 Kgs 18–20, and 2 Chr 32. These similarities consist of shared contents with differences in details, and of individual shared words with at most two consecutive words shared in syntactical similarity. Most similarities could also be limited to Isa 1–39, and an intertextual reference to all of Isa 1–66 cannot be substantiated.

At the same time, individual words as well as two consecutive words in syntactical similarity in Sir 48:17–25 are shared with texts among the Dead Sea Scrolls, but not with any texts in the Hebrew Bible. While this also does not suffice to substantiate any direct intertextual references, extant sources outside the Hebrew Bible show that the vocabulary may not have been Ben Sira's invention as it definitely existed in extant ancient texts. In addition, the Hebrew Bible also mentions other texts not extant today. For example, 2 Kgs 20:20 says about Hezekiah's deeds הלא הם כתובים על ספר דברי הימים למלכי יהודה "Are these not written in the book of the words of the days regarding the kings of Judah?".[214]

While it is sometimes argued that in describing Isaiah Ben Sira uses only texts in the Hebrew Bible and then intentionally changes most of their words and content,[215] an easier explanation is that Ben Sira uses a range of contemporary

---

[213] This is also noted by ZAPFF 2010, 365. BEENTJES 2006b, 155, comments on Sir 48:23 as follows: "On the one hand, the whole line unmistakably recalls the biblical accounts. [...] On the other hand, Ben Sira has nevertheless created something special of his own: another internal parallel within the 'Laus Patrum'."

[214] On these sources cf. WEINGART 2017.

[215] Thus STADELMANN 1980, 205–206; HÖFFKEN 2000, 172–173; BEENTJES 2006b, 155–158.

6.5 Job (Sir 49:9)

6.5.1 Hebrew and Greek Text

Sir 49:9 mentions Job between Ezekiel (Sir 49:8) and the twelve prophets (Sir 49:10). Sir 49:9 reads in the Hebrew Manuscript B:[216]

Sir 49:9   וגם הזכיר את איוב נ[ב]יֹא   And he also remembered Job, a p[roph]et,
המכלכל כל דֹ[רכי צ]דֹק: the one supporting all w[ays of righ]tness.

The last letter of איוֹב "Job" and the word following it which is sometimes reconstructed as נֹ[ב]יֹא "prophet" are damaged.[217] While "prophet" can be reconstructed, "Job" is clearly visible on Manuscript B.[218] The subject of the first verb "he remembered" is probably Ezekiel who is the subject of the preceding verse.[219]

In Greek, Sir 49:9[LXX] reads:[220]

Sir 49:9[LXX]   καὶ γὰρ ἐμνήσθη τῶν ἐχθρῶν   For he also was reminded of the enemies
ἐν ὄμβρῳ καὶ ἀγαθῶσαι τοὺς   in a rainstorm, and to do good to those
εὐθύνοντας ὁδούς.   making straight ways.

It seems that the Septuagint here instead of איוב "Job" translates a plural form of the Hebrew word אויב "enemy", an alternative spelling of איב "enemy".[221] It is unclear if the subject that "was reminded" is Ezekiel who is the subject of the first half of Sir 49:8, or the unnamed subject showing Ezekiel a vision in the second half of the verse, most likely God.

Overall, in the Hebrew text Job is definitely mentioned between Ezekiel and the twelve prophets, and possibly explicitly designated as a prophet himself, while the Greek text does not mention Job at all.[222]

---

[216] Cf. the transcription by ABEGG in RENDSBURG/BINSTEIN 2013, Manuscript B XVIII verso. The letters in square brackets are not reconstructed in BEENTJES 1997, 88.

[217] For a summary of different reconstructions cf. WITTE 2015a, 29–30.

[218] Cf. the images of Manuscript B XVIII verso in RENDSBURG/BINSTEIN 2013 and BODLEIAN LIBRARIES [2017].

[219] Thus also WITTE 2015a, 30 n. 32.

[220] Cf. ZIEGLER 1980, 355.

[221] Cf. GESENIUS 2013, s.v. אֹיֵב u. אוֹיֵב. Thus also PETERS 1913, 421; BECKER/FABRY/REITEMEYER 2011, 2262; WITTE 2015a, 33–34; CORLEY 2019, 224; BEENTJES 2021, 75.

[222] Thus also WITTE 2015a, 37. Job but not as a prophet is mentioned in the Syriac Peshitta of Sir 49:9, cf. WITTE 2015a, 35.

178 6. Ben Sira 44–50: Case Studies

6.5.2 References to the Books of Ezekiel and Job?

Two books now in the Hebrew Bible are usually connected with Sir 49:9: Ezekiel and Job.[223] It is often argued that the mention of Job in Sir 49:9 is a reference to Ezekiel 14:14, 20.[224] Ezek 14:14, 20 mentions Job – as well as Noah and Daniel – as individuals whose righteousness would save their lives during God's punishment. If there is a reference to Ezek 14:14, 20, Noah and Daniel are left out. This is sometimes explained as follows: Noah appears separately in Sir 44–50, the Book of Daniel was not yet completed, and later sources also mention Job as a prophet.[225] Both explanations presuppose a knowledge of later sources including the Hebrew Bible, while it is debated if the figures in Ezek 14 are even identical with those in other books of the Hebrew Bible.[226]

The Book of Job is also seen as referred to in Sir 49:9.[227] It is sometimes argued that Ben Sira here refers to the Book of Job as a part of the "Prophets" part of the canon.[228] The opposite argument is also given: Ben Sira knew the Book of Job but here only refers to Ezekiel as Job is not included in the "Prophets" section of his canon.[229] All of these arguments presuppose that Ben Sira refers to a canon in Sir 44–50, even where it is noted that Ben Sira only mentions figures and not texts.[230] Similar problems appear in studies on Ben Sira and the Book of Job: only the Book of Job in the Hebrew Bible is compared to Ben Sira.[231]

6.5.3 Comparison with the Hebrew Bible

The name איוב "Job" only appears in Ezek 14:14, 20 and in the Book of Job within the Hebrew Bible. Nowhere in the Hebrew Bible are the name איוב "Job" and the word נביא "prophet" combined. The phrase דרכי צדק "ways of rightness" does not appear in the Hebrew Bible at all, כול in a Pilpel form "to provide" is not used in either Ezekiel or Job. The content of Ezek 14:13–20 is a divine threat of destruction and death through רעב "famine", חיה רעה "wild animal", חרב

---

[223] Cf. KAISER 2005, 188; WITTE 2017a, 343–344.

[224] Thus PETERS 1913, 421; EBERHARTER 1925, 156; SAUER 2000, 334; DI LELLA 2006, 166; ZAPFF 2010, 371; BECKER/FABRY/REITEMEYER 2011, 2262; WITTE 2015a, 30.

[225] Thus SKEHAN/DI LELLA 1987, 544; WITTE 2015a, 31–32. Some scholars (SMEND 1906, 471; SKEHAN/DI LELLA 1987, 544; ZAPFF 2010, 371) further argue that Josephus, Ag. Ap. 1.8 (but probably meaning Ag. Ap. 1.40) also counts Job among the thirteen prophetic books, but Job is not actually mentioned there, only the number of thirteen unnamed prophetic books, as WITTE 2015a, 36, notes. For the Greek text and an English translation of Josephus, Ag. Ap. 1.40, cf. THACKERAY 1926, 178–179. On Josephus in general see Chapter 2 Note 88.

[226] Cf. NOTH 1951; WAHL 1992.

[227] Cf. SCHMITT 2011, 449, who takes Sir 49:9 as the *terminus ad quem* for the Book of Job.

[228] Thus SMEND 1906, 471; GOSHEN-GOTTSTEIN 2002, 242; as a possibility also WITTE 2017a, 343–344.

[229] Thus BOX/OESTERLEY 1913, 505; STECK 1991, 136–137; GUILLAUME 2005, 13.

[230] Thus STECK 1991, 136.

[231] Thus EGGER-WENZEL 1996, 203; REITERER 2007, 345–347.

6.5 Job (Sir 49:9)   179

"sword", and דבר "plague" (Ezek 14:13, 15, 17, 19), from which only נח "Noah", דנאל "Daniel", and איוב "Job" (Ezek 14:14, 20) save themselves בצדקתם "through their righteousness" (Ezek 14:14, 20). In Ezek 14:14, 20, the word צדקה "righteousness" is used, similar to Sir 49:9 with the word צדק "rightness", but only the name איוב "Job" is actually shared between these two passages. Job is described as righteous in Ezek 14:14, 20, but not as a prophet. The main content of death and destruction is not shared at all with Sir 49:9.

In the Book of Job, the word נביא "prophet" does not appear. The word צדק "rightness" is used regarding Job, for example in Job 29:14, as is the word דרך "way", for example in Job 31:4, but not in combination. The name יחזקאל "Ezekiel" does not appear in the Book of Job. Job is described as righteous in the Book of Job, but not as a prophet or as connected with Ezekiel.

Overall, neither for Ezek 14:14, 20 nor for the Book of Job, shared words or shared content indicate an intertextual connection with Sir 49:9. Job's righteousness is the only aspect of content shared between the texts.

6.5.4 Comparison with the Greek Septuagint

The combination of ἐχθρός "enemy" and ὄμβρος "rainstorm" is not used anywhere else in the Septuagint.[232] The word ὄμβρος "rainstorm" is not used in either Ezekiel or Job in the Septuagint, neither ἀγαθόω "to do good". In the context of stormy weather, the frequent word ἐχθρός "enemy" is used in Job 38:23[LXX]. Ezek 14:13–20[LXX] does not use stormy weather as a possible threat but rather λιμός "famine", θηρία "wild animals", ῥομφαία "sword", and θάνατος "death" (Ezek 14:13, 15, 17, 19[LXX]). Enemies in a rainstorm play no role in either Ezekiel or Job in the Septuagint, and neither shared words nor shared content indicate an intertextual reference to these books.

6.5.5 Comparison with the Dead Sea Scrolls

Ezekiel 14:13–20 is not extant in the Dead Sea Scrolls,[233] while some parts of the Book of Job are preserved.[234] Job is not designated as a prophet anywhere in the

---

[232] Corley 2019, 224, states: "the strange mention of ὄμβρος 'rainstorm' could be an allusion to God's action in Deut 32:2 and Ezek 38:22, or to the theophany in Job 38:1." However, Deut 32:2[LXX] uses ὄμβρος "rainstorm" without mentioning any enemies, and the word ὄμβρος "rainstorm" is not used in either Ezek 38:22[LXX] or Job 38:1[LXX].

[233] Cf. Ulrich 2002a, 194.

[234] Cf. Ulrich 2002a, 199–200. Job 31:4 is not extant, cf. Ulrich 2002a, 199. 4Q101 (4QpaleoJob^c) contains some parts of Job 13–14 and is dated to 225–150 BCE, cf. Ulrich 2002a, 199; Webster 2002, 379. The word צדק "rightness" is not extant in the preserved parts of Job 29:14 in 11Q10 (11QtgJob), cf. García Martínez/Tigchelaar/van der Woude 1998a, 113–114.

180   6. Ben Sira 44–50: Case Studies

Dead Sea Scrolls.[235] The phrase דרכי צדק "ways of rightness" occurs in the Dead Sea Scrolls, in contrast to the Hebrew Bible where it is not used at all.[236]

6.5.6 Comparison within the Book of Ben Sira

In Hebrew or Greek, the name "Job" does not appear anywhere else in the Book of Ben Sira (on the term "prophet" see Chapter 3.4). In Greek, in the context of stormy weather, the frequent word ἐχθρός "enemy" is used in Sir 46:5^{LXX} regarding Joshua. The words ὄμβρος "rainstorm" and ἀγαθόω "to do good" are not used anywhere else in the Greek Book of Ben Sira. εὐθύνω "to make straight" with the object ὁδός "way" is only used in the Book of Ben Sira within the Septuagint, in Sir 2:6; 37:15; 49:9^{LXX}.

6.5.7 Conclusion

No intertextual connection can be substantiated between Sir 49:9 and the Books of Ezekiel and Job in the Hebrew Bible: there are no significant shared words and several differences in content, with the only similarity in content being Job's righteousness. At the same time, two consecutive words in syntactical similarity which are not contained in the Hebrew Bible are shared with the Dead Sea Scrolls. Sir 49:9^{LXX} does not mention Job at all.

6.6 Twelve Prophets (Sir 49:10)

6.6.1 Hebrew and Greek Text

"The twelve prophets" are mentioned in Sir 49:10. In Hebrew, these verses are not extant in the Masada Manuscript (Mas1h). In Manuscript B, Sir 49:10 is partly damaged and reads as follows:[237]

Sir 49:10	וגם שנים עשר הנביאׁים תהי	And also the twelve prophets – may be
	עצמתם פר[חות מתח[תׁם: אשר	their bones spr[outing from] their pla[ces
	החלימו את יעקב וישעׁוהו ב[...]	below] – who made strong Jacob and saved him in […]

In the Greek Septuagint, Sir 49:10^{LXX} reads as follows:[238]

---

[235] Job is explicitly called a prophet in later texts from the Common Era, cf. WITTE 2015a, 32–33; WITTE 2017a, 333. The name איוב "Job" itself is extant in 11Q10 (11QtgJob), cf. GARCÍA MARTÍNEZ/TIGCHELAAR/VAN DER WOUDE 1998a, 100–101, 125–126, 146–147, 160–161, 168–171.

[236] Cf. NEEF 2011, 723.

[237] Cf. the transcription by ABEGG in RENDSBURG/BINSTEIN 2013, Manuscript B XVIII verso. The letters in square brackets are not reconstructed in BEENTJES 1997, 89, an uncertainty in the reading הנביאׁים "the prophets" is not noted there.

[238] Cf. ZIEGLER 1980, 355.

6.6 Twelve Prophets (Sir 49:10)

Sir 49:10^{LXX} καὶ τῶν δώδεκα προφητῶν[239] τὰ ὀστᾶ ἀναθάλοι ἐκ τοῦ τόπου αὐτῶν· παρεκάλεσαν γὰρ τὸν Ιακωβ[240] καὶ ἐλυτρώσαντο αὐτοὺς ἐν πίστει ἐλπίδος.[241]

And the bones of the twelve prophets may sprout again from their place, for they comforted Jacob and redeemed them with faith of hope.

6.6.2 References to the Book of the Twelve Prophets?

The mention of "the twelve prophets" in Sir 49:10 is usually seen, in research on both Ben Sira and the Twelve Prophets, as the earliest extant evidence for "the Twelve Prophets" as the fixed literary unit now found in the Hebrew Bible,[242] placed after Isaiah, Jeremiah, and Ezekiel in the Masoretic order.[243] Sir 49:10 is sometimes used as a *terminus ante quem* for dating the unit of the Twelve Prophets,[244] even where it is also noted that other roughly contemporary texts do not mention such a unit.[245] Some scholars also assume that Ben Sira knew the Masoretic sequence of the twelve prophetic books in this literary unit.[246] This is rejected by others who note that there is no information on such an order in Sir 49:10.[247] Some arguments for a reference to the literary unit of "the Twelve Prophets" are that words related to נביא "prophet" are not mentioned in the Book of Ben Sira after Sir 49:10,[248] or that the Twelve Prophets do not fit into the chronology of Sir 44–50[249] (presupposing that they are identical with those

---

[239] Some Greek manuscripts read φυλῶν "tribes" instead of προφητῶν "prophets" and also add εἴη τὸ μνημόσυνον ἐν εὐλογίαις "may the remembrance be in blessings" similar to Sir 46:11^{LXX}, cf. ZIEGLER 1980, 355.

[240] Some Greek manuscripts and the Syriac Peshitta read Ισραηλ "Israel" instead of Ιακωβ "Jacob", cf. ZIEGLER 1980, 355.

[241] Some Greek manuscripts here add εἴη τὸ μνημόσυνον αὐτῶν ἐν εὐλογίαις "may their remembrance be in blessings" as in Sir 46:11^{LXX}, cf. ZIEGLER 1980, 355.

[242] Thus BOX/OESTERLEY 1913, 505; PETERS 1913, 421; HAMP 1951, 135; KOOLE 1965, 384; SKEHAN/DI LELLA 1987, 41; CHILDS 1979, 64; STECK 1991, 137; WISCHMEYER 1994, 257; JONES 1995, 8; CARR 1996, 39; FULLER 1996, 91; CRENSHAW 1997a, 631; RENDTORFF 1998, 186; SCHART 1998, 4; STEINMANN 1999, 39; CHAPMAN 2000, 260; SAUER 2000, 316, 334; GOSHEN-GOTT-STEIN 2002, 241–242; MOPSIK 2003, 47–48; WATSON 2004, 80–81; BEENTJES 2006a, 171; WÖHRLE 2006, 1; McDONALD 2007, 83; ZAPFF 2010, 371; MARTTILA 2008, 448; CARR 2011, 192; REITERER 2011c, 95; CORLEY 2013, 140; WRIGHT 2013b, 2343; DINES 2015, 439; ZENGER 2016, 631; FABRY 2018, 4; ZAPFF 2018, 81 n. 14; BEENTJES 2021, 75.

[243] Thus SNAITH 1974, 246; SAUER 1981, 629; SKEHAN/DI LELLA 1987, 544; STECK 1991, 137, 142–144; NOGALSKI 1993, 2, 281; HILDESHEIM 1996, 214, 216; STECK 1996, 130; SAUER 2000, 334; CORLEY 2011, 69–70; BECKER/FABRY/REITEMEYER 2011, 2262; EGGER-WENZEL 2011, 247; SCHMITT 2011, 365; STEMBERGER 2019, 36.

[244] Thus JONES 1995, 8; SCHART 1998, 4.

[245] Thus JONES 1995, 1; DINES 2015, 451.

[246] Thus STECK 1991, 144; SEITZ 2009, 39–40.

[247] Thus PAJUNEN/WEISSENBERG 2015, 733.

[248] Thus STECK 1991, 137–138; BEENTJES 2006d, 220.

[249] Thus STECK 1991, 137.

182   *6. Ben Sira 44–50: Case Studies*

in the Hebrew Bible). The supposed quotation of Mal 3:23–24 in Sir 48:10 (see Chapter 5.5.2) is seen by some scholars as supporting evidence for Ben Sira's knowledge of the Twelve Prophets as a whole,[250] while others argue that Ben Sira could also have had access to individual books instead, and warn against circular arguments.[251] Regarding the content of positive effects on Jacob (Israel), some scholars list passages from selected books in the Twelve Prophets which contain messages of hope,[252] even though others note that much of the content of the Twelve Prophets is actually rather negative for Israel and contains judgment.[253]

6.6.3 Comparison with the Hebrew Bible

Regarding words shared between Sir 49:10 and the Hebrew Bible, a combination of שׁנים עשׂר "twelve" and נביא "prophet" does not appear anywhere in the Hebrew Bible. A combination of עצמות "bones" and פרח "to sprout" is used once, in Isa 66:14, for those rejoicing in the restoration of Jerusalem, but nowhere in the Book of the Twelve Prophets. חלם₁ "to be strong" is not used anywhere in the Book of the Twelve Prophets (the root חלם₂ "to dream" appears once, in Joel 3:1), but only in Isa 38:16 in a hiphil form regarding Hezekiah, and in Job 39:4 in a qal form regarding young animals.[254] It is not combined with יעקב "Jacob" anywhere in the Hebrew Bible. ישׁע "to save" is not combined with יעקב "Jacob" in the Book of the Twelve Prophets, but only in the Book of Jeremiah (Jer 30:7, 10; 31:7; 46:27).

Overall, there are no shared words indicating intertextual connections with the Book of the Twelve Prophets in the Hebrew Bible. Regarding content, the main focus on comfort and hope in Sir 49:10 stands in contrast to the Book of the Twelve Prophets. In the Book of the Twelve Prophets, messages of comfort and hope are the exception rather than the rule amongst messages of threat.[255] The main content is thus not shared between Sir 49:10 and the Book of the Twelve Prophets.

6.6.4 Comparison with the Greek Septuagint

Regarding words shared with other books in the Septuagint, a combination of δώδεκα "twelve" and προφήτης "prophet" does not appear anywhere else in the Septuagint. The same applies to a combination of ὀστέον "bone" and ἀναθάλλω

---

[250] Thus STECK 1991, 141; JONES 1995, 8; SKA 2009, 193 n. 35; CORLEY 2011, 69–70.

[251] Thus BEN ZVI 1996, 130–131 n. 18, 137–138.

[252] Thus HILDESHEIM 1996, 216 (referring to EBERHARTER 1911, 20); CRENSHAW 1997a, 856; SKA 2009, 192–193; ZAPFF 2010, 372.

[253] Thus SNAITH 1974, 246; SKEHAN/DI LELLA 1987, 544; RENDTORFF 1998, 186; SKA 2009, 192–193.

[254] Cf. GESENIUS 2013, s. v. חלם₁, חלם₂.

[255] See Notes 252–253.

6.6 Twelve Prophets (Sir 49:10)183

"to sprout again". In Bar 2:24^{LXX}, τὰ ὀστᾶ "the bones" of kings and fathers are carried ἐκ τοῦ τόπου αὐτῶν "out of their place" rather than sprouting again. The words παρακαλέω "to comfort" and Ἰακωβ "Jacob" appear in one other verse in the Septuagint, Lam 1:17^{LXX}, but there the verb's object is Zion rather than Jacob. The combination of λυτρόω "to redeem" and Ἰακωβ "Jacob" is not found in the Twelve Prophets in the Septuagint, only in Ps 76:16^{LXX} (= Ps 80:16^{MT}) which summarizes Israel's history, and in Isaiah and Jeremiah (Isa 41:14; 43:1; 44:23; Jer 38:11^{LXX}). No other combination of πίστις "faith" and ἐλπίς "hope" is used in the Septuagint. There are no shared words indicating intertextual connection, and as in the Hebrew Bible, the main content is also not shared.

6.6.5 Comparison with the Dead Sea Scrolls

No combination of words for "twelve" and "prophet" is found in the Dead Sea Scrolls. שְׁנִים עָשָׂר "twelve" is frequently used as an important number in other contexts.[256] פרח "to sprout" is used in Dead Sea Scrolls regarding the memory of people,[257] but not combined with עצם "bone". חלם "to be strong" can be used in this meaning rather than as "to dream",[258] but neither this verb nor ישׁע "to save" are combined with יעקב "Jacob".

A Book of Twelve Prophets is not extant in the Dead Sea Scrolls. Fragments of all of the twelve individual books are extant, but no scroll contains parts of all twelve books.[259] Where more than one book is preserved on the same scroll, the order of some of the twelve individual books differs between the Masoretic Text, the Septuagint, and a part of the Dead Sea Scrolls.[260] For example, in 4Q76 (4QXII^a), the preserved parts of Malachi 3,[261] rather than standing at the end of the scroll, are followed by preserved parts of Jonah 1[262] or some other text.[263] A stable collection of "the Twelve Prophets" cannot be materially proven.[264] Never-

---

[256] Cf. FABRY 2016, 238–239.

[257] Cf. DAHMEN 2016, 328–330.

[258] Cf. DiTOMMASO 2011, 988–989.

[259] Cf. ULRICH 2002a, 195–196.

[260] Cf. JONES 1995, esp. 223; FULLER 1996, 91–93, 96; PAJUNEN/WEISSENBERG 2015, 737, 750–751. In Septuagint manuscripts, the order of the Twelve Prophets and their placement before or after Isaiah, Jeremiah, and Ezekiel also differs, cf. SCHART 2011, 2277–2279. The manuscript evidence overall stands in contrast to the one unrivalled ordered unit of the Twelve Prophets assumed by SEITZ 2009, 39–40 (referring to WATSON 2004, 78–88).

[261] Cf. FULLER 1997, 228–230. 4Q76 (4QXII^a) is dated to around 150–125 BCE, cf. FULLER 1997, 221.

[262] Thus FULLER 1997, 222.

[263] Thus PAJUNEN/WEISSENBERG 2015, 749–751.

[264] Cf. PAJUNEN/WEISSENBERG 2015, 750–751. On later Pesharim of some of the Twelve Prophets see Chapter 1 Note 153 and Chapter 2 Note 129.

184 *6. Ben Sira 44–50: Case Studies*

theless, even where the material evidence of the Dead Sea Scrolls is recognized, Sir 49:10 is still argued to be a reference to all of the Twelve Prophets.[265]

6.6.6 Comparison within the Book of Ben Sira

In the Hebrew Book of Ben Sira, שנים עשר "twelve" also appears in Sir 44:23 regarding the twelve tribes of Jacob, while in Sir 44:23[LXX] the form δέκα δύο "ten-two" rather than δώδεκα "twelve" is used. In the Hebrew Book of Ben Sira, amongst other passages outside the "Praise of the Ancestors", the verb ישע "to save" is also used for God through the hand of Isaiah in Sir 48:20.

In the Greek Book of Ben Sira, amongst other passages outside the "Praise of the Ancestors", the verb παρακαλέω "to comfort" and λυτρόω "to redeem" appear in Sir 48:20, 24[LXX] regarding Isaiah, and the noun πίστις "faith" is used in Sir 45:4[LXX] regarding Moses and in Sir 46:15[LXX] regarding Samuel. None of these three prophetic figures are among the Twelve Prophets in the Hebrew Bible.[266] No other combination of πίστις "faith" and ἐλπίς "hope" is used in the Greek Book of Ben Sira, and ἐλπίς "hope" is not used elsewhere in the "Praise of the Ancestors". The Greek verse Sir 46:12[LXX] about the judges shares the content of sprouting bones with the Hebrew and Greek versions of Sir 49:10. In Greek, the whole phrase τὰ ὀστᾶ (αὐτῶν) ἀναθάλοι ἐκ τοῦ τόπου αὐτῶν "(their) bones may sprout again from their place" is also shared between Sir 46:12[LXX] (including αὐτῶν "their") and Sir 49:10[LXX] (without αὐτῶν "their"). The Hebrew Sir 46:11–12 differs from the Greek and shares no words or content with Sir 49:10 (see Chapter 6.3.6).

Overall, in the Greek (but not the Hebrew) Book of Ben Sira, there is a whole phrase shared between the description of the judges in Sir 46:12[LXX] and the description of the twelve prophets in Sir 49:10[LXX]. Shared words connect the twelve prophets with other prophetic figures such as Moses, Samuel, and Isaiah, rather than with any prophetic books.

6.6.7 Conclusion

No text written by any of the twelve prophets is mentioned in Sir 49:10. Rather, the mention of bones shows that the verse refers to persons, not texts. Nevertheless, scholars who explicitly note this reference to persons rather than texts still hold the view that Ben Sira refers to the Twelve Prophets as a literary unit,[267] sometimes based on the Prologue to Ben Sira.[268]

---

[265] Cf. HARTOG 2018, 423.

[266] For the term "prophet" in the Book of Ben Sira see Chapter 3.4.2.

[267] Thus STECK 1991, 136–137; WATSON 2004, 81; McDONALD 2007, 82–83. STECK 1991, 117, argues for a fixed sequence of scrolls containing Isaiah, Jeremiah, Ezekiel, and the Twelve Prophets, but does not explain how given the material nature of scrolls they could be kept in a fixed sequence.

[268] Thus JONES 1995, 8–9.

Shared words between Sir 49:10 and the Twelve Prophets now in the Hebrew Bible are lacking, and the content of Sir 49:10 has an entirely different focus on comfort rather than threat. The Dead Sea Scrolls do not contain a Book of Twelve Prophets as a literary unit. Within the Greek Book of Ben Sira, a shared phrase about the sprouting of bones connects the twelve prophets with the judges. The argument that Ben Sira knew the Twelve Prophets now in the Hebrew Bible presupposes the existence of a literary unit of the Twelve Prophets rather than proving it.

6.7 Conclusion

Case studies of the passages most frequently used to argue for Ben Sira's reference to whole books in the Hebrew Bible – Sir 44:16 and 49:14 about Enoch, Sir 46:11–12 about the judges, Sir 48:17–25 about Isaiah, Sir 49:9 about Job, and Sir 49:10 about the twelve prophets –, do not confirm any intertextual references to the Hebrew Bible or other texts outside the Book of Ben Sira. The five passages do not actually refer to any books at all. They only contain a few shared words with books in the Hebrew Bible. They also differ from the Hebrew Bible in their contents, even on a conceptual level. In the case of Enoch, contents in Ben Sira which differ from the Hebrew Bible such as Enoch's uniqueness or Enoch as a sign of knowledge are preserved in other extant ancient literature. In the case of the judges, the main content in Ben Sira may differ fundamentally from the Hebrew Bible if some judges themselves turn away from God rather than saving the people. Job is most likely designated as a prophet, and the twelve prophets are connected with hope rather than threat. A comparison of the five passages in their Greek translation with the Septuagint also does not reveal any intertextual references. At the same time, the five passages share both words and contents which are not found in the Hebrew Bible with extant texts outside the Hebrew Bible.

The lack of intertextual references to the Hebrew Bible shown in the five case studies could be seen as a negative result: if no intertextual references can be substantiated, the question of Ben Sira's intentional or unintentional use of texts now in the Hebrew Bible cannot be answered.[269] No reception or interpretation of authoritative texts now in the Hebrew Bible can be studied in those passages. At the same time, the case studies show that extant traditions outside the Hebrew Bible share similarities with Ben Sira which are not shared with the Hebrew Bible. This highlights a positive aspect of widening the focus beyond the canon of today's Hebrew Bible. MROCZEK formulates this idea as follows:

---

[269] Cf. similarly WRIGHT 2012, 385 (see Chapter 1 Note 210).

186   *6. Ben Sira 44–50: Case Studies*

"Undoing biblical hegemony is not merely a negative project. Rather, loosening the Bible's hold can uncover *more* possibilities for interpreting the ancient evidence."[270]

One such possibility is that Ben Sira did not invent all the material not shared with today's Hebrew Bible himself, in an intentional deviation from authoritative texts changing most of their words and contents, but instead used a wide range of contemporary traditions. There is extant evidence for such traditions in ancient manuscripts, and oral traditions generally play an explicit role in the Book of Ben Sira (see Chapter 2.3). This does not exclude the possibility that the range of traditions included texts now in the Hebrew Bible. But this is neither necessarily the case[271] nor the only option. There is no necessary priority of the canon of the Hebrew Bible. Rather than seeing all other possible references as additions to references to texts in the Hebrew Bible,[272] the possibility that there are references to other texts but no references to texts in the Hebrew Bible also has to be considered. In addition, aspects such as the materiality and fluidity of ancient texts have to be taken into account.[273]

The five case studies show that a reference to the whole canon of the Hebrew Bible / Old Testament cannot be substantiated based on those passages most frequently used to argue for it. Of course, five case studies do not suffice to argue that Ben Sira had no knowledge of any texts now in the Hebrew Bible at all. Futher detailed studies comparing parts of Sir 44–50 to texts in- and outside the Hebrew Bible would be desirable. The same would be desirable for other chapters in the Book of Ben Sira.[274] It remains possible that references to texts now in Hebrew Bible can be found in the Book of Ben Sira. However, the same is true for texts not now in the Hebrew Bible. Given that the case studies show shared words and contents in Ben Sira and other extant texts which are not shared with the Hebrew Bible, future studies should not compare Sir 44–50 with the canon of the Hebrew Bible only, taking for granted that this canon forms the sole and authoritative basis of the "Praise of the Ancestors". Instead, individual passages in today's Hebrew Bible should be assessed separately and in their ancient sources rather than as a whole canon, and other ancient texts not now included in the Hebrew Bible should be taken into account.

---

[270] MROCZEK 2015, 33.

[271] In contrast, ZAPFF 2019, 97, only asks how, not if, the Book of Ben Sira refers to texts in the Hebrew Bible.

[272] Thus MARBÖCK 1995d, 143.

[273] See Chapter 2. On textual fluidity see Chapter 1 Note 102 and Chapter 3 Note 60.

[274] For examples comparing Sir 16 with 1 Enoch see Note 32.

7. Results

7.1 The Beginning of the Biblical Canon and Ben Sira

The Book of Ben Sira – today included in the Old Testament in some but not all Christian traditions, and not included in the Jewish Hebrew Bible – was written in the early 2nd century BCE. It is usually seen as the earliest evidence for the tripartite canon of today's Hebrew Bible: Law, Prophets, and Writings. This view has to be revised in light of the ancient Dead Sea Scrolls which were re-discovered in the mid-20th century CE. The Dead Sea Scrolls comprise around a thousand fragmentary manuscripts dating from the 3rd century BCE to the 1st century CE. Some of these manuscripts contain texts now in the Hebrew Bible in a variety of different forms while most contain other texts, including parts of the Book of Ben Sira.

7.1.1 Hebrew and Greek Sources

The Book of Ben Sira was written in Hebrew, but for centuries mainly trans-mitted in translations into other languages, most importantly in the ancient Greek translation preserved in the Septuagint (LXX) which also includes a Greek Prologue to this translation. In rediscoveries near Cairo at the end of the 19th century CE and near the Dead Sea in the mid-20th century CE, Hebrew frag-ments of the Book of Ben Sira came to light and were subsequently published in editions and photographs. Today, large parts of the book are available in He-brew, although some chapters are only partly preserved in Hebrew, and some chapters – for example Sir 24 – are not preserved in Hebrew at all.

Three key passages in the Book of Ben Sira are usually used to argue for Ben Sira as the first evidence for a tripartite canon: the Prologue to the Greek trans-lation, Sir 38:24–39:11, and the "Praise of the Ancestors" Sir 44–50. The com-parative analysis of both the available Hebrew texts and the fully extant ancient Greek Septuagint translation shows that two of these three passages are not avail-able in Hebrew: the Hebrew text of most of Sir 38:24–39:11 is not extant, and the Prologue to the Greek translation only exists in Greek. Only Sir 44–50 is mostly extant in Hebrew.

188   7. Results

7.1.2 Anachronism of Biblical Canon

The view that Ben Sira is the earliest evidence for a biblical canon often relies
on concepts developed before the rediscovery of the ancient Dead Sea Scrolls
in the mid-20th century CE. Rather than proving the existence of "the" Bible, the
Dead Sea Scrolls attest to the diversity and variability of texts in antiquity. In
addition, material limitations of ancient writing practices, especially the use of
scrolls rather than codices, exclude the possibility of writing the entire Hebrew
Bible or a significant part thereof on one document before the Common Era. The
terms "Bible" and "canon" are anachronistic for the 2nd century BCE when the
Book of Ben Sira was written. Alternative terms such as "scriptures" and "authoritative texts" are suggested in research on the Dead Sea Scrolls for texts which are
quoted and referred to in ways implying textual authority. However, the Book of
Ben Sira does not include any explicit references to textual authority except for
references to itself. It does not include a single quotation of any text in- or outside
today's Hebrew Bible. At the same time, oral teaching is explicitly mentioned and
plays an important role in the Book of Ben Sira. Only the Greek Prologue refers
to specific groups of books.

7.1.3 Key Passages: Greek Prologue, Sir 38:24–39:11, Sir 44–50

Only the Greek Prologue, written later than the Book of Ben Sira itself, mentions
three categories of books as authoritative for Israel: "the law and the prophets
and the other ancestral books". This seems similar to the tripartite canon of
today's Hebrew Bible. However, the content of the three categories of books is not
actually mentioned in the Prologue, and the Book of Ben Sira itself is described
as having some of the same authority.

Sir 38:24–39:11, mostly extant in Greek only, does not show any references
to a canon in its description of a scribe's activities. God's "law" is referred to
as an especially important source of wisdom, but a written form or the content
of the "law" are not mentioned. Other sources of wisdom including travel and
divine inspiration explicitly play an important role. If compared to the Hebrew
Bible, at most a one-part canon of "Law" can be seen in the Greek text of Sir
38:24–39:11[LXX]. However, the "law" is not equated there with today's Pentateuch.
The passage does not explicitly refer to any written texts, and does not mention
writing or reading among the scribe's activities.

Sir 44–50, the "Praise of the Ancestors", contains some of the same figures as
the first two parts of the tripartite canon of the Hebrew Bible, while figures found
in the "Writings" part of this canon are mostly missing. If compared to the Hebrew Bible, at most a bipartite canon of "Law" and "Prophets" can be seen in Sir
44–50. However, the order of figures praised differs from the Hebrew Bible, for
example regarding the mentions of David, Job, and Phineas, and the lack of any
mentions of Saul or Ezra. Sir 44–50 does not refer to the authority of any written

texts except the Book of Ben Sira itself. Sir 48:10 about Elijah does not contain a quotation of Mal 3:23–24 and shares words and contents with a variety of extant texts. The five passages on Enoch, the judges, Isaiah, Job, and the twelve prophets – which are frequently used to argue for canonical references – only refer to persons, never books. They do not contain intertextual references to the Hebrew Bible or the Greek Septuagint or any other texts. Their contents also differ significantly from those found in the Hebrew Bible. At the same time, the passages share words and contents not found in the Hebrew Bible with other literature prior and contemporary to Ben Sira such as 1 Enoch and Jubilees. Since there are numerous differences between these passages in Ben Sira and the Hebrew Bible and, at the same time, similarities with other extant texts, it is unlikely that Ben Sira refers to the Hebrew Bible only and invents changes to most of its words and contents himself in an intentional deviation from the Hebrew Bible. More probably, Ben Sira uses a wide range of contemporary traditions.

The study of the three key passages also demonstrates that even if the Hebrew and Greek texts of Ben Sira are combined, today's canon of the Hebrew Bible is taken as a point of comparison, and the strongest similarities are highlighted, the Prologue, Sir 38:24–39:11, and Sir 44–50 only indicate a tripartite, one-part, and bipartite canon, rather than any common canon at all. But more importantly, the Greek Prologue contains the only explicit mentions of authoritative written texts. The two key passages in Book of Ben Sira itself show hardly any interest in written texts at all, and do not refer to any textual authority other than the Book of Ben Sira itself.

7.2 Implications

7.2.1 Historical Implications

The Book of Ben Sira in the early 2nd century BCE cannot be used as the earliest evidence for a biblical canon. It is possible that texts now in the Hebrew Bible already existed in the early 2nd century BCE, and for very few passages this is proven by extant ancient manuscripts. But the existence of a biblical canon cannot be taken for granted at the time of Ben Sira. Those sources currently known as references to a canon are later than Ben Sira. In particular, around two whole centuries separate Ben Sira from Philo and Josephus. The Second Temple Period cannot be seen as one monolithic block, and developments during this long period have to be considered.

The place of the Greek Prologue to Ben Sira in reconstructions of the history of the canon of the Hebrew Bible could be reassessed in two ways depending on the date of the Prologue. The date of the Prologue depends on answers given to the question whether the date given in the Prologue itself with reference to a late

2nd century BCE king is correct or pseudepigraphic. It cannot be proven that the Prologue is pseudepigraphic as it does not contain definite anachronisms itself, but as it also shows similarities with ancient pseudepigraphic texts the possibility of pseudepigraphy cannot be excluded either. One Greek word in the Prologue is not otherwise used before the 1st century CE. Materially, the Prologue is not attested in manuscripts before the 4th century CE. If the Prologue does date to the late 2nd century BCE while the Book of Ben Sira dates to the early 2nd century BCE, the difference between the two could support reconstructions which see the Maccabean revolts around 167 BCE as a key factor in the history of the canon. This could also be supported by the extensive praise of the High Priest Simon in Sir 50: rather than textual authority, priestly authority was important for the Hebrew Book of Ben Sira. This may have changed after the Maccabean revolts. However, neither the Prologue nor the Greek translation of the Book of Ben Sira contain any reference to the Maccabean revolts. If the date given in the Prologue is pseudepigraphic, the Prologue could have been written much later than the late 2nd century BCE. This could support reconstructions which date the formation of a tripartite canon to the 1st century CE. Either way, the content of the three categories of books is not mentioned in the Prologue, and no specific canonical list can be derived from it.

7.2.2 Methodological Implications

Further studies of the Book of Ben Sira in Hebrew and Greek, especially on the numerous figures in Sir 44–50, and on the relation of the Book of Ben Sira and the Hebrew Bible and Septuagint as well as the Dead Sea Scrolls would be desirable. In such studies, scholarship on the Dead Sea Scrolls and the Hebrew Bible should be combined, and the spectrum of orality and literacy in antiquity as well as extant texts which today are outside the Hebrew Bible be taken seriously. Since the Book of Ben Sira as the supposed earliest evidence does not prove the existence of a biblical canon, it cannot be taken for granted that all texts in this canon were available, combined, or authoritative at Ben Sira's time. The same applies to the assumption of oral traditions basically identical with the written texts now in the Hebrew Bible. This does not exclude the possibility that references to individual passages which now form a part of the Hebrew Bible may still be found in the Book of Ben Sira, both in the "Praise of the Ancestors" and other parts of the book. However, for each passage now in the Hebrew Bible, the possible availability and textual fluidity of the particular passage, the combination with other passages now in the canon of the Hebrew Bible, and the authority of the passage at Ben Sira's time has to be assessed. In addition, an argument has to be made why a passage now in the Hebrew Bible seems a more likely reference text than other ancient texts, using the same criteria for both.

For future research on the Hebrew Bible / Old Testament as well as the Dead Sea Scrolls more generally, three methodological implications are of particular relevance. First, ancient texts transmitted in more than one language, for example in Hebrew and Greek versions, have to be analyzed by comparing rather than conflating the different languages.

Second, rather than taking the later concept of a biblical canon and applying it equally to centuries before the Common Era, other extant written sources, knowledge about the material limitations of ancient writing practices, textual fluidity, and explicit mentions of oral tradition have to be taken into account. This can serve to avoid circular reasoning where today's Hebrew Bible rather than ancient material evidence serves as both the start and end point of an argument. Even today, as the inclusion or exclusion of the Book of Ben Sira shows, different Jewish and Christian traditions use different biblical canons. And even the concept of canon today is not always restricted to a fixed group of texts. In extant ancient texts, similar words and contents can be found in other ancient texts outside as well as inside different later canons. Rather than assuming that texts included today in the Hebrew Bible or another canon are the point of reference of ancient texts without further arguments, texts for comparison should not be restricted to texts canonical today from the outset. Instead, all extant texts close in their languages and regions should be taken into account. Such sources may in some cases indeed show the authority of texts which now form a part of the Hebrew Bible. However, an argument about the existence and authority of particular texts has to be made for each period of time studied. It cannot be taken for granted that all of the Hebrew Bible was authoritative at all times. Instead, ancient textual authority and criteria for recognizing authoritative texts merit further study.

Third, using the same criteria for detecting intertextual references for texts in and beyond the Hebrew Bible can help to avoid circular reasoning. While the criteria themselves may well be developed further in future research, they should not be applied differently to texts in and beyond the Hebrew Bible without prior explicit arguments giving reasons for such different applications for the particular texts and periods of time which are studied.

7.3 Concluding Summary

The Book of Ben Sira cannot serve as evidence for the tripartite canon of today's Hebrew Bible / Old Testament in the early 2nd century BCE. The Book of Ben Sira places an explicit emphasis on oral teaching. It also contains words and contents which are not shared with today's Hebrew Bible but with other ancient texts, especially texts extant in the Dead Sea Scrolls. Rather than proving the existence of the biblical canon, the Book of Ben Sira attests to a wide range of traditions in the early 2nd century BCE.

Bibliography

ABEGG, Martin G. 2002. "Concordance of Proper Nouns in the Non-Biblical Texts from Qumran." In *The Texts from the Judaean Desert: Indices and an Introduction to the Discoveries in the Judaean Desert Series*, edited by Emanuel Tov, 229–284. Discoveries in the Judaean Desert 39. Oxford: Clarendon.

Accordance 13: Bible Software. 2020. Altamonte Springs, FL: OakTree Software.

ADAMS, Samuel L. 2008. *Wisdom in Transition: Act and Consequence in Second Temple Instructions.* Supplements to the Journal for the Study of Judaism 125. Leiden: Brill.

ADAMS, Samuel L. 2016. "Sage as Prophet? Allusion and Reconfiguration in Ben Sira and Other Second Temple Wisdom Texts." In *Tracing Sapiential Traditions in Ancient Judaism*, edited by Hindy Najman, Jean-Sébastien Rey, and Eibert J.C. Tigchelaar, 89–105. Supplements to the Journal for the Study of Judaism 174. Leiden: Brill.

ADAMS, Samuel L. 2017. "Reassessing the Exclusivism of Ben Sira's Jewish Paideia." In *Second Temple Jewish 'Paideia' in Context*, edited by Jason Zurawski and Gabriele Boccaccini, 47–58. Beihefte zur Zeitschrift für die neutestamentliche Wissenschaft und die Kunde der älteren Kirche 228. Berlin: De Gruyter.

ADAMS, Samuel L. 2021. "Where Is Ezra? Ben Sira's Surprising Omission and the Selective Presentation in the Praise of the Ancestors." In *Sirach and its Contexts: The Pursuit of Wisdom and Human Flourishing*, edited by Samuel L. Adams, Greg S. Goering, and Matthew J. Goff, 151–166. Supplements to the Journal for the Study of Judaism 196. Leiden: Brill.

AITKEN, James K. 2000. "Biblical Interpretation as Political Manifesto: Ben Sira in his Seleucid Setting." *Journal of Jewish Studies* 51 (2): 191–208.

AITKEN, James K. 2011. "The Literary Attainment of the Translator of Greek Sirach." In *The Texts and Versions of the Book of Ben Sira: Transmission and Interpretation*, edited by Jean-Sébastien Rey and Jan Joosten, 95–126. Supplements to the Journal for the Study of Judaism 150. Leiden: Brill.

AITKEN, James K. 2018. "The Synoptic Problem and the Reception of the Ben Sira Manuscripts." In *Discovering, Deciphering and Dissenting: Ben Sira Manuscripts after 120 Years*, edited by James K. Aitken, Renate Egger-Wenzel, and Stefan C. Reif, 147–167. Deuterocanonical and Cognate Literature Yearbook 2018. Berlin: De Gruyter.

AITKEN, James K. 2021. "The Origins and Social Context of the Septuagint." In *The T&T Clark Handbook of Septuagint Research*, edited by William A. Ross and W.E. Glenny, 9–20. London: T&T Clark.

ALEXANDER, Loveday. 1993. *The Preface to Luke's Gospel: Literary Convention and Social Context in Luke 1.1–4 and Acts 1.1.* Society for New Testament Studies Monograph Series 78. Cambridge: Cambridge University Press.

194   *Bibliography*

ALEXANDER, Philip S. 1998. "From Son of Adam to Second God: Transformations of the Biblical Enoch." In *Biblical Figures Outside the Bible*, edited by Michael E. Stone, 87–122. Harrisburg, PA: Trinity Press International.

ALEXANDER, Philip S. 2007. "The Formation of the Biblical Canon in Rabbinic Judaism." In *The Canon of Scripture in Jewish and Christian Tradition*, edited by Philip S. Alexander and Jean-Daniel Kaestli, 57–80. Publications de l'Institut Romand des Sciences Bibliques 4. Lausanne: Éditions du Zèbre.

ALEXANDER, Philip S./VERMES, Geza. 1998. "279. 4QFour Lots." In *Qumran Cave 4, XIX, Sereh Ha-Yaḥad and Two Related Texts*, edited by Philip S. Alexander and Geza Vermes, 217–223, Pl. XXIII. Discoveries in the Judaean Desert 26. Oxford: Clarendon.

ALLEGRO, John M., ed. 1968. *Qumrân Cave 4 I (4Q158–4Q186)*. Discoveries in the Judaean Desert 5. Oxford: Clarendon.

AMELING, Walter. 2001a. "Ptolemaios III. Euergetes I." In *Der Neue Pauly. Enzyklopädie der Antike, Band 10*, edited by Hubert Cancik and Helmuth Schneider, 537–538. Stuttgart: Metzler.

AMELING, Walter. 2001b. "Ptolemaios VIII. Euergetes II." In *Der Neue Pauly. Enzyklopädie der Antike, Band 10*, edited by Hubert Cancik and Helmuth Schneider, 542–544. Stuttgart: Metzler.

ANGEL, Joseph L. 2013. "New Jerusalem." In *Outside the Bible: Ancient Jewish Writing Related to Scripture, Vol. 3*, edited by Louis H. Feldman, James L. Kugel, and Lawrence H. Schiffman, 3152–3171. Lincoln; Philadelphia: University of Nebraska Press; Jewish Publication Society.

ARGALL, Randal A. 1995. *1 Enoch and Sirach: A Comparative Literary and Conceptual Analysis of the Themes of Revelation, Creation and Judgment*. Early Judaism and Its Literature 8. Atlanta, GA: Scholars Press.

ARGALL, Randal A. 2002. "Competing Wisdoms: 1 Enoch and Sirach." *Henoch* 24: 169–178.

ARNETH, Martin. 2015. "Zur 'Kanonisierung' der Hebräischen Bibel." *Verkündigung und Forschung* 60 (1): 42–51.

ARNOLD, Bill T. 2014. *Introduction to the Old Testament*. Cambridge: Cambridge University Press.

ASALE, Bruk A. 2016. "The Ethiopian Orthodox Tewahedo Church Canon of the Scriptures: Neither Open nor Closed." *The Bible Translator* 67 (2): 202–222.

ASKIN, Lindsey A. 2016. "The Qumran Psalms Scroll Debate and Ben Sira: Considering the Evidence of Textual Reuse in Sir 43:11–19." *Dead Sea Discoveries* 23 (1): 27–50.

ASKIN, Lindsey A. 2018a. "What Did Ben Sira's Bible and Desk Look Like?" In *Ancient Readers and Their Scriptures: Engaging the Hebrew Bible in Early Judaism and Christianity*, edited by Garrick V. Allen and John A. Dunne, 3–26. Ancient Judaism and Early Christianity 107. Leiden: Brill.

ASKIN, Lindsey A. 2018b. *Scribal Culture in Ben Sira*. Supplements to the Journal for the Study of Judaism 184. Leiden: Brill.

ASLANOFF, Cyrille. 1998. "Les prologues conservés du Siracide." In *Entrer en matière: Les prologues*, edited by Jean-Daniel Dubois, 167–183. Patrimoines. Paris: Éditions du Cerf.

ASSMANN, Jan. 1992. *Das kulturelle Gedächtnis: Schrift, Erinnerung und politische Identität in frühen Hochkulturen*. München: Beck.

ATTRIDGE, Harold W. 2013. "Philo, the Epic Poet." In *Outside the Bible: Ancient Jewish Writing Related to Scripture, Vol. 1*, edited by Louis H. Feldman, James L. Kugel, and Lawrence H. Schiffman, 726–729. Lincoln; Philadelphia: University of Nebraska Press; Jewish Publication Society.

Bibliography

AUNE, David E. 2012. "Reconceptualizing the Phenomenon of Ancient Pseudepigraphy: An Epilogue." In *Pseudepigraphie und Verfasserfiktion in frühchristlichen Briefen: Pseudepigraphy and Author Fiction in Early Christian Letters*, edited by Michaela Engelmann, Jörg Frey, Jens Herzer, Martina Janßen, and Clare K. Rothschild, 789–824. Wissenschaftliche Untersuchungen zum Neuen Testament 246. Tübingen: Mohr Siebeck.

AUNE, David E. 2013. "Pseudo-Orpheus." In *Outside the Bible: Ancient Jewish Writing Related to Scripture, Vol. 1*, edited by Louis H. Feldman, James L. Kugel, and Lawrence H. Schiffman, 743–749. Lincoln; Philadelphia: University of Nebraska Press; Jewish Publication Society.

AUVRAY, P. 1957. "Notes sur le prologue de l'Ecclesiastique." In *Mélanges bibliques*, edited by André Robert, 281–287. Travaux de l'Institut Catholique de Paris 4. Paris: Bloud & Gay.

BABOTA, Vasile. 2014. *The Institution of the Hasmonean High Priesthood*. Supplements to the Journal for the Study of Judaism 165. Leiden: Brill.

BAGNALL, Roger S. 2002. "Alexandria: Library of Dreams." *Proceedings of the American Philosophical Society* 146 (4): 348–362.

BAILLET, Maurice. 1962. "Textes des Grottes 2Q, 3Q, 6Q, 7Q à 10Q." In *Les "petites grottes" de Qumran: Exploration de la falaise, les grottes 2Q, 3Q, 5Q, 6Q, 7Q à 10Q, le rouleau de cuivre, Textes*, edited by Maurice Baillet, J. T. Milik, Roland De Vaux, and H. W. Baker, 45–145. Discoveries in the Judaean Desert 3. Oxford: Clarendon.

BAILLET, Maurice. 1982a. "482. Livre des Jubilés (?)." In *Qumrân Grotte 4 III (4Q482–4Q520)*, edited by Maurice Baillet, 1–2, Pl. I. Discoveries in the Judaean Desert 7. Oxford: Clarendon.

BAILLET, Maurice. 1982b. "504. Paroles des Luminaires (i)." In *Qumrân Grotte 4 III (4Q482–4Q520)*, edited by Maurice Baillet, 137–168, Pl. XLIX–LIII. Discoveries in the Judaean Desert 7. Oxford: Clarendon.

BAILLET, Maurice / MILIK, J. T. / DE VAUX, Roland / BAKER, H. W., eds. 1962. *Les "petites grottes" de Qumran: Exploration de la falaise, les grottes 2Q, 3Q, 5Q, 6Q, 7Q à 10Q, le rouleau de cuivre, Planches*. Discoveries in the Judaean Desert 3. Oxford: Clarendon.

BARTELMUS, Rüdiger. 2011. "הָיָה." In *Theologisches Wörterbuch zu den Qumrantexten [ThWQ], Band I*, edited by Heinz-Josef Fabry and Ulrich Dahmen, 762–779. Stuttgart: Kohlhammer.

BARTON, John. 1986. *Oracles of God: Perceptions of Ancient Prophecy in Israel after the Exile*. London: Darton Longman and Todd.

BARTON, John. 1987. "Book Review: The Old Testament Canon of the New Testament Church." *Theology* 90: 63–65.

BARTON, John. 1996. "The Significance of a Fixed Canon of the Hebrew Bible." In *Hebrew Bible / Old Testament: The History of Its Interpretation, Vol. 1,1*, edited by Magne Sæbø, C. Brekelmans, Menahem Haran, Michael A. Fishbane, Jean L. Ska, and Peter Machinist, 67–83. Göttingen: Vandenhoeck & Ruprecht.

BARTON, John. 1997. *Holy Writings, Sacred Text: The Canon in Early Christianity*. Louisville, KY: Westminster John Knox Press.

BARTON, John. 2013. "The Old Testament Canons." In *The New Cambridge History of the Bible, Volume I, From the Beginnings to 600*, edited by James C. Paget and Joachim Schaper, 145–164. Cambridge: Cambridge University Press.

BARTON, John. 2019. *A History of the Bible*. London: Allen Lane.

BAUER, Walter/ALAND, Barbara/ALAND, Kurt. 1988. *Griechisch-deutsches Wörterbuch zu den Schriften des Neuen Testaments und der frühchristlichen Literatur.* 6., völlig neu bearbeitete Auflage. Berlin: De Gruyter.

BAUKS, Michaela. 2019. "Intratextualität, Intertextualität und Rezeptionsgeschichte: Was tragen 'transpositional techniques' und 'empirical evidences' zur literarischen Genese der Urgeschichte aus?" In *Neue Wege der Schriftauslegung*, edited by Michaela Bauks, Ulrich Berges, Daniel Krochmalnik, and Manfred Oeming, 13–63. Altes Testament und Moderne 24. Berlin; Münster: Lit.

BAUM, Armin D. 2001. *Pseudepigraphie und literarische Fälschung im frühen Christentum: Mit ausgewählten Quellentexten samt deutscher Übersetzung.* Wissenschaftliche Untersuchungen zum Neuen Testament 138. Tübingen: Mohr Siebeck.

BAUMGARTEN, Joseph M. 1999. "265. 4QMiscellaneous Rules." In *Qumran Cave 4, XXV, Halakhic Texts*, edited by Joseph M. Baumgarten and Józef T. Milik, 57–78, Pl. V–VIII. Discoveries in the Judaean Desert 35. Oxford: Clarendon.

BAUMGARTEN, Joseph M./SCHWARTZ, Daniel R. 1995. "Damascus Document (CD)." In *The Dead Sea Scrolls, Hebrew, Aramaic, and Greek Texts with English Translations, Volume 2, Damascus Document, War Scroll, and Related Documents*, edited by James H. Charlesworth, 12–57. Princeton Theological Seminary Dead Sea Scrolls Project 2. Tübingen: Mohr.

BAUMGARTEN, Joseph M./CHARLESWORTH, James H./NOVAKOVIC, Lidija/RIETZ, Henry W. M. 2006. "Damascus Document, 4Q266–273 (4QD^{a-h}), Introduction." In *The Dead Sea Scrolls, Hebrew, Aramaic, and Greek Texts with English Translations, Volume 3, Damascus Document II, Some Works of the Torah, and Related Documents*, edited by James H. Charlesworth and Henry W. M. Rietz, 1–5. Princeton Theological Seminary Dead Sea Scrolls Project 3. Tübingen: Mohr Siebeck.

BAUMGARTEN, Joseph M./MILIK, Józef T./PFANN, Stephen J./YARDENI, Ada, eds. 1996. *Qumran Cave 4 XIII, The Damascus Document (4Q266–273).* Discoveries in the Judaean Desert 18. Oxford: Clarendon.

BAUTCH, Kelley C. 2011. "חֲנוֹךְ." In *Theologisches Wörterbuch zu den Qumrantexten [ThWQ], Band I*, edited by Heinz-Josef Fabry and Ulrich Dahmen, 1016–1021. Stuttgart: Kohlhammer.

BAYNES, Leslie. 2012. "Enoch and Jubilees in the Canon of the Ethiopian Orthodox Church." In *A Teacher for All Generations: Essays in Honor of James C. VanderKam, Vol. 2*, edited by Eric F. Mason, 799–818. Supplements to the Journal for the Study of Judaism 153/II. Leiden: Brill.

BECKER, Eve-Marie/FABRY, Heinz-Josef/REITEMEYER, Michael. 2011. "Sophia Sirach/ Ben Sira/Ecclesiasticus/Das Buch Jesus Sirach, Erläuterungen." In *Septuaginta Deutsch: Erläuterungen und Kommentare zum griechischen Alten Testament, Band II, Psalmen bis Daniel*, edited by Martin Karrer and Wolfgang Kraus, 2172–2272. Stuttgart: Deutsche Bibelgesellschaft.

BECKER, Hans-Jürgen. 1998. "Bibel, II. Altes Testament, 2. Sammlung und Kanonisierung, a) Jüdischer Kanon." In *Religion in Geschichte und Gegenwart [RGG⁴], Band 1*, edited by Hans D. Betz, Don S. Browning, Bernd Janowski, and Eberhard Jüngel. 4. Aufl., 1408–1410. Tübingen: Mohr Siebeck.

BECKER, Hans-Jürgen. 2001. "Talmud." In *Theologische Realenzyklopädie [TRE], Band 32*, edited by Gerhard Müller, 626–636. Berlin: De Gruyter.

BECKER, Hans-Jürgen. 2012. "Bible, II. Old Testament, 2. Collection and Formation of the Canon, a. Jewish Canon." In *Religion Past and Present [RPP]: Encyclopedia of Theology and Religion, Vol. I*, edited by Hans D. Betz. 4th edition, English edition, 2–3. Leiden: Brill.

BECKER, Michael. 2013. "סתר." In *Theologisches Wörterbuch zu den Qumrantexten [ThWQ], Band II*, edited by Heinz-Josef Fabry and Ulrich Dahmen, 1121–1126. Stuttgart: Kohlhammer.

BECKWITH, Roger T. 1985. *The Old Testament Canon of the New Testament Church and its Background in Early Judaism*. Grand Rapids, MI: Eerdmans.

BECKWITH, Roger T. 1988. "Formation of the Hebrew Bible." In *Mikra: Text, Translation, Reading and Interpretation of the Hebrew Bible in Ancient Judaism and Early Christianity*, edited by Martin J. Mulder and Harry Sysling, 39–86. Compendia Rerum Iudaicarum ad Novum Testamentum. Assen/Maastricht; Philadelphia: Van Gorcum; Fortress Press.

BECKWITH, Roger T. 1991. "A Modern Theory of the Old Testament Canon." *Vetus Testamentum* 41 (4): 385–395.

BEENTJES, Pancratius C. 1981. *Jesus Sirach en tenach*. Nieuwegen: Selbstverlag.

BEENTJES, Pancratius C. 1984. "De stammen van Israël herstellen: Het portret van Elia bij Jesus Sirach." *Amsterdamse cahiers voor exegese en bijbelse theologie* 5: 147–155.

BEENTJES, Pancratius C. 1997. *The Book of Ben Sira in Hebrew: A Text Edition of All Extant Hebrew Manuscripts and a Synopsis of All Parallel Hebrew Ben Sira Texts*. Supplements to Vetus Testamentum 68. Leiden: Brill.

BEENTJES, Pancratius C. 2002. "Errata et Corrigenda." In *Ben Sira's God: Proceedings of the International Ben Sira Conference, Durham, Ushaw College 2001*, edited by Renate Egger-Wenzel, 375–377. Beihefte zur Zeitschrift für die alttestamentliche Wissenschaft 321. Berlin: De Gruyter.

BEENTJES, Pancratius C. 2006a. "Canon and Scripture in the Book of Ben Sira (Jesus Sirach, Ecclesiasticus)." In *"Happy the One who Meditates on Wisdom" (Sir. 14,20): Collected Essays on the Book of Ben Sira*, 169–186. Contributions to Biblical Exegesis and Theology 43. Leuven: Peeters.

BEENTJES, Pancratius C. 2006b. "Hezekiah and Isaiah: A Study on Ben Sira 48,15–25." In *"Happy the One who Meditates on Wisdom" (Sir. 14,20): Collected Essays on the Book of Ben Sira*, 145–158. Contributions to Biblical Exegesis and Theology 43. Leuven: Peeters.

BEENTJES, Pancratius C. 2006c. "In Search of Parallels: Ben Sira and the Book of Kings." In *"Happy the One who Meditates on Wisdom" (Sir. 14,20): Collected Essays on the Book of Ben Sira*, 187–199. Contributions to Biblical Exegesis and Theology 43. Leuven: Peeters.

BEENTJES, Pancratius C. 2006d. "Prophets and Prophecy in the Book of Ben Sira." In *"Happy the One who Meditates on Wisdom" (Sir. 14,20): Collected Essays on the Book of Ben Sira*, 207–229. Contributions to Biblical Exegesis and Theology 43. Leuven: Peeters.

BEENTJES, Pancratius C. 2006e. "Relations between Ben Sira and the Book of Isaiah: Some Methodological Observations." In *"Happy the One who Meditates on Wisdom" (Sir. 14,20): Collected Essays on the Book of Ben Sira*, 201–206. Contributions to Biblical Exegesis and Theology 43. Leuven: Peeters.

BEENTJES, Pancratius C. 2006f. "Scripture and Scribe: Ben Sira 38:34c–39:11." In *"Happy the One who Meditates on Wisdom" (Sir. 14,20): Collected Essays on the Book of Ben Sira*, 115–122. Contributions to Biblical Exegesis and Theology 43. Leuven: Peeters.

BEENTJES, Pancratius C. 2006g. "Some Major Topics in Ben Sira Research." In *"Happy the One who Meditates on Wisdom" (Sir. 14,20): Collected Essays on the Book of Ben Sira*, 3–18. Contributions to Biblical Exegesis and Theology 43. Leuven: Peeters.

198 Bibliography

BEENTJES, Pancratius C. 2006h. "The 'Praise of the Famous' and its Prologue: Some Observations on Ben Sira 44:1–15 and the Question on Enoch in 44:16." In *"Happy the One who Meditates on Wisdom" (Sir. 14,20): Collected Essays on the Book of Ben Sira*, 123–144. Contributions to Biblical Exegesis and Theology 43. Leuven: Peeters.

BEENTJES, Pancratius C. 2008. "Ben Sira 44:19–23 – The Patriarchs: Text, Tradition, Theology." In *Studies in the Book of Ben Sira: Papers of the Third International Conference on the Deuterocanonical Books, Shime'on Centre, Pápa, Hungary, 18–20 May, 2006*, edited by Géza G. Xeravits and József Zsengellér, 209–228. Supplements to the Journal for the Study of Judaism 127. Leiden: Brill.

BEENTJES, Pancratius C. 2017a. "Ben Sira and Song of Songs: What about Parallels and Echoes?" In *"With All Your Soul Fear the Lord" (Sir. 7:27): Collected Essays on the Book of Ben Sira II*, 143–156. Contributions to Biblical Exegesis and Theology 87. Leuven: Peeters.

BEENTJES, Pancratius C. 2017b. "Ben Sira and the Book of Deuteronomy, or: the Limits of Intertextuality." In *"With All Your Soul Fear the Lord" (Sir. 7:27): Collected Essays on the Book of Ben Sira II*, 103–123. Contributions to Biblical Exegesis and Theology 87. Leuven: Peeters.

BEENTJES, Pancratius C. 2017c. "Ben Sira's View of Elijah (Sir. 48:1–11)." In *"With All Your Soul Fear the Lord" (Sir. 7:27): Collected Essays on the Book of Ben Sira II*, 89–99. Contributions to Biblical Exegesis and Theology 87. Leuven: Peeters.

BEENTJES, Pancratius C. 2019. "Intertextuality between the Book of Ben Sira and the Book of Proverbs." In *Reading Proverbs Intertextually*, edited by Katharine Dell and Will Kynes, 141–154. Library of Hebrew Bible/Old Testament Studies. London: T&T Clark.

BEENTJES, Pancratius C. 2021. "Ben Sira and his Grandson on Prophets and Prophecy." In *Prophecy and Hellenism*, edited by Hannes Bezzel and Stefan Pfeiffer, 69–81. Forschungen zum Alten Testament, 2. Reihe 129. Tübingen: Mohr Siebeck.

BEGG, C. T. 1988. "Ben Sirach's Non-Mention of Ezra." *Biblische Notizen* 42: 14–18.

BEN ZVI, Ehud. 1996. "Twelve Prophetic Books or 'The Twelve': A Few Preliminary Considerations." In *Forming Prophetic Literature: Essays on Isaiah and the Twelve in Honor of John D. W. Watts*, edited by James W. Watts and Paul R. House, 125–156. Journal for the Study of the Old Testament Supplement Series 235. Sheffield: Sheffield Academic.

BENDLIN, Andreas. 1998. "Intertextualität." In *Der Neue Pauly. Enzyklopädie der Antike, Band 5*, edited by Hubert Cancik and Helmuth Schneider, 1044–1047. Stuttgart: Metzler.

BERG, Shane. 2013. "Ben Sira, the Genesis Creation Accounts, and the Knowledge of God's Will." *Journal of Biblical Literature* 132 (1): 139–157.

BERGREN, Theodore A. 1998. "Ezra and Nehemiah Square Off in the Apocrypha and Pseudepigrapha." In *Biblical Figures Outside the Bible*, edited by Michael E. Stone, 340–365. Harrisburg, PA: Trinity Press International.

BERLEJUNG, Angelika. 2012a. "Sources (Translation by Thomas Riplinger)." In *T&T Clark Handbook of the Old Testament: An Introduction to the Literature, Religion and History of the Old Testament*, edited by Jan C. Gertz, Angelika Berlejung, Konrad Schmid, and Markus Witte, 3–30. London: T&T Clark.

BERLEJUNG, Angelika. 2012b. "The Books of Maccabees (Translation by Thomas Riplinger)." In *T&T Clark Handbook of the Old Testament: An Introduction to the Literature, Religion and History of the Old Testament*, edited by Jan C. Gertz, Angelika Berlejung, Konrad Schmid, and Markus Witte, 745–764. London: T&T Clark.

BERLEJUNG, Angelika. 2019. "Erster Hauptteil: Quellen und Methoden." In *Grundinformation Altes Testament*, edited by Jan C. Gertz. 6., überarbeitete und erweiterte Auflage, 21–58. UTB 2745. Göttingen: Vandenhoeck & Ruprecht.

BERRIN, Shani L. 2000. "Pesharim." In *Encyclopedia of the Dead Sea Scrolls*, edited by James C. VanderKam, 644–647. Oxford: Oxford University Press.

BERTHELOT, Katell. 2006. "4QMMT et la question du canon de la Bible hébraïque." In *From 4QMMT to Resurrection: Mélanges qumraniens en hommage à Émile Puech*, edited by Florentino García Martínez, Annette Steudel, and Eibert J. C. Tigchelaar, 1–14. Studies on the Texts of the Desert of Judah 61. Leiden: Brill.

BERTRAND, P. H. E. / GANDT, Lois, eds. 2018. *Vitae Antonii Versiones latinae: Vita beati Antonii abbatis Euagrio interprete edidit P. H. E. Bertrand, Versio ueustissima edidit Lois Gandt.* Corpus Christianorum Series Latina 170. Turnhout: Brepols.

BEYER, Andrea. 2014. *Hoffnung in Bethlehem: Innerbiblische Querbezüge als Deutungshorizonte im Ruthbuch.* Beihefte zur Zeitschrift für die alttestamentliche Wissenschaft 463. Berlin: De Gruyter.

Biblia Sacra: Iuxta Latinam Vulgatam Versionem, Vol. 12, Sapientia Salomonis, Liber Hiesu Filii Sirach. 1964. Rom: Typis polyglottis Vaticanis.

BINDER, Vera. 2001. "Schreiber, III. Griechenland und Rom." In *Der Neue Pauly. Enzyklopädie der Antike, Band 11*, edited by Hubert Cancik and Helmuth Schneider, 223–226. Stuttgart: Metzler.

BIRD, Graeme D. 2010. *Multitextuality in the Homeric Iliad: The Witness of the Ptolemaic Papyri.* Hellenic Studies 43. Cambridge, MA: Harvard University Press.

BLACHORSKY, Joshua A. [2014]. "The Book of Ben Sira: Index of Passages." Accessed August 23, 2021. http://bensira.org/pdf/indexOfPassages/indexOfPassages.pdf.

BLACK, Matthew. 1970. "Apocalypsis Henochi Graece." In *Apocalypsis Henochi Graece, Fragmenta pseudepigraphorum quae supersunt Graeca una cum historicorum et auctorum Judaeorum Hellenistarum fragmentis*, edited by Matthew Black and Albert-Marie Denis, 1–44. Pseudepigrapha Veteris Testamenti Graece 3. Leiden: Brill.

BOCCACCINI, Gabriele. 2012. "Is Biblical Literature Still a Useful Term in Scholarship?" In *What is Bible?* edited by Karin Finsterbusch and Armin Lange, 41–51. Contributions to Biblical Exegesis and Theology 67. Leuven: Peeters.

BODLEIAN LIBRARIES. [2017]. "MS. Heb. e. 62, Folio 9a [= MS B XVIII Verso]." Accessed August 23, 2021. https://genizah.bodleian.ox.ac.uk/fragments/full/MS_HEB_e_62_9a. jpg.

BÖHMISCH, Franz. 1997. "Die Textformen des Sirachbuches und ihre Zielgruppen." *Protokolle zur Bibel* 6 (2): 87–122.

BOKHORST, Mirjam J. 2021. *Henoch und der Tempel des Todes: 1 Henoch 14–16 zwischen Schriftauslegung und Traditionsverarbeitung.* Beihefte zur Zeitschrift für die alttestamentliche Wissenschaft 530. Berlin: De Gruyter.

BORCHARDT, Francis. 2014. "Prologue of Sirach (Ben Sira) and the Question of Canon." In *Sacra Scriptura: How "Non-Canonical" Texts Functioned in Early Judaism and Early Christianity*, edited by James H. Charlesworth, 64–71. Jewish and Christian Texts in Contexts and Related Studies 20. London: Bloomsbury.

BORCHARDT, Francis. 2015. "Influence and Power: The Types of Authority in the Process of Scripturalization." *Scandinavian Journal of the Old Testament* 29 (2): 182–196.

BOX, George H. / OESTERLEY, William O. E. 1913. "Sirach." In *The Apocrypha and Pseudepigrapha of the Old Testament in English: With Introductions and Critical and*

200   Bibliography

Explanatory Notes to the Several Books, Vol. 1, edited by Robert H. Charles, 268–517. Oxford: Clarendon.

BOYD-TAYLOR, Cameron. 2021. "What is the Septuagint?" In *The Oxford Handbook of the Septuagint*, edited by Alison Salvesen and Timothy M. Law, 12–32. Oxford: Oxford University Press.

BRANDT, Peter. 2001. *Endgestalten des Kanons*. Bonner Biblische Beiträge 131. Berlin: Philo.

BRODERSEN, Alma. 2017. *The End of the Psalter: Psalms 146–150 in the Masoretic Text, the Dead Sea Scrolls, and the Septuagint*. Beihefte zur Zeitschrift für die alttestamentliche Wissenschaft 505. Berlin: De Gruyter.

BRODERSEN, Alma / NEUMANN, Friederike / WILLGREN, David. 2020. "Einführung." In *Intertextualität und die Entstehung des Psalters: Methodische Reflexionen – Theologiegeschichtliche Perspektiven*, edited by Alma Brodersen, Friederike Neumann, and David Willgren, 1–4. Forschungen zum Alten Testament, 2. Reihe 114. Tübingen: Mohr Siebeck.

BROOKE, George J. 1997a. "Explicit Presentation of Scripture in 4QMMT." In *Legal Texts and Legal Issues: Proceedings of the Second Meeting of the International Organization of Qumran Studies Cambridge 1995, Published in Honour of Joseph M. Baumgarten*, edited by Moshe J. Bernstein, 67–88. Studies on the Texts of the Desert of Judah 23. Leiden: Brill.

BROOKE, George J. 1997b. "'The Canon within the Canon' at Qumran and in the New Testament." In *The Scrolls and the Scriptures: Qumran Fifty Years After*, edited by Stanley E. Porter, 242–266. Journal for the Study of the Pseudepigrapha Supplement Series 26. Sheffield: Sheffield Academic.

BROOKE, George J. 2007. "'Canon' in the Light of the Qumran Scrolls." In *The Canon of Scripture in Jewish and Christian Tradition*, edited by Philip S. Alexander and Jean-Daniel Kaestli, 81–98. Publications de l'Institut Romand des Sciences Bibliques 4. Lausanne: Éditions du Zèbre.

BROWN, Teresa R. 2002. "God and Men in Israel's History: God and Idol Worship in Praise of the Fathers (Sir 44–50)." In *Ben Sira's God: Proceedings of the International Ben Sira Conference, Durham, Ushaw College 2001*, edited by Renate Egger-Wenzel, 214–220. Beihefte zur Zeitschrift für die alttestamentliche Wissenschaft 321. Berlin: De Gruyter.

BUHL, Frants. 1891. *Kanon und Text des Alten Testamentes*. Leipzig: Akademische Buchhandlung.

BURKHARDT, Helmut. 1992. *Die Inspiration heiliger Schriften bei Philo von Alexandrien*. 2., überarb. Aufl. Gießen: Brunnen.

BURNS, Joshua E. 2016. "The Wisdom of the Nations and the Law of Israel: Genealogies of Ethnic Difference in Ben Sira and the Mekhilta." In *Sibyls, Scriptures, and Scrolls: John Collins at Seventy*, edited by Joel S. Baden, Hindy Najman, and Eibert Tigchelaar, 241–260. Supplements to the Journal for the Study of Judaism 175/I–II. Leiden: Brill.

BURROWS, Millar, ed. 1950. *The Dead Sea Scrolls of St. Mark's Monastery, Volume 1, The Isaiah Manuscript and the Habakkuk Commentary*. New Haven: American Schools of Oriental Research.

BURROWS, Millar, ed. 1951. *The Dead Sea Scrolls of St. Mark's Monastery, Volume 2, Fasciscle 2, Plates and Transcription of the Manual of Discipline*. New Haven: American Schools of Oriental Research.

BUTTERFIELD, David. 2017. "Ancient Classical Scholarship (Oxford Bibliographies – Classics)." Accessed August 23, 2021. https://www.oxfordbibliographies.com/view/document/obo-9780195389661/obo-9780195389661-0269.xml.

CADBURY, Henry J. 1955. "The Grandson of Ben Sira." *Harvard Theological Review* 48 (4): 219–225.

CAIRD, George B. 1982. "Ben Sira and the Dating of the Septuagint." In *Studia Evangelica, Vol. VII: Papers Presented to the Fifth International Congress on Biblical Studies Held at Oxford, 1973*, edited by Elizabeth A. Livingstone, 95–100. Texte und Untersuchungen zur Geschichte der altchristlichen Literatur 126. Berlin: Akademie-Verlag.

CALDUCH-BENAGES, Núria. 2011. "The Absence of Named Women from Ben Sira's Praise of the Ancestors." In *Rewriting Biblical History: Essays on Chronicles and Ben Sira in Honor of Pancratius C. Beentjes*, edited by Jeremy Corley and Harm van Grol, 301–318. Deuterocanonical and Cognate Literature Studies 7. Berlin: De Gruyter.

CALDUCH-BENAGES, Nuria. 2016. "Ben Sira 24:22 – Decoding a Metaphor." In *Vermittelte Gegenwart: Konzeptionen der Gottespräsenz von der Zeit des Zweiten Tempels bis Anfang des 2. Jahrhunderts n. Chr.*, edited by Andrea Taschl-Erber and Irmtraud Fischer, 57–72. Wissenschaftliche Untersuchungen zum Neuen Testament 367. Tübingen: Mohr Siebeck.

CALDUCH-BENAGES, Núria / FERRER, Joan / LIESEN, Jan, eds. 2003. *La sabiduría del escriba / Wisdom of the Scribe: Edición diplomática de la versión siriaca del libro de Ben Sira según el Códice Ambrosiano, con traducción española e inglesa / Diplomatic Edition of the Syriac Version of the Book of Ben Sira according to Codex Ambrosianus, with Translations in Spanish and English*. 2nd edition. Biblioteca Midrásica 26. Estella: Editorial Verbo Divino.

CAMPBELL, Jonathan G. 2000. "4QMMT^d and the Tripartite Canon." *Journal of Jewish Studies* 51 (2): 181–190.

CARR, David M. 1996. "Canonization in the Context of Community: An Outline of the Formation of the Tanakh and the Christian Bible." In *A Gift of God in Due Season: Essays on Scripture and Community in Honor of James A. Sanders*, edited by Richard D. Weis and David M. Carr, 22–65. Journal for the Study of the Old Testament Supplement Series 225. Sheffield: Sheffield Academic.

CARR, David M. 2005. *Writing on the Tablet of the Heart: Origins of Scripture and Literature*. Oxford: Oxford University Press.

CARR, David M. 2011. *The Formation of the Hebrew Bible: A New Reconstruction*. Oxford: Oxford University Press.

CARR, David M. 2012. "The Many Uses of Intertextuality in Biblical Studies." In *Congress Volume Helsinki 2010*, edited by Martti Nissinen, 519–549. Supplements to Vetus Testamentum 148. Leiden: Brill.

CARR, David M. 2015. "Orality, Textuality *and* Memory: The State of Biblical Studies." In *Contextualizing Israel's Sacred Writings: Ancient Literacy, Orality and Literary Production*, edited by Brian Schmidt, 161–173. Ancient Israel and Its Literature 22. Atlanta, GA: SBL Press.

CARR, David M. 2017. "Method in Determining the Dependence of Biblical on Non-Biblical Texts." In *Subtle Citation, Allusion, and Translation in the Hebrew Bible*, edited by Ziony Zevit, 41–53. Sheffield: Equinox.

CARR, David M. 2020. "Rethinking the Materiality of Biblical Texts: From Source, Tradition and Redaction to a Scroll Approach." *Zeitschrift für die alttestamentliche Wissenschaft* 132 (4): 594–621.

202   *Bibliography*

CAVALLO, Guglielmo. 1997a. "Buch." In *Der Neue Pauly. Enzyklopädie der Antike, Band 2*, edited by Hubert Cancik and Helmuth Schneider, 809–816. Stuttgart: Metzler.

CAVALLO, Guglielmo. 1997b. "Codex, I. Kulturgeschichte." In *Der Neue Pauly. Enzyklopädie der Antike, Band 3*, edited by Hubert Cancik and Helmuth Schneider, 50–53. Stuttgart: Metzler.

CAVALLO, Guglielmo. 2001. "Rolle." In *Der Neue Pauly. Enzyklopädie der Antike, Band 10*, edited by Hubert Cancik and Helmuth Schneider, 1047–1050. Stuttgart: Metzler.

CHANIOTIS, Angelos. 2009. "Greek History: Hellenistic (Oxford Bibliographies – Classics)." Accessed August 23, 2021. https://www.oxfordbibliographies.com/view/docume nt/obo-9780195389661/obo-9780195389661-0022.xml.

CHANIOTIS, Angelos. 2018. *Age of Conquests: The Greek World from Alexander to Hadrian*. Cambridge, MA: Harvard University Press.

CHAPMAN, Stephen B. 2000. *The Law and the Prophets: A Study in Old Testament Canon Formation*. Forschungen zum Alten Testament 27. Tübingen: Mohr Siebeck.

CHILDS, Brevard S. 1979. *Introduction to the Old Testament as Scripture*. Philadelphia: Fortress Press.

CIRAFESI, Wally V. 2017. "'Taken from Dust, Formed from Clay': Compound Allusions and Scriptural Exegesis in 1QHodayot^a 11:20–37; 20:27–39 and Ben Sira 33:7–15." *Dead Sea Discoveries* 24 (1): 81–111.

CLAYMAN, Dee L. 2016. "Hellenistic Literature (Oxford Bibliographies – Classics)." Accessed August 23, 2021. https://www.oxfordbibliographies.com/view/document/obo-9780195389661/obo-9780195389661-0051.xml.

CLINES, David J.A., ed. 1998. *The Dictionary of Classical Hebrew, Vol. IV*. Sheffield: Sheffield Academic.

COGGINS, R. 2007. "Isaiah." In *The Oxford Bible Commentary*, edited by John Barton and John Muddiman, 433–486. Oxford: Oxford University Press.

COLLINS, John J. 1997. *Jewish Wisdom in the Hellenistic Age*. Old Testament Library. Louisville, KY: Westminster John Knox Press.

COLLINS, John J. 2004. *Introduction to the Hebrew Bible*. Minneapolis: Fortress Press.

COLLINS, John J. 2020. "4QMMT and History." In *Interpreting and Living God's Law at Qumran: Miqṣat Maʿaśe Ha-Torah, Some of the Works of the Torah (4QMMT)*, edited by Reinhard G. Kratz, 161–178. SAPERE 37. Tübingen: Mohr Siebeck.

COLPE, Carsten. 1987. "Sakralisierung von Texten und Filiationen von Kanons." In *Kanon und Zensur*, edited by Aleida Assmann and Jan Assmann, 80–92. Archäologie der literarischen Kommunikation 2. München: Fink.

COLPE, Carsten. 1988. "Heilige Schriften." In *Reallexikon für Antike und Christentum, Band 14*, edited by Ernst Dassmann, 184–223. Stuttgart: Hiersemann.

COLPE, Carsten / HANHART, Robert. 2005. "Juden." In *Lexikon des Hellenismus*, edited by Hatto H. Schmitt, 485–506. Wiesbaden: Harrassowitz.

CONYBEARE, F.C. / ST. STOCK, George. 1995. *Grammar of Septuagint Greek: With Selected Readings, Vocabularies, and Updated Indexes*. Reprinted from the edition originally published by Ginn and Company, Boston, 1905. [Peabody, MA]: Hendrickson.

COOK, Edward M. 2015. *Dictionary of Qumran Aramaic*. Winona Lake, IN: Eisenbrauns.

CORLEY, Jeremy. 2004. "An Intertextual Study of Proverbs and Ben Sira." In *Intertextual Studies in Ben Sira and Tobit: Essays in Honor of Alexander A. Di Lella, O.F.M.*, edited by Jeremy Corley, Vincent T.M. Skemp, and Alexander A. Di Lella, 155–182. Catholic Biblical Quarterly Monograph Series 38. Washington, DC: Catholic Biblical Association of America.

CORLEY, Jeremy. 2008a. "Searching for Structure and Redaction in Ben Sira: An Investigation of Beginnings and Endings." In *The Wisdom of Ben Sira: Studies on Tradition, Redaction, and Theology*, edited by Angelo Passaro, 21–47. Deuterocanonical and Cognate Literature Studies 1. Berlin: De Gruyter.

CORLEY, Jeremy. 2008b. "Sirach 44:1–15 as Introduction to the Praise of the Ancestors." In *Studies in the Book of Ben Sira: Papers of the Third International Conference on the Deuterocanonical Books, Shime'on Centre, Pápa, Hungary, 18–20 May, 2006*, edited by Géza G. Xeravits and József Zsengellér, 151–181. Supplements to the Journal for the Study of Judaism 127. Leiden: Brill.

CORLEY, Jeremy. 2011. "Canonical Assimilation in Ben Sira's Portrayal of Joshua and Samuel." In *Rewriting Biblical History: Essays on Chronicles and Ben Sira in Honor of Pancratius C. Beentjes*, edited by Jeremy Corley and Harm van Grol, 57–78. Deuterocanonical and Cognate Literature Studies 7. Berlin: De Gruyter.

CORLEY, Jeremy. 2013. *Sirach*. The New Collegeville Bible Commentary. Old Testament 21. Collegeville, MN: Liturgical Press.

CORLEY, Jeremy. 2019. "Ecclesiasticus/Ben Sira, Greek." In *Textual History of the Bible, Volume 2B, Baruch/Jeremiah, Daniel (Additions), Ecclesiasticus/Ben Sira, Enoch, Esther (Additions), Ezra*, edited by Frank Feder and Matthias Henze, 214–231. Leiden: Brill.

CORLEY, Jeremy / VAN GROL, Harm. 2011. "Preface." In *Rewriting Biblical History: Essays on Chronicles and Ben Sira in Honor of Pancratius C. Beentjes*, edited by Jeremy Corley and Harm van Grol, v–viii. Deuterocanonical and Cognate Literature Studies 7. Berlin: De Gruyter.

CORLEY, Jeremy / GREGORY, Bradley C. 2016. "Sirach (Oxford Bibliographies – Biblical Studies)." Accessed August 23, 2021. http://www.oxfordbibliographies.com/view/document/obo-9780195393361/obo-9780195393361-0100.xml.

CORLEY, Jeremy / SKEMP, Vincent T. M. / DI LELLA, Alexander A., eds. 2004. *Intertextual Studies in Ben Sira and Tobit: Essays in Honor of Alexander A. Di Lella, O. F. M.* Catholic Biblical Quarterly Monograph Series 38. Washington, DC: Catholic Biblical Association of America.

CRAWFORD, Sidnie W. 2019. *Scribes and Scrolls at Qumran*. Grand Rapids, MI: Eerdmans.

CRENSHAW, James L. 1997a. "The Book of Sirach." In *New Interpreter's Bible, Vol. 5*, edited by Leander E. Keck, 601–867. Nashville, TN: Abingdon Press.

CRENSHAW, James L. 1997b. "The Primacy of Listening in Ben Sira's Pedagogy." In *Wisdom, You Are My Sister: Studies in Honor of Roland E. Murphy, O. Carm., on the Occasion of his Eightieth Birthday*, edited by Michael L. Barré, 180–187. Catholic Biblical Quarterly Monograph Series 29. Washington, DC: Catholic Biblical Association of America.

CROSS, Frank M. 1994. "4QExod-Levᶠ." In *Qumran Cave 4, VII, Genesis to Numbers*, edited by Eugene Ulrich, Frank M. Cross, James R. Davila, Nathan Jastram, Judith E. Sanderson, Emanuel Tov, and John Strugnell, 133–144, Pl. XXII. Discoveries in the Judaean Desert 12. Oxford: Clarendon.

CURTIUS, Ernst R. 1984. *Europäische Literatur und lateinisches Mittelalter*. 10. Aufl. Tübingen: Francke.

DAHMEN, Ulrich. 2016. "פָּרַח." In *Theologisches Wörterbuch zu den Qumrantexten [ThWQ], Band III*, edited by Heinz-Josef Fabry and Ulrich Dahmen, 328–330. Stuttgart: Kohlhammer.

DALMAN, Gustaf. 1905. *Grammatik des jüdisch-palästinischen Aramäisch: Nach den Idiomen des palästinischen Talmud, des Onkelostargum und Prophetentargum und der jerusalemischen Targume*. 2. Aufl. Leipzig: Hinrichs.

204 Bibliography

Davies, Philip R. 1998. *Scribes and Schools: The Canonization of the Hebrew Scriptures.* Library of Ancient Israel. Louisville, KY: Westminster John Knox Press.

Davies, Philip R. 2006. "And Enoch Was Not, For Genesis Took Him." In *Biblical Traditions in Transmission: Essays in Honour of Michael A. Knibb*, edited by Charlotte Hempel and Judith M. Lieu, 97–107. Supplements to the Journal for the Study of Judaism 111. Leiden: Brill.

Davies, William D. / Finkelstein, Louis, eds. 1989. *The Cambridge History of Judaism, Vol. 2, The Hellenistic Age.* Cambridge: Cambridge University Press.

De Vaux, Roland. 1955. "La Poterie." In *Qumran Cave 1*, edited by Dominique Barthélemy and J. T. Milik. Reprint 1964, 8–13. Discoveries in the Judaean Desert 1. Oxford: Clarendon.

Di Lella, Alexander A. 2006. "Ben Sira's Praise of the Ancestors of Old (Sir 44–49): The History of Israel as Parenetic Apologetics." In *History and Identity: How Israel's Later Authors Viewed Its Earlier History*, edited by Núria Calduch-Benages and Jan Liesen, 151–170. Deuterocanonical and Cognate Literature Yearbook 2006. Berlin: De Gruyter.

Dickey, Eleanor. 2007. *Ancient Greek Scholarship: A Guide to Finding, Reading, and Understanding Scholia, Commentaries, Lexica, and Grammatical Treatises, from Their Beginnings to the Byzantine Period.* American Philological Association Classical Resource Series 7. Oxford: Oxford University Press.

Diebner, Bernd J. 1982. "Mein Großvater Jesus." *Dielheimer Blätter zum Alten Testament* 16: 1–37.

Dietrich, Walter / Mathys, Hans-Peter / Römer, Thomas / Smend, Rudolf, eds. 2014. *Die Entstehung des Alten Testaments.* Theologische Wissenschaft 1. Stuttgart: Kohlhammer.

Dimant, Devorah. 1988. "Use and Interpretation of Mikra in the Apocrypha and Pseudepigrapha." In *Mikra: Text, Translation, Reading and Interpretation of the Hebrew Bible in Ancient Judaism and Early Christianity*, edited by Martin J. Mulder and Harry Sysling, 379–419. Compendia Rerum Iudaicarum ad Novum Testamentum. Assen/Maastricht; Philadelphia: Van Gorcum; Fortress Press.

Dines, Jennifer. 2015. "The Minor Prophets." In *The T&T Clark Companion to the Septuagint*, edited by James K. Aitken, 438–455. Bloomsbury Companions. London: T&T Clark.

DiTommaso, Lorenzo. 2011. "חָלַם." In *Theologisches Wörterbuch zu den Qumrantexten [ThWQ], Band I*, edited by Heinz-Josef Fabry and Ulrich Dahmen, 988–993. Stuttgart: Kohlhammer.

DiTommaso, Lorenzo. 2013. "Demetrius the Chronographer." In *Outside the Bible: Ancient Jewish Writing Related to Scripture, Vol. 1*, edited by Louis H. Feldman, James L. Kugel, and Lawrence H. Schiffman, 669–674. Lincoln; Philadelphia: University of Nebraska Press; Jewish Publication Society.

Drawnel, Henryk. 2011. *The Aramaic Astronomical Book (4Q208–4Q211) from Qumran: Text, Translation, and Commentary.* Oxford: Oxford University Press.

Drawnel, Henryk, ed. 2019. *Qumran Cave 4: The Aramaic Books of Enoch, 4Q201, 4Q202, 4Q204, 4Q205, 4Q206, 4Q207, 4Q212.* Oxford: Oxford University Press.

Dubielzig, Uwe. 2005. "Buchwesen." In *Lexikon des Hellenismus*, edited by Hatto H. Schmitt, 212–217. Wiesbaden: Harrassowitz.

Dubischar, Markus. 2015. "Typology of Philological Writings." In *Brill's Companion to Ancient Greek Scholarship, Vol. 1, History, Disciplinary Profiles*, edited by Franco

Montanari, Stefanos Matthaios, and Antonios Rengakos, 545–599. Brill's Companions in Classical Studies. Leiden: Brill.

DUGGAN, Michael W. 2004. "Ezra, Scribe and Priest and the Concerns of Ben Sira." In *Intertextual Studies in Ben Sira and Tobit: Essays in Honor of Alexander A. Di Lella, O.F.M.*, edited by Jeremy Corley, Vincent T.M. Skemp, and Alexander A. Di Lella, 201–210. Catholic Biblical Quarterly Monograph Series 38. Washington, DC: Catholic Biblical Association of America.

DUNCAN, Julie A. 1995. "29. 4QDeut[b]." In *Qumran Cave 4 IX, Deuteronomy, Joshua, Judges, Kings*, edited by Eugene Ulrich, Frank M. Cross, Sidnie W. Crawford, Julie A. Duncan, Patrick W. Skehan, Emanuel Tov, and Julio Trebolle Barrera, 9–14, Pl. II. Discoveries in the Judaean Desert 14. Oxford: Clarendon.

EBERHARTER, Andreas. 1911. *Der Kanon des Alten Testaments zur Zeit des Ben Sira: Auf Grund der Beziehungen des Sirachbuches zu den Schriften des A.T. dargestellt.* Alttestamentliche Abhandlungen III 3. Münster: Aschendorff.

EBERHARTER, Andreas. 1925. *Das Buch Jesus Sirach oder Ecclesiasticus.* Heilige Schrift des Alten Testamentes 6. Bd., 5. Abt. Bonn: Hanstein.

EDER, Walter. 1998. "Hellenismus." In *Der Neue Pauly. Enzyklopädie der Antike, Band 5*, edited by Hubert Cancik and Helmuth Schneider, 312–314. Stuttgart: Metzler.

EDER, Walter / QUACK, Joachim F. 2004. "Dynastie der Ptolemaier." In *Herrscherchronologien der antiken Welt*, edited by Walter Eder, 46–48. Stuttgart: Metzler.

EGGER-WENZEL, Renate. 1996. "Der Gebrauch von תמם bei Ijob und Ben Sira: Ein Vergleich zweier Weisheitsbücher." In *Freundschaft bei Ben Sira: Beiträge des Symposions zu Ben Sira Salzburg 1995*, edited by Friedrich V. Reiterer, 203–238. Beihefte zur Zeitschrift für die alttestamentliche Wissenschaft 244. Berlin: De Gruyter.

EGGER-WENZEL, Renate. 2011. "Josiah and His Prophet(s) in Chronicles and Ben Sira. An Intertextual Comparison." In *Rewriting Biblical History: Essays on Chronicles and Ben Sira in Honor of Pancratius C. Beentjes*, edited by Jeremy Corley and Harm van Grol, 231–256. Deuterocanonical and Cognate Literature Studies 7. Berlin: De Gruyter.

EGO, Beate. 1999. "Der Strom der Tora: zur Rezeption eines tempeltheologischen Motivs in frühjüdischer Zeit." In *Gemeinde ohne Tempel. Community without Temple: Zur Substituierung und Transformation des Jerusalemer Tempels und seines Kults im Alten Testament, antiken Judentum und frühen Christentum*, edited by Beate Ego, Armin Lange, and Peter Pilhofer, 205–214. Wissenschaftliche Untersuchungen zum Neuen Testament 118. Tübingen: Mohr Siebeck.

EGO, Beate. 2001. "Sirach." In *Der Neue Pauly. Enzyklopädie der Antike, Band 11*, edited by Hubert Cancik and Helmuth Schneider, 591–592. Stuttgart: Metzler.

EGO, Beate. 2009. "Im Schatten hellenistischer Bildung. Ben Siras Lern- und Lehrkonzeption zwischen Mündlichkeit und Schriftlichkeit." In *Die Textualisierung der Religion*, edited by Joachim Schaper, 203–221. Forschungen zum Alten Testament 62. Tübingen: Mohr Siebeck.

EISSFELDT, Otto. 1964. *Einleitung in das Alte Testament.* 3., neubearb. Aufl. Neue theologische Grundrisse. Tübingen: Mohr.

ELLIGER, Karl / RUDOLPH, Wilhelm, eds. 1997. *Biblia Hebraica Stuttgartensia [BHS].* 5. verb. Aufl., verkleinerte Ausg. Stuttgart: Deutsche Bibelgesellschaft.

EMADI, Samuel. 2015. "Intertextuality in New Testament Scholarship: Significance, Criteria, and the Art of Intertextual Reading." *Currents in Biblical Research* 14 (1): 8–23.

206   *Bibliography*

ENGEL, Helmut. 2016. "Die Bücher der Makkabäer." In *Einleitung in das Alte Testament*, edited by Erich Zenger and Christian Frevel. 9., aktualisierte Aufl., 389–406. Kohlhammer Studienbücher Theologie 1,1. Stuttgart: Kohlhammer.

ERHO, Ted M. / STUCKENBRUCK, Loren T. 2013. "A Manuscript History of Ethiopic Enoch." *Journal for the Study of the Pseudepigrapha* 23 (2): 87–133.

FABRY, Heinz-Josef. 1999. "Die Qumrantexte und das biblische Kanonproblem." In *Recht und Ethos im Alten Testament – Gestalt und Wirkung: Festschrift für Horst Seebass zum 65. Geburtstag*, edited by Stefan Beyerle, Günter Mayer, and Hans Strauß, 251–271. Neukirchen-Vluyn: Neukirchener.

FABRY, Heinz-Josef. 2009. "Sophia Sirach, Ben Sira, Das Buch Jesus Sirach." In *Septuaginta Deutsch: Das griechische Alte Testament in deutscher Übersetzung*, edited by Wolfgang Kraus and Martin Karrer, 1090–1163. Stuttgart: Deutsche Bibelgesellschaft.

FABRY, Heinz-Josef. 2013. "יַד." In *Theologisches Wörterbuch zu den Qumrantexten [ThWQ]*, *Band II*, edited by Heinz-Josef Fabry and Ulrich Dahmen, 54–69. Stuttgart: Kohlhammer.

FABRY, Heinz-Josef. 2016. "עָשַׂר." In *Theologisches Wörterbuch zu den Qumrantexten [ThWQ], Band III*, edited by Heinz-Josef Fabry and Ulrich Dahmen, 233–240. Stuttgart: Kohlhammer.

FABRY, Heinz-Josef. 2018. "'Gewalt über Gewalt': Die dunklen Seiten Gottes im Zwölfprophetenbuch." In *The Books of the Twelve Prophets: Minor Prophets, Major Theologies*, edited by Heinz-Josef Fabry, 3–29. Bibliotheca Ephemeridum Theologicarum Lovaniensium 295. Leuven: Peeters.

FELDMAN, Louis H. / KUGEL, James L. / SCHIFFMAN, Lawrence H., eds. 2013. *Outside the Bible: Ancient Jewish Writings Related to Scripture*. 3 vols. Lincoln; Philadelphia: University of Nebraska Press; Jewish Publication Society.

FINSTERBUSCH, Karin. 2011. "Aufsummierte Tora: Zur Bedeutung von תורה als Bezeichnung für eine Gesetzessammlung im Pentateuch." *Journal of Ancient Judaism* 2 (1): 1–28.

FINSTERBUSCH, Karin. 2016. "תּוֹרָה." In *Theologisches Wörterbuch zu den Qumrantexten [ThWQ], Band III*, edited by Heinz-Josef Fabry and Ulrich Dahmen, 1110–1118. Stuttgart: Kohlhammer.

FISCHER, Georg. 1998. "Bibel, II. Altes Testament, 1. Bestand und Zusammensetzung." In *Religion in Geschichte und Gegenwart [RGG⁴], Band 1*, edited by Hans D. Betz, Don S. Browning, Bernd Janowski, and Eberhard Jüngel. 4. Aufl., 1407–1408. Tübingen: Mohr Siebeck.

FLINT, Peter W. 1997. *The Dead Sea Psalms Scrolls and the Book of Psalms*. Studies on the Texts of the Desert of Judah 17. Leiden: Brill.

FLINT, Peter W. 2003. "Scriptures in the Dead Sea Scrolls: The Evidence from Qumran." In *Emanuel: Studies in Hebrew Bible, Septuagint, and Dead Sea Scrolls in Honor of Emanuel Tov*, edited by Shalom M. Paul, Robert A. Kraft, Lawrence H. Schiffman, and Weston W. Fields, 269–304. Supplements to Vetus Testamentum 94. Leiden: Brill.

FORSTER, A. H. 1959. "The Date of Ecclesiasticus." *Anglican Theological Review* 41: 1–9.

FORTE, Anthony J., ed. 2014/2021. *Sirach (Ecclesiasticus): Pars altera, Fascicles I–II*. Vetus Latina 11/2. Freiburg: Herder.

FOULKES, Pamela A. 1994. "'To Expound Discipline or Judgement': The Portrait of the Scribe in Ben Sira." *Pacifica* 7: 75–84.

FRANKLINOS, Tristan / FULKERSON, Laurel. 2020. "Authoring, Reading, and Exploring an *Appendix*: Some Introductory Thoughts." In *Constructing Authors and Readers in the Appendices Vergiliana, Tibulliana, and Ouidiana*, edited by Tristan Franklinos and Laurel Fulkerson, 1–23. Pseudepigrapha Latina. Oxford: Oxford University Press.

FREVEL, Christian. 2018. *Geschichte Israels.* 2. erweiterte und überarbeitete Auflage. Kohlhammer Studienbücher Theologie. Stuttgart: Kohlhammer.

FRITZSCHE, Otto F. 1859. *Kurzgefasstes exegetisches Handbuch zu den Apokryphen des Alten Testamentes, 5. Lieferung, Die Weisheit Jesus-Sirach's erklärt und übersetzt.* Leipzig: Hirzel.

FRUHSTORFER, K. 1941. "Des Weisen curriculum vitae nach Sirach (39,1–5)." *Theologischpraktische Quartalschrift* 94: 140–142.

FULLER, Russell. 1996. "The Form and Formation of the Book of the Twelve: The Evidence from the Judean Desert." In *Forming Prophetic Literature: Essays on Isaiah and the Twelve in Honor of John D. W. Watts*, edited by James W. Watts and Paul R. House, 86–101. Journal for the Study of the Old Testament Supplement Series 235. Sheffield: Sheffield Academic.

FULLER, Russell E. 1997. "79. 4QXII^a." In *Qumran Cave 4 X, The Prophets*, edited by Eugene Ulrich, Frank M. Cross, Russell E. Fuller, Judith E. Sanderson, Patrick W. Skehan, and Emanuel Tov, 221–232, Pl. XL–XLII. Discoveries in the Judaean Desert 15. Oxford: Clarendon.

GALLAGHER, Edmon L. / MEADE, John D. 2017. *The Biblical Canon Lists from Early Christianity: Texts and Analysis.* Oxford: Oxford University Press.

GARCÍA MARTÍNEZ, Florentino. 2010. "Rethinking the Bible: Sixty Years of Dead Sea Scrolls Research and Beyond." In *Authoritative Scriptures in Ancient Judaism*, edited by Mladen Popović, 19–36. Supplements to the Journal for the Study of Judaism 141. Leiden: Brill.

GARCÍA MARTÍNEZ, Florentino / TIGCHELAAR, Eibert J. C. / VAN DER WOUDE, Adam S. 1998a. "10. 11QtargumJob." In *Qumran Cave 11, II, 11Q2–18, 11Q20–31*, edited by Florentino García Martínez, Eibert J. C. Tigchelaar, and Adam S. van der Woude, 79–180, Pl. IX–XXI. Discoveries in the Judaean Desert 23. Oxford: Clarendon.

GARCÍA MARTÍNEZ, Florentino / TIGCHELAAR, Eibert J. C. / VAN DER WOUDE, Adam S. 1998b. "12. 11QJubilees." In *Qumran Cave 11, II, 11Q2–18, 11Q20–31*, edited by Florentino García Martínez, Eibert J. C. Tigchelaar, and Adam S. van der Woude, 207–220, Pl. XXVI. Discoveries in the Judaean Desert 23. Oxford: Clarendon.

GARCÍA MARTÍNEZ, Florentino / TIGCHELAAR, Eibert J. C. / VAN DER WOUDE, Adam S. 1998c. "13. 11QMelchizedek." In *Qumran Cave 11, II, 11Q2–18, 11Q20–31*, edited by Florentino García Martínez, Eibert J. C. Tigchelaar, and Adam S. van der Woude, 221–241, Pl. XXVII. Discoveries in the Judaean Desert 23. Oxford: Clarendon.

GARNER, Lori A. 2017. "Traditional Referentiality." In *The Dictionary of the Bible and Ancient Media*, edited by Tom Thatcher, Chris Keith, Raymond F. Person, Elsie R. Stern, and Judith Odor, 425–428. London: Bloomsbury.

GÄRTNER, Hans A. 2001. "Prooimion." In *Der Neue Pauly. Enzyklopädie der Antike, Band 10*, edited by Hubert Cancik and Helmuth Schneider, 409–412. Stuttgart: Metzler.

GASSER, Johann C. 1903. *Das althebräische Spruchbuch und die Sprüche Jesu Ben Sira: In Bezug auf einige wesentliche Merkmale ihrer historischen Verschiedenheit untersucht.* Gütersloh: Bertelsmann.

GEHRKE, Hans-Joachim. 2008. *Geschichte des Hellenismus.* 4., durchges. Aufl. Oldenbourg Grundriss der Geschichte 1B. München: Oldenbourg.

GELSTON, Anthony. 2010. *Biblia Hebraica Quinta [BHQ], Vol. 13, The Twelve Minor Prophets.* Stuttgart: Deutsche Bibelgesellschaft.

208 *Bibliography*

GERTZ, Jan C. 2012. "The Partial Compositions (Translation by Peter Altmann)." In *T&T Clark Handbook of the Old Testament: An Introduction to the Literature, Religion and History of the Old Testament*, edited by Jan C. Gertz, Angelika Berlejung, Konrad Schmid, and Markus Witte, 293–382. London: T&T Clark.

GERTZ, Jan C. / BERLEJUNG, Angelika / SCHMID, Konrad / WITTE, Markus, eds. 2012. *T&T Clark Handbook of the Old Testament: An Introduction to the Literature, Religion and History of the Old Testament*. London: T&T Clark.

GESCHE, Bonifatia / RABO, Gabriel / LUSTIG, Christian. [2018]. "Eine Synopse zum Buch Jesus Sirach." Accessed August 23, 2021. http://www.sirach-synopse.uni-saarland.de.

GESENIUS, Wilhelm. 2013. *Hebräisches und Aramäisches Handwörterbuch über das Alte Testament*. 18. Aufl. Berlin: Springer.

GESENIUS, Wilhelm / KAUTZSCH, E. 1909. *Wilhelm Gesenius' Hebräische Grammatik*. 28. vielfach verb. und verm. Aufl. Leipzig: Vogel.

GILBERT, Maurice. 1974. "L'Éloge de la Sagesse (Siracide 24)." *Revue théologique de Louvain* 5 (3): 326–348.

GILBERT, Maurice. 1984. "Wisdom Literature." In *Jewish Writings of the Second Temple Period: Apocrypha, Pseudepigrapha, Qumran Sectarian, Writings, Philo, Josephus*, edited by Michael E. Stone, 283–324. Compendia Rerum Iudaicarum ad Novum Testamentum. Assen: Van Gorcum.

GILBERT, Maurice. 2011. "The Review of History in Ben Sira 44–50 and Wisdom 10–19." In *Rewriting Biblical History: Essays on Chronicles and Ben Sira in Honor of Pancratius C. Beentjes*, edited by Jeremy Corley and Harm van Grol, 319–334. Deuterocanonical and Cognate Literature Studies 7. Berlin: De Gruyter.

GOERING, Greg S. 2009. *Wisdom's Root Revealed: Ben Sira and the Election of Israel*. Supplements to the Journal for the Study of Judaism 139. Leiden: Brill.

GOFF, Matthew J. 2005. "Hellenistic Instruction in Palestine and Egypt: Ben Sira and Papyrus Insinger." *Journal for the Study of Judaism* 36 (2): 147–172.

GOFF, Matthew J. 2010. "Ben Sira and the Giants of the Land: A Note on Ben Sira 16:7." *Journal of Biblical Literature* 129 (4): 645–655.

GOFF, Matthew. 2018. "Ben Sira – Biblical Sage, Rabbi, and Payyeṭan: The Figure and Text of Ben Sira in Rabbinic Judaism." In *Discovering, Deciphering and Dissenting: Ben Sira Manuscripts after 120 Years*, edited by James K. Aitken, Renate Egger-Wenzel, and Stefan C. Reif, 183–199. Deuterocanonical and Cognate Literature Yearbook 2018. Berlin: De Gruyter.

GOSHEN-GOTTSTEIN, Alon. 2002. "Ben Sira's Praise of the Fathers: A Canon-Conscious Reading." In *Ben Sira's God: Proceedings of the International Ben Sira Conference, Durham, Ushaw College 2001*, edited by Renate Egger-Wenzel, 235–267. Beihefte zur Zeitschrift für die alttestamentliche Wissenschaft 321. Berlin: De Gruyter.

GRABBE, Lester L. 2000. *Judaic Religion in the Second Temple Period: Belief and Practice from the Exile to Yavneh*. London: Routledge.

GRABBE, Lester L. 2004. *A History of the Jews and Judaism in the Second Temple Period, Vol. 1, Yehud: A History of the Persian Province of Judah*. Library of Second Temple Studies 47. London: T&T Clark.

GRABBE, Lester L. 2006. "The Law, the Prophets, and the Rest: The State of the Bible in Pre-Maccabean Times." *Dead Sea Discoveries* 13 (3): 319–338.

GRABBE, Lester L. 2008. *A History of the Jews and Judaism in the Second Temple Period, Vol. 2, The Coming of the Greeks: The Early Hellenistic Period (335–175 BCE)*. Library of Second Temple Studies 68. London: T&T Clark.

Bibliography   209

GRABBE, Lester L. 2012. "Hellenistic Jewish Literature (Oxford Bibliographies – Jewish Studies)." Accessed August 23, 2021. https://www.oxfordbibliographies.com/view/document/obo-9780199840731/obo-9780199840731-0048.xml.

GRABBE, Lester L. 2020. *A History of the Jews and Judaism in the Second Temple Period, Vol. 3, The Maccabaean Revolt, Hasmonaean Rule, and Herod the Great (175–4 BCE)*. Library of Second Temple Studies 95. London: Bloomsbury.

GRAETZ, H. 1871. *Kohélet קהלת oder der Salomonische Prediger: Übersetzt und kritisch erläutert*. Leipzig: Winter.

GREGORY, Bradley. 2019. "Ecclesiasticus/Ben Sira, Latin." In *Textual History of the Bible, Volume 2B, Baruch/Jeremiah, Daniel (Additions), Ecclesiasticus/Ben Sira, Enoch, Esther (Additions), Ezra*, edited by Frank Feder and Matthias Henze, 243–255. Leiden: Brill.

GRUEN, Erich S. 2010. "Jewish Literature." In *A Companion to Hellenistic Literature*, edited by James J. Clauss and Martine Cuypers, 415–428. Blackwell Companions to the Ancient World. Chichester: Wiley-Blackwell.

GRUEN, Erich S. 2013. "Artapanus." In *Outside the Bible: Ancient Jewish Writing Related to Scripture, Vol. 1*, edited by Louis H. Feldman, James L. Kugel, and Lawrence H. Schiffman, 675–685. Lincoln; Philadelphia: University of Nebraska Press; Jewish Publication Society.

GUILLAUME, Philippe. 2005. "New Light on the Nebiim from Alexandria: A Chronography to Replace the Deuteronomistic History." *Journal of Hebrew Scriptures* 5: Article 9, 1–51.

GÜTHENKE, Constanze / HOLMES, Brooke. 2018. "Hyperinclusivity, Hypercanonicity, and the Future of the Field." In *Marginality, Canonicity, Passion*, edited by Marco Formisano and Christina S. Kraus, 57–73. Classical Presences. Oxford: Oxford University Press.

GUTZWILLER, Kathryn. 2007. *A Guide to Hellenistic Literature*. Blackwell Guides to Classical Literature. Malden, MA: Blackwell.

HAGENBICHLER (PAUL), Elfriede. 1992. "Bescheidenheitstopos." In *Historisches Wörterbuch der Rhetorik, Bd. 1*, edited by Gert Ueding, 1491–1495. Tübingen: Niemeyer.

HAMP, Vinzenz. 1951. *Sirach*. Echter Bibel, Das Alte Testament 13. Würzburg: Echter.

HANHART, Robert. 1994. "Textgeschichtliche Probleme der LXX von ihrer Entstehung bis Origenes." In *Die Septuaginta zwischen Judentum und Christentum*, edited by Martin Hengel and Anna M. Schwemer, 1–19. Wissenschaftliche Untersuchungen zum Neuen Testament 72. Tübingen: Mohr Siebeck.

HARDING, James E. 2016. "Ben Sira on Friendship: Notes on Intertextuality and Method." In *Perspectives on Israelite Wisdom: Proceedings of the Oxford Old Testament Seminar*, edited by John Jarick, 439–462. Library of Hebrew Bible/Old Testament Studies 618. London: Bloomsbury.

HART, John H.A. 1907. "The Prologue to Ecclesiasticus." *Jewish Quarterly Review* 19 (2): 284–297.

HART, John H.A. 1909. *Ecclesiasticus: The Greek Text of Codex 248: Edited with a Textual Commentary and Prolegomena*. Cambridge.

HARTENSTEIN, Friedhelm. 2019. "Kanongeschichte(n) und Geltungsfragen: Ein alttestamentlicher Beitrag zum 'Primat der Praxis' für eine Theologie der Schrift." In *Kanon: Marburger Jahrbuch Theologie XXXI*, edited by Elisabeth Gräb-Schmidt and Volker Leppin, 1–35. Marburger Theologische Studien 131. Leipzig: Evangelische Verlagsanstalt.

HARTOG, Pieter B. 2018. "Reading and Copying the Minor Prophets in the Late Second Temple Period." In *The Books of the Twelve Prophets: Minor Prophets, Major Theologies*, edited by Heinz-Josef Fabry, 411–423. Bibliotheca Ephemeridum Theologicarum Lovaniensium 295. Leuven: Peeters.

Hays, Christopher B. 2008. "Echoes of the Ancient Near East? Intertextuality and the Comparative Study of the Old Testament." In *The Word Leaps the Gap: Essays on Scripture and Theology in Honor of Richard B. Hays*, edited by J. Ross Wagner, C. Kavin Rowe, and A. Katherine Grieb, 20–43. Grand Rapids, MI: Eerdmans.

Hays, Richard B. 1989. *Echoes of Scripture in the Letters of Paul*. New Haven: Yale University Press.

Hayward, Robert, ed. 1996. *The Jewish Temple: A Non-Biblical Sourcebook*. London: Routledge.

Hearon, Holly. 2016. "Orality and Literacy (Oxford Bibliographies – Biblical Studies)." Accessed August 23, 2021. https://www.oxfordbibliographies.com/view/document/ob o-9780195393361/obo-9780195393361-0224.xml.

Hengel, Martin. 1988. *Judentum und Hellenismus: Studien zu ihrer Begegnung unter besonderer Berücksichtigung Palästinas bis zur Mitte des 2. Jh.s v. Chr.* 3., durchges. Auflage. Wissenschaftliche Untersuchungen zum Neuen Testament 10. Tübingen: Mohr Siebeck.

Hengel, Martin. 1994. "Die Septuaginta als 'christliche Schriftensammlung', ihre Vorgeschichte und das Problem ihres Kanons." In *Die Septuaginta zwischen Judentum und Christentum*, edited by Martin Hengel and Anna M. Schwemer, 182–284. Wissenschaftliche Untersuchungen zum Neuen Testament 72. Tübingen: Mohr Siebeck.

Herrmann, Klaus. 2000. "Henoch." In *Religion in Geschichte und Gegenwart [RGG⁴]*, Band 3, edited by Hans D. Betz, Don S. Browning, Bernd Janowski, and Eberhard Jüngel. 4. Aufl., 1626–1627. Tübingen: Mohr Siebeck.

Heszer, Catherine. 2020. "Literacy and Reading." In *T&T Clark Encyclopedia of Second Temple Judaism*. Vol. 2, edited by Loren T. Stuckenbruck and Daniel M. Gurtner, 438–440. London: T&T Clark.

Hildesheim, Ralph. 1996. *Bis daß ein Prophet aufstand wie Feuer: Untersuchungen zum Prophetenverständnis des Ben Sira in Sir 48,1–49,16*. Trierer theologische Studien 58. Trier: Paulinus.

Hilgert, Markus. 2016. "Materiale Textkulturen: Textbasierte historische Kulturwissenschaften nach dem *material culture turn*." In *Materialität: Herausforderungen für die Sozial- und Kulturwissenschaften*, edited by Herbert Kalthoff, Torsten Cress, and Tobias Röhl, 255–267. Paderborn: Fink.

Höffken, Peter. 1975. "Warum schwieg Jesus Sirach über Esra?" *Zeitschrift für die alttestamentliche Wissenschaft* 87 (2): 184–202.

Höffken, Peter. 2000. "Jesus Sirachs Darstellung der Interaktion des Königs Hiskija und des Propheten Jesaja (Sir 48:17–25)." *Journal for the Study of Judaism* 31 (2): 162–175.

Horgan, Maurya P. 2002. "Pesharim: Introduction." In *The Dead Sea Scrolls, Hebrew, Aramaic, and Greek Texts with English Translations, Volume 6B, Pesharim, Other Commentaries, and Related Documents*, edited by James H. Charlesworth, 1–5. Princeton Theological Seminary Dead Sea Scrolls Project 6B. Tübingen: Mohr Siebeck.

Horsley, Richard A. 2007. *Scribes, Visionaries, and the Politics of Second Temple Judea*. Louisville, KY: Westminster John Knox Press.

Horsley, Richard A./Tiller, Patrick. 2002. "Ben Sira and the Sociology of the Second Temple." In *Second Temple Studies III: Studies in Politics, Class and Material Culture*, edited by Philip R. Davies and John M. Halligan, 74–107. Journal for the Study of the Old Testament Supplement Series 340. London: Sheffield Academic.

Bibliography

HOSE, Martin. 1999. "Literatur, III. Griechisch." In *Der Neue Pauly. Enzyklopädie der Antike, Band 7*, edited by Hubert Cancik and Helmuth Schneider, 272–288. Stuttgart: Metzler.

HUPPING, Carol/OESTREICH, Julia/LISS, Janet/NROMAN, Robin/PELC, Julie/CORMAN, Debra, eds. 2008. *The Jewish Bible*. JPS Guide. Philadelphia: Jewish Publication Society.

ISRAEL ANTIQUITIES AUTHORITY. 2013. "Mas 1h – Mas Sir: Plate *238, B-371464, Taken November 2013, Photographer: Shai Halevi, Image Type: Color Photograph, Side: Recto." Accessed August 23, 2021. https://www.deadseascrolls.org.il/explore-the-arch ive/image/B-371464.

JACOBSON, Howard. 2013. "Ezekiel, the Tragedian." In *Outside the Bible: Ancient Jewish Writing Related to Scripture, Vol. 1*, edited by Louis H. Feldman, James L. Kugel, and Lawrence H. Schiffman, 730–742. Lincoln; Philadelphia: University of Nebraska Press; Jewish Publication Society.

JANßEN, Martina. 2011. "Pseudepigraphie, in: Das Wissenschaftliche Bibellexikon im Internet (WiBiLex)." Accessed August 23, 2021. https://www.bibelwissenschaft.de/stichwort/53905/.

JASTROW, Marcus. 1903. *A Dictionary of Targumim, Talmud and Midrashic Literature*. London: Luzac.

JELLICOE, Sidney. 1968. *The Septuagint and Modern Study*. Oxford: Clarendon.

JONES, Barry A. 1995. *The Formation of the Book of the Twelve: A Study in Text and Canon*. Society of Biblical Literature Dissertation Series 149. Atlanta, GA: Scholars Press.

JOÜON, Paul/MURAOKA, Takamitsu. 2011. *A Grammar of Biblical Hebrew*. 3rd repr. of the 2nd ed., with corr. Subsidia Biblica 27. Roma: Gregorian & Biblical Press.

KAHLE, Paul. 1959. *The Cairo Geniza*. 2nd ed. Schweich Lectures. Oxford: Blackwell.

KAISER, Otto. 2005. *Weisheit für das Leben: Das Buch "Jesus Sirach". Übersetzt und eingeleitet*. Stuttgart: Radius.

KALTHOFF, Herbert/CRESS, Torsten/RÖHL, Tobias. 2016. "Einleitung: Materialität in Kultur und Gesellschaft." In *Materialität: Herausforderungen für die Sozial- und Kulturwissenschaften*, edited by Herbert Kalthoff, Torsten Cress, and Tobias Röhl, 11–41. Paderborn: Fink.

KEARNS, Conleth. 2011. *The Expanded Text of Ecclesiasticus: Its Teaching on the Future Life as a Clue to Its Origin*. Edited by Pancratius C. Beentjes. Deuterocanonical and Cognate Literature Studies 11. Berlin: De Gruyter.

KEITH, Chris. 2020a. "Scribes and Scribalism." In *T&T Clark Encyclopedia of Second Temple Judaism*. Vol. 2, edited by Loren T. Stuckenbruck and Daniel M. Gurtner, 712–713. London: T&T Clark.

KEITH, Chris. 2020b. "Writing." In *T&T Clark Encyclopedia of Second Temple Judaism*. Vol. 2, edited by Loren T. Stuckenbruck and Daniel M. Gurtner, 831–833. London: T&T Clark.

KELLERMANN, Ulrich. 2017. *Elia als Toralehrer und Versöhner: Mal 3,22–24 und das Motiv der Zuwendung der Herzen von Vätern und Söhnen durch Elia im frühen Judentum*. Beiträge zum Verstehen der Bibel 32. Berlin: Lit.

KELLY, Joseph R. 2017. "Identifying Literary Allusions: Theory and the Criterion of Shared language." In *Subtle Citation, Allusion, and Translation in the Hebrew Bible*, edited by Ziony Zevit, 22–40. Sheffield: Equinox.

KESSLER, Rainer. 2011. *Maleachi*. Herders theologischer Kommentar zum Alten Testament. Freiburg: Herder.

212   *Bibliography*

Kieweler, Hans Volker. 1992. *Ben Sira zwischen Judentum und Hellenismus: Eine Aus-einandersetzung mit Th. Middendorp.* Beiträge zur Erforschung des Alten Testaments und des antiken Judentums 30. Frankfurt: Lang.

Kieweler, Hans-Volker. 1998. "Benehmen bei Tisch." In *Der Einzelne und seine Gemeinschaft bei Ben Sira,* edited by Renate Egger-Wenzel, 191–215. Beihefte zur Zeitschrift für die alttestamentliche Wissenschaft. Berlin: De Gruyter.

Kister, Menahem. 1999. "Some Notes on Biblical Expressions and Allusions and the Lexicography of Ben Sira." In *Sirach, Scrolls, and Sages: Proceedings of a Second International Symposium on the Hebrew of the Dead Sea Scrolls, Ben Sira, and the Mishnah, Held at Leiden University, 15–17 December 1997,* edited by T. Muraoka and J. F. Elwolde, 160–187. Studies on the Texts of the Desert of Judah 33. Leiden: Brill.

Knibb, Michael A. 1997. "Isaianic Traditions in the Apocrypha and Pseudepigrapha." In *Writing and Reading the Scroll of Isaiah: Studies of an Interpretive Tradition, Vol. 2,* edited by Craig C. Broyles and Craig A. Evans, 633–650. Supplements to Vetus Testamentum 70,2. Leiden: Brill.

Knibb, Michael A. 2010. "Reflections on the Status of the Early Enochic Writings." In *Authoritative Scriptures in Ancient Judaism,* edited by Mladen Popović, 143–154. Supplements to the Journal for the Study of Judaism 141. Leiden: Brill.

Knight, Jonathan. 1995. *The Ascension of Isaiah.* Guides to Apocrypha and Pseudepigrapha. Sheffield: Sheffield Academic.

Koenen, Klaus. 2017. "Aaron / Aaroniden, in: Das wissenschaftliche Bibellexikon im Internet (WiBiLex)." Accessed August 23, 2021. https://www.bibelwissenschaft.de/stich wort/11012/.

Koet, Bart J. 2011. "Elijah as Reconciler of Father and Son: From 1 Kings 16:34 and Malachi 3:22–24 to Ben Sira 48:1–11 and Luke 1:13–17." In *Rewriting Biblical History: Essays on Chronicles and Ben Sira in Honor of Pancratius C. Beentjes,* edited by Jeremy Corley and Harm van Grol, 173–190. Deuterocanonical and Cognate Literature Studies 7. Berlin: De Gruyter.

Koole, J. L. 1965. "Die Bibel des Ben Sira." In כה: *1940–1965,* edited by P. A. H. De Boer, 374–396. Oudtestamentische Studiën 14. Leiden: Brill.

Koole, J. L. 1977. "Gestaltung des alttestamentlichen Kanons." *Gereformeerd theologisch tijdschrift* 77: 224–238.

Kraft, Robert A. 1996. "Scripture and Canon in Jewish Apocrypha and Pseudepigrapha." In *Hebrew Bible / Old Testament: The History of Its Interpretation, Vol. 1,1,* edited by Magne Sæbø, C. Brekelmans, Menahem Haran, Michael A. Fishbane, Jean L. Ska, and Peter Machinist, 199–216. Göttingen: Vandenhoeck & Ruprecht.

Kratz, Reinhard G. 2020a. "Introduction." In *Interpreting and Living God's Law at Qumran: Miqṣat Maʿaśe Ha-Torah, Some of the Works of the Torah (4QMMT),* edited by Reinhard G. Kratz, 3–30. SAPERE 37. Tübingen: Mohr Siebeck.

Kratz, Reinhard G. 2020b. "Law and Narrative: 4QMMT and the Hebrew Bible." In *Interpreting and Living God's Law at Qumran: Miqṣat Maʿaśe Ha-Torah, Some of the Works of the Torah (4QMMT),* edited by Reinhard G. Kratz, 85–104. SAPERE 37. Tübingen: Mohr Siebeck.

Kratz, Reinhard G. 2020c. "Miqṣat Maʿaśe Ha-Torah (4QMMT), Some of the Works of the Torah: Reconstructed Text (According to the Format of 4Q394)." In *Interpreting and Living God's Law at Qumran: Miqṣat Maʿaśe Ha-Torah, Some of the Works of the Torah (4QMMT),* edited by Reinhard G. Kratz, 32–53. SAPERE 37. Tübingen: Mohr Siebeck.

KRATZ, Reinhard G. / STEUDEL, Annette / KOTTSIEPER, Ingo, eds. 2017/2018. *Hebräisches und aramäisches Wörterbuch zu den Texten vom Toten Meer: Einschließlich der Manuskripte aus der Kairoer Geniza, Band 1–2.* Berlin: De Gruyter.

KRAUSE, Joachim J. 2014. *Exodus und Eisodus: Komposition und Theologie von Josua 1–5.* Supplements to Vetus Testamentum 161. Leiden: Brill.

KRAUß, Anna / LEIPZIGER, Jonas / SCHÜCKING-JUNGBLUT, Friederike. 2020. "Material Aspects of Reading and Material Text Cultures: An Introduction." In *Material Aspects of Reading in Ancient and Medieval Cultures,* edited by Anna Krauß, Jonas Leipziger, and Friederike Schücking-Jungblut, 1–8. Materiale Textkulturen 26. Berlin: De Gruyter.

KREUZER, Siegfried. 2009. "Der Prolog des Buches Ben Sira (Weisheit des Jesus Sirach) im Horizont seiner Gattung: Ein Vergleich mit dem Euagoras des Isokrates." In *Geschehen und Gedächtnis: Die hellenistische Welt und ihre Wirkung. Festschrift für Wolfgang Orth zum 65. Geburtstag,* edited by Jens-Frederik Eckholdt, Marcus Sigismund, and Susanne Sigismund, 135–160. Antike Kultur und Geschichte 13. Berlin: Lit.

KREUZER, Siegfried. 2015. "Papyrus 967: Bemerkungen zu seiner buchtechnischen, textgeschichtlichen und kanongeschichtlichen Bedeutung." In *Geschichte, Sprache und Text: Studien zum Alten Testament und seiner Umwelt,* 437–456. Beihefte zur Zeitschrift für die alttestamentliche Wissenschaft 479. Berlin: De Gruyter.

KREUZER, Siegfried. 2016. "Entstehung und Überlieferung der Septuaginta." In *Einleitung in die Septuaginta,* edited by Siegfried Kreuzer, 29–88. Handbuch zur Septuaginta LXX.H 1. Gütersloh: Gütersloher Verlagshaus.

KREUZER, Siegfried / SIGISMUND, Marcus. 2016. "Überblick zu den Textzeugen der Septuaginta." In *Einleitung in die Septuaginta,* edited by Siegfried Kreuzer, 89–94. Handbuch zur Septuaginta LXX.H 1. Gütersloh: Gütersloher Verlagshaus.

KREVANS, Nita / SENS, Alexander. 2006. "Language and Literature." In *The Cambridge Companion to the Hellenistic World,* edited by Glenn R. Bugh, 186–207. Cambridge: Cambridge University Press.

KÜHNERT, Friedmar / VOGT, Ernst. 2005. "Philologie." In *Lexikon des Hellenismus,* edited by Hatto H. Schmitt, 789–800. Wiesbaden: Harrassowitz.

KUMPMANN, Christina. 2016. "עֶלְיוֹן." In *Theologisches Wörterbuch zu den Qumrantexten [ThWQ], Band III,* edited by Heinz-Josef Fabry and Ulrich Dahmen, 117–123. Stuttgart: Kohlhammer.

KVANVIG, Helge S. 1988. *Roots of Apocalyptic: The Mesopotamian Background of the Enoch Figure and of the Son of Man.* Wissenschaftliche Monographien zum Alten und Neuen Testament 61. Neukirchen-Vluyn: Neukirchener.

KVANVIG, Helge S. 2011. *Primeval History: Babylonian, Biblical, and Enochic: An Intertextual Reading.* Supplements to the Journal for the Study of Judaism 149. Leiden: Brill.

KWON, JiSeong J. 2016. *Scribal Culture and Intertextuality: Literary and Historical Relationships between Job and Deutero-Isaiah.* Forschungen zum Alten Testament, 2. Reihe 85. Tübingen: Mohr Siebeck.

KYNES, Will. 2012. *My Psalm Has Turned into Weeping: Job's Dialogue with the Psalms.* Beihefte zur Zeitschrift für die alttestamentliche Wissenschaft 437. Berlin: De Gruyter.

LABENDZ, Jenny R. 2006. "The Book of Ben Sira in Rabbinic Literature." *AJS Review* 30 (2): 347–392.

LANGE, Armin. 2002. "The Status of the Biblical Texts in the Qumran Corpus and the Canonical Process." In *The Bible as Book: The Hebrew Bible and the Judaean Desert Discoveries,* edited by Edward D. Herbert and Emanuel Tov, 21–30. London: British Library.

214 Bibliography

LANGE, Armin. 2003. "Qumran." In *Religion in Geschichte und Gegenwart [RGG⁴], Band 6*, edited by Hans D. Betz, Don S. Browning, Bernd Janowski, and Eberhard Jüngel. 4th ed., 1873–1896. Tübingen: Mohr Siebeck.

LANGE, Armin. 2004. "From Literature to Scripture: The Unity and Plurality of the Hebrew Scriptures in Light of the Qumran Library." In *One Scripture or Many? Canon from Biblical, Theological, and Philosophical Perspectives*, edited by Christine Helmer and Christof Landmesser, 51–107. Oxford: Oxford University Press.

LANGE, Armin. 2006. "Pre-Maccabean Literature from the Qumran Library and the Hebrew Bible." *Dead Sea Discoveries* 13 (3): 277–305.

LANGE, Armin. 2008. "'The Law, the Prophets, and the Other Books of the Fathers' (Sir, Prologue) Canonical Lists in Ben Sira and Elsewhere?" In *Studies in the Book of Ben Sira: Papers of the Third International Conference on the Deuterocanonical Books, Shime'on Centre, Pápa, Hungary, 18–20 May, 2006*, edited by Géza G. Xeravits and József Zsengellér, 55–80. Supplements to the Journal for the Study of Judaism 127. Leiden: Brill.

LANGE, Armin. 2009. *Handbuch der Textfunde vom Toten Meer, Band 1: Die Handschriften biblischer Bücher von Qumran und den anderen Fundorten*. Tübingen: Mohr Siebeck.

LANGE, Armin. 2013a. "Wisdom Literature from the Qumran Library, Instruction-like Composition B." In *Outside the Bible: Ancient Jewish Writing Related to Scripture, Vol. 3*, edited by Louis H. Feldman, James L. Kugel, and Lawrence H. Schiffman, 2414–2417. Lincoln; Philadelphia: University of Nebraska Press; Jewish Publication Society.

LANGE, Armin. 2013b. "Wisdom Literature from the Qumran Library, Musar leMevin." In *Outside the Bible: Ancient Jewish Writing Related to Scripture, Vol. 3*, edited by Louis H. Feldman, James L. Kugel, and Lawrence H. Schiffman, 2417–2443. Lincoln; Philadelphia: University of Nebraska Press; Jewish Publication Society.

LANGE, Armin / WEIGOLD, Matthias. 2011. *Biblical Quotations and Allusions in Second Temple Jewish Literature*. Journal of Ancient Judaism Supplements 5. Göttingen: Vandenhoeck & Ruprecht.

LARSON, Erik. 2000. "465. 4QpapText Mentioning Samson?" In *Qumran Cave 4 XXVI, Cryptic Texts and Miscellanea, Part 1*, edited by Stephen J. Pfann and Philip Alexander, 394–395, Pl. XXVII. Discoveries in the Judaean Desert 36. Oxford: Clarendon.

LARSON, Erik W. 2005. "The LXX and Enoch: Influence and Interpretation in Early Jewish Literature." In *Enoch and Qumran Origins: New Light on a Forgotten Connection*, edited by Gabriele Boccaccini, 84–89. Grand Rapids, MI: Eerdmans.

LAUBER, Stephan. 2013. *Weisheit im Widerspruch: Studien zu den Elihu-Reden in Ijob 32–37*. Beihefte zur Zeitschrift für die alttestamentliche Wissenschaft Band 454. Berlin: De Gruyter.

LEBRAM, J. C. H. 1968. "Aspekte der alttestamentlichen Kanonbildung." *Vetus Testamentum* 18 (2): 173–189.

LEE, Thomas R. 1986. *Studies in the Form of Sirach 44–50*. Society of Biblical Literature Dissertation Series 75. Atlanta, GA: Scholars Press.

LEHNUS, Luigi. 1999. "Kallimachos [3], Kallimachos aus Kyrene, hell. Dichter und Grammatiker." In *Der Neue Pauly. Enzyklopädie der Antike, Band 6*, edited by Hubert Cancik and Helmuth Schneider, 188–194. Stuttgart: Metzler.

LEIMAN, Sid Z. 1976. *The Canonization of Hebrew Scripture: The Talmudic and Midrashic Evidence*. Transactions of the Connecticut Academy of Arts and Sciences 47. Hamden: Archon.

LEONARD, Jeffery M. 2008. "Identifying Inner-Biblical Allusions: Psalm 78 as a Test Case." *Journal of Biblical Literature* 127: 241–265.

LIATSI, Maria. 2017. "Platons *Siebter Brief* als Gegenstand des Unechtheitsverdachtes: Ein hermeneutisches Missverständnis." In *Verleugnete Rezeption: Fälschungen antiker Texte*, edited by Wolfgang Kofler and Anna A. Novokhatko, 53–61. Pontes 7. Freiburg: Rombach.

LIDDELL, Henry G. / SCOTT, Robert / JONES, Henry S. [1940]. "A Greek-English Lexicon [LSJ]." Accessed August 23, 2021. http://www.tlg.uci.edu/lsj.

LIESEN, Jan. 2000. *Full of Praise: An Exegetical Study of Sir 39, 12–35*. Supplements to the Journal for the Study of Judaism 64. Leiden: Brill.

LIESEN, Jan. 2008. "A Common Background of Ben Sira and the Psalter: The Concept of תּוֹרָה in Sir 32:14–33:3 and the Torah Psalms." In *The Wisdom of Ben Sira: Studies on Tradition, Redaction, and Theology*, edited by Angelo Passaro, 179–208. Deuterocanonical and Cognate Literature Studies 1. Berlin: De Gruyter.

LIM, Timothy H. 2001. "The Alleged Reference to the Tripartite Division of the Hebrew Bible." *Revue de Qumrân* 20 (1): 23–37.

LIM, Timothy H. 2002. *Pesharim*. Companion to the Qumran Scrolls 3. London: Bloomsbury Publishing.

LIM, Timothy H. 2010. "Authoritative Scriptures and the Dead Sea Scrolls." In *The Oxford Handbook of the Dead Sea Scrolls*, edited by Timothy H. Lim and John J. Collins, 303–322. Oxford: Oxford University Press.

LIM, Timothy H. 2013. *The Formation of the Jewish Canon*. The Anchor Yale Bible Reference Library. New Haven: Yale University Press.

LISS, Hanna. 2019. *Tanach: Lehrbuch der jüdischen Bibel*. 4., völlig neu überarbeitete Auflage. Schriften der Hochschule für Jüdische Studien Heidelberg 8. Heidelberg: Universitätsverlag Winter.

LÓPEZ MARQUÉS, Eva. 1992. "Prolog." In *Historisches Wörterbuch der Rhetorik, Bd. 6*, edited by Gert Ueding, 201–208. Tübingen: Niemeyer.

LÜHRMANN, Dieter. 1975. "Henoch und die Metanoia." *Zeitschrift für die Neutestamentliche Wissenschaft und die Kunde der Älteren Kirche* 66 (1): 103–116.

LUNDHAUG, Hugo / LIED, Liv I. 2017. "Studying Snapshots: On Manuscript Culture, Textual Fluidity, and New Philology." In *Snapshots of Evolving Traditions: Jewish and Christian Manuscript Culture, Textual Fluidity, and New Philology*, edited by Liv I. Lied and Hugo Lundhaug, 1–19. Texte und Untersuchungen zur Geschichte der altchristlichen Literatur 175. Berlin: De Gruyter.

LUST, Johan / EYNIKEL, Erik / HAUSPIE, Katrin. 2003. *A Greek-English Lexicon of the Septuagint [LEH]*. Revised Edition. Stuttgart: Deutsche Bibelgesellschaft.

MACHIELA, Daniel A. 2009. *The Dead Sea Genesis Apocryphon: A New Text and Translation with Introduction and Special Treatment of Columns 13–17*. Studies on the Texts of the Desert of Judah 79. Leiden: Brill.

MACK, Burton L. 1982. "Under the Shadow of Moses. Authorship and Authority in Hellenistic Judaism." *Society of Biblical Literature Seminar Papers* 21: 299–318.

MACK, Burton L. 1985. *Wisdom and the Hebrew Epic: Ben Sira's Hymn in Praise of the Fathers*. Chicago: University of Chicago Press.

MACKENZIE, Roderick A. F. 1983. *Sirach*. Wilmington, DE: Glazier.

MAGNESS, Jodi. 2004. "Why Scroll Jars?" In *Religion and Society in Roman Palestine: Old Questions, New Approaches*, edited by Douglas R. Edwards, 146–161. London: Routledge.

216   *Bibliography*

MAIER, Johann. 2007. "7. Bezeugung der Bibel." In *Kulturgeschichte der Bibel*, edited by Anton Grabner-Haider, 181–211. Göttingen: Vandenhoeck & Ruprecht.

MAIR, A. W., ed. 1960. *Callimachus: Hymns and Epigrams, Lycophron, with an English Translation by A. W. Mair; Aratus, with an English Translation by G. R. Mair.* Loeb Classical Library. London; Cambridge, MA: Heinemann; Harvard University Press.

MANDEL, Paul D. 2017. *The Origins of Midrash: From Teaching to Text.* Supplements to the Journal for the Study of Judaism 180. Leiden: Brill.

MÄNNLEIN-ROBERT, Irmgard. 1992. "Prooemium." In *Historisches Wörterbuch der Rhetorik, Bd. 6*, edited by Gert Ueding, 247–256. Tübingen: Niemeyer.

MARBÖCK, Johann. 1971. *Weisheit im Wandel.* Bonner Biblische Beiträge 37. Bonn: Hanstein.

MARBÖCK, Johannes. 1993. "Die 'Geschichte Israels' als 'Bundesgeschichte' nach dem Sirachbuch." In *Der Neue Bund im Alten: Studien zur Bundestheologie der beiden Testamente*, edited by Erich Zenger, 177–197. Quaestiones Disputatae 146. Freiburg: Herder.

MARBÖCK, Johannes. 1995a. "Gebet um die Rettung Zions in Sir 36,1–22 (G: 33,1–13a; 36,16b–22) im Zusammenhang der Geschichtsschau Ben Siras." In *Gottes Weisheit unter uns: Zur Theologie des Buches Sirach*, edited by Irmtraud Fischer, 149–166. Herders biblische Studien 6. Freiburg: Herder.

MARBÖCK, Johannes. 1995b. "Gesetz und Weisheit. Zum Verständnis des Gesetzes bei Jesus Ben Sira." In *Gottes Weisheit unter uns: Zur Theologie des Buches Sirach*, edited by Irmtraud Fischer, 52–72. Herders biblische Studien 6. Freiburg: Herder.

MARBÖCK, Johannes. 1995c. "Gottes Weisheit unter uns. Sir 24 als Beitrag zur biblischen Theologie." In *Gottes Weisheit unter uns: Zur Theologie des Buches Sirach*, edited by Irmtraud Fischer, 73–87. Herders biblische Studien 6. Freiburg: Herder.

MARBÖCK, Johannes. 1995d. "Henoch – Adam – der Thronwagen. Zur frühjüdischen pseudepigraphischen Tradition bei Ben Sira." In *Gottes Weisheit unter uns: Zur Theologie des Buches Sirach*, edited by Irmtraud Fischer, 133–143. Herders biblische Studien 6. Freiburg: Herder.

MARBÖCK, Johannes. 1995e. "Sir 38,24–39,11: Der schriftgelehrte Weise. Ein Beitrag zu Gestalt und Werk Ben Siras." In *Gottes Weisheit unter uns: Zur Theologie des Buches Sirach*, edited by Irmtraud Fischer, 25–51. Herders biblische Studien 6. Freiburg: Herder.

MARBÖCK, Johannes. 2000. "Jesaja in Sirach 48,15–25: Zum Prophetenverständnis in der späten Weisheit." In *Schriftauslegung in der Schrift: Festschrift für Odil Hannes Steck zu seinem 65. Geburtstag*, edited by Odil H. Steck, Konrad Schmid, Reinhard G. Kratz, and Thomas Krüger, 305–319. Beihefte zur Zeitschrift für die alttestamentliche Wissenschaft 300. Berlin: De Gruyter.

MARBÖCK, Johannes. 2003. "Text und Übersetzung – Horizonte einer Auslegung im Prolog zum griechischen Sirach." In *Horizonte biblischer Texte: Festschrift für Josef M. Oesch zum 60. Geburtstag*, edited by Andreas Vonach, 99–116. Orbis biblicus et orientalis 196. Fribourg: Academic Press.

MARBÖCK, Johannes. 2008. "Mit Hand und Herz: Der schriftgelehrte Weise und das Handwerk in Sir 38,24–34." *Biblische Notizen* 139: 39–60.

MARBÖCK, Johannes. 2010. *Jesus Sirach 1–23.* Herders theologischer Kommentar zum Alten Testament. Freiburg: Herder.

MARCUS, Ralph, ed. 1933. *Josephus, Vol. VII, Jewish Antiquities, Books XII–XIV: With an English Translation.* Reprinted 1986. Loeb Classical Library 365. Cambridge, MA, London: Harvard University Press; Heinemann.

Bibliography

MARSHALL, John W. 2016. "Pseudepigraphy, Early Christian (Oxford Bibliographies – Biblical Studies)." Accessed August 23, 2021. https://www.oxfordbibliographies.com/view/document/obo-9780195393361/obo-9780195393361-0219.xml.

MARTIN, James D. 1986. "Ben Sira – A Child of his Time." In *A Word in Season: Essays in Honour of William McKane*, edited by James D. Martin and Philip R. Davies, 141–161. Library of Hebrew Bible/Old Testament Studies 42. London: Bloomsbury.

MARTTILA, Marko. 2008. "Die Propheten Israels in Ben Siras 'Lob der Väter'." In *Houses Full of All Good Things: Essays in Memory of Timo Veijola*, edited by Juha Pakkala and Martti Nissinen, 434–450. Publications of the Finnish Exegetical Society 93. Helsinki, Göttingen: Finnish Exegetical Society; Vandenhoeck & Ruprecht.

MARTTILA, Marko / PAJUNEN, Mika S. 2013. "Wisdom, Israel and Other Nations." *Journal of Ancient Judaism* 4 (1): 2–26.

MASON, Steve. 2007. "Jews, Judaeans, Judaizing, Judaism: Problems of Categorization in Ancient History." *Journal for the Study of Judaism* 38 (4–5): 457–512.

McDONALD, Lee M. 2002. "Appendix A: Primary Sources for the Study of the Old Testament/Hebrew Bible." In *The Canon Debate*, edited by Lee M. McDonald and James A. Sanders, 580–582. Peabody, MA: Hendrickson.

McDONALD, Lee M. 2007. *The Biblical Canon: Its Origin, Transmission, and Authority.* Updated & rev. 3rd ed. Peabody, MA: Hendrickson Publishers.

MEADE, John D. 2021. "The Septuagint and the Biblical Canon." In *The T&T Clark Handbook of Septuagint Research*, edited by William A. Ross and W. E. Glenny, 207–230. London: T&T Clark.

MEIER, Mischa. 1998. "Euergetes." In *Der Neue Pauly. Enzyklopädie der Antike, Band 4*, edited by Hubert Cancik and Helmuth Schneider, 228. Stuttgart: Metzler.

MERMELSTEIN, Ari. 2014. *Creation, Covenant, and the Beginnings of Judaism: Reconceiving Historical Time in the Second Temple Period.* Supplements to the Journal for the Study of Judaism 168. Leiden: Brill.

METSO, Sarianna. 2019. *The Community Rule: A Critical Edition with Translation.* Early Judaism and Its Literature 51. Atlanta, GA: SBL Press.

METZENTHIN, Christian. 2013. "כָּתַב." In *Theologisches Wörterbuch zu den Qumrantexten [ThWQ], Band II*, edited by Heinz-Josef Fabry and Ulrich Dahmen, 455–460. Stuttgart: Kohlhammer.

MICHELAKIS, Pantelis. 2020. "Introduction: Classical Antiquity, Media Histories, Media Theories." In *Classics and Media Theory*, edited by Pantelis Michelakis, 1–28. Classical Presences. Oxford: Oxford University Press.

MIDDENDORP, Theophil. 1973. *Die Stellung Jesu Ben Siras zwischen Judentum und Hellenismus.* Leiden: Brill.

MIGNE, Jacques-Paul, ed. 1887. *Patrologia Graeco-Latina, Series Graeca, Vol. 28.* Paris: Garnier.

MILIK, Józef T. 1962a. "Le Rouleau de Cuivre Provenant de la Grotte 3Q (3Q15), Commentaire et Texte." In *Les "petites grottes" de Qumran: Exploration de la falaise, les grottes 2Q, 3Q, 5Q, 6Q, 7Q à 10Q, le rouleau de cuivre, Textes*, edited by Maurice Baillet, J. T. Milik, Roland De Vaux, and H. W. Baker, 211–302. Discoveries in the Judaean Desert 3. Oxford: Clarendon.

MILIK, Józef T. 1962b. "Textes de la Grotte 5Q." In *Les "petites grottes" de Qumran: Exploration de la falaise, les grottes 2Q, 3Q, 5Q, 6Q, 7Q à 10Q, le rouleau de cuivre, Textes*, edited by Maurice Baillet, J. T. Milik, Roland De Vaux, and H. W. Baker, 167–197. Discoveries in the Judaean Desert 3. Oxford: Clarendon.

218   Bibliography

MILIK, Józef T. 1976. *The Books of Enoch: Aramaic Fragments of Qumrân Cave 4*. Oxford: Clarendon.

MILLER, Geoffrey D. 2011. "Intertextuality in Old Testament Research." *Currents in Biblical Research* 9 (3): 283–309.

MILLER, Shem. 2019. *Dead Sea Media: Orality, Textuality, and Memory in the Scrolls from the Judean Desert*. Studies on the Texts of the Desert of Judah 129. Leiden: Brill.

MITCHELL, Christine. 2011. "Chronicles and Ben Sira: Questions of Genre." In *Rewriting Biblical History: Essays on Chronicles and Ben Sira in Honor of Pancratius C. Beentjes*, edited by Jeremy Corley and Harm van Grol, 1–25. Deuterocanonical and Cognate Literature Studies 7. Berlin: De Gruyter.

MOPSIK, Charles. 2003. *La sagesse de Ben Sira*. Lagrasse, Aude: Verdier.

MORGENSTERN, Matthew J./SEGAL, Michael. 2013. "The Genesis Apocryphon." In *Outside the Bible: Ancient Jewish Writing Related to Scripture, Vol. 1*, edited by Louis H. Feldman, James L. Kugel, and Lawrence H. Schiffman, 237–262. Lincoln; Philadelphia: University of Nebraska Press; Jewish Publication Society.

MORLA, Víctor. 2012. *Los manuscritos hebreos de Ben Sira: Traducción y notas*. Asociación Bíblica Española, Tesis y monografías 59. Estella: Editorial Verbo Divino.

MROCZEK, Eva. 2015. "The Hegemony of the Biblical in the Study of Second Temple Literature." *Journal of Ancient Judaism* 6 (1): 2–35.

MROCZEK, Eva. 2016. *The Literary Imagination in Jewish Antiquity*. Oxford: Oxford University Press.

MROCZEK, Eva. 2020. "Pseudepigraphy." In *T&T Clark Encyclopedia of Second Temple Judaism*. Vol. 2, edited by Loren T. Stuckenbruck and Daniel M. Gurtner, 637–639. London: T&T Clark.

MULDER, Otto. 2003. *Simon the High Priest in Sirach 50: An Exegetical Study of the Significance of Simon the High Priest as Climax to the Praise of the Fathers in Ben Sira's Concept of the History of Israel*. Supplements to the Journal for the Study of Judaism 78. Leiden: Brill.

MULDER, Otto. 2011. "New Elements in Ben Sira's Portrait of the High Priest Simon in Sirach 50." In *Rewriting Biblical History: Essays on Chronicles and Ben Sira in Honor of Pancratius C. Beentjes*, edited by Jeremy Corley and Harm van Grol, 273–290. Deuterocanonical and Cognate Literature Studies 7. Berlin: De Gruyter.

MÜLLER, Matthias. 2005. *Edujot (Zeugenaussagen)*. Die Mischna, Textkritische Ausgabe mit deutscher Übersetzung und Kommentar. Ein Karem, Jerusalem: Lee Achim Sefarim.

MURADYAN, Gohar/TOPCHYAN, Aram. 2013. "Pseudo-Philo, On Samson and On Jonah." In *Outside the Bible: Ancient Jewish Writing Related to Scripture, Vol. 1*, edited by Louis H. Feldman, James L. Kugel, and Lawrence H. Schiffman, 750–775. Lincoln; Philadelphia: University of Nebraska Press; Jewish Publication Society.

MURAOKA, Takamitsu. 2011. *A Grammar of Qumran Aramaic*. Ancient Near Eastern Studies Supplement 38. Leuven: Peeters.

MURAOKA, Takamitsu. 2016. *A Syntax of Septuagint Greek*. Leuven: Peeters.

NAJMAN, Hindy/TIGCHELAAR, Eibert J.C. 2014. "A Preparatory Study of Nomenclature and Text Designation in the Dead Sea Scrolls." *Revue de Qumrân* 26 (3 (103)): 305–325.

NEEF, Heinz-Dieter. 2011. "דֶּרֶךְ." In *Theologisches Wörterbuch zu den Qumrantexten [ThWQ], Band I*, edited by Heinz-Josef Fabry and Ulrich Dahmen, 716–725. Stuttgart: Kohlhammer.

Bibliography

NESSELRATH, Heinz-Günther. 2013. "Das Museion und die Große Bibliothek von Alexandria." In *Alexandria*, edited by Tobias Georges, Felix Albrecht, and Reinhard Feldmeier, 65–88. Civitatum Orbis MEditerranei Studia 1. Tübingen: Mohr Siebeck.

NESTLE, E. 1897. "Zum Prolog des Ecclesiasticus." *Zeitschrift für die alttestamentliche Wissenschaft* 17 (1): 123–124.

NESTLE, Eb. 1901. "Miscellen." *Zeitschrift für die alttestamentliche Wissenschaft* 21: 327–336.

Nestle-Aland, ed. 2012. *Novum Testamentum Graece: Begründet von Eberhard und Erwin Nestle, herausgegeben von Barbara und Kurt Aland, Johannes Karavidopoulos, Carlo M. Martini, Bruce M. Metzger.* 28. revidierte Auflage. Stuttgart: Deutsche Bibelgesellschaft.

NETZ, Reviel. 2018. "The Greek Canon: A Few Data, Observations, Limits." In *Marginality, Canonicity, Passion*, edited by Marco Formisano and Christina S. Kraus, 203–230. Classical Presences. Oxford: Oxford University Press.

NEWMAN, Judith H. 2017. "Hybridity, Hydrology, and Hidden Transcript: Sirach 24 and the Judean Encounter with Ptolemaic Isis Worship." In *Jewish Cultural Encounters in the Ancient Mediterranean and Near Eastern World*, edited by Mladen Popović, Myles Schoonover, and Marijn Vandenberghe, 157–176. Supplements to the Journal for the Study of Judaism 178. Leiden: Brill.

NEWMAN, Judith H. 2018. *Before the Bible: The Liturgical Body and the Formation of Scriptures in Early Judaism.* Oxford: Oxford University Press.

NEWSOM, Carol. 1996. "379. 4QApocryphon of Joshua[b]." In *Qumran Cave 4, XVII, Parabiblical Texts, Part 3*, edited by George J. Brooke, John Collins, Torleif Elgvin, Peter W. Flint, Jonas C. Greenfield, Erik W. Larson, Carol Newsom et al., 263–288 Pl. XXI–XXV. Discoveries in the Judaean Desert 22. Oxford: Clarendon.

NICKELSBURG, George W. E. 2001. *1 Enoch 1: A Commentary on the Book of 1 Enoch, Chapters 1–36; 81–108.* Hermeneia. Minneapolis: Fortress Press.

NICKELSBURG, George W. E. 2005. *Jewish Literature between the Bible and the Mishnah: A Historical and Literary Indroduction.* 2nd ed. Minneapolis: Fortress Press.

NICKELSBURG, George W. E. 2013. "Tobit." In *Outside the Bible: Ancient Jewish Writing Related to Scripture, Vol. 3*, edited by Louis H. Feldman, James L. Kugel, and Lawrence H. Schiffman, 2631–2661. Lincoln; Philadelphia: University of Nebraska Press; Jewish Publication Society.

NICKELSBURG, George W. E. / VANDERKAM, James C. 2012a. *1 Enoch 2: A Commentary on the Book of 1 Enoch, Chapters 37–82.* Hermeneia. Minneapolis: Fortress Press.

NICKELSBURG, George W. E. / VANDERKAM, James C. 2012b. *1 Enoch: The Hermeneia Translation.* Minneapolis: Fortress Press.

NIDITCH, Susan. 1996. *Oral World and Written Word: Ancient Israelite Literature.* Library of Ancient Israel. Louisville, KY: Westminster John Knox Press.

NIDITCH, Susan. 2010. "Hebrew Bible and Oral Literature: Misconceptions and New Directions." In *The Interface of Orality and Writing: Speaking, Seeing, Writing in the Shaping of New Genres*, edited by Annette Weissenrieder and Robert B. Coote, 3–18. Wissenschaftliche Untersuchungen zum Neuen Testament 260. Tübingen: Mohr Siebeck.

NIEHOFF, Maren. 2011. *Jewish Exegesis and Homeric Scholarship in Alexandria.* Cambridge: Cambridge University Press.

220 Bibliography

NIELSEN, Inge. 1997. "Bibliothek, I. Bibliotheksgebäude." In *Der Neue Pauly. Enzyklopädie der Antike, Band 2*, edited by Hubert Cancik and Helmuth Schneider, 634–639. Stuttgart: Metzler.

NILSEN, Tina D. 2018. *The Origins of Deuteronomy 32: Intertextuality, Memory, Identity.* New York: Peter Lang.

NISSINEN, Martti. 2009. "Wisdom as Mediatrix in Sirach 24: Ben Sira, Love Lyrics, and Prophecy." In *Of God(s), Trees, Kings, and Scholars: Neo-Assyrian and Related Studies in Honour of Simo Parpola*, edited by Mikko Luukko, Saana Svärd, and Raija Mattila, 377–390. Studia Orientalia 106. Helsinki: Finnish Oriental Society.

NITZAN, Bilhah. 2013. "Pesher Habakuk." In *Outside the Bible: Ancient Jewish Writing Related to Scripture, Vol. 1*, edited by Louis H. Feldman, James L. Kugel, and Lawrence H. Schiffman, 363–666. Lincoln; Philadelphia: University of Nebraska Press; Jewish Publication Society.

NOGALSKI, James. 1993. *Literary Precursors to the Book of the Twelve.* Beihefte zur Zeitschrift für die alttestamentliche Wissenschaft 217. Berlin: De Gruyter.

NOTH, Martin. 1951. "Noah, Daniel Und Hiob in Ezechiel XIV." *Vetus Testamentum* 1 (1): 251–260.

NRSV: Holy Bible, New Revised Standard Version [NRSV], Containing the Old and New Testaments and the Deuterocanonical Books. 1989. Second Printing Hendrickson Publishers Edition 2007. Peabody, MA: Hendrickson Bibles.

ÖHLER, Markus. 1997. *Elia im Neuen Testament: Untersuchungen zur Bedeutung des alttestamentlichen Propheten im frühen Christentum.* Beihefte zur Zeitschrift für die neutestamentliche Wissenschaft und die Kunde der älteren Kirche 88. Berlin: De Gruyter.

OLSZOWY-SCHLANGER, Judith. 2018. "The 'Booklet' of Ben Sira: Codicological and Paleographical Remarks on the Cairo Genizah Fragments." In *Discovering, Deciphering and Dissenting: Ben Sira Manuscripts after 120 Years*, edited by James K. Aitken, Renate Egger-Wenzel, and Stefan C. Reif, 67–96. Deuterocanonical and Cognate Literature Yearbook 2018. Berlin: De Gruyter.

OLYAN, Saul. 1994. "382. 4Qpap paraKings et al." In *Qumran Cave 4: VIII, Parabiblical Texts, Part 1*, edited by Harold W. Attridge, Torleif Elgvin, Jozef Milik, Saul Olyan, John Strugnell, Emanuel Tov, James VanderKam, and Sidnie White, 363–416, Pl. XXXVIII–XLI. Discoveries in the Judaean Desert 13. Oxford: Clarendon.

ORLINSKY, Harry M. 1991. "Some Terms in the Prologue to Ben Sira and the Hebrew Canon." *Journal of Biblical Literature* 110 (3): 483–490.

ORPANA, Jessi. 2016. "Transmission and Reinterpretation of Scriptural Imagery and Traditions on the Creation of Humanity in the Book of Ben Sira." *Henoch* 38 (1): 4–14.

OSSÁNDON WIDOW, Juan C. 2019. *The Origins of the Canon of the Hebrew Bible: An Analysis of Josephus and 4 Ezra.* Supplements to the Journal for the Study of Judaism 186. Leiden: Brill.

OTTO, Eckart. 2003a. "Pentateuch." In *Religion in Geschichte und Gegenwart [RGG⁴], Band 6*, edited by Hans D. Betz, Don S. Browning, Bernd Janowski, and Eberhard Jüngel. 4th ed., 1089–1102. Tübingen: Mohr Siebeck.

OTTO, Eckart. 2003b. "Priestertum, II. Religionsgeschichtlich, 1. Alter Orient und Altes Testament." In *Religion in Geschichte und Gegenwart [RGG⁴], Band 6*, edited by Hans D. Betz, Don S. Browning, Bernd Janowski, and Eberhard Jüngel. 4th ed., 1646–1649. Tübingen: Mohr Siebeck.

OWENS, Robert J. 1989. "The Early Syriac Text of Ben Sira in the Demonstrations of Aphrahat." *Journal of Semitic Studies* 34 (1): 39–75.

OWENS, Robert J. 2011. "Christian Features in the Peshitta Text of Ben Sira: the Question of Dependency on the Syriac New Testament." In *The Texts and Versions of the Book of Ben Sira: Transmission and Interpretation*, edited by Jean-Sébastien Rey and Jan Joosten, 177–196. Supplements to the Journal for the Study of Judaism 150. Leiden: Brill.

OXFORD ENGLISH DICTIONARY [OED] ONLINE. 1888/2021. "canon, n.[1]." Accessed August 23, 2021. www.oed.com/view/Entry/27148.

PAGANINI, Simone / JÖRIS, Steffen. 2016. "שָׁפַט." In *Theologisches Wörterbuch zu den Qumrantexten [ThWQ], Band III*, edited by Heinz-Josef Fabry and Ulrich Dahmen, 1044–1051. Stuttgart: Kohlhammer.

PAJUNEN, Mika S. 2014. "Perspectives on the Existence of a Particular Authoritative Book of Psalms in the Late Second Temple Period." *Journal for the Study of the Old Testament* 39 (2): 139–163.

PAJUNEN, Mika S. / WEISSENBERG, Hanne von. 2015. "The Book of Malachi, Manuscript 4Q76 (4QXIIa), and the Formation of the 'Book of the Twelve'." *Journal of Biblical Literature* 134 (4): 731–751.

PANTELIA, Maria C. 2014. "Thesaurus Linguae Graecae [TLG]: Digital Library." Accessed August 23, 2021. http://stephanus.tlg.uci.edu/.

PARK, Song S. 2009. "Tradition, Oral, A. Old Testament." In *The New Interpreter's Dictionary of the Bible, Vol. 5*, edited by Katharine D. Sakenfeld, 645–646. Nashville, TN: Abingdon Press.

PEIRANO, Irene. 2012. *The Rhetoric of the Roman Fake: Latin Pseudepigrapha in Context.* Cambridge: Cambridge University Press.

PERDUE, Leo G. 2004. "Ben Sira and the Prophets." In *Intertextual Studies in Ben Sira and Tobit: Essays in Honor of Alexander A. Di Lella, O.F.M.*, edited by Jeremy Corley, Vincent T. M. Skemp, and Alexander A. Di Lella, 132–154. Catholic Biblical Quarterly Monograph Series 38. Washington, DC: Catholic Biblical Association of America.

PERSON, Raymond F. 2017. "Scribal Memory." In *The Dictionary of the Bible and Ancient Media*, edited by Tom Thatcher, Chris Keith, Raymond F. Person, Elsie R. Stern, and Judith Odor, 352–355. London: Bloomsbury.

PERSON, Raymond F. / KEITH, Chris. 2017. "Media Studies and Biblical Studies: An Introduction." In *The Dictionary of the Bible and Ancient Media*, edited by Tom Thatcher, Chris Keith, Raymond F. Person, Elsie R. Stern, and Judith Odor, 1–15. London: Bloomsbury.

PETERS, Norbert. 1913. *Das Buch Jesus Sirach oder Ecclesiasticus übersetzt und erklärt.* Exegetisches Handbuch zum Alten Testament 25. Münster: Aschendorff.

PEZZOLI-OLGIATI, Daria. 2001. "Kanon, I. Religionsgeschichtlich." In *Religion in Geschichte und Gegenwart [RGG⁴], Band 4*, edited by Hans D. Betz, Don S. Browning, Bernd Janowski, and Eberhard Jüngel. 4. Aufl., 767. Tübingen: Mohr Siebeck.

PFEIFFER, Rudolf. 1968. *History of Classical Scholarship: From the Beginnings to the End of the Hellenistic Age.* Oxford: Clarendon.

PIETERSMA, Albert / WRIGHT, Benjamin G., eds. 2007. *A New English Translation of the Septuagint, and other Greek Translations Traditionally Included under that Title [NETS].* Oxford: Oxford University Press. (Also available online. Accessed August 23, 2021. http://ccat.sas.upenn.edu/nets/edition.)

222   *Bibliography*

POPOVIĆ, Mladen. 2010. "Introducing *Authoritative Scriptures in Ancient Judaism.*" In *Authoritative Scriptures in Ancient Judaism*, edited by Mladen Popović, 1–17. Supplements to the Journal for the Study of Judaism 141. Leiden: Brill.

PRATO, G.L. 1987. "Classi lavorative e 'otium' sapienziale: Il significato teologico di una dicotomia sociale secondo Ben Sira (38,24–39,11)." In *Lavoro e riposo nella Bibbia*, edited by Antonio Fanuli and Giuseppe De Gennaro, 149–175. Napoli: Edizioni Dehoniane.

PRATO, G.L. 2000. "Scrittura divina e scrittura umana in Ben Sira: dal fenomeno grafico al testo sacro." *Ricerche storico bibliche* 12: 75–97.

PRESTEL, Peter / SCHORCH, Stefan. 2011. "Genesis / Das erste Buch Mose." In *Septuaginta Deutsch: Erläuterungen und Kommentare zum griechischen Alten Testament, Band I, Genesis bis Makkabäer*, edited by Martin Karrer and Wolfgang Kraus, 145–257. Stuttgart: Deutsche Bibelgesellschaft.

PRITCHARD, James B. 1969. *Ancient Near Eastern Texts relating to the Old Testament [ANET]*. 3rd ed. with suppl. Princeton, NJ: Princeton University Press.

PUECH, Émile. 1998. *Qumrân Grotte 4: Textes Hebreux (4Q521–4Q528, 4Q576–4Q579)*. Discoveries in the Judaean Desert 25. Oxford: Clarendon.

PUECH, Émile. 2009a. "558. 4QpapVision[b] ar." In *Qumrân Grotte 4 XXVII, Textes Araméens, Deuxième Partie 4Q550–4Q575a, 4Q580–4Q587 et Appendices*, edited by Emile Puech, 179–262. Discoveries in the Judaean Desert 37. Oxford: Clarendon.

PUECH, Émile. 2009b. "559. 4QpapChronologie biblique ar." In *Qumrân Grotte 4 XXVII, Textes Araméens, Deuxième Partie 4Q550–4Q575a, 4Q580–4Q587 et Appendices*, edited by Emile Puech, 263–290, Pl. XV. Discoveries in the Judaean Desert 37. Oxford: Clarendon.

QIMRON, Elisha / CHARLESWORTH, James H. 1994. "Rule of the Community (1QS)." In *The Dead Sea Scrolls, Hebrew, Aramaic, and Greek Texts with English Translations, Volume 1, Rule of the Community and Related Documents*, edited by James H. Charlesworth, 1–51. Princeton Theological Seminary Dead Sea Scrolls Project 1. Tübingen: Mohr.

QIMRON, Elisha / CHARLESWORTH, James H. / HUME, Douglas A. / MILLER, John B.F. / PFANN, Stephen J. / RIETZ, Henry W.M. 2006. "Some Works of the Torah: 4Q391–399 (=4QMMT[a–f]) and 4Q313." In *The Dead Sea Scrolls, Hebrew, Aramaic, and Greek Texts with English Translations, Volume 3, Damascus Document II, Some Works of the Torah, and Related Documents*, edited by James H. Charlesworth and Henry W.M. Rietz, 187–223. Princeton Theological Seminary Dead Sea Scrolls Project 3. Tübingen: Mohr Siebeck.

QIMRON, Elisha / STRUGNELL, John, eds. 1994. *Qumran Cave 4, V, Miqṣat Maʿaśe Ha-Torah*. Discoveries in the Judaean Desert 10. Oxford: Clarendon.

QUICK, Laura E. 2014. "Recent Research on Ancient Israelite Education: A Bibliographic Essay." *Currents in Biblical Research* 13 (1): 9–33.

RADL, Walter. 2002. "Lukasevangelium." In *Religion in Geschichte und Gegenwart [RGG⁴]*, Band 5, edited by Hans D. Betz, Don S. Browning, Bernd Janowski, and Eberhard Jüngel. 4th ed., 546–550. Tübingen: Mohr Siebeck.

RAHLFS, Alfred / HANHART, Robert, eds. 2006. *Septuaginta: Id est Vetus Testamentum graece iuxta LXX interpretes*. Ed. altera. Stuttgart: Deutsche Bibelgesellschaft.

REED, Annette Y. 2012. "Second Temple Judaism (Oxford Bibliographies – Biblical Studies)." Accessed August 23, 2021. https://www.oxfordbibliographies.com/view/document/obo-9780195393361/obo-9780195393361-0087.xml.

REED, Annette Y. 2020. "Pseudepigrapha, 'Old Testament'." In *T&T Clark Encyclopedia of Second Temple Judaism*. Vol. 2, edited by Loren T. Stuckenbruck and Daniel M. Gurtner, 634–638. London: T&T Clark.

REIF, Stefan C. 1997. "The Discovery of the Cambridge Genizah Fragments of Ben Sira: Scholars and Texts." In *The Book of Ben Sira in Modern Research: Proceedings of the First International Ben Sira Conference, 28–31 July 1996 Soesterberg, Netherlands*, edited by Pancratius C. Beentjes, 1–22. Beihefte zur Zeitschrift für die alttestamentliche Wissenschaft 255. Berlin: De Gruyter.

REITEMEYER, Michael. 2000. *Weisheitslehre als Gotteslob: Psalmentheologie im Buch Jesus Sirach*. Bonner Biblische Beiträge 127. Berlin: Philo.

REITEMEYER, Michael. 2011. "Sophia Sirach / Ben Sira / Ecclesiasticus / Das Buch Jesus Sirach, Einleitung 1–5." In *Septuaginta Deutsch: Erläuterungen und Kommentare zum griechischen Alten Testament, Band II, Psalmen bis Daniel*, edited by Martin Karrer and Wolfgang Kraus, 2158–2165. Stuttgart: Deutsche Bibelgesellschaft.

REITERER, Friedrich V. 1980. *Urtext und Übersetzungen: Sprachstudie über Sir 44, 16–45, 26 als Beitrag zur Siraforschung*. Arbeiten zu Text und Sprache im Alten Testament 12. St. Ottilien: EOS.

REITERER, Friedrich V. 2007. "Das Verhältnis Ijobs und Ben Siras." In *"Alle Weisheit stammt vom Herrn ...": Gesammelte Studien zu Ben Sira*, edited by Renate Egger-Wenzel, 345–375. Beihefte zur Zeitschrift für die alttestamentliche Wissenschaft 375. Berlin: De Gruyter.

REITERER, Friedrich V. 2008a. "Das Verhältnis der חכמה zur תורה im Buch Ben Sira: Kriterien zu gegenseitigen Bestimmung." In *Studies in the Book of Ben Sira: Papers of the Third International Conference on the Deuterocanonical Books, Shime'on Centre, Pápa, Hungary, 18–20 May, 2006*, edited by Géza G. Xeravits and József Zsengellér, 97–133. Supplements to the Journal for the Study of Judaism 127. Leiden: Brill.

REITERER, Friedrich V. 2008b. "The Interpretation of the Wisdom Tradition of the Torah within Ben Sira." In *The Wisdom of Ben Sira: Studies on Tradition, Redaction, and Theology*, edited by Angelo Passaro, 209–231. Deuterocanonical and Cognate Literature Studies 1. Berlin: De Gruyter.

REITERER, Friedrich V. 2008c. "The Sociological Significance of the Scribe as the Teacher of Wisdom in Ben Sira." In *Sages, Scribes, and Seers in Israel and the Ancient Near East: An Introduction*, edited by Leo G. Perdue, 218–244. Forschungen zur Religion und Literatur des Alten und Neuen Testaments 219. Göttingen: Vandenhoeck & Ruprecht.

REITERER, Friedrich V. 2011a. "Aaron's Polyvalent Role according to Ben Sira." In *Rewriting Biblical History: Essays on Chronicles and Ben Sira in Honor of Pancratius C. Beentjes*, edited by Jeremy Corley and Harm van Grol, 27–56. Deuterocanonical and Cognate Literature Studies 7. Berlin: De Gruyter.

REITERER, Friedrich V. 2011b. "Der Pentateuch in der spätbiblischen Weisheit Ben Siras." In *"Die Vollendung der Gottesfurcht ist Weisheit" (Sir 21,11): Studien zum Buch Ben Sira (Jesus Sirach)*, 45–67. Stuttgarter biblische Aufsatzbände 50. Stuttgart: Katholisches Bibelwerk.

REITERER, Friedrich V. 2011c. "Prophet und Prophetie in Tobit und Ben Sira. Berührungspunkte und Differenzen." In *"Die Vollendung der Gottesfurcht ist Weisheit" (Sir 21,11): Studien zum Buch Ben Sira (Jesus Sirach)*, 83–99. Stuttgarter biblische Aufsatzbände 50. Stuttgart: Katholisches Bibelwerk.

REITERER, Friedrich V. 2011d. "The Influence of the Book of Exodus on Ben Sira." In *"Die Vollendung der Gottesfurcht ist Weisheit" (Sir 21,11): Studien zum Buch Ben Sira*

224 *Bibliography*

(Jesus Sirach), 69–82. Stuttgarter biblische Aufsatzbände 50. Stuttgart: Katholisches Bibelwerk.

REITERER, Friedrich V. 2013. "Ein unkonventioneller Umgang mit der biblischen Autorität. Siras Art in hellenistischer Umgebung aus seiner Bibel zu denken und zu sprechen." In *Scriptural Authority in Early Judaism and Ancient Christianity*, edited by Geza G. Xeravits, Tobias Nicklas, and Isaac Kalimi, 129–166. Berlin: De Gruyter.

RENDSBURG, Gary A./BINSTEIN, Jacob. 2013. "The Book of Ben Sira, ספר בן סירא [www. bensira.org]." Accessed August 23, 2021. www.bensira.org.

RENDTORFF, Rolf. 1998. "Alas for the Day! The 'Day of the LORD' in the Book of the Twelve." In *God in the Fray: A Tribute to Walter Brueggemann*, edited by Tod Linafelt and Timothy K. Beal, 186–197. Minneapolis: Fortress Press.

REY, Jean-Sébastien. 2016. "Knowledge Hidden and Revealed: Ben Sira between Wisdom and Apocalyptic Literature." *Hebrew Bible and Ancient Israel* 5 (3): 255–272.

REY, Jean-Sébastien/DHONT, Marieke. 2018. "Scribal Practices in Ben Sira Manuscript B: Codicological Reconstruction and Material Typology of Marginal Readings." In *Discovering, Deciphering and Dissenting: Ben Sira Manuscripts after 120 Years*, edited by James K. Aitken, Renate Egger-Wenzel, and Stefan C. Reif, 97–123. Deuterocanonical and Cognate Literature Yearbook 2018. Berlin: De Gruyter.

REYMOND, Eric D. 2011. "גָּבַר." In *Theologisches Wörterbuch zu den Qumrantexten [ThWQ]*, *Band I*, edited by Heinz-Josef Fabry and Ulrich Dahmen, 565–573. Stuttgart: Kohlhammer.

REYMOND, Eric D. 2019. "Ecclesiasticus/Ben Sira, Hebrew." In *Textual History of the Bible, Volume 2B, Baruch/Jeremiah, Daniel (Additions), Ecclesiasticus/Ben Sira, Enoch, Esther (Additions), Ezra*, edited by Frank Feder and Matthias Henze, 199–213. Leiden: Brill.

RICKENBACHER, Otto. 1973. *Weisheitsperikopen bei Ben Sira*. Orbis biblicus et orientalis 1. Fribourg: Universitätsverlag.

ROGERS, Jessie. 2004. "'It Overflows Like the Euphrates with Understanding': Another Look at the Relationship between Law and Wisdom in Sirach." In *Of Scribes and Sages: Early Jewish Interpretation and Transmission of Scripture, Vol. 1, Ancient Versions and Traditions*, edited by Craig A. Evans, 114–121. Library of Second Temple Studies 50. London: T&T Clark International.

ROLLSTON, Chris A. 1992. "The Non-Encomiastic Features of Ben Sira 44–50." M.A. Thesis, Emmanuel School of Religion, Johnson City, TN. Accessed August 23, 2021. https://www.academia.edu/10484718/The_Non_Encomiastic_Features_of_Ben_Sira _44_50.

ROLLSTON, Chris A. 2001. "Ben Sira 38:24–39:11 and the Egyptian Satire of the Trades: A Reconsideration." *Journal of Biblical Literature* 120 (1): 131–139.

RÖSLER, Wolfgang. 2001. "Schriftlichkeit–Mündlichkeit." In *Der Neue Pauly. Enzyklopädie der Antike, Band 11*, edited by Hubert Cancik and Helmuth Schneider, 241–246. Stuttgart: Metzler.

ROSS, William A. 2021. "Introduction." In *The T&T Clark Handbook of Septuagint Research*, edited by William A. Ross and W. E. Glenny, 1–8. London: T&T Clark.

RÜGER, Hans P. 1984. "Le Siracide: Un livre à la frontière du canon." In *Le canon de l'Ancien Testament: Sa formation et son histoire*, edited by Jean-Daniel Kaestli and Otto Wermelinger, 47–69. Le monde de la Bible. Genève: Labor et fides.

RUNIA, David T. 2000. "Philon, [12] Ph. von Alexandreia (Philo Iudaeus)." In *Der Neue Pauly. Enzyklopädie der Antike, Band 9*, edited by Hubert Cancik and Helmuth Schneider, 850–856. Stuttgart: Metzler.

Bibliography 225

RÜPKE, Jörg. 1999. "Literatur, I. Allgemein." In *Der Neue Pauly. Enzyklopädie der Antike, Band 7*, edited by Hubert Cancik and Helmuth Schneider, 266–267. Stuttgart: Metzler.

RYLE, Herbert E. 1892. *The Canon of the Old Testament: An Essay on the Gradual Growth and Formation of the Hebrew Canon of Scripture*. London: Macmillan.

RYSSEL, Victor. 1900. "Die Sprüche Jesus', des Sohnes Sirachs." In *Die Apokryphen und Pseudepigraphen des Alten Testaments, Band I*, edited by Emil Kautzsch, 230–475. Tübingen: Mohr.

SANDERS, Jack T. 1983. *Ben Sira and Demotic Wisdom*. Society of Biblical Literature Monograph Series 28. Chico, CA: Scholars Press.

SANDERS, James A. 1965. *The Psalms Scroll of Qumran Cave 11 (11QPs^a)*. Discoveries in the Judaean Desert 4. Oxford: Clarendon.

SANDERS, James A. 1972. *Torah and Canon*. Philadelphia: Fortress Press.

SAUER, Georg. 1981. *Jesus Sirach (Ben Sira)*. Jüdische Schriften aus hellenistisch-römischer Zeit 3,5. Gütersloh: Mohn.

SAUER, Georg. 2000. *Jesus Sirach – Ben Sira*. Das Alte Testament Deutsch, Apokryphen 1. Göttingen: Vandenhoeck & Ruprecht.

SCARSO, Teresa. 2020. "The Intertextuality of the Figure of Elijah in the Qumran Texts." *Judaïsme Ancien – Ancient Judaism* 8: 233–248.

SCHAPER, Joachim. 2000. "Hohepriester, I. Altes Testament." In *Religion in Geschichte und Gegenwart [RGG^4], Band 3*, edited by Hans D. Betz, Don S. Browning, Bernd Janowski, and Eberhard Jüngel. 4. Aufl., 1835–1836. Tübingen: Mohr Siebeck.

SCHART, Aaron. 1998. *Die Entstehung des Zwölfprophetenbuchs: Neubearbeitungen von Amos im Rahmen schriftenübergreifender Redaktionsprozesse*. Beihefte zur Zeitschrift für die alttestamentliche Wissenschaft 260. Berlin: De Gruyter.

SCHART, Aaron. 2011. "Dodekapropheton. Das Zwölfprophetenbuch." In *Septuaginta Deutsch: Erläuterungen und Kommentare zum griechischen Alten Testament, Band II, Psalmen bis Daniel*, edited by Martin Karrer and Wolfgang Kraus, 2275–2286. Stuttgart: Deutsche Bibelgesellschaft.

SCHECHTER, S. 1899. "Introduction, III. The Relation of Ben Sira to the Old Testament." In *The Wisdom of Ben Sira: Portions of the Book Ecclesiasticus from Hebrew Manuscripts in the Cairo Genizah Collection*, edited by S. Schechter and C. Taylor, 12–38. Cambridge: University Press.

SCHECHTER, S. 1908a. *Studies in Judaism: Second Series*. Philadelphia: Jewish Publication Society of America.

SCHECHTER, S. 1908b. "The Study of the Bible." In *Studies in Judaism: Second Series*, 31–54. Philadelphia: Jewish Publication Society of America.

SCHECHTER, S./TAYLOR, C., eds. 1899. *The Wisdom of Ben Sira: Portions of the Book Ecclesiasticus from Hebrew Manuscripts in the Cairo Genizah Collection*. Cambridge: University Press.

SCHERER, Andreas. 2005. "Richter / Richterbuch, in: Das Wissenschaftliche Bibellexikon im Internet (WiBiLex)." Accessed August 23, 2021. https://www.bibelwissenschaft.de/stichwort/11857/.

SCHIFFMAN, Lawrence H. 1995. *Reclaiming the Dead Sea Scrolls: The History of Judaism, the Background of Christianity, the Lost Library of Qumran*. Anchor Bible Reference Library. New York: Doubleday.

SCHILDENBERGER, Johannes. 1950. "Die Bedeutung von Sir 48,24 f. für die Verfasserfrage von Is 40–66." In *Alttestamentliche Studien*, edited by Hubert Junker, 188–204. Bonner Biblische Beiträge 1. Bonn: Hanstein.

226 *Bibliography*

SCHINDLER, Alfred. 2001. "Kanon, II. Kirchengeschichtlich." In *Religion in Geschichte und Gegenwart [RGG⁴], Band 4*, edited by Hans D. Betz, Don S. Browning, Bernd Janowski, and Eberhard Jüngel. 4. Aufl., 767–770. Tübingen: Mohr Siebeck.

SCHMID, Konrad. 2011. "Schriftgelehrte Arbeit an der Schrift: Historische Überlegungen zum Vorgang innerbiblischer Exegese." In *Schriftgelehrte Traditionsliteratur*, 35–60. Forschungen zum Alten Testament 77. Tübingen: Mohr Siebeck.

SCHMID, Konrad. 2012a. "The Book of Isaiah (Translation by Jennifer Adams-Maß-mann)." In *T&T Clark Handbook of the Old Testament: An Introduction to the Literature, Religion and History of the Old Testament*, edited by Jan C. Gertz, Angelika Berlejung, Konrad Schmid, and Markus Witte, 401–429. London: T&T Clark.

SCHMID, Konrad. 2012b. "The Canon and the Cult: The Emergence of Book Religion in Ancient Israel and the Gradual Sublimation of the Temple Cult." *Journal of Biblical Literature* 131 (2): 289–305.

SCHMID, Konrad / SCHRÖTER, Jens. 2019. *Die Entstehung der Bibel: Von den ersten Texten zu den heiligen Schriften*. München: Beck.

SCHMIDT, A. J. 2019. *Wisdom, Cosmos, and Cultus in the Book of Sirach*. Deuterocanonical and Cognate Literature Studies 42. Berlin: De Gruyter.

SCHMITT, Hans-Christoph. 2011. *Arbeitsbuch zum Alten Testament: Grundzüge der Geschichte Israels und der alttestamentlichen Schriften*. 3., durchges. Aufl. UTB 2146. Göttingen: Vandenhoeck & Ruprecht.

SCHMITT, Hatto H. 2005. "Schrift und Schreiben." In *Lexikon des Hellenismus*, edited by Hatto H. Schmitt, 950–952. Wiesbaden: Harrassowitz.

SCHNABEL, Eckhard J. 1985. *Law and Wisdom from Ben Sira to Paul: A Tradition Historical Enquiry into the Relation of Law, Wisdom, and Ethics*. Wissenschaftliche Untersuchungen zum Neuen Testament, 2. Reihe 16. Tübingen: Mohr.

SCHNELLE, Udo. 1998. "Bibel, I. Zum Begriff." In *Religion in Geschichte und Gegenwart [RGG⁴], Band 1*, edited by Hans D. Betz, Don S. Browning, Bernd Janowski, and Eberhard Jüngel. 4. Aufl., 1407. Tübingen: Mohr Siebeck.

SCHNELLE, Udo. 2012. "Bible, I. Concept." In *Religion Past and Present [RPP]: Encyclopedia of Theology and Religion, Vol. I*, edited by Hans D. Betz. 4th edition, English edition, 1. Leiden: Brill.

SCHNIEDEWIND, William M. 2004. *How the Bible Became a Book: The Textualization of Ancient Israel*. Cambridge: Cambridge University Press.

SCHRADER, Lutz. 1994. *Leiden und Gerechtigkeit: Studien zur Theologie und Textgeschichte des Sirachbuches*. Beiträge zur biblischen Exegese und Theologie 27. Frankfurt am Main: Lang.

SCHRADER, Lutz. 1998. "Beruf, Arbeit und Muße als Sinnerfüllung bei Jesus Sirach." In *Der Einzelne und seine Gemeinschaft bei Ben Sira*, edited by Renate Egger-Wenzel, 117–150. Beihefte zur Zeitschrift für die alttestamentliche Wissenschaft. Berlin: De Gruyter.

SCHREINER, Josef. 2002. *Jesus Sirach 1–24*. Neue Echter Bibel, Altes Testament Lfg. 38. Würzburg: Echter.

SCHULLER, Eileen M. / BERNSTEIN, Moshe J. 2001. "372. 4QNarrative and Poetic Composition[b]." In *Wadi Daliyeh II and Qumran Cave 4 XXVIII: Wadi Daliyeh II, The Samaria Papyri from Wadi Daliyeh, and Qumran Cave 4 XXVIII, Miscellanea, Part 2*, edited by Douglas M. Gropp, Moshe J. Bernstein, Monica Brady, James H. Charlesworth, Peter W. Flint, Haggai Misgav, Stephen J. Pfann, Eileen Schuller, Eibert Tigchelaar, and James VanderKam, 165–197, Pl. XLVII–XLIX. Discoveries in the Judaean Desert 28. Oxford: Clarendon.

SCHULTZ, Richard L. 1999. *The Search for Quotation: Verbal Parallels in the Prophets.* Journal for the Study of the Old Testament Supplement Series 180. Sheffield: Sheffield Academic.

SCHÜRER, Emil. 1986. *The History of the Jewish People in the Age of Jesus Christ (175 B.C.– A.D. 135), Vol. III Part 1: A New English Version Revised and Edited by Géza Vermès, Fergus Millar, Martin Goodman.* Edinburgh: T&T Clark.

SCHWARTZ, Daniel R. 2000. "Hohepriester, II. Antikes Judentum." In *Religion in Geschichte und Gegenwart [RGG⁴], Band 3,* edited by Hans D. Betz, Don S. Browning, Bernd Janowski, and Eberhard Jüngel. 4. Aufl., 1836. Tübingen: Mohr Siebeck.

SEITZ, Christopher R. 2009. *The Goodly Fellowship of the Prophets: The Achievement of Association in Canon Formation.* Grand Rapids, MI: Baker Academic.

SEPTUAGINTA-UNTERNEHMEN. 2012. "Offizielles Verzeichnis der Rahlfs-Sigeln: Herausgegeben vom Septuaginta-Unternehmen der Akademie der Wissenschaften zu Göttingen, Stand: Dezember 2012." Accessed August 23, 2021. http://rep.adw-goe.de/bitstre am/handle/11858/00-001S-0000-0022-A30C-8/Rahlfs-Sigeln_Stand_Dezember_2012 .pdf?sequence=1.

SHEPPARD, Gerald T. 1980. *Wisdom as a Hermeneutical Construct: A Study in the Sapientializing of the Old Testament.* Beihefte zur Zeitschrift für die alttestamentliche Wissenschaft 151. Berlin: De Gruyter.

SIEGERT, Folker. 2001. *Zwischen Hebräischer Bibel und Altem Testament: Eine Einführung in die Septuaginta.* Münsteraner judaistische Studien 9. Münster: Lit.

SIEGERT, Folker. 2019. *Einleitung in die hellenistisch-jüdische Literatur: Apokrypha, Pseudepigrapha und Fragmente verlorener Autorenwerke.* Berlin: De Gruyter.

SKA, Jean L. 2009. "The Praise of the Fathers in Sirach (Sir 44–50) and the Canon of the Old Testament." In *The Exegesis of the Pentateuch: Exegetical Studies and Basic Questions,* edited by Jean-Louis Ska, 184–195. Forschungen zum Alten Testament 66. Tübingen: Mohr Siebeck.

SKEHAN, Patrick W. / ULRICH, Eugene. 1997a. "56. 4QIsa^b." In *Qumran Cave 4 X, The Prophets,* edited by Eugene Ulrich, Frank M. Cross, Russell E. Fuller, Judith E. Sanderson, Patrick W. Skehan, and Emanuel Tov, 19–43, Pl. III–VI. Discoveries in the Judaean Desert 15. Oxford: Clarendon.

SKEHAN, Patrick W. / ULRICH, Eugene. 1997b. "58. 4QIsa^d." In *Qumran Cave 4 X, The Prophets,* edited by Eugene Ulrich, Frank M. Cross, Russell E. Fuller, Judith E. Sanderson, Patrick W. Skehan, and Emanuel Tov, 75–88, Pl. XIII–XV. Discoveries in the Judaean Desert 15. Oxford: Clarendon.

SKEHAN, Patrick W. / ULRICH, Eugene. 1997c. "66. 4QIsa^m." In *Qumran Cave 4 X, The Prophets,* edited by Eugene Ulrich, Frank M. Cross, Russell E. Fuller, Judith E. Sanderson, Patrick W. Skehan, and Emanuel Tov, 131–132, Pl. XXII. Discoveries in the Judaean Desert 15. Oxford: Clarendon.

SKEHAN, Patrick W. / DI LELLA, Alexander A. 1987. *The Wisdom of Ben Sira: A New Translation with Notes by Patrick W. Skehan, Introduction and Commentary by Alexander A. di Lella, O. F. M.* Anchor Bible 39. New York: Doubleday.

SKEHAN, Patrick W. / ULRICH, Eugene / SANDERSON, Judith E. 1992. "11. 4QpaleoGenesis–Exodus^l." In *Qumran Cave 4, IV, Palaeo-Hebrew and Greek Biblical Manuscripts,* edited by Patrick W. Skehan, Eugene C. Ulrich, and Judith E. Sanderson, 17–50, Pl. I–VI. Discoveries in the Judaean Desert 9. Oxford: Clarendon.

SKEHAN, Patrick W. / ULRICH, Eugene / FLINT, Peter W. 2000. "4QPs^a." In *Qumran Cave 4, XI, Psalms to Chronicles,* edited by Eugene Ulrich, Frank M. Cross, Joseph

228   *Bibliography*

A. Fitzmyer, and Peter W. Flint, 7–22, Pl. I–II. Discoveries in the Judaean Desert 16. Oxford: Clarendon.

SMEND, Rudolf. 1906. *Die Weisheit des Jesus Sirach erklärt.* Berlin: Reimer.

SMYTH, Herbert W./ MESSING, Gordon M. 1956. *Greek Grammar.* Cambridge, MA: Harvard University Press.

SNAITH, John G. 1967. "Biblical Quotations in the Hebrew of Ecclesiasticus." *Journal of Theological Studies* 18 (1): 1–12.

SNAITH, John G. 1974. *Ecclesiasticus: Or The Wisdom of Jesus Son of Sirach.* Cambridge: Cambridge University Press.

SPEYER, Wolfgang. 1971. *Die literarische Fälschung im heidnischen und christlichen Altertum: Ein Versuch ihrer Deutung.* Handbuch der Altertumswissenschaft Abteilung 1, Teil 2. München: Beck.

STADEL, Christian. 2011. "הָלַד." In *Theologisches Wörterbuch zu den Qumrantexten [ThWQ], Band I*, edited by Heinz-Josef Fabry and Ulrich Dahmen, 782–789. Stuttgart: Kohlhammer.

STADELMANN, Helge. 1980. *Ben Sira als Schriftgelehrter: Eine Untersuchung zum Berufsbild des vor-makkabäischen Sôfēr unter Berücksichtigung seines Verhältnisses zu Priester-, Propheten- und Weisheitslehrertum.* Wissenschaftliche Untersuchungen zum Neuen Testament 2. Tübingen: Mohr.

STECK, Odil H. 1991. *Der Abschluß der Prophetie im Alten Testament: Ein Versuch zur Frage der Vorgeschichte des Kanons.* Biblisch-Theologische Studien 17. Neukirchen-Vluyn: Neukirchener.

STECK, Odil H. 1992. "Der Kanon des hebräischen Alten Testamentes. Historische Materialien für eine ökumenische Perspektive." In *Verbindliches Zeugnis I*, edited by Wolfgang Pannenberg, 11–33. Dialog der Kirchen. Freiburg: Herder.

STECK, Odil H. 1996. *Die Prophetenbücher und ihr theologisches Zeugnis: Wege der Nachfrage und Fährten zur Antwort.* Tübingen: Mohr.

STEINMANN, Andrew E. 1999. *The Oracles of God: The Old Testament Canon.* St. Louis, MO: Concordia.

STEINS, Georg. 1995. *Die Chronik als kanonisches Abschlußphänomen.* Bonner Biblische Beiträge 93. Weinheim: Beltz Athenäum.

STEMBERGER, Günter. 2001. "Tanach." In *Theologische Realenzyklopädie [TRE], Band 32*, edited by Gerhard Müller, 636–639. Berlin: De Gruyter.

STEMBERGER, Günter. 2019. "Hermeneutik der jüdischen Bibel." In *Hermeneutik der Jüdischen Bibel und des Alten Testaments.* 2. Auflage, 29–141. Stuttgart: Kohlhammer Verlag.

STIPP, Hermann-Josef. 2021. "Die Erkennbarkeit intentionaler innerbiblischer Intertextualität am Beispiel von Jeremia 26 und 36." In *Exegetik des Alten Testaments: Bausteine für eine Theorie der Exegese*, edited by Joachim J. Krause and Kristin Weingart, 127–160. Forschungen zum Alten Testament, 2. Reihe 127. Tübingen: Mohr Siebeck.

STÖKL BEN EZRA, Daniel. 2016. *Qumran: Die Texte vom Toten Meer und das antike Judentum.* Jüdische Studien 3. Tübingen: Mohr Siebeck.

STONE, Michael E. 1978. "The Book of Enoch and Judaism in the Third Century B.C.E." *Catholic Biblical Quarterly* 40 (4): 479–492.

STONE, Michael E. 2010. "The Book(s) Attributed to Noah." In *Noah and His Book(s)*, edited by Michael E. Stone, 7–25. Early Judaism and Its Literature 28. Atlanta, GA: Society of Biblical Literature.

Bibliography

Stone, Michael E. / Eshel, Esther. 2013. "Aramaic Levi Document." In *Outside the Bible: Ancient Jewish Writing Related to Scripture, Vol. 2*, edited by Louis H. Feldman, James L. Kugel, and Lawrence H. Schiffman, 1490–1506. Lincoln; Philadelphia: University of Nebraska Press; Jewish Publication Society.

Strack, Hermann L. / Billerbeck, Paul. 1928. *Kommentar zum Neuen Testament aus Talmud und Midrasch, Vierter Band: Exkurse zu einzelnen Stellen des Neuen Testaments, Abhandlungen zur neutestamentlichen Theologie und Archäologie, Erster Teil*. München: Beck.

Strawn, Brent A. 2016. "תָּמַם." In *Theologisches Wörterbuch zu den Qumrantexten [ThWQ], Band III*, edited by Heinz-Josef Fabry and Ulrich Dahmen, 1135–1143. Stuttgart: Kohlhammer.

Stuckenbruck, Loren T. 2007. *1 Enoch 91–108*. Commentaries on Early Jewish Literature. Berlin: De Gruyter.

Stuckenbruck, Loren T. 2013a. "The *Book of Enoch*: Its Reception in Second Temple Jewish and in Christian Tradition." *Early Christianity* 4 (1): 7–40.

Stuckenbruck, Loren T. 2013b. "The Book of Giants." In *Outside the Bible: Ancient Jewish Writing Related to Scripture, Vol. 1*, edited by Louis H. Feldman, James L. Kugel, and Lawrence H. Schiffman, 221–236. Lincoln; Philadelphia: University of Nebraska Press; Jewish Publication Society.

Stuckenbruck, Loren T. 2016. "1 Enoch 1: A Comparison of Two Translations." In *New Vistas on Early Judaism and Christianity: From Enoch to Montreal and Back*, edited by Lorenzo DiTommaso, 25–40. Jewish and Christian Texts in Contexts and Related Studies 22. London: Bloomsbury T&T Clark.

Stuckenbruck, Loren T. 2020. "What Is Second Temple Judaism?" In *T&T Clark Encyclopedia of Second Temple Judaism*. Vol. 1, edited by Loren T. Stuckenbruck and Daniel M. Gurtner, 1–19. London: T&T Clark.

Stuckenbruck, Loren T. / Erho, Ted M. 2019. *The Significance of Ethiopic Witnesses for the Text Tradition of 1 Enoch: Problems and Prospects [Manuscript for Publication the 2019 IOSOT Congress Volume Edited by Joachim Schaper (Forthcoming)]*.

Stuttgarter Erklärungsbibel: Mit Apokryphen. 2005. Stuttgart: Deutsche Bibelgesellschaft.

Sukenik, E. L., ed. 1955. *The Dead Sea Scrolls of the Hebrew University*. Jerusalem: Magnes.

Sundberg, Albert C. 1968. "The 'Old Testament': a Christian Canon." *Catholic Biblical Quarterly* 30: 143–155.

Sundberg, Albert C. 2002. "The Septuagint: The Bible of Hellenistic Judaism." In *The Canon Debate*, edited by Lee M. McDonald and James A. Sanders, 68–90. Peabody, MA: Hendrickson.

Swanson, Theodore N. 1970. *The Closing of the Collection of Holy Scriptures: A Study in the History of the Canonization of the Old Testament*. Nashville, TN, Vanderbilt University: PhD Dissertation.

Swete, Henry B. 1900. *An Introduction to the Old Testament in Greek: With an Appendix Containing the Letter of Aristeas, Edited by Henry St. John Thackeray*. Cambridge: Cambridge University Press.

Tal, Abraham, ed. 2015. *Biblia Hebraica Quinta [BHQ], Vol. 1, Genesis*. Stuttgart: Deutsche Bibelgesellschaft.

Talabardon, Susanne. 2012. "Midrasch, in: Das Wissenschaftliche Bibellexikon im Internet (WiBiLex)." Accessed August 23, 2021. https://www.bibelwissenschaft.de/stichwort/27721/.

230   Bibliography

Tångberg, Arvid. 1994. "Nehemia/Nehemiabuch." In *Theologische Realenzyklopädie [TRE], Band 24*, edited by Horst R. Balz, 242–246. Berlin: De Gruyter.

Taylor, Charles/Hart, John H.A. 1903. "Two Notes on Enoch in Sir. XLIV 16." *Journal of Theological Studies* 4 (16): 589–591.

Thackeray, H. St. J., ed. 1926. *Josephus, Vol. I, The Life, Against Apion: With an English Translation*. Reprinted 1976. Loeb Classical Library 186. Cambridge, MA; London: Harvard University Press; Heinemann.

Thiele, Walter. 1987. *Sirach (Ecclesiasticus)*. Vetus Latina 11/2. Freiburg: Herder.

Tigchelaar, Eibert. 2020. "Material Construction and Palaeographic Dating of 4QMMT: The Evidence of the Manuscripts." In *Interpreting and Living God's Law at Qumran: Miqṣat Ma'aśe Ha-Torah, Some of the Works of the Torah (4QMMT)*, edited by Reinhard G. Kratz, 57–65. SAPERE 37. Tübingen: Mohr Siebeck.

Tilly, Michael. 2007. "Aristeasbrief, in: Das Wissenschaftliche Bibellexikon im Internet (WiBiLex)." Accessed August 23, 2021. https://www.bibelwissenschaft.de/stichwort/13793/.

Tov, Emanuel. 1998. "The Dimensions of the Qumran Scrolls." *Dead Sea Discoveries* 5 (1): 69–91.

Tov, Emanuel. 2002. "Categorized List of the 'Biblical Texts'." In *The Texts from the Judaean Desert: Indices and an Introduction to the Discoveries in the Judaean Desert Series*, edited by Emanuel Tov, 165–183. Discoveries in the Judaean Desert 39. Oxford: Clarendon.

Tov, Emanuel. 2004. *Scribal Practices and Approaches Reflected in the Texts Found in the Judean Desert*. Studies on the Texts of the Desert of Judah 54. Leiden: Brill.

Tov, Emanuel. 2010. *Revised Lists of the Texts from the Judaean Desert*. Leiden: Brill.

Tov, Emanuel. 2012. *Textual Criticism of the Hebrew Bible*. 3rd edition, revised and expanded. Minneapolis: Fortress Press.

Trebolle Barrera, Julio. 2000. "118. 4QChr." In *Qumran Cave 4, XI, Psalms to Chronicles*, edited by Eugene Ulrich, Frank M. Cross, Joseph A. Fitzmyer, and Peter W. Flint, 295–297, Pl. XXXVIII. Discoveries in the Judaean Desert 16. Oxford: Clarendon.

Trebolle Barrera, Julio. 2002. "Origins of a Tripartite Old Testament Canon." In *The Canon Debate*, edited by Lee M. McDonald and James A. Sanders, 128–145. Peabody, MA: Hendrickson.

Trebolle Barrera, Julio. 2006. "Canon of the Old Testament." In *The New Interpreter's Dictionary of the Bible, Vol. 1*, edited by Katharine D. Sakenfeld, 548–563. Nashville, TN: Abingdon Press.

Trypanis, C.A., ed. 1975. *Callimachus: Aetia, Iambi, Lyric Poems, Hecale, Minor Epic and Elegiac Poems, Fragments of Epigrams, Fragments of Uncertain Location: Text, Translation and Notes*. Loeb Classical Library 421. Cambridge, MA; London: Harvard University Press; Heinemann.

Tzoref, Shani B. 2013. "Pesher Nahum." In *Outside the Bible: Ancient Jewish Writing Related to Scripture, Vol. 1*, edited by Louis H. Feldman, James L. Kugel, and Lawrence H. Schiffman, 623–635. Lincoln; Philadelphia: University of Nebraska Press; Jewish Publication Society.

Ueberschaer, Frank. 2007. *Weisheit aus der Begegnung: Bildung nach dem Buch Ben Sira*. Beihefte zur Zeitschrift für die alttestamentliche Wissenschaft 379. Berlin: De Gruyter.

Ueberschaer, Frank. 2016. "Sophia Sirach/ Ben Sira/ Das Buch Jesus Sirach." In *Einleitung in die Septuaginta*, edited by Siegfried Kreuzer, 437–455. Handbuch zur Septuaginta LXX.H 1. Gütersloh: Gütersloher Verlagshaus.

Ulrich, Eugene. 1992. "The Canonical Process, Textual Criticism, and Latter Stages in the Composition of the Bible." In *"Sha'arei Talmon": Studies in the Bible, Qumran, and the Ancient Near East Presented to Shemaryahu Talmon*, edited by Michael A. Fishbane, Emanuel Tov, Weston W. Fields, and Shemaryahu Talmon, 267–291. Winona Lake, IN: Eisenbrauns.

Ulrich, Eugene. 1994. "The Bible in the Making: The Scriptures at Qumran." In *The Community of the Renewed Covenant: The Notre Dame Symposium on the Dead Sea Scrolls*, edited by Eugene Ulrich and James C. VanderKam, 77–94. Christianity and Judaism in Antiquity 10. Notre Dame, IN: University of Notre Dame Press.

Ulrich, Eugene. 1999. "Pluriformity in the Biblical Text, Text Groups, and Questions of Canon." In *The Dead Sea Scrolls and the Origins of the Bible*, 79–98. Grand Rapids, MI: Eerdmans.

Ulrich, Eugene. 2000. "Canon." In *Encyclopedia of the Dead Sea Scrolls*, edited by James C. VanderKam, 117–120. Oxford: Oxford University Press.

Ulrich, Eugene. 2002a. "Index of Passages in the 'Biblical Texts'." In *The Texts from the Judaean Desert: Indices and an Introduction to the Discoveries in the Judaean Desert Series*, edited by Emanuel Tov, 185–201. Discoveries in the Judaean Desert 39. Oxford: Clarendon.

Ulrich, Eugene. 2002b. "The Notion and Definition of Canon." In *The Canon Debate*, edited by Lee M. McDonald and James A. Sanders, 21–35. Peabody, MA: Hendrickson.

Ulrich, Eugene. 2003a. "Qumran and the Canon of the Old Testament." In *The Biblical Canons*, edited by J.-M. Auwers and H. J. de Jonge, 57–80. Bibliotheca Ephemeridum Theologicarum Lovaniensium 163. Leuven: Leuven University Press; Peeters.

Ulrich, Eugene. 2003b. "The Non-Attestation of a Tripartite Canon in 4QMMT." *Catholic Biblical Quarterly* 65 (2): 202–214.

Ulrich, Eugene, ed. 2010. *The Biblical Qumran Scrolls: Transcriptions and Textual Variants*. Supplements to Vetus Testamentum 134. Leiden: Brill.

van der Kooij, Arie. 1998. "The Canonization of Ancient Books Kept in the Temple of Jerusalem." In *Canonization and Decanonization: Papers Presented to the International Conference of the Leiden Institute for the Study of Religions (LISOR), Held at Leiden 9–10 January 1997*, edited by Arie van der Kooij and Karel van der Toorn, 17–40. Studies in the History of Religions. Leiden: Brill.

van der Kooij, Arie. 2003. "Canonization of Ancient Hebrew Books and Hasmonaean Politics." In *The Biblical Canons*, edited by J.-M. Auwers and H. J. de Jonge, 27–38. Bibliotheca Ephemeridum Theologicarum Lovaniensium 163. Leuven: Leuven University Press; Peeters.

van der Kooij, Arie. 2010. "Authoritative Scriptures and Scribal Culture." In *Authoritative Scriptures in Ancient Judaism*, edited by Mladen Popović, 55–71. Supplements to the Journal for the Study of Judaism 141. Leiden: Brill.

van der Kooij, Arie. 2012. "The Claim of Maccabean Leadership and the Use of Scripture." In *Jewish Identity and Politics between the Maccabees and Bar Kokhba: Groups, Normativity, and Rituals*, edited by Benedikt Eckhardt, 29–49. Supplements to the Journal for the Study of Judaism 155. Leiden: Brill.

van der Toorn, Karel. 2007. *Scribal Culture and the Making of the Hebrew Bible*. Cambridge, MA: Harvard University Press.

van der Woude, Adam S. 1992. "Pluriformity and Uniformity: Reflections on the Transmission of the Text of the Old Testament." In *Sacred History and Sacred Texts in Early Judaism: A Symposium in Honour of A. S. van der Woude*, edited by Jan N. Bremmer and

232 Bibliography

Florentino García Martínez, 151–169. Contributions to Biblical Exegesis and Theology. Kampen: Kok.

VAN KOOTEN, George H. 2010. "Ancestral, Oracular and Prophetic Authority: 'Scriptural Authority' According to Paul and Philo." In *Authoritative Scriptures in Ancient Judaism*, edited by Mladen Popović, 267–308. Supplements to the Journal for the Study of Judaism 141. Leiden: Brill.

VAN PEURSEN, W. T. 2007. *Language and Interpretation in the Syriac Text of Ben Sira: A Comparative Linguistic and Literary Study*. Monographs of the Peshitta Institute Leiden 16. Leiden: Brill.

VAN PEURSEN, Wido. 2019. "Ecclesiasticus/Ben Sira, Syriac." In *Textual History of the Bible, Volume 2B, Baruch/Jeremiah, Daniel (Additions), Ecclesiasticus/Ben Sira, Enoch, Esther (Additions), Ezra*, edited by Frank Feder and Matthias Henze, 232–242. Leiden: Brill.

VAN WIERINGEN, Archibald L. H. M. 2011. "Sirach 48:17–25 and the Isaiah-Book: Hezekiah and Isaiah in the Book of Sirach and the Reader-Oriented Perspective of the Isaiah-Book." In *Rewriting Biblical History: Essays on Chronicles and Ben Sira in Honor of Pancratius C. Beentjes*, edited by Jeremy Corley and Harm van Grol, 191–210. Deuterocanonical and Cognate Literature Studies 7. Berlin: De Gruyter.

VANDERKAM, James C. 1984. *Enoch and the Growth of an Apocalyptic Tradition*. Catholic Biblical Quarterly Monograph Series 16. Washington, DC: Catholic Biblical Association of America.

VANDERKAM, James C. 1989a. *The Book of Jubilees: A Critical Text*. Corpus Scriptorum Christianorum Orientalium 510. Leuven: Peeters.

VANDERKAM, James C. 1989b. *The Book of Jubilees: Translated*. Corpus Scriptorum Christianorum Orientalium 511. Leuven: Peeters.

VANDERKAM, James C. 1995. *Enoch, a Man for All Generations*. Studies on Personalities of the Old Testament. Columbia, SC: University of South Carolina Press.

VANDERKAM, James C. 1998. "Authoritative Literature in the Dead Sea Scrolls." *Dead Sea Discoveries* 5 (3): 382–402.

VANDERKAM, James C. 2000. "Simon the Just: Simon I or Simon II?" In *From Revelation to Canon: Studies in the Hebrew Bible and Second Temple Literature*, 224–240. Supplements to the Journal for the Study of Judaism 62. Leiden: Brill.

VANDERKAM, James C. 2001. *An Introduction to Early Judaism*. Grand Rapids, MI: Eerdmans.

VANDERKAM, James C. 2002. "Questions of Canon Viewed through the Dead Sea Scrolls." In *The Canon Debate*, edited by Lee M. McDonald and James A. Sanders, 91–109. Peabody, MA: Hendrickson.

VANDERKAM, James C. 2004. *From Joshua to Caiaphas: High Priests after the Exile*. Minneapolis; Assen: Fortress Press; Van Gorcum.

VANDERKAM, James C. 2010. *The Dead Sea Scrolls Today*. Second Edition. Grand Rapids, MI: Eerdmans.

VANDERKAM, James C. 2018. *Jubilees 1: A Commentary on the Book of Jubilees, Chapters 1–21*. Hermeneia. Minneapolis: Fortress Press.

VANDERKAM, James C. / MILIK, J. T. 1994a. "219. 4QJubilees^d." In *Qumran Cave 4: VIII, Parabiblical Texts, Part 1*, edited by Harold W. Attridge, Torleif Elgvin, Jozef Milik, Saul Olyan, John Strugnell, Emanuel Tov, James VanderKam, and Sidnie White, 39–53, Pl. IV. Discoveries in the Judaean Desert 13. Oxford: Clarendon.

VANDERKAM, James C. / MILIK, J. T. 1994b. "220. 4QJubilees^e." In *Qumran Cave 4: VIII, Parabiblical Texts, Part 1*, edited by Harold W. Attridge, Torleif Elgvin, Jozef Milik, Saul

Olyan, John Strugnell, Emanuel Tov, James VanderKam, and Sidnie White, 55–61, Pl. V. Discoveries in the Judaean Desert 13. Oxford: Clarendon.

VEIJOLA, Timo. 2006. "Law and Wisdom: The Deuteronomistic Heritage in Ben Sira's Teaching of the Law." In *Ancient Israel, Judaism, and Christianity in Contemporary Perspective: Essays in Memory of Karl-Johan Illman*, edited by Jacob Neusner, Alan J. Avery-Peck, Antti Laato, Risto Nurmela, and Karl-Gustav Sandelin, 144–164. Studies in Judaism. Lanham: University Press of America.

VELTRI, Giuseppe. 1994. *Eine Tora für den König Talmai*. Texts and Studies in Ancient Judaism 41. Tübingen: Mohr.

VELTRI, Giuseppe. 2006. *Libraries, Translations, and 'Canonic' Texts: The Septuagint, Aquila and Ben Sira in the Jewish and Christian Traditions*. Supplements to the Journal for the Study of Judaism 109. Leiden: Brill.

VOITILA, Anssi. 2008. "For Those Who Love Learning: How the Reader is Persuaded to Study the Book of Ben Sira as a Translation." In *Houses Full of All Good Things: Essays in Memory of Timo Veijola*, edited by Juha Pakkala and Martti Nissinen, 451–460. Publications of the Finnish Exegetical Society 93. Helsinki; Göttingen: Finnish Exegetical Society; Vandenhoeck & Ruprecht.

VOS, J. Cornelis de. 2006. "'Wer Weisheit lernt, braucht viel Zeit': Arbeit und Muße in Sirach 38,24–39,11." In *Arbeit in der Antike, in Judentum und Christentum*, edited by Detlev Dormeyer, 39–56. Münsteraner judaistische Studien 20. Münster: Lit.

VÖSSING, Konrad. 1997. "Bibliothek, II. Bibliothekswesen, B. Griechenland, Rom, christliche Bibliotheken." In *Der Neue Pauly. Enzyklopädie der Antike, Band 2*, edited by Hubert Cancik and Helmuth Schneider, 640–647. Stuttgart: Metzler.

WAGNER, Christian. 1999. *Die Septuaginta-Hapaxlegomena im Buch Jesus Sirach: Untersuchungen zu Wortwahl und Wortbildung unter besonderer Berücksichtigung des textkritischen und übersetzungstechnischen Aspekts*. Beihefte zur Zeitschrift für die alttestamentliche Wissenschaft 282. Berlin: De Gruyter.

WAHL, Harald-Martin. 1992. "Noah, Daniel und Hiob in Ezechiel XVI 12–20 (21–3): Anmerkungen zum traditionsgeschichtlichen Hintergrund." *Vetus Testamentum* 42 (4): 542–553.

WALLACE, Daniel B. 1996. *Greek Grammar Beyond the Basics: An Exegetical Syntax of the New Testament with Scripture, Subject, and Greek Word Indexes*. Grand Rapids, MI: Zondervan.

WANDREY, Irina. 1998. "Iosephos, [4] I. Flavios." In *Der Neue Pauly. Enzyklopädie der Antike, Band 5*, edited by Hubert Cancik and Helmuth Schneider, 1089–1091. Stuttgart: Metzler.

WANKE, Gunther. 1980. "Bibel I." In *Theologische Realenzyklopädie [TRE], Band 6*, edited by Gerhard Müller, 1–8. Berlin: De Gruyter.

WATSON, Francis. 2004. *Paul and the Hermeneutics of Faith*. London: T&T Clark International.

WEARNE, Gareth J. 2020. "What Was the Book of Moses in 4QMMT?" *Catholic Biblical Quarterly* 82 (2): 237–255.

WEBER, Robert / GRYSON, Roger, eds. 2007. *Biblia Sacra: Iuxta Vulgatam Versionem*. 5., verb. Aufl. Stuttgart: Deutsche Bibelgesellschaft.

WEBSTER, B. 2002. "Chronological Index of the Texts from the Judaean Desert." In *The Texts from the Judaean Desert: Indices and an Introduction to the Discoveries in the Judaean Desert Series*, edited by Emanuel Tov, 351–446. Discoveries in the Judaean Desert 39. Oxford: Clarendon.

234   *Bibliography*

WEINGART, Kristin. 2015. "Erkennst du auch, was du liest? Zur Markierung von Zitaten im Alten Testament." In *Methodik im Diskurs: Neue Perspektiven für die Alttestamentliche Exegese*, edited by Raik Heckl, 143–170. Biblisch-Theologische Studien 156. Neukirchen-Vluyn: Neukirchener.

WEINGART, Kristin. 2017. "Annalen (AT), in: Das Wissenschaftliche Bibellexikon im Internet (WiBiLex)." Accessed August 23, 2021. https://www.bibelwissenschaft.de/stichwort/13421/.

WEISSENBERG, Hanne von. 2009. *4QMMT: Reevaluating the Text, the Function, and the Meaning of the Epilogue*. Studies on the Texts of the Desert of Judah 82. Leiden: Brill.

WICKE-REUTER, Ursel. 2000. *Göttliche Providenz und menschliche Verantwortung bei Ben Sira und in der Frühen Stoa*. Beihefte zur Zeitschrift für die alttestamentliche Wissenschaft 298. Berlin: De Gruyter.

WILCKEN, Ulrich. 1906. "Rezension von W. Dittenberger, Orientis Graeci Inscriptiones Selectae." *Archiv für Papyrusforschung und verwandte Gebiete* 3 (2): 313–336.

WILLIAMS, David S. 1994. "The Date of Ecclesiasticus." *Vetus Testamentum* 44 (4): 563–566.

WILLIAMS, Rowan. 1998. "Athanasius." In *Religion in Geschichte und Gegenwart [RGG⁴]*, Band 1, edited by Hans D. Betz, Don S. Browning, Bernd Janowski, and Eberhard Jüngel. 4. Aufl., 870–873. Tübingen: Mohr Siebeck.

WISCHMEYER, Oda. 1994. *Die Kultur des Buches Jesus Sirach*. Beihefte zur Zeitschrift für die neutestamentliche Wissenschaft und die Kunde der älteren Kirche 77. Berlin: De Gruyter.

WISE, M.O. 1997. "To Know the Times and the Seasons: A Study of the Aramaic Chronograph 4Q559." *Journal for the Study of the Pseudepigrapha* 15: 3–51.

WISSMANN, Jessica. 2010. "Education." In *A Companion to Hellenistic Literature*, edited by James J. Clauss and Martine Cuypers, 62–77. Blackwell Companions to the Ancient World. Chichester: Wiley-Blackwell.

WITTE, Markus. 2006. "Die Gebeine Josefs." In *Auf dem Weg zur Endgestalt von Genesis bis II Regum: Festschrift Hans-Christoph Schmitt zum 65. Geburtstag*, edited by Martin Beck, 139–156. Beihefte zur Zeitschrift für die alttestamentliche Wissenschaft 370. Berlin: De Gruyter.

WITTE, Markus. 2012a. "Der 'Kanon' heiliger Schriften des antiken Judentums im Spiegel des Buches Ben Sira/Jesus Sirach." In *Kanon in Konstruktion und Dekonstruktion: Kanonisierungsprozesse religiöser Texte von der Antike bis zur Gegenwart. Ein Handbuch*, edited by Eve-Marie Becker and Stefan Scholz, 229–257. Berlin: De Gruyter.

WITTE, Markus. 2012b. "Jesus Sirach (Ben Sira) (Translation by Mark Biddle)." In *T&T Clark Handbook of the Old Testament: An Introduction to the Literature, Religion and History of the Old Testament*, edited by Jan C. Gertz, Angelika Berlejung, Konrad Schmid, and Markus Witte, 725–739. London: T&T Clark.

WITTE, Markus. 2012c. "The Book of Daniel (Translation by Mark Biddle)." In *T&T Clark Handbook of the Old Testament: An Introduction to the Literature, Religion and History of the Old Testament*, edited by Jan C. Gertz, Angelika Berlejung, Konrad Schmid, and Markus Witte, 643–668. London: T&T Clark.

WITTE, Markus. 2015a. "Ist auch Hiob unter den Propheten? Grundsätzliche Probleme der Sirachexegese am Beispiel von Sir 49,8–10." In *Texte und Kontexte des Sirachbuchs: Gesammelte Studien zu Ben Sira und zur frühjüdischen Weisheit*, 23–37. Forschungen zum Alten Testament 98. Tübingen: Mohr Siebeck.

WITTE, Markus. 2015b. "Wege der Sirachforschung." In *Texte und Kontexte des Sirachbuchs: Gesammelte Studien zu Ben Sira und zur frühjüdischen Weisheit*, 1–20. Forschungen zum Alten Testament 98. Tübingen: Mohr Siebeck.

WITTE, Markus. 2017a. "Hiob als jüdisches, christliches und paganes Werk: Überlegungen zur Hermeneutik heiliger Schriften." In *Congress Volume Stellenbosch 2016*, edited by Louis C. Jonker, Gideon R. Kotzé, and Christl M. Maier, 329–353. Supplements to Vetus Testamentum 177. Leiden: Brill.

WITTE, Markus. 2017b. "Key Aspects and Themes in Recent Scholarship on the Book of Ben Sira." In *Texts and Contexts of the Book of Sirach*, edited by Gerhard Karner, Frank Ueberschaer, and Burkard M. Zapff, 1–31. Septuagint and Cognate Studies 66. Atlanta, GA: SBL Press.

WITTE, Markus. 2019a. "Jesus Sirach (Ben Sira)." In *Grundinformation Altes Testament*, edited by Jan C. Gertz. 6., überarbeitete und erweiterte Auflage, 555–567. UTB 2745. Göttingen: Vandenhoeck & Ruprecht.

WITTE, Markus. 2019b. "Menschenbilder des Sirachbuches." In *Theology and Anthropology in the Book of Sirach*, edited by Bonifatia Gesche, Christian Lustig, and Gabriel Rabo, 1–36. Septuagint and Cognate Studies 73. Atlanta, GA: SBL Press.

WITTE, Markus. 2020. "Beobachtungen zum Abrahamporträt des Sirachbuchs (Sir 44,19–21)." In *Fortgeschriebenes Gotteswort: Studien zu Geschichte, Theologie und Auslegung des Alten Testaments, Festschrift für Christoph Levin zum 70. Geburtstag*, edited by Reinhard Müller, Urmas Nõmmik, and Juha Pakkala, 397–413. Tübingen: Mohr Siebeck.

WÖHRLE, Jakob. 2006. *Die frühen Sammlungen des Zwölfprophetenbuches: Entstehung und Komposition*. Beihefte zur Zeitschrift für die alttestamentliche Wissenschaft 360. Berlin: De Gruyter.

WRIGHT, Benjamin G. 1989. *No Small Difference: Sirach's Relationship to its Hebrew Parent Text*. Septuagint and Cognate Studies 26. Atlanta, GA: Scholars Press.

WRIGHT, Benjamin G. 1997. "'Fear the Lord and Honor the Priest': Ben Sira as Defender of the Jerusalem Priesthood." In *The Book of Ben Sira in Modern Research: Proceedings of the First International Ben Sira Conference, 28–31 July 1996 Soesterberg, Netherlands*, edited by Pancratius C. Beentjes, 189–222. Beihefte zur Zeitschrift für die alttestamentliche Wissenschaft 255. Berlin: De Gruyter.

WRIGHT, Benjamin G. 2003a. "Access to the Source: Cicero, Ben Sira, the Septuagint and Their Audience." *Journal for the Study of Judaism* 34 (1): 1–27.

WRIGHT, Benjamin G. 2003b. "Why a Prologue? Ben Sira's Grandson and His Greek Translation." In *Emanuel: Studies in Hebrew Bible, Septuagint, and Dead Sea Scrolls in Honor of Emanuel Tov*, edited by Shalom M. Paul, Robert A. Kraft, Lawrence H. Schiffman, and Weston W. Fields, 633–644. Supplements to Vetus Testamentum 94. Leiden: Brill.

WRIGHT, Benjamin G. 2006a. "Eschatology without a Messiah in the Wisdom of Ben Sira." In *The Septuagint and Messianism*, edited by Michael A. Knibb, 313–323. Leuven: Leuven University Press; Peeters.

WRIGHT, Benjamin G. 2006b. "Putting the Puzzle Together: Some Suggestions Concerning the Social Location of the Wisdom of Ben Sira." In *Conflicted Boundaries in Wisdom and Apocalypticism*, edited by Benjamin G. Wright and Lawrence M. Wills, 89–112. Society of Biblical Literature Symposium Series 35. Leiden: Brill.

236   *Bibliography*

WRIGHT, Benjamin G. 2007a. "1 Enoch and Ben Sira: Wisdom and Apocalypticism in Relationship." In *The Early Enoch Literature*, edited by Gabriele Boccaccini and John Collins, 159–176. Supplements to the Journal for the Study of Judaism 121. Leiden: Brill.

WRIGHT, Benjamin G. 2007b. "Wisdom of Iesous Son of Sirach." In *A New English Translation of the Septuagint, and other Greek Translations Traditionally Included under that Title [NETS]*, edited by Albert Pietersma and Benjamin G. Wright, 715–762. Oxford: Oxford University Press. (Also available online. Accessed August 23, 2021. http://ccat. sas.upenn.edu/nets/edition.)

WRIGHT, Benjamin G. 2008. "The Use and Interpretation of Biblical Tradition in Ben Sira's Praise of the Ancestors." In *Studies in the Book of Ben Sira: Papers of the Third International Conference on the Deuterocanonical Books, Shime'on Centre, Pápa, Hungary, 18–20 May, 2006*, edited by Géza G. Xeravits and József Zsengellér, 183–207. Supplements to the Journal for the Study of Judaism 127. Leiden: Brill.

WRIGHT, Benjamin G. 2009. "Jubilees, Sirach, and Sapiential Tradition." In *Enoch and the Mosaic Torah: The Evidence of Jubilees*, edited by Gabriele Boccaccini and Giovanni Ibba, 116–130. Grand Rapids, MI: Eerdmans.

WRIGHT, Benjamin G. 2011. "Translation Greek in Sirach in Light of the Grandson's Prologue." In *The Texts and Versions of the Book of Ben Sira: Transmission and Interpretation*, edited by Jean-Sébastien Rey and Jan Joosten, 75–94. Supplements to the Journal for the Study of Judaism 150. Leiden: Brill.

WRIGHT, Benjamin G. 2012. "Biblical Interpretation in Ben Sira." In *A Companion to Biblical Interpretation in Early Judaism*, edited by Matthias Henze, 363–388. Grand Rapids, MI: Eerdmans.

WRIGHT, Benjamin G. 2013a. "Torah and Sapiential Pedagogy in the Book of Ben Sira." In *Wisdom and Torah: The Reception of 'Torah' in the Wisdom Literature of the Second Temple Period*, edited by Bernd U. Schipper and D.A. Teeter, 157–186. Supplements to the Journal for the Study of Judaism 163. Leiden: Brill.

WRIGHT, Benjamin G. 2013b. "Wisdom of Ben Sira." In *Outside the Bible: Ancient Jewish Writing Related to Scripture, Vol. 3*, edited by Louis H. Feldman, James L. Kugel, and Lawrence H. Schiffman, 2208–2352. Lincoln; Philadelphia: University of Nebraska Press; Jewish Publication Society.

WRIGHT, Benjamin G. 2015. *The Letter of Aristeas: 'Aristeas to Philocrates' or 'On the Translation of the Law of the Jews'*. Commentaries on Early Jewish Literature. Berlin: De Gruyter.

WRIGHT, Benjamin G. 2019. "Ecclesiasticus/Ben Sira, Textual History of Ben Sira." In *Textual History of the Bible, Volume 2B, Baruch/Jeremiah, Daniel (Additions), Ecclesiasticus/Ben Sira, Enoch, Esther (Additions), Ezra*, edited by Frank Feder and Matthias Henze, 187–198. Leiden: Brill.

WRIGHT, Benjamin G./ MROCZEK, Eva. 2021. "Ben Sira's Pseudo-Pseudepigraphy: Idealizations from Antiquity to the Early Middle Ages." In *Sirach and its Contexts: The Pursuit of Wisdom and Human Flourishing*, edited by Samuel L. Adams, Greg S. Goering, and Matthew J. Goff, 213–239. Supplements to the Journal for the Study of Judaism 196. Leiden: Brill.

WÜRTHWEIN, Ernst. 1988. *Der Text des Alten Testaments: Eine Einführung in die Biblia Hebraica*. 5., neubearb. Aufl. Stuttgart: Deutsche Bibelgesellschaft.

XERAVITS, Géza G. 2013. "נבא." In *Theologisches Wörterbuch zu den Qumrantexten [ThWQ], Band II*, edited by Heinz-Josef Fabry and Ulrich Dahmen, 847–852. Stuttgart: Kohlhammer.

YADIN, Yigael. 1999. "The Ben Sira Scroll from Masada: Introduction, Emendations and Commentary." In *Masada VI, Yigael Yadin Excavations 1963–1965, Final Reports: Hebrew Fragments from Masada, The Ben Sira Scroll from Masada*, edited by Shemaryahu Talmon and Yigael Yadin, 151–252. The Masada Reports. Jerusalem: Israel Exploration Society.

ZAHN, Molly M. 2010. "Rewritten Scripture." In *The Oxford Handbook of the Dead Sea Scrolls*, edited by Timothy H. Lim and John J. Collins, 323–336. Oxford: Oxford University Press.

ZAHN, Molly M. 2011a. "Talking About Rewritten Texts: Some Reflections on Terminology." In *Changes in Scripture: Rewriting and Interpreting Authoritative Traditions in the Second Temple Period*, edited by Hanne von Weissenberg, Juha Pakkala, and Marko Marttila, 93–119. Beihefte zur Zeitschrift für die alttestamentliche Wissenschaft 419. Berlin: De Gruyter.

ZAHN, Molly M. 2011b. *Rethinking Rewritten Scripture: Composition and Exegesis in the 4QReworked Pentateuch Manuscripts*. Studies on the Texts of the Desert of Judah 95. Leiden: Brill.

ZAHN, Molly M. 2012. "Identifying Reuse of Scripture in the Temple Scroll: Some Methodological Reflections." In *A Teacher for All Generations: Essays in Honor of James C. VanderKam, Vol. 1*, edited by Eric F. Mason, 341–358. Supplements to the Journal for the Study of Judaism 153/I. Leiden: Brill.

ZAHN, Molly M. 2016. "Innerbiblical Exegesis – The View from beyond the Bible." In *The Formation of the Pentateuch*, edited by Jan C. Gertz, 107–120. Forschungen zum Alten Testament 111. Tübingen: Mohr Siebeck.

ZAHN, Molly M. 2020a. *Genres of Rewriting in Second Temple Judaism: Scribal Composition and Transmission*. Cambridge: Cambridge University Press.

ZAHN, Molly M. 2020b. "Pentateuch." In *T&T Clark Encyclopedia of Second Temple Judaism*. Vol. 1, edited by Loren T. Stuckenbruck and Daniel M. Gurtner, 419–422. London: T&T Clark.

ZAHN, Molly M. 2020c. "Torah, Traditioning of." In *T&T Clark Encyclopedia of Second Temple Judaism*. Vol. 2, edited by Loren T. Stuckenbruck and Daniel M. Gurtner, 804–806. London: T&T Clark.

ZAHN, Molly M. 2021. "The Relevance of Moses Traditions in the Second Temple Period." In *The Oxford Handbook of the Pentateuch*, edited by Joel S. Baden and Jeffrey Stackert, 79–94. Oxford: Oxford University Press.

ZAPFF, Burkard M. 2010. *Jesus Sirach 25–51*. Neue Echter Bibel, Altes Testament Lfg. 38. Würzburg: Echter.

ZAPFF, Burkard M. 2018. "Rückschlüsse aus der Entstehung der Michaschrift auf das Werden des Zwölfprophetenbuches." In *The Books of the Twelve Prophets: Minor Prophets, Major Theologies*, edited by Heinz-Josef Fabry, 79–101. Bibliotheca Ephemeridum Theologicarum Lovaniensium 295. Leuven: Peeters.

ZAPFF, Burkard M. 2019. "Anthropologische Konzepte der biblischen Urgeschichte bei Jesus Sirach." In *Theology and Anthropology in the Book of Sirach*, edited by Bonifatia Gesche, Christian Lustig, and Gabriel Rabo, 95–118. Septuagint and Cognate Studies 73. Atlanta, GA: SBL Press.

ZENGER, Erich. 2008. "A. Heilige Schrift der Juden und Christen." In *Einleitung in das Alte Testament*, edited by Erich Zenger. 7., durchges. und erw. Aufl., 11–33. Kohlhammer Studienbücher Theologie 1,1. Stuttgart: Kohlhammer.

238 *Bibliography*

ZENGER, Erich. 2016. "Das Zwölfprophetenbuch." In *Einleitung in das Alte Testament*, edited by Erich Zenger and Christian Frevel. 9., aktualisierte Aufl., 630–709. Kohlhammer Studienbücher Theologie 1,1. Stuttgart: Kohlhammer.

ZENGER, Erich / FREVEL, Christian. 2016. "Heilige Schrift der Juden und der Christen." In *Einleitung in das Alte Testament*, edited by Erich Zenger and Christian Frevel. 9., aktualisierte Aufl., 11–36. Kohlhammer Studienbücher Theologie 1,1. Stuttgart: Kohlhammer.

ZENNER, J. K. 1896. "Der Prolog des Buches Ecclesiasticus." *Zeitschrift für katholische Theologie* 20: 571–574.

ZIEGLER, Joseph, ed. 1980. *Sapientia Iesu Filii Sirach*. 2., durchges. Aufl. Septuaginta 12,2. Göttingen: Vandenhoeck & Ruprecht.

ZIMMERMANN, Bernhard. 2001. "Prolog." In *Der Neue Pauly. Enzyklopädie der Antike, Band 10*, edited by Hubert Cancik and Helmuth Schneider, 398–400. Stuttgart: Metzler.

ZÖCKLER, Otto. 1891. "Die Weisheit Jesus Sirachs." In *Die Apokryphen des Alten Testaments*, edited by Otto Zöckler, 255–354. Kurzgefaßter Kommentar zu den heiligen Schriften Alten und Neuen Testamentes sowie zu den Apokryphen A 9. München: Beck.

Index of Sources

Varying numbers given in brackets are explained in footnotes on the respective pages.

Book of Ben Sira

Ben Sira – Hebrew (Sir)

1–2	6
3:17	156
3:29	52
4:24	52
6	7
6:33	53
6:35	53
7:6	156
9:13	156
9:15	73
10:1–2	164
10:5	54
10:17	164
10:24	164
14:14	156
15–16	149
15:1	72
16	186
16:7	25, 146–147
16:24	53
17	6
24	6
27–29	6
30–36	2
31:8	36, 156
31:31	36
32:5	36
32:15	72
32:17	73
32:18	73
32:24	72
33:2	72
33:3	72
33:10	156
35:22	164
36	35
36:13 (36:11)	136
36:20 (36:15)	74
36:21 (36:16)	73
38:16–23	104
38:24–39:11	8, 34, 82, 85, 99–113, 187–189
38:24–27	99–100, 103–105, 113
38:24	10, 54, 100, 103–105
38:25–26	105
38:25	103, 105
38:26	100, 105
38:27	100, 104–105
39–44	6
39	32
39:15–35	104
39:15	99
39:32	53–54
41:4	73
41:8	72
42:15–49:16	123
42:2	72
42:7	53–54
43	117
44–50	5–6, 8, 25, 31, 34, 53, 83, 115–190
44–49	3–4, 11, 20, 56, 83, 123–125, 132–133
44–45	122
44	117, 131, 144, 154–155

44:1–45:26	124	46:11–12	119, 123, 126, 143, 159–165, 184–185
44:1–15	116, 119, 122		
44:1	115, 119, 121	46:11	119, 159, 161
44:3	74	46:12	159
44:4	53	46:13–20	119
44:5	53–54	46:13	73–74, 119, 159, 164
44:10–15	158	46:15	73
44:13	164	46:19	121
44:14	156	46:20	73–74, 156
44:15	144	47	131
44:16–45:26	122	47:1–11	120
44:16	119, 143–158, 185	47:1	74, 119–120
44:17–18	119	47:2	120
44:17	116, 119, 145, 156, 164	47:5	175
44:19–21	119	47:8	175
44:19–20	132	47:9	123
44:19	119	47:12–23	120
44:20	72, 132, 156	47:13	120
44:22–23	119	47:14–17	123
44:22	119	47:14–15	121
44:23–45:5	119	47:17–20	121
44:23	116, 119, 184	47:23–24	120
45–50	117	47:23	120
45	131–132	47:24	120
45:1	119	47:24–48:11	120
45:5	72	48	131, 167
45:6–22	119, 132	48:1	73
45:6	119	48:4	54, 73, 120–121, 134–135
45:11	54		
45:17	73	48:8	73, 164
45:19	121	48:9	146, 152, 156
45:23–24	119	48:10–11	108
45:23	119	48:10	10, 23, 29, 54, 123, 125–126, 133–142, 182, 189
45:24	35		
45:25	119		
45:25–26	119, 121–122, 124, 132, 146	48:11	121
		48:12	120
46–50	122	48:13	74
46–49	4	48:17–25	143, 165–177, 185
46	131	48:17–22	120
46:1–49:16	122	48:17	120, 165, 168, 175
46:1–49:10	124, 127	48:18–21	168
46:1–7	119	48:18	165, 168–169
46:1	74, 119, 124, 156	48:19	165, 169
46:4	175	48:20–23	172
46:5	175	48:20	165, 169, 171, 174–175, 184
46:7–10	119		
46:7	119	48:21	165, 170–171, 173

Index of Sources

48:22–25	120, 172	51:1	117
48:22–24	165	51:12i	35
48:22	120, 165, 170, 175	51:19	73
48:23	165, 176	51:23–30	57
48:24–25	167, 171	51:23	52
48:24	108, 165, 170–172, 174	51:30	2
48:25	165, 171, 174–175		
49	131, 155	*Ben Sira – Greek (Sir^{LXX})*	
49:1–6	120	Prologue	2–8, 11, 32, 34,
49:1	36, 120		37–38, 55–56, 58–97,
49:4	72, 175		99, 107–109, 112,
49:7	73, 120, 156, 175		122–123, 125, 184,
49:8–10	6		187–190
49:8	120, 152, 177	l. 1–14	68–69, 83
49:9	73, 85, 116, 120,	l. 1–2	68–69, 87
	143–144, 177–180, 185	l. 1	59, 74, 77, 81–82
49:10	56, 73, 108, 120, 123,	l. 2	59, 70, 79, 81, 87
	125–126, 143–144,	l. 3	59, 67–69, 86, 93
	164–165, 180–185	l. 4–6	68
49:11	120	l. 4	55, 59, 69, 93
49:11–50:21	124	l. 5	55, 59, 69, 86, 93
49:12	120, 175	l. 6	55, 59, 90
49:13	58, 120–121, 146	l. 7–12	68
49:14–16	122, 131	l. 7	3, 59, 61, 66, 68, 83, 88,
49:14	120, 143–158, 185		94
49:15–16	146	l. 8–10	68–69, 81
49:15	120	l. 8	59, 74
49:16	117, 120, 127, 155	l. 9	59, 77, 81–82
50	35, 37, 115, 117–118,	l. 10	55, 60, 68–70, 74, 77,
	121, 131–133, 190		79–81, 83, 88, 93
50:1–24	122	l. 11	60
50:1–21	117, 120	l. 12	55, 60, 68–69, 86–88,
50:1	35, 37, 120, 146, 155		93
50:3	175	l. 13–14	68, 91
50:4	175	l. 13	60, 69, 86–87, 91, 94
50:19	175	l. 14	60, 69, 84–85, 90–91,
50:22–24	120		94
50:22–23	117, 120–121	l. 15–26	68–70, 86, 93
50:22	35	l. 15–17	66
50:23–24	122	l. 15	60, 68
50:24	35, 117, 120, 131	l. 16	60
50:25–26	117, 121	l. 17	55, 60, 69, 88, 93
50:25	121	l. 18	60
50:27–29	117, 121	l. 19–22	89
50:27	2, 53, 121	l. 19–20	68
50:28	53, 121	l. 19	60, 88–89
50:29	117	l. 20	60, 89
51	7, 35, 117	l. 21–26	70

l. 21–22	68, 89
l. 21	60, 68, 89, 94
l. 22	60, 68, 70, 89
l. 23–26	68, 83, 89
l. 23–25	68
l. 23	60, 88–89
l. 24–26	89
l. 24–25	68–70, 88
l. 24	60, 70, 74, 77, 79, 81–82, 84, 88–89
l. 25	55, 60, 70, 74, 77, 79–81
l. 26	55, 60, 68
l. 27–36	68–69
l. 27–28	62, 68
l. 27	60, 62
l. 28	3, 60, 62–63, 66
l. 29	60, 66, 68–69, 90, 93
l. 30	55, 60–61, 63, 67–68
l. 31–34	68
l. 31	60, 69, 93–94
l. 32	61, 63
l. 33	55, 61, 67–68
l. 34	61, 66–67, 69, 91, 93
l. 35–36	68
l. 35	60
l. 36	60, 67, 69, 84–85, 91, 94
1:4^{LXX}	157
2:6^{LXX}	180
2:10^{LXX}	83, 110
2:11^{LXX}	175
2:16^{LXX}	74, 83
3:29^{LXX}	54, 110
4:24^{LXX}	54
6:9^{LXX}	157
6:33^{LXX}	54
6:35^{LXX}	54
9:10^{LXX}	83
9:15^{LXX}	74, 83
10:1–2^{LXX}	164
10:5^{LXX}	54
10:24^{LXX}	164
14:21^{LXX}	176
15:1^{LXX}	74
16:7^{LXX}	83, 147
16:8^{LXX}	67
16:24^{LXX}	54
17:11^{LXX}	74
19:17^{LXX}	74
19:20^{LXX}	74
19:24^{LXX}	74
20:27^{LXX}	87
21:11^{LXX}	74
21:15^{LXX}	91
23:23^{LXX}	74
24^{LXX}	76
24:1–22^{LXX}	75
24:23^{LXX}	31, 55, 73–77, 108, 110
24:33^{LXX}	74, 77, 88, 112, 157
30–36^{LXX}	2, 7
31:8^{LXX} (34:8^{LXX})	74
32:1^{LXX} (32:15^{LXX})	74
32:15^{LXX} (35:12^{LXX})	164
32:17^{LXX}	73
33:3^{LXX} (36:22^{LXX})	175
34:31^{LXX} (31:31^{LXX})	36
35:5^{LXX} (32:5^{LXX})	36
35:15^{LXX} (32:24^{LXX})	74
35:24^{LXX} (35:1^{LXX})	74
36:2–3^{LXX} (33:2–3^{LXX})	74
36:10^{LXX} (33:10^{LXX})	136, 157
36:14^{LXX}	74
36:15^{LXX}	73
36:20^{LXX} (36:14^{LXX})	77
36:21^{LXX} (36:15^{LXX})	77, 83
37:15^{LXX}	180
38:12^{LXX}	157
38:16–23^{LXX}	104
38:24–39:11^{LXX}	99–113, 126, 187–189
38:24–34^{LXX}	105
38:24^{LXX}	10, 54, 100, 104–106, 111
38:25–26^{LXX}	105–106
38:25^{LXX}	100, 106–107
38:26–28^{LXX}	83
38:26^{LXX}	101
38:27^{LXX}	55, 101, 104, 106
38:28^{LXX}	101, 105–106
38:29–30^{LXX}	101, 105–106
38:29^{LXX}	101
38:30^{LXX}	83, 101, 106
38:31–34^{LXX}	101–102, 106
38:31^{LXX}	101

38:32[LXX] (38:33[LXX])	101	44:19[LXX]	119
38:33[LXX] (38:34[LXX])	102	44:20[LXX]	74
38:34–39:11[LXX]	105–106	44:22[LXX]	119
38:34–39:3[LXX]	106, 111	44:23[LXX]	116, 119, 184
38:34–39:1[LXX]	5, 6, 20, 83, 99, 107–109, 111–113, 122	45:1[LXX]	119, 164
		45:3[LXX]	176
38:34[LXX] (39:1[LXX])	73–74, 83, 102, 106–107, 110, 113	45:4[LXX]	184
		45:5[LXX]	74
39:1–8[LXX]	111	45:6[LXX]	119
39:1–3[LXX]	83	45:11[LXX]	54
39:1[LXX]	74, 77, 102, 106–107, 109–112	45:17[LXX]	74
		45:23[LXX]	119
39:2–5[LXX]	111	45:24[LXX]	35
39:2–3[LXX]	109–111	45:25[LXX]	119
39:2[LXX]	102, 109	45:26[LXX]	119, 121, 157
39:3[LXX]	102, 110–111, 176	46:1[LXX]	77, 119, 124
39:4[LXX]	102, 106	46:2[LXX]	175
39:5[LXX]	83, 102, 106–107	46:4[LXX]	176
39:6[LXX]	102–103, 106–107, 112	46:5[LXX]	180
39:7–8[LXX]	106	46:7[LXX]	119
39:7[LXX]	103, 176	46:11–12[LXX]	159–165
39:8[LXX]	73–74, 103–104, 107, 112–113	46:11[LXX]	119, 159, 162, 181
		46:12[LXX]	159–160, 162, 164–165, 184
39:9–11[LXX]	106		
39:9–10[LXX]	106	46:13[LXX]	77, 119
39:9[LXX]	103, 157	46:14[LXX]	74, 164
39:10[LXX]	103, 106	46:15[LXX]	77, 175–176, 184
39:11[LXX]	103–104	46:18[LXX]	116, 175
39:12–35[LXX]	104	46:19[LXX]	121
39:29[LXX]	157	46:20[LXX]	77, 176
39:32[LXX]	54	47:1–2[LXX]	120
41:5[LXX]	67	47:1[LXX]	77, 119
41:8[LXX]	74	47:4[LXX]	175
42:2[LXX]	74	47:7[LXX]	175
42:7[LXX]	54	47:13[LXX]	120
42:19[LXX]	176	47:14–20[LXX]	121
44–50[LXX]	115–190	47:15[LXX]	110
44[LXX]	126	47:16[LXX]	116
44:1[LXX]	119, 121	47:17[LXX]	110
44:3–4[LXX]	111	47:23–25[LXX]	120
44:3[LXX]	77, 111	47:23[LXX]	120
44:4[LXX]	54	47:25[LXX]	116
44:5[LXX]	54	48–49[LXX]	131
44:7[LXX]	157	48:1–12[LXX]	120
44:12[LXX]	116	48:1[LXX]	77, 120, 135
44:14[LXX]	157	48:4[LXX]	54, 120–121, 135
44:16[LXX]	119, 144–158	48:8[LXX]	77
44:17[LXX]	119	48:9[LXX]	152, 157

244 — *Index of Sources*

48:10[LXX]	10, 54, 134–142	49:12[LXX]	117, 120
48:11[LXX]	120–121	49:13[LXX]	120–121
48:12[LXX]	116, 120, 175	49:14[LXX]	120, 144–158
48:17–25[LXX]	165–177	49:15[LXX]	120
48:13[LXX]	77	49:16[LXX]	117, 120
48:17[LXX]	120, 165, 172, 175	50:1[LXX]	35–37, 120
48:18[LXX]	165, 172, 175	50:4[LXX]	176
48:19[LXX]	165, 172, 175	50:11[LXX]	157
48:20[LXX]	120, 165, 172–173, 175, 184	50:15[LXX]	116
		50:19[LXX]	175
48:21[LXX]	165, 170, 173, 175	50:20[LXX]	175
48:22[LXX]	73, 77, 120, 165, 173, 175–176	50:21[LXX]	118
		50:22–24[LXX]	118, 120–121
48:23[LXX]	165, 173, 176	50:22[LXX]	121
48:24[LXX]	165, 173, 184	50:23[LXX]	121
48:25[LXX]	165, 173, 176	50:24[LXX]	35, 117–118, 175
49:1[LXX]	36, 120	50:25[LXX]	121
49:4[LXX]	74	50:27[LXX]	2, 35, 55, 121, 141–142
49:7[LXX]	120	50:28–29[LXX]	121
49:7[LXX]	77	50:29[LXX]	8, 116–117
49:8[LXX]	120, 176	51:2[LXX]	175
49:9[LXX]	116, 177–180	51:11[LXX]	87
49:10[LXX]	77, 120, 160, 164–165, 173, 175, 180–185	51:19[LXX]	74, 175
		51:23[LXX]	52
49:11[LXX]	116–117, 120	51:30[LXX]	3

Hebrew Bible (Masoretic Text, MT)

Genesis (Gen)		12–36	128
Book of Genesis	18, 25, 39, 41, 45, 51, 128–130, 132, 141, 143, 146–150, 153, 155	14:18–20	169
		14:22–24	169
		14:22	169
2–3	129	16	130
3–4	130	17	132
4:17–18	147	17:1	148–149
5–9	128	21	130
5	129	24:40	148
5:21–24	146–149, 153, 156–158	37–50	129
5:21	147	48:15	148
5:22	147–148, 152		
5:23	147, 152	*Exodus (Exod)*	
5:24	146–148, 153	Book of Exodus	41, 44, 47–48, 51, 128
6	146–147	1–19	51
6:1–4	25, 141	7:1	125
6:9	148–149	32	128, 130
6:13–21	149		

Index of Sources

Leviticus (Lev)
Book of Leviticus 22, 44–45, 127–128

Numbers (Num)
Book of Numbers 39, 128–130, 161
6:24–26 44
14 128
25 128–129
25:5 161

Deuteronomy (Deut)
Book of Deuteronomy
18, 29–30, 44, 48, 75, 77, 123, 127–128, 140
19:17–18 160
28:58 140
29:19–20 140
29:26 140
29:28 171
30:10 140
32:2 179
33:4 75–77
34:10 125

Joshua (Josh)
Book of Joshua 3–4, 123–124, 127–130, 161
1:8 140
8:34 140
14–15 128
15:17 161, 163
23:6 140
24 129

Judges (Judg)
Book of Judges 4, 123, 126, 128, 143, 159–165, 185, 189
1:13 161, 163
2:16–19 161
2:16–18 160
2:19 160
3 163
3:7–11 161–162
3:8 163
3:9–10 161
3:9 163
3:10 163
3:11 163

3:12 163
3:14–15 163
3:15–16 163
3:17 163
3:20–21 163
3:23 163
3:26 163
3:31 163
4:1 163
4:4 160
5:6 163
8:27 160, 162
8:31 161
13:24 161
16:20 160

1 Samuel (1 Sam)
Book of 1 Samuel 125, 128, 130, 161
1 128
1:9 161
4:18 161
12:11 161
17 128

2 Samuel (2 Sam)
Book of 2 Samuel 128, 130
7 128

1 Kings (1 Kgs)
Book of 1 Kings 129, 135
1–22 129

2 Kings (2 Kgs)
Book of 2 Kings 41, 125, 127, 129, 135, 169
1–9 129
13:20–21 160
18–20 129, 168–172, 174, 176
18–19 169, 172
18:13 168
18:17 168
18:27 168
18:36 169
19:1–4 169
19:4 168–169
19:6 169
19:14–20 169
19:14 169

246 Index of Sources

19:19	169	36:1–2	174
19:22	169	36:1	168
19:35	170	36:2	168
20:1–11	173	36:12	168
20:3	170	36:21	169
20:4–6	173	37:1–4	169
20:8–11	173	37:4	168–169
20:20	19, 168, 176	37:6	169
21:13	169	37:8–12	174
22–23	129	37:14–21	169
22:2	170	37:14	169
22:13	140	37:20	169
23:3	140	37:23	169
23:22	160	37:29–32	174
23:24	140	37:36	170
		38:1–8	173
Isaiah (Isa)		38:3	170, 173
Book of Isaiah	4, 18, 40, 129, 136, 139,	38:4–6	173
	143, 158, 165–177,	38:12–22	174
	181, 184–185, 189	38:16	182
1–66	40, 167, 172, 176	39:1–8	174
1–39	129, 167, 170, 172, 176	40–66	167, 172
1:1	167	40–55	167, 170–171
1:15	169	40	174
1:24	172	40:1	170–172
1:27	172	42:9	171
1:26	161	44:28	167
2:2	170, 172	45:1	167
3:16	172	45:12	169
3:17	172	46:10	170, 172
3:26	172	49:6	135–137, 140
4:3	139–140	56–66	108, 167
5:25	169	61:1	170, 172
11:2	170, 172	61:2–3	170–171
14:14	169	61:2	170–172
20:2	169	61:3	170–172
21:10	172	66:14	182
22:9	168		
22:11	168	*Jeremiah (Jer)*	
24:4	172	Book of Jeremiah	4, 129, 181–182, 184
24:7	172	17:1	39
24:23	172	25:13	140
28:28	170	30:7	182
34:16	172	30:10	182
34:17	149	31:7	182
36–39	168, 170, 172, 174	32:12	140
36–38	172	46:27	182
36–37	168–169	51:60	140

Index of Sources

247

Ezekiel (Ezek)

Book of Ezekiel	4, 6, 46–47, 129, 178, 180–181, 184
10	129
14	129, 133, 178
14:13–20	178–179
14:13	179
14:14	178–179
14:15	179
14:17	179
14:19	179
14:20	178–179
20	118
20:21	169
38:22	179
40–48	47

Twelve Prophets

Book of the Twelve Prophets	3–4, 6, 108, 124, 126, 129, 141, 143, 180–185, 189

Joel (Joel)

3:1	182
4:20	149

Jonah (Jonah)

1	183

Haggai (Hag)

Book of Haggai	129
1:1	62
2:1	62

Zechariah (Zech)

Book of Zechariah	129
1:1	62

Malachi (Mal)

Book of Malachi	125, 134–142
3	183
3:16	47
3:23–24	54, 123, 126, 134–142, 182, 189
3:23	108, 134–135, 138
3:24	135, 137–138, 140
4:5–6 NRSV = 3:23–24 MT	

Psalms (Ps)

Book of Psalms	5, 7, 18, 32–33, 41, 49, 57, 72, 123, 129, 169
19:13	171
37:26	161
66:19	169
68	118
77–78	118
78:35	169
105–106	118
135–136	118

Job (Job)

Book of Job	5–6, 122–123, 127, 129–130, 133, 143, 177–180, 188–189
13–14	179
29:14	179
31:4	179
38:1	179
39:4	182

Proverbs (Prov)

Book of Proverbs	5, 30–31, 123, 129
3:3	39
7:3	39
10:7	160–161

Ruth (Ruth)

Book of Ruth	22, 129–130
1:1	160

Song of Songs (Song)

Book of Song of Songs	17, 22, 129

Ecclesiastes (Eccl)

Book of Ecclesiastes	47, 129

Lamentations (Lam)

Book of Lamentations	129

Esther (Esth)

Book of Esther	18, 22, 125, 129–130

248 Index of Sources

Daniel (Dan)
Book of Daniel 11, 17, 22, 44, 80, 125,
            129, 178

Ezra (Ezra)
Book of Ezra 5, 22, 129–130, 188
7:10 108

Nehemiah (Neh)
Book of Nehemiah 5, 22, 122–123, 125,
            129–130
8:8–9 108

1 Chronicles (1 Chr)
Book of 1 Chronicles
            125, 127–128
1:3 147
4:41 140
11–29 128
16:40 140
17:10 161

2 Chronicles (2 Chr)
Book of 2 Chronicles
            125, 127, 129, 135, 169
11:17 170
17:3 170
19:6 160–161
29–32 168–171, 173
29:1–3 174
29:3 168
31:20 170
32 168–169, 172, 176
32:5 168
32:11 169
32:20 169
32:21 170
32:22 169
32:24–26 173
32:30 168–169
34:2 170
34:21 140
34:24 140
34:31 140

Septuagint (LXX)

Genesis^{LXX} (Gen^{LXX})
5:21–24^{LXX} 146–149
5:21^{LXX} 148
5:22^{LXX} 148
5:23^{LXX} 148
5:24^{LXX} 148

Exodus^{LXX} (Exod^{LXX})
Book of Exodus^{LXX} 45

Leviticus^{LXX} (Lev^{LXX})
Book of Leviticus^{LXX}
            45

Numbers^{LXX} (Num^{LXX})
Book of Numbers^{LXX}
            45
11:26^{LXX} 140
25:5^{LXX} 162

Deuteronomy^{LXX} (Deut^{LXX})
Book of Deuteronomy^{LXX}
            45
29:28^{LXX} 173
32:2^{LXX} 179
33:4^{LXX} 75–77

Judges^{LXX} (Judg^{LXX})
Book of Judges^{LXX} 162
2:17^{LXX} 162
2:19^{LXX} 162
8:27^{LXX} 162
8:33^{LXX} 162

1 Kings^{LXX} (1 Kgs^{LXX}) = 3 Kingsdoms^{LXX}
5:10^{LXX} 110

2 Kings^{LXX} (2 Kgs^{LXX}) = 4 Kingdoms^{LXX}
Book of 2 Kings^{LXX} 172
13:20–21^{LXX} 162
18–20^{LXX} 173

Index of Sources

18:12^{LXX}	173		2:19–32^{LXX}	67
19:19^{LXX}	173		10:1^{LXX}	86
19:35^{LXX}	173		15:37–39^{LXX}	67
20:1–11^{LXX}	173			
20:1^{LXX}	173		*Psalms^{LXX} (Ps^{LXX})*	
20:3^{LXX}	173		1^{LXX}	110
20:4–6^{LXX}	173		1:2^{LXX}	110
20:20^{LXX}	172		18:13^{LXX} (= 19:13^{MT})	
21:8^{LXX}	173			173
21:13^{LXX}	172		36:26^{LXX} (= 37:26^{MT})	
				162
2 Chronicles^{LXX} (2 Chr^{LXX})			76:16^{LXX} (= 80:16^{MT})	
Book of 2 Chronicles^{LXX}				183
	172			
29–32^{LXX}	173		*Proverbs^{LXX} (Prov^{LXX})*	
31:20^{LXX}	173		10:7^{LXX}	162
32^{LXX}	172		31:25^{LXX}	71
32:5^{LXX}	172			
32:21^{LXX}	173		*Job^{LXX} (Job^{LXX})*	
32:22^{LXX}	173		Book of Job^{LXX}	179
32:24–26^{LXX}	173		38:1^{LXX}	179
34:2^{LXX}	173		38:23^{LXX}	179
1 Esdras^{LXX} (1 Esd^{LXX})			*Wisdom of Solomon^{LXX} (Wis^{LXX})*	
9:13^{LXX}	162		4:10–11^{LXX}	147
			10–19^{LXX}	118
Esther^{LXX} (Esth^{LXX})			19:10^{LXX}	67
10:3^{ILXX}	67			
			Twelve Prophets^{LXX}	
Tobit^{LXX} (Tob^{LXX})			Book of the Twelve Prophets^{LXX}	
Book of Tobit	46, 55			45, 183
1 Maccabees^{LXX} (1 Macc^{LXX})			*Haggai^{LXX} (Hag^{LXX})*	
2^{LXX}	118		1:1^{LXX}	62
2:49–68^{LXX}	118		1:15^{LXX}	62
2:54^{LXX}	35		2:10^{LXX}	62
3:7^{LXX}	162			
13:42^{LXX}	62		*Zechariah^{LXX} (Zech^{LXX})*	
14:27^{LXX}	62		1:1^{LXX}	62
			1:7^{LXX}	62
2 Maccabees^{LXX} (2 Macc^{LXX})			7:1^{LXX}	62
Book of 2 Maccabees^{LXX}				
	42, 67		*Malachi^{LXX} (Mal^{LXX})*	
2:2–3^{LXX}	82		3:22–23^{LXX} (= 3:23–24^{MT})	
2:13–15^{LXX}	42–43, 57, 84			134–142
2:13^{LXX}	42–43, 82		3:22^{LXX}	135
2:14^{LXX}	42		3:23^{LXX}	135, 140
2:15^{LXX}	42			

250 Index of Sources

Isaiah^{LXX} (Isa^{LXX})
Book of Isaiah^{LXX} 172–173, 183
1:15^{LXX} 172
11:2^{LXX} 173
22:11^{LXX} 172
36–39^{LXX} 173
36–37^{LXX} 172
37:14^{LXX} 172
37:20^{LXX} 173
37:36^{LXX} 173
38:1–8^{LXX} 173
38:3^{LXX} 173
38:4–6^{LXX} 173
38:8^{LXX} 173
41:14^{LXX} 183
42:9^{LXX} 173
43:1^{LXX} 183
44:23^{LXX} 183
49:6^{LXX} 136
61:3^{LXX} 173
65:2^{LXX} 172

Jeremiah^{LXX} (Jer^{LXX})
Book of Jeremiah^{LXX}
183
38:11^{LXX} 183

Baruch^{LXX} (Bar^{LXX})
2:24^{LXX} 183

Lamentations^{LXX} (Lam^{LXX})
1:17^{LXX} 183

Epistle of Jeremiah^{LXX} (Ep Jer^{LXX})
Book of the Epistle of Jeremiah ^{LXX}
45

Ezekiel^{LXX} (Ezek^{LXX})
Book of Ezekiel^{LXX} 172, 179, 183
14:13–20^{LXX} 179
14:13^{LXX} 179
14:15^{LXX} 179
14:17^{LXX} 179
14:19^{LXX} 179
38:22^{LXX} 179

Daniel^{LXX} (Dan^{LXX})
2:45^{LXX} 173

New Testament

Luke
Book of Luke 80
1:1–4 67
1:17 138, 141–142
24:32 82
24:44 80

Hebrews
11 118

Jude
14–15 49

Dead Sea Scrolls

1Q8 (1QIsa^b) 136, 174
1Q20 (1QapGen ar) 46–47, 155–158, 174
1QIsa^a, Isaiah Scroll 40–41, 136, 139, 168–171, 174
1QpHab 47

1QS, Rule of the Community 139
2Q18 (2QSir) 6–7
3Q15 (3QCopper Scroll) 140
4Q11 (4QpaleoGen–Exod^l) 41

Index of Sources

251

4Q15 (4QExod^d) — 44
4Q17 (4QExod–Lev^f) — 44–45
4Q29 (4QDeut^b) — 140
4Q46 (4QpaleoDeut^s) — 44
4Q52 (4QSam^b) — 44
4Q56 (4QIsa^b) — 168–169, 174
4Q58 (4QIsa^d) — 136
4Q66 (4QIsa^m) — 171
4Q70 (4QJer^a) — 44
4Q76 (4QXII^a) — 135, 141, 183
4Q83 (4QPs^a) — 169
4Q101 (4QpaleoJob^c) — 179
4Q118 (4QChr) — 174
4Q122 (4QLXXDeut) — 45
4Q169 (4QpNah) — 47–48
4Q174 (4QFlor) — 125
4Q201 (4QEn^a ar) — 44–45, 150, 157
4Q208 (4QEnastr^a ar) — 44–45
4Q212 (En^g ar) — 151–152
4Q219 (4QJub^d) — 155
4Q220 (4QJub^e) — 155
4Q258 (4QS^d) — 139
4Q265 (4QMiscellaneous Rules) — 139
4Q266 (4QD^a) — 71–72
4Q268 (4QD^c) — 174
4Q279 (4QFour Lots) — 139
4Q365 (4QRP^c) — 46
4Q372 (4QapocrJoseph^b) — 174

4Q379 (4QapocrJosh^b) — 72
4Q382 (4Qpap paraKings et al.) — 138, 140–142
4Q394–399 (4QMMT^a–f) — 48
4Q397 (4QMMT^d) — 46, 48–49, 72
4Q424 (4QInstruction-like Work) — 46
4Q465 (4QpapText Mentioning Samson?) — 163
4Q482 (4Qpap Jub^i?) — 169
4Q504 (4QDibHam^a) — 139
4Q521 (4QMessianic Apocalypse) — 137, 140, 142
4Q558 (4QpapVision^b ar) — 137–138, 140, 142
4Q559 (4QpapBibChronology ar) — 163, 165
5Q3 (5QIsa) — 174
6Q1 (6QpaleoGen) — 149
11Q5 (11QPs^a) — 7, 32–33, 57, 72
11Q10 (11QtgJob) — 179–180
11Q13 (11QMelch) — 140
11Q19 (11QT^a), Temple Scroll — 40, 71
Mas1h (MasSir), Masada Manuscript — 6, 116–117, 119, 131, 144–145, 159, 165, 180

Further Sources

1 Enoch (1 En)
Book of 1 Enoch — 13, 17–18, 33, 46, 49–51, 53–54, 58, 141, 146–147, 149–153, 155, 157–158, 163, 186, 189
1–36 — 49–50, 149
1–10 — 45
1:1 — 150
1:2 — 150
6–11 — 146–147
12:1–2 — 153
12:1 — 153

12:4 — 150
15:1 — 150
19:3 — 150–151
14–16 — 51
14 — 152
14:21 — 152–153
37–71 — 49–50
37:1–5 — 151
37:4 — 150–151
39:3–4 — 153
39:3 — 153
65:1–3 — 154
65:9 — 154

70:1–2	153	*Damascus Document (CD),*	
71:1	153	*see also* 4Q266, 4Q268	
71:5	153	7:17	71–72
71:14	150		
72–82	49–50, 149	*Mishnah*	
72:32	151	Eduyyot 8:7	138
73	45		
74:10	151	*Jubilees (Jub)*	
74:12	151	Book of Jubilees	18, 33, 46–47, 49,
80–82	50		51–52, 71, 149,
81:5–6	153		153–155, 157–158,
82	151		174, 189
82:1–3	151	4:16–17	51
82:1–2	151	4:18	153–154
82:6	151	4:23–24	154
83–90	49–50	4:23	154
85–90	118	4:24	154
91–108	51	4:25	155
91–105	49–50, 149	7	154
91:1–10	50	7:38–39	154
91:1–2	152	10:17	154
91:11–17	50	13:29	169
91:18–19	50	19	154–155
92:1–5	50	19:23–24	154–155
92:1	53–54, 151–152	19:27	155
92:3	152	21	154
93:1–10	50	21:10	19, 155–156
93:11–14	50	21:20	174
94:1–105:2	50		
94:1–4	152	*Josephus*	
94:1	152	Ag. Ap. 1.37–45	44, 72, 80
99:10	152	Ag. Ap. 1.38–40	44, 80
106–107	49–50	Ag. Ap. 1.40	44, 178
108	50	Ant. 12.138–144	37, 44
108:1	54	Ant. 12.138–142	42, 44

Index of Subjects

Aaron 35, 46, 117, 119, 125, 128, 130–132
Abel 130
Abraham 46–47, 74, 119, 128, 131–132,
  148–149, 154–156
Adam 49, 120, 127, 129, 131, 146, 155–157
Alexandria 62, *see also* Library – Alexan-
  dria
Anachronism of Biblical Canon 11–17, 21,
  30–31, 39, 57–58, 133, 147, 155, 188
Anachronisms in Pseudepigraphic Texts
  64, 190
Antiochus III Megas 36–37, 42
Antiochus IV Epiphanes 35–37, 49
Apocrypha 1–2, 42, 88, 155
– Genesis Apocryphon *see* Index of
  Sources – 1Q20
Apology 67, 94–95
Aramaic
– 1 Enoch 49–51, 149–153
– Ben Sira 3, 9
– Genesis Apocryphon *see* Index of
  Sources – 1Q20
– Language 14, 32–33, 89
Aramaic Levi Document 46–47
Artapanus 46
Ascension of Isaiah 171
Authoritative Texts 11–23, 31–33, 49, 71,
  188–191, *see also* Criteria for Author-
  itative Texts
– Ben Sira 38:24-39:11 113
– Ben Sira 44-50 126–127, 133, 140–142,
  147, 158, 185–186
– Greek Prologue to Ben Sira 80, 84–85,
  87, 93–94, 96–97

Ben Sira *see also* Creativity of Ben Sira;
  Orality – Ben Sira
– Date 1–2, 35–38, 61–66
– Languages 6–10

– Manuscripts 6–10
– Name 2–3
– Structure 1–2, 29, 67–69, 105–107,
  119–122
Bible 14–16, *see also* Biblical Canon;
  Hebrew Bible
– Definitions 1, 14–15
Biblical Canon 1–23, 26–27, 31, 34, 39–41,
  45–49, 56–57, 64, 187–191, *see also*
  Canon; Intertextuality – Canonical
  Restriction; Septuagint – Canon
– Definitions 11–14
– Ben Sira 38:24-39:11 107–113, 187–188
– Ben Sira 44-50 122–144, 147, 178,
  185–189
– Greek Prologue to Ben Sira 66, 78–97,
  178–189
– History 3–6, 10–11, 41–43, 66, 78–79,
  95–97, 189–190
Blessing 44, 117, 119–122, 124, 132, 154–155,
  159–162, 181
Book of Giants 46
Book of Noah 155
Books 1–2, 14–15, 40–41, 51–55, 58
– Biblical Books 1–6, 40–43, 128–130
– Definitions 14–15, 40–41, 55
– Mentions in Ben Sira 52–55, 58,
  123–124, 133, 143–144, 185–186, 188–191
– Mentions in the Greek Prologue to Ben
  Sira 55, 58–61, 69–70, 75–78, 96–97
– Unknown Books 47, 51, 155–156, 176

Caleb 119, 128, 130–131, 161–163, 165
Cain 130, 147
Cairo Genizah *see* Genizah
Canon *see also* Biblical Canon
– Definitions 11–14
– Non-Biblical Canons 11–12, 43, 64

254   *Index of Subjects*

Circular Reasoning 66, 82–83, 132–133,
   137, 142, 182, 191
Codex 14–15, 40–41
– Codex Leningradensis (L) 40
– Codex Sinaiticus (S) 7, 40, 61, 92, 103, 116
– Codex Vaticanus (B) 7, 40, 61, 92, 103,
   116
– Materiality 14–15, 40–41, 55, 58, 97, 188
Creativity of Ben Sira 23, 47, 131–132, 158,
   167, 176–177, 185–186, 189
Criteria for Authoritative Texts 18–20, 49,
   97, 113, 142, 191
Criteria for Intertextuality 27–31, 34, 190

David 42, 49, 72, 119–120, 123, 128,
   130–131, 145, 165–166, 170, 173, 175, 188
Dead Sea Scrolls 14, 33–34, 39, 44–49, 57
– Definitions 14
– Comparisons with Ben Sira 32–33,
   149–158, 163–165, 174–177, 179–180,
   183–184
– Impact on the History of the Biblical
   Canon 15, 18–21, 26–27, 187–188, 190–191
– Key Terms 70–72, 139–140, 142
– Materiality 40–41
– Oldest Manuscripts 44–45
Demetrius the Chronographer 46
Deuterocanonical Books 1–2, *see also*
   Apocrypha
Divine Passive 86–87

Egypt 32–33, 36, 41–42, 104–105
– Greek Prologue to Ben Sira 3, 60,
   62–67, 69, 76, 90, 93
Elijah 54, 73, 77, 120–121, 129, 131, 134–141,
   146, 148, 152, 156–157, 189
Elisha 77, 116, 120, 129, 131, 160, 162, 175
Enoch *see also* Index of Sources – 1 Enoch
– Figure 46, 51, 53–54, 63, 116, 118–120,
   128–131, 143–158, 163, 185–186, 189
Enosh 117, 120, 129, 131, 146, 155
Ethiopian Orthodox Tewahedo Church
   13, 15–16, 49
Ethiopic 9, 49–51, 150, 153
Ezekiel *see also* Index of Sources –
   Ezekiel; Ezekiel^LXX
– Figure 46–47, 116, 120, 129, 131, 152,
   176–177, 179

Ezekiel the Tragedian 46–47
Ezra *see also* Index of Sources – Ezra
– 4 Ezra 13
– Figure 108, 129–130, 162, 188

Figures 19–20, 46–48, 63, 115–133,
   141–142, 145, 154–155, 161–165, 176, 178,
   184, 188, 190
Fluidity 14, 45–46, 71, 141, 186, 190–191

Geʿez *see* Ethiopic
Genesis Apocryphon *see* Index of Sources
   – 1Q20
Genizah 2, 6–7, 10, 66
Giants 83, 141, 147, *see also* Book of Giants
Grandfather 3–5, 37, 59, 61–66, 68–69,
   82–83, 87–88, 92–94, 189–190, *see also*
   Grandson
Grandson 3–5, 8, 61–66, 68–69, 82,
   93–94, 189–190, *see also* Grandfather
Greek Canon *see* Septuagint – Canon

Hapax Legomena *see* Septuagint – Hapax
   Legomena
Hebrew Bible, 1–6, 10–11, 14–15, 18–34,
   39–40, 47–49, 53, 56, 187–191, *see also*
   Bible; Biblical Canon
– Comparisons with Ben Sira 127–142,
   143–144, 147–149, 160–162, 168–172,
   178–179, 182, 185–186
– Definitions 1, 14–15
– Manuscripts 40–45
Hellenism 32, 36–39, 41–43, 57–58, 64,
   118–119, 158
– Definition 36
Hezekiah 120, 129, 131, 165–177, 182
History 8–10, 33–38, 88, 118–119, 124–125,
   154, 183, 189–190, *see also* Ben Sira
   – Date; Biblical Canon – History;
   Hellenism; Second Temple Period
Homer 32, 43, 89

Inspiration
– Ben Sira 86, 106–107, 112–113, 188
– Biblical Canon 12, 18, 79, 167
Intention
– Ben Sira *see* Creativity of Ben Sira
– Intertextuality 26, 28, 185–186, 189

Index of Subjects

Intertextuality 22–34, 189–191, *see also* Criteria for Intertextuality; Intention – Intertextuality
– Canonical Restriction 20–21, 26–27, 29–31, 131–133, 191
– Case Studies 75–77, 134–141, 143–186
– Definitions 25–27
Instruction *see also* Teaching
– 4QInstruction *see* Musar leMevin
– Ben Sira 31, 52–53, 104
– Instruction-like Composition B *see* Index of Sources – 4Q424
Invention *see* Creativity of Ben Sira
Isaac 119, 128, 131, 148, 155
Isaiah *see also* Index of Sources – Isaiah; Isaiah^{LXX}
– Figure 77, 120, 129, 131, 143, 165–177, 185, 189
Ishmael 128, 130

Jacob
– Figure 46, 116, 119, 128, 131, 154–155
– Israel 74, 76, 134, 136–138, 180–184
Jar *see* Scroll Jar
Jeremiah *see also* Index of Sources – Jeremiah; Jeremiah^{LXX}
– Figure 73, 77, 120, 129, 131, 175
Jeroboam 120, 129, 131
Jerusalem 2–3, 11, 35–38, 42–43, 50–52, 56–58, 121, 168–169, 175, 182, *see also* Library – Jerusalem
Jeshua 117, 120, 129, 131
Job *see also* Index of Sources – Job; Job^{LXX}
– Figure 73, 85, 116–117, 120, 124, 129–131, 143, 177–180, 185, 188–189
Joseph 46–47, 120, 129, 131, 146
Josephus 13, 37, 42, 44, 72, 80, 178, 189, *see also* Index of Sources – Josephus
Joshua *see also* Index of Sources – Joshua
– Figure 74, 77, 119, 124, 128, 130–131, 156, 175–176, 180
Josiah 120, 129, 131, 170–173, 175
Jubilees *see* Index of Sources – Jubilees
Judas Maccabaeus 42–43, 162
Judges *see also* Index of Sources – Judges; Judges^{LXX}
– Figures 119, 123, 126, 128, 131, 133, 143, 159–165, 184–185, 189

Language 19, 28, 33–34, 43–45, 50–52, 58, 187, 191, *see also* Aramaic; Ben Sira – Languages; Ethiopic; Latin; Syriac
– Greek Prologue to Ben Sira 60, 65, 70, 89
Latin 1, 8–10, 14, 67, 118, 154
– Vetus Latina 8–9
– Vulgate 8–9, 102, 144–145, 154, 159
Law *see also* Pentateuch; Torah
– Ben Sira 38:24-39:11 102–103, 107–113
– Definitions 1, 70–78
– Greek Prologue to Ben Sira 59–61, 67–69, 78–97
– Law identified with Torah/Pentateuch 1, 3–6, 10–11, 32, 69–78, 142, 187–188
– Law not identified with Torah/Pentateuch 54, 69–78, 96, 113, 132–133, 140, 175, 188–189
– Other laws 11–12, 17, 54, 140
Library 41–43
– Alexandria 41–43
– Jerusalem 42–43, 56–58
Literacy *see* Writing – Literacy
Literature 43–48, 189
– Ben Sira 38:24-39:11 109–111
– Biblical Canon 16–17, 44–45
– Definitions 43
– Greek Prologue to Ben Sira 68, 82–83, 85, 90
– Hellenism 32, 43
– Second Temple Period 26–27, 32–34, 44–48, 143, 157–158, 185, 189
Lists
– Canon 5, 12–14
– Greek Prologue to Ben Sira 70, 74, 77, 81, 190
– Figures 127–133, 163
– References in Ben Sira 22–25, 29–30, 32, 182

Maccabean Revolts 11, 37–38, 58, 65–66, 82, 190
Masada 2, 6–7
Masada Manuscript *see* Index of Sources – Mas1h
Masoretic Text XIV, 71, 127, 134, 147, 181, 183
Midrash 119

256 *Index of Subjects*

Mishnah 12, 138
Moses 46–47, 49, 63, 74, 76, 81, 119, 124–125, 128, 131, 164, 173, 184
– Law of Moses 55, 70–71, 74, 76, 81
Musar leMevin 46–47

Nathan 77, 119, 128, 131
Nehemiah *see also* Index of Sources – Nehemiah
– Figure 42–43, 57–58, 120–121, 129–131, 146
New Jerusalem 46–47
New Testament 10, 14, 25–26, 49, 63–64, 67, 71–72, 78, 87, 118, 138
Noah *see also* Book of Noah
– Figure 46, 116, 119, 124, 128, 131, 144–145, 148–149, 154–156, 164, 178–179

Old Testament 1–2, 14, 16, 92, 124, 186–187, 191, *see also* Bible
Orality 18, 25, 38–40, 43, 141–142, 190
– Ben Sira 52–58, 188, 191
– Lack of Recordings 39–40
– Oral Traditions identified with Bible 39, 190
– Oral Traditions not identified with Bible 19–20, 25, 31, 75, 77, 90, 109, 127, 141–142, 157, 186, 188, 190–191

Papyrus Insinger 32
Pentateuch 1, 41–42, 45, 48, 70–78, 84, 96, 188, *see also* Law; Torah
– Septuagint Pentateuch 23, 45, 92–93, 96
Pesharim 19, 47–48
Philo 44, 189
Philo the Epic Poet 47
Phineas 35, 119–120, 128–131, 145, 161, 188
Professions 38–39, 54, 73–74, 104–107, 111–113
Prologue
– Definitions 61
– Greek Prologue to Ben Sira 2–8, 11, 32, 34, 37–38, 55–56, 58–97, 108–109, 112, 123, 125, 184, 187–190
– Minuscule 248 61
Prophets *see also* Job; Twelve Prophets

– Biblical Canon 1, 10–11, 41, 69–78, 96–97, 122–125, 132–133, 136–137, 140, 142–143, 187–189
– Definitions 1, 69–78
Pseudepigraphy 63–66, 96, 189–190
Pseudo-Orpheus 47
Pseudo-Philo 47

Qumran 2, 6, 15, 23, *see also* Dead Sea Scrolls
Quotation 19, 23–24, 26–31, 47, 49, 56–57, 71, 75–77, 133, 188
– Ben Sira 48:10 134–142, 189

Rehoboam 120, 129, 131, 170–171

Samuel *see also* Index of Sources – 1–2 Samuel
– Figure 73–74, 77, 119, 121, 128, 131, 156, 159, 161–162, 164–165, 175–176, 184
Satire on the Trades 32, 104
Saul 128, 130, 188
Scribe 42, 53–54, 73–74, 77, 99–113, 126, 151, 188
Scriptures 12–13, 15–17, 56, 188, *see also* Authoritative Texts; Biblical Canon
– Definitions 15–17
Scroll *see also* Dead Sea Scrolls
– Materiality 14–15, 40–43, 55, 57–58, 97, 183–184, 188
Scroll Jar 15, 41
Second Temple Period 9–11, 15, 20, 36–39, 42–52, 58, 63, 70–71, 189, *see also* Literature – Second Temple Period
– Definitions 36
– History 36–37, 58
Septuagint 2, 23, 40, 67, 69–78, 92–93, 96–97, 189–190, *see also* Prologue – Greek Prologue to Ben Sira
– Book of Ben Sira 7–10, 131, 187
– Date 45, 92
– Definitions XIV, 2, 40
– Canon 2, 92–95, 112–113, 126
– Codices *see* Codex – Codex Sinaiticus (S); Codex Vaticanus (B)
– Comparisons with Ben Sira 69–78, 96–97, 134–141, 143–144, 147–149, 162, 172–173, 179, 182–183, 185

Index of Subjects

– Hapax Legomena 65, 86, 89–90
Seth 117, 120, 129, 131, 146, 155
Shem 117, 120, 129, 131, 146, 155
Simon the High Priest 35–37, 115, 117–118,
  120–122, 129–133, 146, 155, 157, 175–176,
  190
Solomon 110, 120–121, 123, 129, 131
Syriac 8–10, 145
– Peshitta 8–10, 76–77, 102, 145, 177, 181

Teaching 38–39, 52–58, 77, 103–104,
  106–107, 112, 118, 142, 188, 191
Texts *see also* Writing
– Definitions 25
Textual Authority *see* Authoritative Texts
Textual Fluidity *see* Fluidity
Theognis 32
Twelve Prophets *see also* Index of Sources
  – Twelve Prophets; Twelve Prophets^{LXX}
– Figures 73, 77, 116, 120, 123–125, 131,
  143, 160, 164–165, 173, 175, 177, 180–185,
  189
Torah 1, 42–43, 56, 73, 132–133, *see also*
  Law; Pentateuch

Translation *see also* Grandfather;
  Grandson; Language; Septuagint
– Book of Ben Sira *see* Ben Sira –
  Languages
– Greek Prologue to the Book of Ben
  Sira 3, 60–70, 83, 85–86, 88–97

Writing *see also* Books; Literature; Quo-
  tation; Scribe
– Greek Prologue to Ben Sira 59–60, 86,
  90–91, 96–97
– Literacy 38–40, 52–58, 113, 141–142,
  188–191
– Materiality 40–43, 57–58, 157–158, 164,
  183, 186, 188, 190–191
– Rewriting 15, 19, 47–48
Writings *see also* Authoritative Texts
– Biblical Canon 1, 10, 48–49, 122, 124,
  129–130, 142, 187–189
– Definitions 1, 69–78

Zerubbabel 117, 120, 129, 131
Zion 165–166, 170–173, 183, *see also*
  Jerusalem

Forschungen zum Alten Testament

Edited by
Corinna Körting (Hamburg) · Konrad Schmid (Zürich)
Mark S. Smith (Princeton) · Andrew Teeter (Harvard)

FAT I publishes works that give important momentum to Old Testament research all over the world. There are no religious or denominational preferences, and the series has no limits defined by certain positions. The sole determining factor for the acceptance of a manuscript is its high level of scholarship. Monographs, including habilitations, essay collections by established scholars and conference volumes on key subjects from the fields of theology and religious history define the profile of the series.

FAT II makes a point of publishing outstanding works of scholars at the beginning of their career and welcomes explorative research. As in *FAT I,* there are no religious or denominational preferences, and the series has no limits defined by certain positions. In addition to dissertations and monographs by recent doctorates and established scholars, *FAT II* publishes conference volumes on subjects from the fields of theology and religious history with an interdisciplinary focus.

FAT I:
ISSN: 0940-4155
Suggested citation: FAT I
All published volumes at
www.mohrsiebeck.com/fat1

FAT II:
ISSN: 1611-4914
Suggested citation: FAT II
All published volumes at
www.mohrsiebeck.com/fat2

Mohr Siebeck
www.mohrsiebeck.com